THE ETHICS OF THE NEW TESTAMENT

THE

ETHICS

OF THE
NEW TESTAMENT

WOLFGANG SCHRAGE

Translated by David E. Green

FORTRESS PRESS   PHILADELPHIA

Translated by David E. Green from the German *Ethik des Neuen Testaments*. Copyright © Vandenhoeck & Ruprecht, Göttingen 1982.

ENGLISH TRANSLATION COPYRIGHT © 1988 BY FORTRESS PRESS

First paperback edition 1990

Library of Congress Cataloging-in-Publication Data

Schrage, Wolfgang.
    The ethics of the New Testament.

    Translation of: Ethik des Neuen Testaments.
    Bibliography: p.
    Includes index.
    1. Ethics in the Bible.   2. Bible.   N.T.—Theology.
    3. Christian ethics—History—Early church, ca. 30–600.
    I. Title.
    BS2545.E8S2613   1987   241.5   86–45922
    ISBN 0–8006–0835–6 (cloth)
    ISBN 0–8006–2477–7 (paper)

Printed in the United States of America   1-2477

94   93   92   91   90   2   3   4   5   6   7   8   9   10

To my wife

CONTENTS

A bibliography of works dealing with the ethics of the entire New Testament appears at the end of this book. Separate bibliographies pertinent to each chapter or section appear at the beginning of each. More specialized discussions are cited in the footnotes.

Normally the bibliographical reference in a note refers to the entries at the beginning of each section, or to the general bibliography when it is followed by the subunit in which the item appears. That is, *Ethics* (B) in n. 2 of chap. 1 has its full entry in the B (General) subsection of the book's Bibliography (pp. 349–53).

ABBREVIATIONS

The abbreviations in this volume follow Siegfried Schwertner's *Internationales Abkürzungsverzeichnis für Theologie und Grenzgebiete* (Berlin: de Gruyter, 1974).

The abbreviations of biblical literature and other ancient literature are those found in the *Journal of Biblical Literature*, Hermeneia, and *Harvard Theological Review*.

AnBib	Analecta Biblica
ANRW	*Aufstieg und Niedergang der römischen Welt*
ARM	*Archives royales de Mari*
ASTI	*Annual of the Swedish Theological Institute in Jerusalem*
AThANT	Arbeiten zur Theologie des Alten und Neuen Testaments
BEThL	Bibliotheca ephemeridum theologicarum lovaniensium
BEvTh	Beiträge zur evangelischen Theologie
BFChTh	Beiträge zur Förderung christlicher Theologie
BHTh	Beiträge zur historischen Theologie
BiLe	*Bibel und Leben*
BLA	Bampton Lectures in America
BR	*Biblical Research*
BSt	Biblische Studien
BTB	*Biblical Theology Bulletin*
BU	Biblische Untersuchungen
BZ	*Biblische Zeitschrift*
BZNW	Beihefte zur Zeitschrift für die neutestamentliche Wissenschaft
Cath	*Catholicisme*
CBQ	*Catholic Biblical Quarterly*
CBQ.M	Catholic Biblical Quarterly Monograph Series
CThM	Calwer theologische Monographien
CV	*Communio viatorum*

CwH	Calwer Hefte zur Förderung biblischen Glaubens und christlichen Lebens
ED	*Euntes docete*
EETh	Einführung in die evangelische Theologie
EHS.T	Europäische Hochschulschriften. Reihe 23: Theologie
EKKNT	Evangelisch-Katholischer Kommentar zum Neuen Testament (Neukirchen: Neukirchener; Zurich: Benziger)
ET	*Expository Times*
EtB	Etudes bibliques
ETL	*Emphemerides Theologicae Lovanienses*
EvTh	*Evangelische Theologie*
FBESG	Forschungen und Berichte der evangelischen Studiengemeinschaft
FRLANT	Forschungen zur Religion und Literatur des Alten und Neuen Testaments
FThSt	Frieburger theologische Studien
FzB	Forschung zur Bibel
GNT	Grundrisse zum Neuen Testament
GTA	Göttinger theologische Arbeiten
HeyJ	*Heythrop Journal*
HMT	*Handbuch der Moraltheologie*
HNT	Handbuch zum Neuen Testament (Tübingen: Mohr)
HThK	Herders theologischer Kommentar (Freiburg: Herder)
HThR	*Harvard Theological Review*
JAAR	*Journal of the American Academy of Religion*
JBL	*Journal of Biblical Literature*
JR	*Journal of Religion*
JSNT	*Journal for the Study of the New Testament*
KBANT	Kommentare und Beiträge zum Alten und Neuen Testament
KEK	Kritisch-exegetischer Kommentar über das Neue Testament (Göttingen: Vandenhoeck & Ruprecht)
KuD	*Kerygma und Dogma*
LR	*Lutherische Rundschau*
LTh	Library of Theology
LTP	*Laval théologique et philosophique*
LUA	*Lunds Universitets Årskrift*
LXX	Septuagint
MThSt	Marburger theologische Studien
MThZ	*Münchener theologische Zeitschrift*
NKS	*Nederlands(che) katholieke stemmen*
NT	*Novum Testamentum*
NT.S	Supplements to Novum Testamentum
NTA	Neutestamentliche Abhandlungen

NTD	Das Neue Testament Deutsch (Göttingen: Vandenhoeck & Ruprecht)
NTF	Neutestamentliche Forschung
NTG	Neue theologische Grundrisse
NTL	New Testament Library
NTS	*New Testament Studies*
ÖTK	Ökumenischer Taschenbuchkommentar zum Neuen Testament
Qumran	Dead Sea Scrolls
CD	*Damascus Document*
1QM	*War Scroll*
1QS	*Manual of Discipline*
RAC	*Reallexikon für Antike und Christentum*
RGG³	*Die Religion in Geschichte und Gegenwart.* 3d ed.
RNT	Regensburger Neues Testament (Regensburg: Pustet)
RSV	Revised Standard Version
RThPh	*Revue de théologie et de philosophie*
RTR	*Reformed Theological Review*
SBLDS	Society of Biblical Literature Dissertation Series
SBM	Stuttgarter biblische Monographien
SBS	Stuttgarter Bibel-Studien
SBT	Studies in Biblical Theology
ScEs	*Science et esprit*
SGV	Sammlung gemeinverständlicher Vorträge und Schriften
SJTh	*Scottish Journal of Theology*
SNTSMS	Society for New Testament Studies Monograph Series
StANT	Studien zum Alten und Neuen Testament
StEv	*Studia Evangelica*
StNT	Studien zum Neuen Testament
StTh	*Studia Theologica* (Lund)
SWJT	*Southwestern Journal of Theology*
TDNT	*Theological Dictionary of the New Testament*
TDOT	*Theological Dictionary of the Old Testament*
Test.	Testament
ThB	*Theologische Beiträge*
ThF	Theologische Forschung
ThGl	*Theologie und Glaube*
ThHK	Theologischer Handkommentar zum Neuen Testament (Berlin: Evangelische Verlaganstalt)
ThLZ	*Theologische Literaturzeitung*
ThQ	*Theologische Quartalschrift*
ThR	*Theologische Rundschau*
ThTh	Themen der Theologie
ThViat	*Theologia viatorum*

TRE	*Theologische Real-Enzyklopädie*
TThSt	Trierer theologische Studien
TThZ	*Trierer theologische Zeitschrift*
TU	Texte und Untersuchungen zur Geschichte der altchristlichen Literatur
UNT	Untersuchungen zum Neuen Testament
VF	*Verkündigung und Forschung*
WA	Martin Luther. *Werke*. Kritische Gesamtausgabe (Weimar Ausgabe)
WBTh	Wiener Beiträge zur Theologie
WMANT	Wissenschaftliche Monographien zum Alten und Neuen Testament
WPKG	Wissenschaft und Praxis in Kirche und Gesellschaft
WuA	*Wort und Antwort* (Salzburg)
WuD	*Wort und Dienst*
WUNT	Wissenschaftliche Untersuchungen zum Neuen Testament
ZdZ	*Zeichen der Zeit*
ZEE	*Zeitschrift für evangelische Ethik*
ZNW	*Zeitschrift für die neutestamentliche Wissenschaft*
ZSTh	*Zeitschrift für systematische Theologie*
ZThK	*Zeitschrift für Theologie und Kirche*

INTRODUCTION

The subject matter dealt with by an ethics of the New Testament is the question of how life was lived in the earliest Christian communities: what were the foundations, the support for, and the criteria and principles for this way of acting and living. In an age of uncertainty and drift, reconsideration of New Testament ethics seems especially urgent. Despite all the committees, synods, and reports dealing with ethical questions, there seems to be a substantial need for breathing space; once again, for example, we hear voices criticizing too much social action and insisting that what matters is not action but faith, as though they were mutually exclusive. Of course salvation is by faith alone—but this faith works through love (Gal. 5:6). The Son of man when he returns will not ask what we have had faith in but what we have done or failed to do (Matt. 25:31ff.). For the New Testament, faith is not primarily speculation or assent to ideas and theories, not fulfillment of cultic obligations or mystical ecstasy, but hearing God's Word and doing God's will. Faith and practice are indissolubly linked. With varying emphases, the church has always had to fight on two fronts, lest "those without faith devote themselves to vain works, or those without works take refuge in faith."[1] The danger of activism without faith must not be minimized. At the same time, we must certainly be on our guard when the Christian faith, adapting to the sentimentality of bourgeois prosperity and widespread narcissism, threatens to be reduced to private subjectivity or narrow ecclesiasticism, or, out of hopelessness occasioned by the world about us, threatens to take refuge in otherworldliness. At least the New Testament cannot be blamed for such a development. The early church was neither a mystery cult, a monastic movement, nor a philosophical party. It was a community of witness and service, a church for God and "a church for others." Jesus, for example, did not suggest that his followers lead a monastic life in the desert like the Essenes. He did not commend to them an inward or transcendent kingdom of

1. Martin Luther, WA 45:689, on John 15:10ff.

1

speculation or soul like that of the mystics and Gnostics. He sent them into the world and to their immediate neighbors.

But even when we take seriously the fact that the actions and life style of Christians in everyday realities are crucially important, the question often remains whether we always give the fundamental ideas and leitmotifs of the New Testament due attention, whether we are following its lead. It is true that we cannot espouse a simplistic biblicism that brings New Testament precepts into our own day. Here we must confront difficult hermeneutical and theological questions. For example, those who consider New Testament eschatology obsolete, in light of the close connection in the New Testament between eschatology and ethics, will follow Sanders[2] in rejecting New Testament ethics as well. And those who confuse "faithfulness in this world" with mere accommodation to the earthly order and refuse to hear the contradiction spoken by God's promise and commandment likewise have no need for New Testament ethics and will consider the New Testament itself potentially expendable, if they do not in fact reject it out of hand as an instrument of authoritarian oppression. Of course the proper relationship of scriptural authority to the authority of reason and the contemporary world is far from clear. But there should be no doubt within the church or among theologians that, despite the changed situation and different problems, the New Testament must still be taken as an absolute standard if the conduct required of Christians today is still to be Christian conduct, grounded in the name of Jesus Christ. Even in an age when as almost never before new paradigms for action are needed and—to use Martin Luther's language—new Decalogues must be framed, the new answers remain answerable to the New Testament. The New Testament is not a foundation for logical deduction, but it is the crucial point of reference, because it bears witness to the eschatological revelation of God's will in Jesus Christ, who is not only Savior and Redeemer, but also sovereign Lord. If only for this reason, any Christian ethics must pursue the direction established by the New Testament.

Now the New Testament is certainly not a handbook or compendium of Christian ethics, with universal rules or detailed descriptions of conduct. It does not contain philosophic teaching about norms or virtues, or definitions and legitimations deriving from some kind of natural law governing justice and property, labor and society. Nowhere—or almost nowhere—do we find any interest in universal moral principles, eternally valid statements about what constitutes a just social and political order or the relationship between the sexes, or programs and handy guidelines for dealing with other ethical problems. But in the various documents, each seeking in its own way to bear witness to the salvation given in Jesus Christ and the sovereignty of God that has dawned in him, we hear a repeated call to appropriate conduct on the part

2. *Ethics* (B), 29; cf. 129.

of Christians—and not just to individual morality in the private sphere. Despite many lacunae in the realm of social ethics, there are, at least in outline, patterns for social relationships and structures that are clearly not exempt from renewal. Of course one can be a "new creature" even in an old setting, but for "representatives of this new world"[3] the new world need not be merely an object of hope or a utopia. It can be reality, fragmentarily and proleptically. The church has long enough left to so-called fanatics faith in the transforming power of the kingdom of God and of love, while being content with ethical and spiritual introversion.[4] Only those who confuse eschatology with a dualism based on a godless world and a worldless god can see a dichotomy between changing the heart and changing the world. Personal renewal must occasion a corresponding structural renewal. But the main emphasis of this outline—and this is largely consonant with the conclusions reached by New Testament ethics—will be neither on structural transformation nor on the way of life that relates to God (as in prayer and praise) or focuses on personal development and integration. Of course freedom and self-discipline, forgiveness and freedom from anxiety, are central ethical themes; the works of love described in Matthew 25 include not only corporeal and material assistance but also psychical and spiritual aid such as comfort and encouragement. But the primary emphasis is on giving food and drink, providing shelter and clothing, and visiting.

Considered concretely, the practical conclusions people derive from God's saving act for their own conduct toward their neighbors, society, and the world may be very different and in part contradictory. There is no such thing as *the* ethics of the New Testament, any more than *the* theology or *the* christology of the New Testament. This does not mean that New Testament ethics cannot have a guiding principle, certain points of convergence and confluence. But we must always remember that nearly everything is still in flux. In New Testament ethics we cannot simply equate all the evidence, combining Jesus with Paul or James with John. The proper methodology is to see that each individual voice is heard, so that the various early Christian models are not forced into a single mold or submerged in an imaginary New Testament ethics. Only so will the freedom and plurality of ethical concepts offered by the New Testament be sufficiently visible, even though the limits of primitive Christian "orthopraxy" must not be ignored.

We shall take as our primary point of departure the texts bearing on the theme at hand. This is necessary because for the most part, except for Jesus' own practice, we have only the ethical instructions contained in the texts; only very indirectly is it possible to reconstruct the actual practice of the earliest Christian communities. But this procedure is also proper because New Testament ethics is in the first instance prescriptive rather than ana-

3. Martin Dibelius, *The Sermon on the Mount* (New York: Scribner's, 1940), 59.
4. Cf. Wendland, *Ethik* (B), 19.

lytical and descriptive. Better put, its purpose is to inspire new reflections, attitudes, and actions by opening new horizons and perspectives. The primary subject of our study will therefore not be the practical realization of ethical principles, the early Christian ethos, but the theological motivation and justification of New Testament ethics, its basic criteria and concrete requirements. Of course there can be no difference in principle between the two questions,[5] because, as Schlatter says, what we think and what we do go hand in hand; and it may well be that on occasion the ethos has been responsible for shaping an interpretative ethics to justify it, instead of itself developing out of the ethics.[6] But it would be wrong to tie ourselves too closely to the schema of theory versus practice, especially since it is unlikely that "ethical instructions will continue to be preserved and handed down very long if no one takes them seriously, if no one makes the least attempt to put them into practice."[7] In any case, the New Testament itself is more prescriptive than descriptive with respect to practice (cf. the Sermon on the Mount). Even though the recounting of true-to-life examples may carry more conviction today than reflection on ethical principles and decisions, it is impossible to evade the fact that, many "exemplary narratives" notwithstanding, an argumentative ethics stands in the foreground of the New Testament, not a narrative ethics. This does not mean that ethical questions are examined merely ideologically and intellectually; it is just that the inability to say much about how an ethics is to be realized is not in itself a reductio ad absurdum. This is not to deny that absence of realization or failure in practice calls the ethics involved into question. In particular, the historical consequences of New Testament texts that have not served to instruct the church in the practice of love must compel critical judgments. But even this must not divert our attention from ethics to ethos, especially because it is likely that, as a rule, ethos followed ethics. No one in the New Testament considered thought a substitute for action or confused talk and action. Many early Christian writers expressly denounced the dichotomy between deeds and words, the absence of a *christopraxy* corresponding to christology. Modern doubts as to whether the demands of the New Testament are realizable (especially with regard to the Sermon on the Mount) must not keep us from seeing that the New Testament writers in general quite naturally assume that Christians do God's will. That the directives of the New Testament are intended only to suggest the proper attitude or even to confront everyone with failure are modern hypotheses that for the most part function only as theological alibis and repressions.

Less important than ethos for an understanding of New Testament ethics, therefore, is the situation addressed. It is obvious that the New Testament

5. Kümmel, "Sittlichkeit" (B), 70.
6. Leander E. Keck, "On the Ethos of the Early Christians," *JAAR* 42 (1974): 435–52.
7. G. Theissen, "Wanderradikalismus," *ZThK* 70 (1973): 247.

writers did not build castles in the air, constructing ideal but unfulfillable demands. They did not voice their thoughts abstractly, idealistically, and independently of the problems of those whom they were addressing. They confronted specific occasions and situations, and can be understood only in their historical and sociological context. New Testament ethics is contextual ethics, ethics in the context of specific situations. The institution of slavery, for example, was such an oppressive reality for certain members of the Christian community that many New Testament writers could not evade it. On the other hand, there are many problems of modern life for answers to which one will obviously search the New Testament in vain. It is not by accident, for example, that we find only admonitions urging proper conduct toward the state and its authorities but no instructions directed to Christians with political responsibility. This is not simply because the early Christian community looked for an imminent eschaton, but because it was generally a marginal group without influence; it could hardly have had members in high places who could exert political influence on affairs of state, an institution that was then totally non-Christian. The preachers and teachers of the New Testament do not entertain the notion that it makes sense to preach into the blue, even though their message is anything but anxious defensiveness and a retreat mentality. Nor were they much concerned about the persuasiveness of their guidelines among non-Christians or accusations that they were preaching a private ecclesiastical morality. By the nature of the case, only members of the community were addressed; no general moral principles were proclaimed. The real subject of New Testament ethics is neither society nor the individual, but the community (cf. the introduction to Philemon). When Paul addresses the problem of divorce, he does so not in general terms but solely with reference to Christians married to other Christians or to non-Christians (1 Cor. 7:10ff.). The ethical problems, furthermore, arose primarily from the local soil of the individual communities. This limitation does not detract from the message's claim to universality; community ethics is not conventicle ethics. In any case, no one can doubt that acute problems within the communities account for much, albeit not everything. New Testament ethics is not a mere reflex of the life and circumstances of the early Christian communities, but, although it cannot be derived from such problems as economic distress, political dependency, uprooted homelessness, and persecution, it cannot be understood apart from them.

The situational background also explains why New Testament ethics is fragmentary and not systematic. For this reason we should really use the term "ethics" in quotation marks; the same is true for concepts such as formal ethics, situation ethics, personal ethics, social ethics, and so forth. Perhaps it would be more appropriate in the case of the New Testament to speak of parenesis or paraclesis, but these terms also do not comprehend the whole, because ethics implies more an element of reflection upon conduct. If "ethics" does not inherently mean ethics that has been subject to dispassionate study and methodical examination but rather reflection on conduct, then we can easily speak (albeit with a grain of salt) of New Testament ethics. The writers of the New Testament certainly reflected as much over the conduct of Christians as over problems of christology, eschatology, ecclesiology, and so forth. They did not, however, develop these thoughts independently, but usually let them issue in concrete admonitions. Therefore the concrete instructions must be examined to determine their premises and implications, their justifications and perspectives. Even if today we no longer feel bound by all the requirements imposed by the New Testament, the texts do not thereby lose their relevance. We must still search out the motives and criteria that determined the special perspective of the New Testament on such problems as slavery and eating food offered to idols.

Although the New Testament does not develop a systematic ethics, it would be wrong to picture the conduct of the first Christians too atomistically and the ethics of the New Testament too situationally. Although we do not find a closed system based on ethical reflection or a reasoned ethics, it is impossible to overlook the high value New Testament ethics itself places on reason and rational knowledge. Although nothing is said explicitly about reason or an immanent logos, and although there is an undeniable difference between New Testament ethics and the Hellenistic Roman ethics that seeks "to solve by rational means the problems of human life in the abstract and in society,"[8] it will not suffice to distinguish New Testament ethics from "rationalistic sophistry" and "clever casuistry," stressing instead the "onset of telos," "involvement," "dynamism," as does Preisker,[9] for example. We shall therefore return to the rationality of Christian conduct when we examine the ethics of Jesus and its sapiential tradition and especially the ethics of Paul with its repeated appeal to reason, wisdom, and knowledge. We shall then investigate whether the presuppositions and foundations of this ethics or merely its subject matter derive from reason, or whether neither is true and the appeal to reason is nothing more than a secondary argument: the persuasive power of rational arguments cannot be dispensed with, but especially in cases of conflict reason cannot have the final word. The plausibility and general acceptance of the "golden rule" (Matt. 7:12 par.), for example, must not be confused with the ethics of the kingdom of God. In addition, reason must be directed by love; only when this criterion of christologically defined love is in force can "the effective identity of loving and rational conduct"[10] be maintained. Reason alone does not guarantee either humanity or love.

Despite the unmistakable importance of reason, it remains the fact that New Testament ethics is not systematic but concrete, exemplary, situational,

8. Dihle, *RAC* 6:647.
9. *Ethos*(B), 24ff.
10. Duchrow, *Christenheit* (B), 117.

intended for a particular time—although we must add at once that the paradigms and models of conduct are not arbitrary and without claim to authority. There is a tendency today to speak of "models of conduct" in order to make it clear that the instructions recorded in the Bible are not legalistic and are not directly applicable to the present. Blank uses the "model" concept to arrive at an ethics "that, without being legalistic, is nevertheless binding."[11] Hoffmann and Eid prefer the term "perspectives," which retains the notion of concreteness while making it "convertible, extensible."[12] Specific paradigms can help master analogous situations. Of course the infinite variation of the human world—cultural, social, and societal—cannot be reduced to a common denominator, but certain crucial fundamental questions and attitudes remain fixed. Despite the variety of specific types of behavior, earliest Christianity displays constant guidelines and standards of conduct that forbid relativism as much as they forbid codified authoritative morality. The law of love and specific individual commandments stand firm before all situational analysis. When situations changed, people did not simply repeat verbatim the words and acts of Jesus; but they did try constantly to put them into practice. The reinterpretations of ethical traditions that appear already in the New Testament show that people were not interested in slavishly reproducing behavioral norms. Instead, with total freedom and innovative ability that supported not only reinterpretation but creation of new material, they sought to preserve the instructions of Jesus and the experience of the earliest community in order to master analogous or new situations.

To address a situation means to be influenced by that situation. This does not mean that the social or socioeconomic reality of the earliest Christian communities or even of the New Testament world constitutes sufficient criterion or basis to explain the ethics of the first Christians. It is true that the decisions recorded in the New Testament are predetermined to some degree by contemporary patterns of thought and action, values and goals. They are also shaped by many forces outside the community. Responsibility must be divided among various factors: religious, cultural, and intellectual as well as economic, political, and social. The criteria for reaching ethical decisions were not established in isolation from the contemporary historical situation, but the New Testament writers were certainly not content with merely mentioning or describing situations as normative. This would be purely tautological and would turn earliest Christianity into nothing more than a mirror of its society. The spirit of the age and the agenda of the day were not the criteria for early Christian ethics, any more than were established customs

11. Josef Blank, "Zum Problem 'ethischer Normen' im Neuen Testament," in *Schriftauslegung in Theorie und Praxis* (Munich: Kösel, 1969), 144–57, esp. 142; cf. also H. Schürmann, "Haben die paulinischen Wendungen und Weisungen Modellcharakter?" in *Orientierungen am NT*, KBANT (Düsseldorf: Patmos, 1978), 89–115.

12. Paul Hoffmann and Volker Eid, *Jesus von Nazareth und eine christliche Moral* (Freiburg: Herder, 1975), 23–24.

and conventional pragmatic norms. Furthermore, the same reality could evoke different responses. Finally, there is a real limit to the situational character of New Testament ethics set by the appearance of general as well as topical parenesis (to use the terminology of Dibelius), admonitions not framed specifically to address a unique situation but tending to transcend the particular and take on a universal or even prophylactic character. The content of the *Haustafeln* in the New Testament was no more determined by specific problems within the communities than was that of the catalogues of virtues and vices. Of course hunger (cf. Acts 11:28; 12:20) and similar hardships (Mealand,[13] e.g., cites the slim chances Galilean fishermen had for employment in Jerusalem and the possibility of a sabbatical year when the fields would lie fallow) led Christian love to find expression in sacrificial acts of charity, but it is also assumed that the poor can "always" be well treated (Mark 14:7). Furthermore, many admonitions are in large measure conventional and traditional.

When we examine the ethical instructions of the New Testament, it is therefore often less important to consider those addressed than the traditional, cultural, social, and religiohistorical background together with the ethical theory and practice of the ancient world. This is all the more true because New Testament ethics in large measure drew upon and incorporated the heritage of classical ethics, albeit with important differences in motivation and presentation of alternative courses of conduct. It is impossible in this study to deal with problems of Jewish or Stoic ethics, but in the context of specific problems and problem areas we shall mention points at which New Testament ethics resembles or differs from the ethics of the ancient world. We shall see that the New Testament does not espouse a middle-of-the-road contemporary morality. The ancient tradition was not only critically received but also repeatedly modified and rejected, not for the sake of originality in Christian conduct but for its substantial adequacy.

As we shall see, the ethics of Jesus, the Synoptics, Paul, and John share one primary common feature: their theological or christological foundation. New Testament ethics is neither autonomous nor teleological. Its criterion and basis is God's saving act in Jesus Christ. Ethics follows from this act and reflects it—is indeed implicit in it. It is even somewhat misleading to speak of sequential ethics, because love and righteousness are not just the consequence but the expression of belonging to Christ. Otherwise we might easily fall into a quantitative misunderstanding, even though both sanctification and justification are the work of God alone, and all quantification misses the dialectical paradox that God does *everything*, and we must therefore do *everything* (Phil. 2:13). We must ask in each instance what it is that inspires

13. David L. Mealand, *Poverty and Expectation in the Gospels*, 8–9, 38ff.

and motivates Christian conduct, what gives Christian conduct its vitality and elan.

There is a widespread view that what is new and peculiar to New Testament ethics, what makes it specifically Christian and binding, has nothing to do with its substance but concerns only the nature of the ethical subject and the grounds on which this subject acts. This is an oversimplification, but it can hardly be doubted that the crucial element is the basis, the sign, the motivating force, the indicative of salvation that precedes all imperatives. It would be contrary to the nature of the New Testament to develop ethics independently; even the primarily ethical orientation of the Letter of James would not support such an approach. The foundations and motives are not displayed explicitly in all cases, but New Testament ethics absolutely demands a theological context and an appeal to New Testament dogmatics. Considerations of space make it impossible to develop this relationship with theology in detail here, but the primary motifs and the fundamental soteriological questions giving rise to them cannot and must not be passed over if New Testament ethics is not to be left hanging in the air or reduced to mere legalistic morality. This holds true especially with respect to christology and eschatology, because they are associated intimately with ethics. The basis and goal of Christian conduct are God's sovereignty and Jesus' cross and resurrection.

In any case, the difficulty of communicating New Testament ethics on a rationally plausible basis must not tempt us into reshaping our exegetical findings to satisfy the taste of present-day theology. Furthermore, there is good reason to suggest that the real task of Christian ethics today should be to emphasize its awkward and difficult aspects. What Barth wrote in 1922 in his commentary on Romans appears to be still topical, above all for ethics: "Those who urge us to shake ourselves free from theology and to think—and more particularly to speak and write—only what is immediately intelligible to the general public seem to me to be suffering from a kind of hysteria and to be entirely without discernment."[14] The conflicts over the peace movement today have made the Sermon on the Mount topical for many, especially in its apparently irrational, utopian, and rigoristic injunctions that often seem out of place in the real world.

None of these considerations, of course, is intended to put "theology" in second place. Even when we consider that the christological traditions of the Christ hymns in Philippians 2 or 1 Peter 2 and 3 were incorporated for the sole purpose of justifying Christian conduct, so that even the christological confession of faith does not appear for its own sake, it would be wrong to suppose that the "theology" is, as it were, only the introduction, that the New Testament does not really hit its stride until it deals with ethics, which could

14. Karl Barth, *The Epistle to the Romans* (London: Oxford Univ. Press, 1933), vii.

even do without "religion" and "theology." Today it is commonplace to cite Käsemann's phrase about "worship in everyday life," which suggests that liturgy coincides with ethics, sometimes interpreted in a purely moralistic sense. But Käsemann's words can be read in both directions and must not be allowed to turn the New Testament into a code of morality. To read the New Testament purely as a textbook of ethics is just as misguided as the notion that its primary concern is a theological orthodoxy in which day-to-day conduct is not so important—a position that sometimes appears to have been taken by an orthodox Protestantism that thought it could dispense with works of love and justice. Even a document like the Letter of James with its vital concern that faith be realized in living, which does not always totally escape the danger of moralism, cannot simply be disregarded as being a handbook of prosaic morality. Even this letter can cite truly theological reasons for its admonitions, whether convincing or not.

The New Testament itself shows that it is not enough to search out the motives and reasons for Christian conduct. We must also look for the criteria and concrete substance of ethics. Because of the problems associated with the static notion of a "norm,"[15] we shall avoid this term and speak instead of "criteria," which are better able to combine dynamically and historically the freedom and constraint of New Testament ethics. The New Testament does not aim solely at a new foundation or a transformation of basic attitudes. It also strives to shape Christian life and concrete conduct in detail. The New Testament does not support a formalistic situation ethics without shape or substance, which leaves all its content up to the individual, ending all too easily in material arbitrariness or conformity to the world. Seneca was of the opinion that whosoever has come to understand philosophical principles "will find the proper precept in each individual case" and needs no further specific admonitions.[16] It is not by chance that this notion comes close to the "ideal vagueness and generality" of Stoic ethics, for which specific circumstances are irrelevant.[17] But this is certainly not true for the New Testament. Käsemann has rightly stressed that "the 'ethic' of the New Testament puts forward without any hesitation single injunctions in almost casuistic fashion."[18] Fear of legalism has often obscured this point. Troeltsch already cautioned that Protestant theologians had become so unfamiliar with the idea of a Christian ethos displaying substantial particularity that "for them the whole of the Christian ethos is exhausted in denunciation of good works and in the right

15. Cf. Christian Link, "Überlegungen zum Problem der Norm in der theologischen Ethik," in *Schöpferische Nachfolge* (Festschrift für Heinz Eduard Tödt) (Heidelberg: Forschungsstätte der evangelischen Studiengemeinschaft, 1978), 95ff.

16. *Epistula* 94.

17. Adolf Bonhoeffer, *Die Ethik des Stoikers Epictet* (Stuttgart: Enke, 1894), 90; cf. also Greeven, *Hauptproblem* (B), 63, 75.

18. Ernst Käsemann, "Principles of the Interpretation of Romans 13," in *NT Questions of Today* (London: SCM Press, 1969), 197.

definition of the grace which imparts moral energy, but, on the side of content, it is entirely indefinite."[19]

This danger is by no means past. It seems to me that adaptation and conformity to the thought and practice of the world have in large measure progressed so far today that Christian ethics in effect often scarcely dares to say anything that does not agree with the dominant morality of society or is not considered "realistic," "effective," and "practical," if it does not in fact seem desperately close to a situational ethical relativism. The New Testament is certainly not concerned to establish an ethical clericalism or a fundamental sectarian nonconformity, but it is concerned that Christians be "the salt of the earth" and "the light of the world" (Matt. 5:13–14; cf. also Phil. 2:15) and maintain their distinctiveness even in their "good works." Matthew 5:46–47 states that what even tax collectors and pagans do is not enough. Without the corrective of the "extraordinary," Christianity would in fact "simply be drowned in the world";[20] and it has reason today to be less fearful of sectarianism than of conformity to the world. Ethical originality, casuistry, and legalism are not the purpose of the New Testament, but neither is reduction to the single admonition to follow one's conscience in every situation. The notion of a "middle axiom" between the Scylla of casuistry and the Charybdis of formalism could therefore be of use in understanding New Testament ethics.[21] In any case, the New Testament contains clear points of reference and guidelines. If there is common agreement that love is the general tenor of New Testament ethics as well as the center and quintessence of all the individual admonitions, it must remain clear that this love implies quite specific content and criteria; it is not an abstract formal principle.

Of course the superior status of the law of love means that there can be no directives to be followed for their own sake, for example, no universally valid law of nonviolence, but love considers the consequences for others correctly only when it refuses to dispense itself from all material implications. Today we can use the concept of love—quite apart from its trivial and emotional definitions—to cover quite contradictory actions. Without giving serious thought to the whole notion of property and ownership, we can apply it to relief programs for the Third and Fourth World that give back a few crumbs that have been taken away from others. This may be in part because we do not have the courage the New Testament had for ethical specificity. It is astonishing how we white adherents of the so-called religion of love observe in silence

---

19. Ernst Troeltsch, *The Social Teachings of the Christian Church* (New York: Macmillan, 1931), 1:198. Cf. also Max Horkheimer, *Kritische Theorie*, 2 vols. (Frankfurt: Fischer, 1968), 1:271: "Religion had so long been robbed of clear, specific content, so formalized, adapted, spiritualized, and shifted to the innermost subjectivity of the subject, that it was compatible with any act and any public praxis that was customary in this atheistic reality."

20. Wendland, "Sozialethik" (B1), 79.

21. Compare J. H. Oldham with Heinz-Dieter Wendland, *Die Kirche in der revolutionären Gesellschaft* (Gütersloh: Mohn, 1967), 34.

the monstrous and loveless acts of cruelty exploiting the starving and wretched of this earth, acts through which we profit and can pour billions into arms while plunging others into misery. It seems to me that our primary problem is not whether to give precedence to deductive or inductive norms, but whether we hear "the cry of the poor."[22] The New Testament does not identify Christian conduct permanently with specific political or social institutions and practices, but when decisions are reached its material directives reveal paradigmatically types, perspectives, and priorities that can point the way to new horizons and forms and encourage us to go forward.[23]

This is especially true when we turn to pneumatology. Those who take account of the renewing and life-giving power of the Spirit, who leads into all truth, will be open to surprising insights and new forms of action. They will not immediately brand as heresy every desire for change in church and society, and will not stick obstinately to what is traditional and familiar. The Spirit of God is the motive force that constantly brings us out of our fortified positions into new insecurity and can never be domesticated or restrained by the church. It is also the Spirit who "recalls" Christ and follows Christ in the New Testament. Thus both inflexibility and arbitrariness are overcome.

We shall discuss the major representatives of New Testament ethics in sequence. This does not automatically imply a negative estimate of the later documents, as though the path from Jesus to the Pastoral and Catholic Letters is to be understood as a decline. Those who would speak, for example, of an increasing tendency on the part of New Testament ethics to moralize, to become middle-class and conformed to the world—often from a very middle-class pulpit indeed—suggesting that New Testament ethics loses its purity with time, will be hard put to deal with the Revelation of John or 1 Peter. It is also wrong to reach unhistorical judgments. We must not, for example, duck the question of how a perverted Paulinism or libertinism and the asceticism of Gnosticism could have been more effectively countered than they actually were, namely through emphasis on "works," through elements of so-called natural ethics, and so forth. This does not mean that we avoid critical judgments. Such judgments are inescapable, for example, with reference to certain patriarchal and androcentric statements, but also with reference to uncharismatic obduracy and threatening legalism. The New Testament itself invites us to make these judgments. But the criterion on which they are based cannot simply be textual primacy or formal radicalism; it can only be the gospel itself and love as encountered in the passing ages.

22. Hiers, *Jesus and Ethics*.
23. Houlden, *Ethics* (B), 119.

I

JESUS'
ESCHATOLOGICAL ETHICS

BIBLIOGRAPHY

General

Berner, Ursula. *Die Bergpredigt.* GTA 12. Göttingen: Vandenhoeck & Ruprecht, 1979.

Bornkamm, Günther. *Jesus von Nazareth.* 12th ed. Stuttgart: Kohlhammer, 1980. Eng. trans. of 3rd German ed: *Jesus of Nazareth.* New York: Harper & Row; London: Hodder & Stoughton, 1960.

Braun, Herbert. *Jesus.* ThTh 1. Stuttgart: Kreuz, 1969. English: *Jesus of Nazareth.* Philadelphia: Fortress Press, 1979.

————. *Spätjüdisch-häretischer und frühchristlicher Radikalismus.* 2d ed. BHTh 24. Tübingen: Mohr, 1979. Cited here from 1st ed. (1957).

Bultmann, Rudolf. *Geschichte der synoptischen Tradition.* 9th ed. FRLANT 29. Göttingen: Vandenhoeck & Ruprecht, 1979. English: *History of the Synoptic Tradition.* Rev. ed. New York: Harper & Row, 1976.

————. *Jesus.* 3d ed. Gütersloh: Mohn, 1977.

Dibelius, Martin. *The Sermon on the Mount.* New York: Scribner's, 1940.

Dietzfelbinger, Christian. *Die Antithesen der Bergpredigt.* Munich: Kaiser, 1975.

Eichholz, Georg. *Auslegung der Bergpredigt.* 2d ed. BSt 46. Neukirchen: Neukirchener Verlag, 1970.

Goppelt, Leonhard. *Theologie des NT.* Göttingen: Vandenhoeck & Ruprecht, 1976. English: *Theology of the NT.* Grand Rapids: Eerdmans, 1981–82.

Hengel, Martin. *Nachfolge und Charisma.* BZNW 34. Berlin: Töpelmann, 1968. English: *The Charismatic Leader and His Followers.* New York: Crossroad; Edinburgh: T. & T. Clark, 1981.

Hiers, Richard H. *Jesus and Ethics.* Philadelphia: Westminster Press, 1968.

Hoffmann, Paul, and Volker Eid. *Jesus von Nazareth und eine christliche Moral.* Freiburg: Herder, 1975.

Jeremias, Joachim. *Die Gleichnisse Jesu.* 8th ed. Göttingen: Vandenhoeck & Ruprecht, 1970. Cited here from the 6th ed. (1962). English: *The Parables of Jesus.* 3d ed. New York: Scribner's; London: SCM Press, 1972.

————. *Neutestamentliche Theologie. I. Die Verkündigung Jesus.* 2d ed. Göttingen: Vandenhoeck & Ruprecht, 1973. English: *New Testament Theology. Part 1, The Proclamation of Jesus.* New York: Scribner, 1971.

Jüngel, Eberhard. *Paulus und Jesus.* 5th ed. Tübingen: Mohr, 1979.

Kümmel, Werner Georg. *Die Theologie des Neuen Testaments nach seine Hauptzeugen Jesus, Paulus, Johannes.* 4th ed. GNT 3. Göttingen: Vandenhoeck & Ruprecht, 1980. Cited here from the 1st ed. (1969). Pp. 20–85. English: *The Theology of the NT According to Its Major Witnesses: Jesus—Paul—John.* Nashville: Abingdon Press, 1973.

Lindeskog, Gösta. *Die Jesusfrage im neuzeitlichen Judentum.* Arbeiten und Mitteilungen aus dem neutestamentlichen Seminar zu Uppsala 8. Darmstadt: Wissenschaftliche Buchgesellschaft, 1973 [1938].

Linnemann, Eta. *Gleichnisse Jesu.* 7th ed. Göttingen: Vandenhoeck & Ruprecht, 1978. Eng. trans. of 3d ed.: *Parables of Jesus.* London: SPCK, 1966 (*Jesus of the Parables* [New York: Harper & Row, 1966]).

Manson, Thomas Walter. *Ethics and the Gospel.* New York: Charles Scribner's Sons, 1960.

Merklein, Helmut. *Die Gottesherrschaft als Handlungsprinzip.* Würzburg: Echter, 1978.

Neuhäusler, Engelbert. *Anspruch und Antwort Gottes.* Düsseldorf: Patmos, 1962.

Percy, Ernst. *Die Botschaft Jesu*. Lund: Gleerup, 1953.

Sanders, Jack T. *Ethics* (B). Pp. 1–29.

Schnackenburg, Rudolf. *Botschaft* (B). Pp. 3–128.

Schottroff, Luise, and Wolfgang Stegemann. *Jesus von Nazareth—Hoffnung der Armen*. Stuttgart: Kohlhammer, 1978. English: *Jesus and the Hope of the Poor*. Maryknoll, N.Y.: Orbis Books, 1986.

Schottroff, Willy, and Wolfgang Stegemann, eds. *Der Gott der kleinen Leute*. Munich: Kaiser, 1979. English: *God of the Lowly: Socio-Historical Interpretations of the Bible*. Maryknoll, N.Y.: Orbis Books, 1984.

Soiron, Thaddäus. *Die Bergpredigt Jesu*. Freiburg: Herder, 1941.

Theissen, Gerd. *Soziologie der Jesusbewegung*. 2d ed. English: *Sociology of Early Palestinian Christianity*. Philadelphia: Fortress Press, 1978.

———. "Wanderradikalismus." *ZThK* 70 (1973): 245–70. Reprinted in *Studien zur Soziologie des Urchistentums*, 245–71. WUNT 19. Tübingen: Mohr, 1979. English: "Itinerant Radikalism," *Radical Religion* II, 213 (1976): 84–93.

Weder, Hans. *Die Gleichnisse Jesu als Metaphern*. FRLANT 120. 2d ed. Göttingen: Vandenhoeck & Ruprecht, 1980.

Wendland, Heinz-Dieter. *Ethik* (B). Pp. 4–33.

Windisch, Hans. *Der Sinn der Bergpredigt*. UNT 16. Leipzig: Hinrichs, 1937. English: *The Meaning of the Sermon on the Mount*. Philadelphia: Westminster Press, 1951.

A. Eschatology and Ethics (pp. 18–40)

Bald, H. "Eschatologische oder theozentrische Ethik?" *VF* 24 (1979): 35–72.

Flender, Helmut. *Die Botschaft Jesu von der Herrschaft Gottes*. Munich: Kaiser, 1968.

Hoffmann, Paul. " 'Eschatologie' und 'Friedenshandeln' in der Jesusverkündigung." In *Eschatologie und Frieden*, ed. G. Liedke, 1:179–233. Texte und Materialien der Forschungsstätte der evangelischen Studiengemeinschaft, ser. A, 6–8. 3 vols. Heidelberg: Forschungsstätte der evangelischen Studiengemeinschaft, 1978.

Schürmann, Heinz. "Eschatologie und Liebesdienst in der Verkündigung Jesu." In *Kaufet die Zeit aus* (Festschrift Theoderich Kampmann), ed. H. Kirchhoff, 39–71. Paderborn: Schöningh, 1959. Cited from Festschrift K. Schubert. 1964. Pp. 203–32.

B. The Will of God and the Law (pp. 40–68)

Banks, Robert J. *Jesus and the Law in the Synoptic Tradition*. SNTSMS, 28. New York and Cambridge: Cambridge Univ. Press, 1975.

Berger, Klaus. *Die Gesetzesauslegung Jesu, I*. WMANT 40. Tübingen: Mohr, 1972.

Betz, Hans Dieter. *Nachfolge* (B6). Pp. 5–47.

Bonhoeffer, Dietrich. *Nachfolge*. 11th ed. Munich: Kaiser, 1976. English: *The Cost of Discipleship*. Rev. ed. New York: Macmillan, 1959.

Hengel, Martin. "Jesus und die Tora." *ThB* 9 (1978): 152–72.

Hübner, Hans. *Das Gesetz in der synoptischen Tradition*. Witten: Luther, 1973.

Kuhn, Heinz W. "Nachfolge nach Ostern." In *Kirche* (Festschrift Günther Bornkamm), 105–32. Tübingen: Mohr, 1980.

Limbeck, Meinrad. *Von der Ohnmacht des Rechts*. Düsseldorf: Patmos, 1972.

Luz, Ulrich, and Rudolf Smend. *Gesetz*. Biblische Konfrontationen. Stuttgart: Kohlhammer, 1981.

Noll, Peter. *Jesus und das Gesetz.* SGV 253. Tübingen: Mohr, 1968.
Osborn, Eric Francis. *Patterns* (B). Pp. 21–28.
Schulz, Anselm. *Nachfolgen und Nachahmen.* StANT 6. Munich: Kösel, 1962. Pp. 17–133.
Schweizer, Eduard. *Erniedrigung und Erhöhung bei Jesus und seinen Nachfolgern.* 2d ed. AThANT 28. Zurich: Zwingli, 1962. Pp. 7–21. Eng. trans. of the 1st ed. (1955): *Lordship and Discipleship.* SBT 28. London: SCM Press, 1960.
Theissen, Gerd. "'Wir haben alles verlassen' (Mc.X.28)." *NT* 19 (1977): 161–96. Reprinted in *Studien zur Soziologie des Urchristentums,* 106–41.

C. The Double Commandment of Love (pp. 68–87)

Becker, Jürgen. "Feindesliebe—Nächstenliebe—Bruderliebe." *ZEE* 25 (1981): 5–17.
Bornkamm, Günther. "Das Doppelgebot der Liebe." In *Geschichte und Glaube* (*Gesammelte Aufsätze,* vol. 3.), 37–45. BEvTh 48. Munich: Kaiser, 1968.
Burchard, Christoph. "Das doppelte Liebesgebot in der frühchristlichen Überlieferung." In *Der Ruf Jesu und die Antwort der Gemeinde* (Festschrift Joachim Jeremias), 409–32. Göttingen: Vandenhoeck & Ruprecht, 1970.
Friedrich, Johannes. *Gott im Bruder?* Stuttgart: Calwer, 1977.
Furnish, Victor Paul. *Love Command* (B6). Pp. 24–69.
Lührmann, Dieter. "Liebet eure Feinde." *ZThK* 69 (1972): 412–38.
Luz, Ulrich. "Einige Erwägungen zur Auslegung Gottes in der ethischen Verkündigung Jesu." *EKKNT* Vorarbeiten Heft 2 (1970): 119–30.
Nissen, Andreas. *Gott und der Nächste im antiken Judentum.* WUNT 15. Tübingen: Mohr, 1974.
Piper, John. *Love Your Enemies.* SNTSMS 38. New York and Cambridge: Cambridge Univ. Press, 1979.
Theissen, Gerd. "Gewaltverzicht und Feindesliebe." In *Studien zur Soziologie des Urschristentums,* 160–97.

D. Concrete Precepts (pp. 87–115)

Baltensweiler, Heinrich. *Ehe* (B2).
Cullmann, Oscar. *Jesus und die Revolutionären seiner Zeit.* Tübingen: Mohr, 1970. English: *Jesus and the Revolutionaries.* New York: Harper & Row, 1970.
———. *Staat* (B5).
Hengel, Martin. *War Jesus Revolutionär?* CwH 110. Stuttgart: Calwer, 1970. English: *Was Jesus a Revolutionist?* Philadelphia: Fortress Press, 1971.
Huuhtanen, Pauli. "Die Perikope vom 'Reichen Jüngling' unter besonderer Berücksichtigung der Akzentuierung des Lukas." In *Theologie aus dem Norden,* ed. A. Fuchs, 79–98. Linz: Fuchs, 1976.
Mealand, David L. *Poverty and Expectation in the Gospels.* London: SPCK, 1980.
O'Neill, Louis. "Dimension politique de la vie de Jésus." In *Le Christ hier, aujourd'hui et demain,* 365–94. Quebec: Presses de l'université Laval, 1976.
Petzke, Gerd. "Der historische Jesus in der sozialethischen Diskussion." In *Jesus Christus in Historie und Theologie* (Festschrift Hans Conzelmann), 223–35. Tübingen: Mohr, 1975.
Schaller, Berndt. "Die Sprüche über Ehescheidung und Wiederheirat in der synoptischen Überlieferung." In *Der Ruf Jesu* (I.C), 226–46.
Schottroff, Luise. "Gewaltverzicht und Feindesliebe in der urchristlichen Jesustradi-

tion." In *Jesus Christus in Historie und Theologie*, 197–221. English: "Non-Violence and the Love of One's Enemies," in *Essays on the Love Commandment* by L. Schottroff et al. (Philadelphia: Fortress Press, 1978).

Schrage, Wolfgang. *Staat* (B5). Pp. 14–49.

Yoder, John Howard. *The Politics of Jesus*. 4th ed. Grand Rapids: Eerdmans, 1977.

A. ESCHATOLOGY AND ETHICS

1. The Kingdom of God as the Foundation and Horizon of Jesus' Ethics

When we ask about the ethics of Jesus, we must first ask about the center of his message, which makes the proclamation and realization of God's will comprehensible and imperative. This center, which also constitutes the sign and purpose of Jesus' entire ministry, is the message of the imminent coming of the kingdom or kingdom of God, marking an eschatological epoch.

1.1 The precise meaning of this kingdom is disputed. A brief survey of Old Testament and Jewish tradition shows that the final eschatological manifestation of God's kingdom was pictured originally in historical terms within the order of the natural world (see, e.g., Isa. 52:7; Zech. 14:9; Obad. 21). Apocalypticism introduced a double perspective. On the one hand, the continued hopes associated with earthly nationalism looked for restoration of the Davidic empire (exemplified by the Targumim and the Eighteen Benedictions). On the other, there was a transcendental expectation of another world associated with the coming eon (exemplified by Ethiopic Enoch). The two overlapped, however, and it would therefore be incorrect to draw too sharp a line between the two expectations and ignore the connection between the present and the future dimensions; the eternal kingdom of God is universally accepted, not only in the Old Testament (see Exod. 15:18; Ps. 10:16) but also in apocalyptic literature (see Dan. 4:31[34]; Ethiopic Enoch 84:2). Even when the coming of God's reign in this world is expected, it often includes supernatural elements; and when the expectation of something totally other is the focus of attention, it is usually associated with earthly elements and sociopolitical manifestations (see Dan. 7:13–14; Assumption of Moses 10). What matters is the universal, definitive, and imminent coming of God as sovereign to transform the world and intervene on behalf of his people. Rabbinic Judaism too speaks of the "kingdom of heaven" in both present and future form. In the present, there is a mysterious governance of God established by the law and acknowledged by human obedience to the law. But Israel also prays (in the Kaddish and Alenu prayers, for example)[1] for the final mighty revelation of God's kingdom in the eyes of all the world. Here again, we find a mixture of historical and supernatural features. The important observation for ethics is that the kingdom of God does not simply represent the dimension of transcendence but has to do with this world.

1.2 Jesus drew upon this eschatological hope for a cosmic universal manifestation of God's kingdom when he preached that God was on the point of establishing final sovereignty over the rebellious cosmos. He also reshaped this expectation, which does not in fact play a dominant role in Judaism. The

---

1. Hermann L. Strack and Paul Billerbeck, *Kommentar zum NT aus Talmud und Midrasch*, 7th ed. (Munich: Beck, 1978), 1:408ff.

Judaism of Jesus' day looked for a historical eschaton; for Jesus, however,
God's kingdom was not connected with sacred times and places, nor was it
limited esoterically and sectarianly to a sacred remnant in Israel.[2] God's
kingdom cannot be calculated on the basis of an apocalyptic timetable, nor
can it be described in speculative detail. Nor can it be imposed by the action
of the Zealots, nor can it be limited to political nationalism. Its most characteristic feature is the temporal dialectic of present and future. This means, for
example, that people can speak of it as imminent and pray for its coming (as
in the second petition of the Lord's Prayer), but can also proclaim its dawning
in the present with Jesus (cf. Matt. 12:28 par.; Luke 17:20). It is now no
longer at hand but has begun; Jesus obviously understood his own ministry
in word and deed as a sign of its appearance, as the proleptic presence of the
future. Jesus is therefore not restricted to either future or present statements
about God's kingdom. "Realized eschatology" is wrong in ascribing all statements concerning the future to secondary restatement of Jesus' message in
apocalyptic terms. The so-called "totally eschatological" interpretation is
equally wrong in looking upon all the statements referring to the present as
post-Easter interpolations.[3] The simultaneity of present and future is characteristic of Jesus.

1.3 The parables of the mustard seed and the seed growing secretly illustrate
the relationship between present and future—not, to be sure, in the sense of
intensive or extensive growth brought about by human agency or against the
background of an evolutionary model, but also not as a simple pair of opposites.

The parable of the mustard seed (Mark 4:30–32), for example, compares
the kingdom of God to a mustard seed, which is smaller than all other kinds
of seed but grows up into the greatest of all shrubs. Unlike the Q version in
Luke 13:18–19, which does not mention the smallness of the seed, Mark 4
accents not the development of the seed into a tree but the contrast between
the tiniest seed and the largest shrub. We are dealing here with a "contrast
parable," which contrasts the insignificant beginning with the enormous end,
without mentioning an interim of biological or historical development.[4]

There is a clear relationship, however, between beginning and end. The
kingdom of God does not simply grow organically and continuously out of
the beginning, but it is certainly impossible to separate beginning and end. It
is even possible to see here traces of a kind of eschatological movement, which
must not be confused with the modern notion of historical progress.[5] In this

2. Hoffmann, "Eschatologie," 185.
3. For further discussion, see Werner G. Kümmel, *Promise and Fulfillment*, 3d ed., SBT 23
(London: SCM Press, 1966); Norman Perrin, *Rediscovering the Teaching of Jesus* (New York:
Harper & Row, 1967), 54ff.; Kümmel, *Theology*, 27ff.
4. See Jeremias, *Parables*, 146ff.; Otto Kuss, *Aufsätze zur Exegese des NT*, vol. 1 of *Auslegung
und Verkündigung* (Regensburg: Pustet, 1963), 78 ff., 85 ff.
5. See Kuss, *Aufsätze*, and 1 Cor. 15:23ff.

sense it is appropriate to speak of an "inaugurated" eschatology.[6] There can be no eschatological shrub without its historical mustard seed, and the seed is what matters. It is therefore out of place to insist that the parable likens the kingdom of God to the final phase of development.[7] The reverse is in fact the case: interest focuses precisely on the beginning, which is astonishingly tiny—quite unlike what one would expect and predict naively by looking at the end. According to Fuchs, Jesus' contemporaries did not have to be told that God's final intervention would be immensely successful. Their question was instead whether it was not more reasonable to assume that the God who concludes so wondrously should also begin wondrously.[8] The insignificant beginning, however, is intimately connected with the ministry of Jesus, in which the eschatological kingdom of God is already present as a sign "in the midst of you" (Luke 17:21). The kingdom of God does not simply manifest itself through a visible continuous process, and certainly not as just the final link in a chain of apocalyptic events. But it is connected indissolubly with the ministry of Jesus and thus impinges on the worldly reality of the present.

This means, however, that the kingdom of God cannot simply be interpreted as a "totally transcendent quantity."[9] On the one hand, it is associated with the terminology of the coming eon (e.g., "come," "enter in"). On the other hand, it reflects present experience (Matt. 12:28). Through his ministry, Jesus brings the effectual presence of the kingdom of God into the realm of historical reality. The involvement of the kingdom with the actual experience of the world makes it impossible to look for the substance and import of Jesus' message in the difference between God and humankind and a consequent separation from the world. The thrust of Jesus' message is rather to show that "the eternal and transcendent kingdom of God is at work here and now."[10] The "transcendent" makes itself "immanent." It seeks to deliver people in this world and impose its claim on them. Wendland in particular has warned against the danger (related to the doctrine of the two kingdoms) of transforming the kingdom of God into "a purely invisible quantity, either beyond this world or within us."[11]

Jesus' refusal to interpret the kingdom of God in political or nationalistic terms is often used far too quickly as evidence that it should be conceived as being not only transcendent but also purely spiritual. But the message of

6. The expression is Haenchen's, cited by Ernst Käsemann, "The Problem of the Historical Jesus," in *Essays on NT Themes*, SBT 41 (London: SCM Press, 1964), 15–47 (quotation from p. 44).

7. Jeremias, *Parables*, 147.

8. Ernst Fuchs, "What Is Interpreted in the Exegesis of the NT?" in *Studies of the Historical Jesus*, SBT 42 (London: SCM Press, 1964), 91–92.

9. Walter Schmithals, "Jesus und die Weltlichkeit des Reiches Gottes," *Evangelische Kommentare* 1 (1968): 313–20 (quotation from 315).

10. Ulrich Wilckens, "Urchristlicher Kommunismus," in *Christentum und Gesellschaft*, ed. W. Lohff (Göttingen: Vandenhoeck & Ruprecht, 1969), 141.

11. Wendland, "Weltherrschaft" (B1), 95.

God's kingdom has social and political dimensions, not just in apocalyptic but in Jesus' own teaching. It is therefore not by accident that throughout the course of history this message has often inspired social blueprints for the future, even though it cannot be translated directly in such a form.[12] Luke 17:20–21 is not to be understood to mean that the kingdom is inward, within people's hearts.[13] Its presence is visible in Jesus' entire ministry (Matt. 11:5–6). Even the statements referring to the future confirm that the kingdom of God is expected to entail deliverance from bodily and social ills and fulfillment of concrete desires (cf. Luke 6:20–21; Matt. 8:11). Flender maintains[14] that Jesus' expectation of the kingdom is to be understood only in this concrete future sense. In my opinion, the phrase "in the midst of you" (Luke 17:21) also goes beyond the person of Jesus. Although he represents the kingdom, which dawns in his ministry, he himself also stands in its service and brings his followers into its service. He himself proclaims the kingdom of God and his exorcisms are signs of its coming,[15] but his disciples are also to proclaim the kingdom and heal.[16] They, too, share secondarily in mediating the presence and reality of the kingdom of God.

1.4 It has often been pointed out that the kingdom of God itself approaches (Mark 1:14–15) and is brought about by God himself. In particular, the parable of the seed growing secretly in Mark 4:26ff. is usually interpreted as suggesting the radical exclusion of all human activity.

This parable compares the kingdom of God to a seed sown by a sower; while the sower sleeps and rises night and day, the seed sprouts and grows *automatē*, "by itself" (Mark 4:28). This is the point of the parable. The farmer has nothing to do with the growing. The coming of the harvest is assured. This means that the kingdom of God comes without visible cause and is not a miracle performed by human agency. But this does not necessarily imply that there is no human contribution, that the kingdom comes independently of human effort and activity. The farmer cannot affect the ripening of the harvest by his waking or sleeping, by his working or waiting—but he is called to sow and (v. 29) harvest with his sickle. Stuhlmann has shown[17] that the point of Mark 4 is not the contrast between active and passive: the parable is not antisynergistic, anti-Zealot, or even quietistic. The word *automatē* in fact means "unfathomably, miraculously, without visible cause." The parable does not aim to exclude human cooperation but to emphasize the certain, inexplicable, imperceptible coming of the kingdom of

12. Heinz Schürmann, "Das eschatologische Heil Gottes und die Weltverantwortung des Menschen," *Geist und Leben* 50 (1977): 26.

13. Luther, Harnack, and others.

14. *Botschaft*, 32.

15. See below, I.A.1.5.

16. See below, I.B.2.4.

17. Rainer Stuhlmann, "Beobachtungen und Überlegungen zu Mk. 4,26–29," *NT* 19 (1973): 153–62.

God, which is beyond all human powers (including the power of understanding); its coming is brought about by God alone. The point is the certain and unfathomable arrival of the harvest. Other passages too assume that, when the Lord's "harvest" comes, humans will be actively involved (Matt. 9:37–38 par.).

There has often been rather too much stress on the notion that one can only pray for the coming of the kingdom. There is some truth in this statement. But just as the third petition of the Lord's Prayer, that God's will may be realized by God himself ("thy will be done"), does not dispense anyone from the need to do God's will, so too with respect to the second petition ("thy kingdom come"). Conzelmann states that the coming of the kingdom of God can be hastened by prayer, which seems only to contradict the principle that God himself inaugurates it: "God alone acts, yet man can intervene and influence God."[18] But this "seeming contradiction" is not limited to prayer (notice the tension between Luke 12:32 and 9:62). We share in the dawning of the kingdom of God. The final coming is reserved to God's initiative; it is not subject to our intervention and direction. But this does not mean that until then we are left with nothing to do but pray or even wait passively. It is possible to conform to the coming of the kingdom, even in what we do. We can and must live it and extend it.

1.5 To define more precisely the meaning of such "conformity," we must first discuss the salvific nature of the kingdom of God. The fact that Jesus mediates the nearness and presence of the kingdom of God through human experience shows that this experience is salvific: the kingdom of God brings salvation for the *entire* person (as exemplified, e.g., by the healings). God establishes his kingdom when Jesus' victory over the demons brings salvation and deliverance to those who are enslaved and when he makes his own the cause of the poor and the lost, the disenfranchised and degraded. When Jesus drives out demons, he is already demonstrating his victory over the forces of evil that hold captive the human race (Mark 3:27); he is, as it were, the "finger of God" with which God delivers humanity from the power of Satan (cf. Luke 11:20 and 10:18). When he takes the side of those who are rejected by society, he makes credible the coming of God's kingdom as the coming of God's love and justice. What kings and prophets longed to see and hear now begins to become reality (Luke 10:23–24). It is not by chance that some figurative sayings, suggesting (like the parables) the mysterious and indirect aspect of the coming of God's kingdom, indicate that with Jesus the day of salvation has dawned: it is already the time of eschatological rejoicing rather than fasting (Mark 2:18–19), it is the time of harvest (Matt. 9:37–38), and so forth.

It is illuminating to compare the message of Jesus with that of John the

18. Conzelmann, *Outline* (B), 110.

Baptist. The focus of John's preaching was not the God of mercy but the God of judgment, not the salvation of God but the coming wrath of God (Luke 3:7ff. par.).[19] Jesus did not simply discard the idea of judgment but integrated it into his preaching (see Matt. 11:22, 24; 12:36; Luke 16:1ff.; 12:16ff.). His message, however, puts primary emphasis on the salvific nature of the kingdom of God, displayed in the message of salvation and the forgiveness of sins, in healings and exorcisms, in table fellowship with sinners and tax collectors, in fulfillment of the prophets' promises, and so forth. Luz rightly claims that the crucial point is the interpretation of the coming of God's kingdom "as God's unlimited and boundless love for the outcasts and marginal people of Israel."[20]

The citation of Isa. 61:1–2 in Matt. 11:5 (see also Luke 4:18–19) is as characteristic of Jesus' message as are the Beatitudes in their original form. It is not by accident that Matthew and Luke, following Q, begin the great discourse that is of the utmost significance for the ethics of Jesus (the Sermon on the Mount and the Sermon on the Plain) with the promise of unconditional salvation in the Beatitudes. Although Matthew has expanded the sayings by adding ethical elements,[21] it is clear that eschatological salvation is promised to the poor, the despised, those who mourn, and those in need. Those who are religiously and socially disadvantaged in the eyes of this world because they have nothing and must depend on God alone in their need receive Jesus' promise of God's kingdom as salvation. "Blessed are you poor" (Luke 6:20).

The concept of "poverty" probably has not only social and economic but also religious significance. This duality is already apparent in certain passages of the Old Testament and other Jewish documents (e.g., Isa. 61:1–2). There is a similarity to the sayings about "receiving the kingdom of God like a child" (Mark 10:15 par.), which does not mean receiving the kingdom "in childlike innocence"—the New Testament never mentions the innocence of children—but in impotence and need, trusting in God's grace rather than in one's own ability and achievements.[22] Jesus' own way of life chimes with the unconditional promise of salvation: his friendship with those made unclean by sickness, with disqualified women, with excluded sinners and Samaritans (Mark 2:17). Tax collectors and prostitutes, who belong to groups ostracized both socially and religiously, will enter the kingdom of God before the devout, and this "precedence" (Matt. 21:31) is to be understood not simply temporally but exclusively.

It is easy to see how shocking such statements must have been. The parable

19. See Jürgen Becker, *Johannes der Taüfer und Jesus von Nazareth*, BS 63 (Neukirchen: Neukirchener Verlag, 1976).
20. Ulrich Luz, "basileia," *Exegetisches Wörterbuch zum NT*, ed. H. Balz and G. Schneider, 3 vols. (Stuttgart: Kohlhammer, 1980–83), 1:486.
21. See below, 151–52.
22. See Merklein, *Gottesherrschaft*, 128–29.

of the laborers in the vineyard (Matt. 20:1ff.) describes the displeasure of those who have worked longest, illustrating the scandal provoked among devout observers of the law, who considered Jesus' attitude toward sinners a transgression of sacred injunctions. Those who are devout wish for a God who will be a guarantor of religious and moral order, who will apportion to all their just desserts, not a God who is totally free to ignore what people have earned (including rewards for ethical behavior) and think they have coming to them, not a God who fills the empty hands of those who stand before him as beggars without any claim. The boundless sovereignty of God's mercy is illustrated by the way the owner of the vineyard treats those who have done the least. The conduct of the father in the parable of Luke 15 is similar: he runs to meet his prodigal son, receives him back home, gives a banquet to celebrate his return—and thus evokes the protest of the elder son.

Jesus thus justifies his own conduct toward the lost by appealing to the mercy God shows sinners. As an important corollary, he claims to realize God's love in his own ministry, indeed to act as God's representative. Fuchs, who stresses the ethical implications of this claim, rightly says: "Jesus dares to affirm the will of God as though he himself stood in God's place."[23] This also confirms his claim to exercise a unique authority in interpreting God's will. It is also significant for Jesus' ethics to note that he proclaimed and lived the salvific arrival of the kingdom of God, and that he is therefore unlikely to have preached an ethics of merit calling on people to earn their salvation through their conduct. His ethics presupposes both the dawning kingdom of God with its gift of salvation and the assurance and expectation of its complete realization.

2. The Relationship of Eschatology and Ethics

No matter how Jesus' eschatology is defined, no one has been able to overlook its significance for his ethics. Weiss and Schweitzer already noted that Jesus' ethics must be explained primarily from the perspective of his eschatology. Even if eschatology is limited to imminent expectation and ethics is defined specifically in the sense of interim ethics,[24] it cannot be denied that Jesus understood his message and his ethics as deriving from the imminent or incipient kingdom of God. In this sense Jesus' ethics is a direct consequence of his eschatological message of the kingdom and mercy of God.[25] The imminent kingdom of God motivates people to act in a way appropriate to this kingdom.

The dependence of Jesus' ethics on his eschatology is not disputed even by

23. Ernst Fuchs, "The Quest of the Historical Jesus," in *Studies*, 21; cf. Jeremias, *Theology* 1:120.
24. See below, 30–31.
25. See Merklein, *Gottesherrschaft*, 15 and passim.

those who interpret this eschatology as being realized; an example is provided by Dodd, who states that the presence of the kingdom lays the foundation for ethics and calls people to appropriate conduct: "History has reached its climax. . . . It is the zero hour, in which decisive action is called for."[26]

Finally, many do not follow Weiss and Schweitzer in interpreting Jesus' eschatology as referring totally to the future or Dodd in interpreting it as being totally realized and present, but take instead a dialectical approach; they, too, see ethical implications. Wendland, for example, finds a double motivation in Jesus' ethics: for Jesus, both "the indicative of present salvation" and "the future of judgment to come" determine conduct;[27] it may remain for now an open question whether these two phrases describe the polarity accurately.

2.1 Of course not all exegetes think that Jesus' ethics is grounded in his eschatology. In particular, Windisch[28] and Schürmann[29] consider ethics and eschatology to be two relatively isolated quantities without any necessary direct relationship. But even if a systematic connection remains problematic and there is usually no direct literary connection between the two entities, the question of a material unity or relationship remains.[30] Such an intentional unity has been seen in the existential understanding of the situation in which decisions are made, in the idea of God, and in an implicit christology.

According to Bultmann, the unity of Jesus' eschatological message and his ethical message lies in the deepest meaning of each: the individual "*now* stands under the necessity of decision."[31] Both eschatology and ethics are based on the same view of humanity and its relationship to God.[32] Since, however, a timeless existentialism cannot be made the key to an understanding of Jesus, it would be better to say that in the coming of salvation "the coming ruler intervenes in the present as the loving Father"; Jesus' ethical demands "always focus radically on God."[33] At the same time, the unity of eschatology and ethics is given in the person of Jesus, who shows the way in both.[34] The truth of this implicitly christological solution consists in the fact that the presence of the salvation brought by the kingdom of God depends upon Jesus, who also claims to act for God and accomplish God's will.[35]

26. Dodd, *Gospel* (B), 60; see also Amos N. Wilder, *Eschatology and Ethics in the Teaching of Jesus*, rev. ed. (New York: Harper & Row, 1950), 160.
27. Wendland, *Ethik* (B), 29; cf. Merklein, *Gottesherrschaft*, 168.
28. *Bergpredigt*, 6ff.
29. *Eschatologie*, 203ff.
30. See below, 33.
31. Bultmann, *Jesus*, 131.
32. Hans Conzelmann, "Jesus Christus," *RGG³*, 3:637 [English: *Jesus* (Philadelphia: Fortress Press, 1973)].
33. Kümmel, *Theology*, 49; cf. also Windisch, *Bergpredigt*, 23.
34. Conzelmann, "Jesus Christus," 637; cf. idem, *Grundriss* (B), 144: indirect Christology is the "common starting point" for the doctrine of God, ethics, and eschatology; cf. also Wendland, *Ethik* (B), 32.
35. Merklein, *Gottesherrschaft*, 41.

The important point here is the significance of ethics in this triangular relationship. It makes little sense to frame the question as though theocentric and eschatological ethics were mutually exclusive,[36] since Jesus' preaching, including his ethics, is both theological and eschatological. It cannot be denied that there is some tension between eschatology and certain statements about God deriving from wisdom tradition, which present God primarily as Creator with less emphasis on his eschatological role.[37] But this tension is not reducible to a treatment of eschatology and theology as mutually exclusive alternatives. It is characteristic, in fact, that both come together in the preaching of the kingdom of God: the eschatological sovereignty of God is the sovereignty of the Father, who in his sovereignty brings forth the saving power of his love.

2.2 Of course there are also passages where we find a direct relationship between eschatology and ethics; the eschatology may be either futuristic or realized. Our first example, Luke 12:58–59, involves a futuristic eschatology. This "crisis parable" warns against appearing unprepared before God's judgment seat.

We need not discuss Matthew's version of this parable (Matt. 5:25–26), which has been reshaped parenetically. Common to both is the advice to come to terms with one's accuser while still on the way to court if one is in debt to him. Once the proceedings begin, the outcome can only be disastrous.[38]

In Luke this material has not yet been allegorized; it is still a parable inculcating proper conduct at the last moment. There is a point at which it is too late, even if the coming judgment is not just a threat but also an opportunity (cf. also Luke 16:1ff.). The time remaining can and must be used for proper behavior in the face of the coming eschaton.

It is unlikely that the parable goes beyond the point of comparison (*tertium comparationis*) and enjoins reconciliation with actual accusers. This reading does not do justice to the heavily emphasized demand (note the use of the imperative, rare in parables) to reach an agreement as quickly as possible. Furthermore it is a commonplace in other passages that reconciliation with one's neighbor is a condition for deliverance in the day of judgment.[39] If this interpretation were correct, the parable would not only be stating a formal requirement of repentance in the face of the approaching end but would be demanding material readiness to forgive and seek reconciliation.[40] In any case, the imminent eschaton with its expected judgment provides the motivation for an ethics, the substance of which, as always, needs further definition. Compare also Luke 13:6ff., where the barren fig tree is given another

36. Bald, "Ethik," 36.
37. See below, 33–34.
38. See Jeremias, *Parables*, 32–33, 132–33; Schürmann, "Eschatologie," 205ff.
39. Schürmann, "Eschatologie."
40. Pace Jeremias, *Parables*, 34ff.

chance, and Luke 16:1ff., where the steward in his present conduct uses every means at his disposal to prepare for the future.

Another example with a similar perspective on human conduct is the concluding parable of the Sermon on the Mount/Plain (Matt. 7:24–27//Luke 6:47–49): doing the words of Jesus—understood as guidelines for how to live—has consequences for final salvation or eternal destiny. It is therefore wise to guide one's conduct now by these words and incorporate this eschatological dimension into one's total manner of life. Those who do not do so are foolish and "great will be their fall"—they will not be saved at the end.

Here belong the so-called entrance sayings,[41] which make entry into the kingdom of God conditional upon fulfillment of certain conditions: not merely acceptance of the kingdom "like a child" (Mark 10:15 par.) or becoming like children (Matt. 18:3), but a way of life (cf. Mark 10:25). These statements chime totally with the inescapable threats of judgment, according to which judgment follows not only rejection of the kingdom of God (e.g., Luke 10:10ff.; 11:31–32) but also concrete misconduct or specific sins of omission (Matt. 25:31ff.). At the last judgment, therefore, people must render account for every careless word (Matt. 12:36), those who judge will be judged (Matt. 7:1–2), the scribes who devour widows' houses and for a pretense make long prayers will be judged strictly (Mark. 12:40), those who are angry with their brothers shall be liable to judgment (Matt. 5:22), and so forth (besides Matt. 25:31ff., see also Luke 19:12ff.). Everyone comes to face this final judgment on the part of God. Everything done and left undone has inescapable consequences for evil or for good, for salvation or perdition.

Above all, the notion of reward belongs to this series of eschatological motifs in Jesus' ethics. The promise of reward, too, is based in part on specific actions, from giving a cup of water (Mark 9:41 par.) to love of enemies (Matt. 5:46; cf. also the parables in Matthew 25).

Protestantism has a prejudice, inherited from Plato and Kant, against the notion of reward. This prejudice has been reinforced by the dispute with Catholicism. But the genuinely biblical notion of reward must be distinguished from idealistic ethics, which claims that doing good has meaning and value in itself, as well as from the doctrine of merit acquired through good works. Luke 17:7–10, the parable of the master and servant, clearly states a fundamental motif of the New Testament concept of reward, which is of particular importance for ethics, when it concludes: "So you also, when you have done all that is commanded you, say, 'We are unworthy servants; we have only done what was our duty.'" This "duty" we owe enshrines the radical claim God has upon us as his servants and our absolute commitment to him. What is "commanded" makes human autonomy and autarchy both illusionary and hubristic. Therefore not even good works can establish a human

---

41. Cf. Hans Windisch, "Die Sprüche vom Eingehen in das Reich Gottes," *ZNW* 27 (1928): 163–92; Merklein, *Gottesherrschaft*, 134.

claim upon God. Reward is a free gift of God (cf. Matt. 20:1ff.). This cuts off at the root all speculative calculation of reward as a motif of ethics while taking seriously humankind in its dependence on God.[42]

All this shows clearly that the eschatological message of Jesus—more precisely, the promise of the unmerited kingdom of God, which cannot be established by human efforts—is a crucial motive for human conduct. "Repent, *for* the kingdom of God is at hand" (Mark 1:15). Human conduct is a consequence, not a condition, of the coming of God's kingdom, but when the kingdom does not lead to appropriate consequential action on the part of humankind, it becomes judgment.

2.3 An examination of comparative material can make the point even clearer, above all the background of rabbinic Judaism, where we find statements resembling Mark 1:15 associating repentance with the eschaton. According to the rabbis, God has determined the day of eschatological deliverance; on the other hand, the messianic era will not come until the moral and religious condition of the people allows it to. It was also widely believed that the coming of the Messiah and of salvation could be hastened by repentance as well as by observance of the law, study of the Torah, and so forth, and could be delayed by the absence of such conduct. Rabbi Eliezer ben Hyrcanus (ca. 90), for example, says in YTaanit 1:1: "If the Israelites do not repent, they will not be redeemed for all eternity." In Sanhedrin 97b, the same rabbi says: "If the Israelites repent, they will be redeemed; but if they do not, they will not be redeemed." In a similar vein, Rabbi Levi (ca. 300) says in the Midrash on Song of Solomon 5:2 (118a): "If the Israelites were to repent only for a day, they would be redeemed at once and the Son of David would come at once."[43]

In apocalyptic literature too, despite its dominant determinism, we hear similar voices. In Syriac Baruch 46:5–6, for example, we read: "But only prepare your hearts to obey the law. . . . For if you do so, the promises will come true for you." In 44:7 also, observance of the law is the precondition for the coming of the eschaton: "If you wait patiently and do not forget his law, the times will be turned into salvation for you." The apocalyptic writers are usually also aware that the kingdom of God can be established only by God's own mighty act; obedience to the law merely prepares humankind to receive the kingdom.

In the Qumran Scrolls and the preaching of John the Baptist, however, we find a different situation; here ethical injuctions are motivated by apocalyptic statements, and the nearness of the eschaton leads to exhortations and warnings. Although there are occasional hints of an eschatological present, the

---

42. See H. Preisker, "misthos," *TDNT* 4:703ff., 719ff.; Günther Bornkamm, "Der Lohngedanke im Neuen Testament," in *Studien zu Antike und Christentum* (*Gesammelte Aufsätze*, vol. 2), 2d ed., BEvTh 28 (Munich: Kaiser, 1962), 69–92.
43. Strack-Billerbeck, *Kommentar* 1:162ff.

parenesis is based primarily on statements referring to the future. Formally, however, the eschaton is the wellspring and foundation of ethics; this structure resembles the relationship between eschatology and ethics found in the preaching of Jesus. In any case, Jesus' message is not: "Repent, *that* the kingdom of God may come," but: "Repent, *for* the kingdom of God is at hand."

2.4 The association just outlined between eschatology and ethics is fully supported by texts like the parable of the treasure in the field and the valuable pearl (Matt. 13:44–46). Here we see the crucial difference between the apocalyptic definition of the relationship between eschatology and ethics and Jesus' definition. Here ethics is based not on the future coming but on the presence of the kingdom of God.

According to Matt. 13:44–46, the kingdom of God/heaven is like a treasure hidden in a field, which someone finds and then hides again. The finder goes in joy and sells all that he has in order to buy the field. The parable of the pearl is similar.[44]

It cannot be said with certainty whether Matthew is responsible for linking the two parables, but their parallel conclusions appear to show that at least for him everything depends on "total commitment" and an either/or.[45] If we disregard the Matthaean setting, however, this interpretation does not appear to be the whole story. Many exegetes rightly point to the phrase "in his joy" (v. 44). But since this "joy" is mentioned explicitly only in the parable of the treasure in the field, one may also say that the point is the unexpected discovery implicit in the finding of the treasure and the pearl. Only this reading makes sense of what the finder decides to do in the light of his stroke of luck, because it is only the discovery that causes the finder to be swept up in his response. Jüngel even says: "Anyone moved by *joy* over the discovery of such a treasure does not need to make a decision. The decision has already been made. The *discovery* has relieved the finder of making it."[46] This is something of an exaggeration, but it does justice to the crucial significance of the discovery, which in truth makes the surrender of everything else the only possible response.[47] In Luke 19:11ff. par., similarly, it is the "minas" that bring the profit.[48]

This means that the kingdom of God when found itself evokes conduct appropriate to the eschaton. The kingdom of God is the foundation of ethics in the sense that it has already irrupted into the present as a joyfully acknowledged discovery, as something that even now brings salvation, joy, and direction. For Jesus, ethics is a consequence of eschatology not merely in

---

44. See Jeremias, *Parables*, 156ff.; Merklein, *Gottesherrschaft*, 65ff.; Weder, *Gleichnisse*, 138ff.
45. Linnemann, *Parables*, 106; Merklein, *Gottesherrschaft*, 67–68; etc.
46. Jüngel, *Paulus*, 143; cf. Weder, *Gottesherrschaft*, 140.
47. Jeremias, *Parables*, 158; cf. also Georg Eichholz, *Gleichnisse der Evangelien*, 3d ed. (Neukirchen: Neukirchener Verlag, 1979), 109ff.
48. See Weder, *Gottesherrschaft*, 205–6.

the sense that it serves to prepare humanity for the imminent eschaton, as in Luke 12:57ff. and the entrance sayings. It is also an inescapable consequence in the sense that it is the only reasonable response to the kingdom of God already at hand in Jesus. Therefore in the dawning day of joy and salvation— wedding guests can hardly mourn and fast during the marriage feast[49]—it is inappropriate to fast ascetically (Mark 2:18–19). Therefore reception of sinners, the unclean, and tax collectors can be grounded in Jesus' reception of the lost (Luke 15:3ff.). Above all, therefore, the new vision of the law, which differs from that of "those of old,"[50] can be understood only on the basis of Jesus' eschatology.[51] We shall encounter (I.A.4 below) a relationship similar to that in Matt. 13:44–46 but with more circumstantial content (e.g., the parable of the wicked servant). But first two qualifications must be noted.

3. Eschatological Ethics—Neither Apocalyptic nor Sapiential

3.1 It has already been pointed out that Weiss and Schweitzer were responsible for rediscovering the eschatological nature of Jesus' message. In the nineteenth century, the kingdom of God was generally understood as a moral kingdom evolving and taking shape within this world; it was spread and advanced by human efforts. Weiss, however, maintained in his study of Jesus' message[52] that the kingdom of God is not immanent and evolutionary; it is not a moral duty and an ethical possibility. It is beyond the scope of human ability and initiative, and can only invade this world through a miraculous act of God. Jesus' call to awake and repent is meant to prepare the way for this act. Jesus' ethics can be understood only from the perspective of a belief that the end of the world is imminent. The critical nature of the present moment, when everything hangs in the balance, compels Jesus to proclaim extraordinary laws to govern the final battle, in which things of this world can only stand in the way.[53] Jesus' ethics is the demand of a man who knows he already stands with one foot in the new age; it is meant for those who expect the world to end at any moment. "He demands mighty acts, sometimes super-human acts, he demands things that would be simply impossible under ordinary circumstances."[54] But even Weiss saw that the "negatively ascetic" aspect of the "fundamental eschatological perspective" does not apply to *all* of Jesus' words, an observation he explains primarily on the psychological grounds of "a calmer mood."[55]

49. Joachim Jeremias, "nymphē," *TDNT* 4:1103–4.
50. See below, 52–53.
51. See Ulrich B. Müller, "Vision und Botschaft," *ZThK* 74 (1977): 416–48, esp. 430ff.; Merklein, *Gottesherrschaft*, 72ff. English: *Jesus' Proclamation of the Kingdom of God*. Philadelphia: Fortress Press; London: SCM Press, 1971.
52. Johannes Weiss, *Die Predigt Jesu vom Reiche Gottes* (Göttingen: Vandenhoeck & Ruprecht, 1892).
53. Ibid., 143.
54. Ibid., 139.
55. Ibid., 134ff.

Schweitzer understands Jesus' eschatology even more radically and consistently as the end of all civilization and its values. For Schweitzer, Jesus' entire ethics falls within the concept of "repentance that prepares the way for the coming of the kingdom."[56] Because catastrophe is imminent and it is a time of crisis, bridges must be burned and the dead must be left to bury their dead. Jesus' eschatological message is the crucial basis and guideline for his ethics. The present is merely an interim, a time of preparation for the kingdom of God. Jesus' ethics is therefore an interim ethics.[57]

3.2 But our discussion at the end of the previous section has already shown that Jesus' eschatology cannot be identified with apocalypticism. Jesus' ethics, therefore, cannot be interpreted as interim ethics. It is clearly not true that Jesus' eschatological sayings are to be interpreted as emergency legislation for a world standing in the smoke and glare of imminent cosmic catastrophe.[58] Jesus was not a prophet of doom or an ethicist of catastrophe, basing his instruction on visions of a holocaust or universal destruction. Weiss and Schweitzer impose on Jesus' words an apocalyptic fire that is obviously foreign to them, as the substance of Jesus' ethics will confirm. The dominant motive and fundamental basis for Jesus' demands is not the apocalyptic end of the world or fear of it (cf. Luke 19:11ff. par., which rejects fear as a response to the coming accounting), but the God who in Jesus has come to save, who brings his final salvation in Jesus and has Jesus proclaim his will with authority. This, not imminent apocalyptic expectation, is what gives meaning, for example, to the commandment to love both neighbor and enemy in Matthew 5 and Luke 6. Apocalyptic expectation and the temporal dimension as such cannot explain it.

The apocalyptic structure of religious and ethical dicta does not lead automatically to a conclusion such as the commandment to love one's enemies, which Weiss[59] sees as part of Jesus' eschatological message. We may compare the Qumran texts, which are dominated by expectation of an imminent eschaton: they repeatedly inculcate not love but "hatred" toward enemies and those who do not belong to the sect (e.g., 1QS 9:21–22; cf. the inner circle ethics of 1QS 10:17ff.). We might also cite other features of Qumran ethics such as its legalism. The Zealot movement, too, was characterized by strong eschatological expectations, which led the Zealots to try to usher in the eschaton by means of violent political action.

All this shows that it is not eschatology alone, or at least not apocalyptic eschatology, that determines Jesus' ethics. Jesus' demands are not based primarily on the shortness of the time remaining but on the fact that it is the

---

56. Albert Schweitzer, *The Mystery of the Kingdom of God* (New York: Dodd, Mead, 1914), 94.
57. Ibid., 97; cf. idem, *The Quest of the Historical Jesus* (New York: Macmillan, 1950), 354ff. For an appreciation of the notion of "interim ethics," see Hiers, *Jesus*, 134ff.; a positive estimate is also found in Sanders, *Ethics*, 11 and passim.
58. Cf. Bornkamm, *Jesus*, 228.
59. *Predigt*, 150.

kingdom of God that comes, the kingdom of the God who acts to save the world.

3.3 Of course it would be wrong to counter the theory of an apocalyptically based interim ethics with the equally one-sided perspective of "realized eschatology," as do such scholars as Dodd and Wilder. Nor, however, is it possible to deal convincingly with the notion of interim ethics by isolating the substance of Jesus' demands from their eschatological context. This would reduce eschatology to the role of a motivating force. The coming of the kingdom could then motivate the general call to repentance, but not specific demands.

"Even if this is in fact earth's latest hour, God's will today is no different from what it has always been."[60] Wendland is somewhat more cautious,[61] deriving the substance of Jesus' demands from God's nature and will rather than from the nearness of the eschaton. According to Schürmann, finally, the imminent end "determines the conduct demanded by Jesus only accidentally; its motivation is practical and parenetic, not ultimate and essential."[62] Wilder says much the same: eschatology is not dominant but secondary, not an "essential sanction" (that is the will of God) but merely a "formal sanction."

None of this is really convincing; although it will certainly not do for us to derive the substance of Jesus' demands from the imminence of the eschaton, neither can we derive it from an eternal and changeless divine will. Not only is the discontinuity between Jesus and the Old Testament with its law too clear, but the concept of God and God's will presupposed by this approach is too formal and vague: it shows no trace of God's eschatological will for salvation. Despite its intended conclusiveness based on the natural order of creation, the statement that God makes his sun rise and sends his rain upon both the evil and the good—the justification in Matthew 5 for the command to love enemies—is not a universal statement anyone might make by observing the natural world but a graphic metaphor of God's eschatological loving will: it must be expounded by Jesus to be convincing. Certainly there is no trace of this radical and fundamental commandment to love enemies in the wisdom tradition, which rests on eternal order and plausibility. The statement that God "made" the Sabbath as a blessing for human well-being (Mark 2:27) is not deduced from the divine order of creation. It carries conviction because it reflects Jesus' absolute authority and consistent praxis of love. The meaning of God's act of creation and the possibility of its providing an epistemological basis for human conduct (cf. Mark 10:6) must first be elucidated by Jesus. Alongside the parallelism between beginning and end— which can be recognized only from the perspective of the end—there is a

60. Conzelmann, "Jesus Christus," 637.
61. *Ethik* (B), 18.
62. "Eschatologie," 212.

sense in which the end surpasses the beginning. Only the eschatological shape of God's boundless love illuminates creation.

It is quite appropriate to speak of theocentric and theonomous ethics,[63] but it must be clearly stated what "God" means in this context. The eschatological and soteriological aspects of God must be kept constantly in mind. The reference can be only to the God who has come to save once for all in Jesus, the God who now lets one discover the precious pearl and make the appropriate response. It is therefore wrong to speak of a notion of God that is only formally eschatological but materially theological, because for Jesus the notion of God and eschatology are inseparable.

Nor, however, can one make a sharp distinction between motive and content in Jesus' ethics. Merklein has rightly emphasized that "at least in basic outline" the ethical message of Jesus must be interpreted materially from the perspective of the eschatological kingdom of God; it demands a "reorientation of conduct."[64] We may recall the example of celibacy[65] or the radical sayings concerning discipleship, which can hardly be supported by a theology based on creation.

3.4 Above all, it misrepresents the eschatological ethics of Jesus to look on the reality of the created world as the common bond or even the broader concept uniting Jesus' ethics and theology. Bald, for example, finds belief in God as Creator to be the unity linking Jesus' future-oriented eschatological sayings with his present-oriented ethical sayings.[66] Our discussion has shown, however, that the broader category integrating Jesus' teaching is not the reality of the created world or belief in the Creator, but the kingdom of God.[67] Above all, God's will cannot be deduced from any universally recognized ontological order, as we must still (or again) insist against attempts to base an ethics on natural law.[68] We admit unreservedly the importance for Jesus of statements dealing with God's creative work, but not their autonomy. In Judaism, the doctrine of creation led to a conservative interpretation of the law in the sense of preserving the status quo. Jesus' eschatological faith, however, leads him to describe models of conduct in harmony with God's new eschatological act.[69]

63. Neuhäusler, *Anspruch*, 48; Schürmann, "Eschatologie," 214ff.; Bald, "Ethik"; and others.
64. Merklein, *Gottesherrschaft*, 42, 47; cf. also 15.
65. Ibid., 93–94.
66. Bald, "Ethik," 45.
67. Cf. Merklein, *Gottesherrschaft*, 37.
68. "An inward affinity between the natural and the moral" (W. D. Davies, "The Relevance of the Moral Teaching of the Early Church," in *Neotestamentica et Semitica* [Festschrift Matthew Black], ed. E. E. Ellis and M. Wilcox [Edinburgh: Clarke, 1969], 30–49, quotation from 36) is a fiction. Schnackenburg rightly calls "natural moral law" an inappropriate category for discussing the ethics of Jesus (Rudolf Schnackenburg, "Die neutestamentliche Sittenlehre in ihrer Eigenart im Vergleich zu einer natürlichen Ethik," in *Moraltheologie und Bibel*, ed. J. Stelzenberger [Paderborn: Schöningh, 1964], 39–69, esp. 49, 52).
69. Hoffmann, "Eschatologie," 190–91.

But how does this square with the observation that the eschatological perspective is far from determining the entire corpus of the ethical tradition? As we have already suggested, Jesus' message includes wisdom traditions that make Jesus resemble a wisdom teacher more than an eschatological prophet, a teacher who teaches without any reference to the eschaton, who in fact appears to count on an enduring world. It is an open question, of course, whether it is legitimate to conclude that where the eschatological kingdom is not mentioned explicitly it cannot be cited exegetically. The objection to isolating the wisdom passages in this manner is that the isolated nature of the individual traditions makes it necessary to apprehend the intellectual unity of Jesus' ethical message through a process of reconstruction. We are dealing with texts that fall within the orbit of wisdom traditio-historically, not in substance.[70] Traditional material at odds with eschatology, such as the almost rationalistic appeal to reason and experience that derives from wisdom, takes on a different meaning and a new appearance in the eschatological context. This is best illustrated by examples. In Matthew 6 and 10, for example, we find sayings and complexes of sayings in which the eschatological motif is not prominent.

In the warning against laying up treasures in Matt. 6:19ff. and Luke 12:16ff., Bultmann and other exegetes see Jesus as a wisdom instructor dominated by the spirit of a popular religiosity.[71] It is indisputable that here Jesus appeals to what might be called common sense. For example, Matt. 6:19 uses a rational argument to call into question the permanence of earthly treasures. What matters is where one's heart is: the heart must not be fixed on earthly things that pass away but on heavenly things that endure. There one's heart must be totally fixed; that is what one can truly rely on. Such treasure, however, is not found on earth but only where God is: in heaven.

But is all this wisdom instruction based on universal human experience and immediately evident to all? This really holds true only for the impermanence of earthly treasures. Common sense can deduce the folly of laying up treasure on earth from general knowledge and experience, but it does not follow by any means that what matters is to lay up treasures in heaven. The logic is at least as likely to end in despair and meaninglessness or the uninhibited enjoyment of reaping the day (carpe diem): "Let us eat and drink, for tomorrow we die" (Isa. 22:13). The appeal to reason and experience can disclose the negative and undermine security, but it cannot lay a positive foundation for love and hope. It has an ancillary function but cannot carry the entire burden.

70. Kümmel, "Sittlichkeit" (B), 72; idem, "Jesusforschung seit 1965, IV: Bergpredigt, Gleichnisse, Wunderberichte," ThR 43 (1978): 253.
71. Harald Riesenfeld, "Vom Schätzesammeln und Sorgen," in Neotestamentica et Patristica (Festschrift Oscar Cullmann), ed. W. C. van Unnik, NT.S 6 (Leiden: Brill, 1962), 47–58, esp. 48.

This is confirmed by the exhortation not to be anxious (Matt. 6:25 par.). Many parallels from popular tradition indicate that by itself this passage could derive from a popular optimistic faith in providence. When the exhortation is based on the argument that mortals are not in control of their own lives and cannot lengthen their life span by anxiety, or when birds and lilies are mentioned as examples of proper freedom from anxiety, we are dealing with wisdom arguments.[72]

Even here, however, these arguments carry little conviction. Above all, insight into the pointlessness of anxiety does not necessarily bring freedom from anxiety, whose power is not overcome by logic and reason alone. The focus of the text, enshrining both the true value and the limitation of the sapiential tradition, is v. 32 ("your heavenly Father knows that you need them all"), which recalls the petition for bread in the Lord's Prayer. It is just those who pray for the eschatological kingdom of God who can be confident of the creator God's care and faithfulness. When the kingdom of God dawns, the power of anxiety is broken. Therefore Matt. 6:33 insists that one must seek first the kingdom of God. Matthew 6:25ff. does not paint an idyllic picture. It illustrates the harshness of a life without home, possession, or protection, lived under the aegis of the kingdom of God.[73]

Matthew, too, clearly expressed the primacy of eschatology by placing the wisdom texts of the Sermon on the Mount in an eschatological setting. Luck interprets the evidence differently; according to him, Matthew "shifts what was originally an eschatological proclamation of divine law to a perspective shaped by the thought-forms of wisdom."[74] But even Luke 12:31 still makes it clear that only the primacy of the kingdom of God makes concern for food and clothing secondary. Even Jewish apocalyptic, which incorporated wisdom elements, never gave precedence to wisdom. Neither do wisdom and its logic ever define the structure of Jesus' world.

In fact, we must go a step beyond such restrictions on the perspective of wisdom: eschatology continually shatters the wisdom tradition (for a much earlier example, see the prophetical criticism of wisdom in Jer. 8:8–9). What may seem to make sense under normal circumstances can be irrational in the light of the coming of God's kingdom. The newness of the eschaton destroys the categories and criteria of ancient tradition (cf. the image of the new patch and the new wine in Mark 2:21–22 and the eschatological reinterpretation of such wisdom proverbs as Mark 4:21ff.).

Discussing Matt. 10:26, Käsemann claims that the insight of practical wisdom has been turned on its head with remarkable audacity: "Nothing is

72. Cf. Prov. 6:6ff. and Zeller, *Mahnsprüche* (B7), 82ff.
73. See Theissen, "Wanderradikalismus," 251; Mealand, *Poverty* (I.D), 85ff.; Schottroff and Stegemann, *Jesus*, 59ff.
74. Ulrich Luck, *Die Vollkommenheitsforderung der Bergpredigt* (Munich: Kaiser, 1968), 38; cf. the criticism in Kümmel, "Jesusforschung," 114.

covered that will not be revealed, or hidden that will not be known." This is
obviously meant to say something like "Murder will out," and is rightly
thought to be a wisdom saying. The saying is probably an admonition to be
circumspect, because secrets rarely remain secret. But this raises the problem
of why v. 27 calls on people to proclaim on the housetops what they have
heard in secret. Käsemann says: "If the point of the proverb in its present
form is that caution must be thrown to the winds at the eschaton, this would
agree excellently with the admonition not to be anxious in Matt. 6:25ff."[75]

It is undoubtedly true that the eschatological revaluation of all values leads
people to do the very things they would otherwise fear and against which they
would otherwise be cautioned. Jesus' demands often enough exceed the
measure of what makes sense (see, e.g., Mark 9:43ff.). This confusion of
normal expectations brings out the novelty of the kingdom of God, which
flies in the face of ordinary conduct. We must of course record the general
reservation that the similarity of Jesus' wisdom sayings to proverbs, popular
adages, and so forth, makes it especially difficult to judge their authenticity.
There can be no doubt, however, that wisdom discourse has been modified by
the eschatological message with its radical and paradoxical demands, nor can
there be any doubt that this eschatological message is not just the announcement of the end of the world but the promise that God the Father is
eschatologically at hand. This saving power of the Father brings to an end the
destroying power of Satan, of whose awful reign of terror the ordered world
of wisdom knows little. The wisdom approach to certain basic phenomena of
human life is thus secondary to the proclamation of the kingdom of God; it
plays a "complementary and supporting role."[76]

According to Zeller, such sayings as Matt. 5:39–40, 44–45 deal with
traditional wisdom subjects but exceed "all reasonable limits."[77] In his discussion, he is trying to establish a particular *Sitz im Leben* for the wisdom
admonitions: they are addressed to those who have already responded to the
call of the kingdom and are now being instructed by Jesus in the practical
consequences of his message, for example, in the renewal of interpersonal
relationships.

It is therefore possible to say that the two perspectives are mutually
complementary.[78] The notion of creation is secondary and subordinate to
eschatology, but is not therefore irrelevant. It is noteworthy that we rarely
find motivations based on natural ethics in Jesus' teaching, even though the

75. Ernst Käsemann, "Das Problem des historischen Jesus," *ZThK* 51 (1954): 147–48
[= *Essays on NT Themes*, 15–47]; cf. also idem, "Die Anfänge christlicher Theologie," *ZThK* 57
(1960): 177–78 [= *NT Questions of Today*, 82–107].
76. Dieter Zeller, "Weisheitliche Überlieferung in der Predigt Jesus," in *Religiöse Grunder-
fahrungen*, ed. W. Strolz (Freiburg: Herder, 1977), 94–111 (quotation from 107); cf. idem,
Mahnsprüche, 182.
77. *Mahnsprüche*, 150.
78. Neuhäusler, *Anspruch*, 40.

appearance of such wisdom motifs with their straightforward simplicity would be appropriate to the explication of God's will. There is no suggestion, for example, that eschatological and rational ethics must necessarily come into conflict, especially since religious wisdom had given rise to ways of life clearly related to an eschatological ethos and distinct from mere rationalism and the doctrine that there are intrinsically and objectively good and evil actions, quite apart from God's will. When one considers human finitude together with the vulnerability of human wealth, even rational economic considerations can be "foolish," as wisdom often insists (see Luke 12:61ff.). Such "foolishness" is not simply an intellectual deficiency but self-delusion, the mistaken assumption that one can make provision for one's own life and salvation. Here there is undoubtedly an affinity between wisdom motifs and the eschatological perspective.

Käsemann has emphasized that when what matters is the relationship between religion and morality, between the cult and daily life, faith and reason fall together for Jesus. "The scandal he provoked did not consist in his . . . presenting impenetrable mysteries to our minds. Instead he bore witness to a God who is not in tune with our ideas and our wishes, a God who breaks our will and with it all rationality that flows from our godless and idolatrous world."[79]

Indeed the limit imposed on wisdom and reason as motive and substance of ethics is not mysterious, ineffable, and speculative. The limit and also the real foundation is the God who reveals himself eschatologically in Jesus' message and ministry as the God of love. What matters, then, is still the eschatological kingdom of God, which cannot be derived from the tradition of wisdom.

4. Eschatological Ethics—Conforming to God's Salvation

If the motive and horizon of Jesus' ethics is realized eschatology in which the salvific kingdom of God is already at hand in Jesus, there remains the question of what this means in practice. Here we must have recourse to the soteriological sayings concerning the promise of salvation, forgiveness of sins, table fellowship, and so forth, as the reflection of God's love. It would be strange if these sayings did not have ethical consequences. And this is in fact the case: according to Jesus, it is the coming of God's kingdom that is to determine human conduct.

The best point of departure is the parable of the wicked servant (Matt. 18:23ff.), which tells of a king who wants to settle accounts with his servants. One of them, probably a governor, owes the king ten thousand talents—an inconceivably large sum, something like the entire tax imposed on a province. When the governor is unable to pay and the king seeks to have him, his family, and all his possessions sold, the governor falls on his knees and

79. *Freedom* (B), 27.

asks for an extension. The king, however, in his generosity forgives him his entire debt. As soon as the governor is released, however, he meets a fellow servant, probably a subordinate official, who owes him a hundred denarii. In words that deliberately echo the earlier scene, he asks the governor for an extension. The governor, however, has him imprisoned immediately, so that he can work off his debt or have it paid by relatives. When the king hears of this, he sends for the governor and charges him once more: "You wicked servant! I forgave you all that debt because you besought me. And should you not have had mercy on your fellow servant, as I had mercy on you?"[80]

In a word, we might say that the parable concerns our obligation to show mercy to others because of the mercy God has shown us when his kingdom comes in Jesus (see, e.g., Matt. 5:7; 9:27 par.). The primary point, therefore, is not the culpability of human intransigence, although there are overtones of judgment. Nor is it the incommensurability between what we owe God and what we owe others, although the enormous difference between the sums mentioned is certainly no accident, and despite the parallelism between the relationships only the governor "falls on his knees" before his master. Nor, finally, is it the "grace period" granted by God, although one may find in God's mercy the gift of time as well as the forgiveness of sins. The crucial point is rather that divine and human mercy correspond. It is not by chance that the king's forgiveness of the debt precedes the governor's demand for payment.

Linnemann rightly states that the "priority of the mercy shown by the king is not just a narrative necessity but has substantial significance." The conduct of the governor—who is guilty of no injustice but is only demanding his rights!—is reprehensible only because he acts without mercy *after* receiving mercy.[81] "If the conduct of the wicked servant were recounted apart from the mercy shown previously by his lord, it would never arouse our protest. The parable shows clearly that the sequence is more than a mere temporal sequence of otherwise independent events."[82]

The experience of God's mercy is therefore the prerequisite, the basis, and the reason for merciful conduct toward others. God's mercy lays the foundation for God's demands—as well as for God's judgment, should this mercy fail to produce results in spite of its incomprehensible freedom from limitations. What God does demands above all corresponding actions on our part. God does not show kindness in order to maintain his superiority, but in order that our kindness may reflect his. The "lead of God's love" cannot be made up, because it "is always ahead of whatever we do";[83] but our conduct must

80. See Linnemann, *Parables,* 105ff; Weder, *Gleichnisse,* 210ff.
81. Linnemann, *Parables,* 177.
82. Ibid., 111.
83. Weder, *Gleichnisse,* 217.

be considered from the perspective of this lead and must aim at love and kindness.

"Every one to whom much is given, of him will much be required; of him to whom men commit much they will demand the more" (Luke 12:48b). We might also cite the parable of the talents (Matt. 25:14ff. par.): an abundance of talents carries an obligation to put them to work. But even if, as seems likely, all the servants originally were given the same amount (cf. Luke 19:11ff.), the parable shows that what matters is a responsible attitude toward the gift of the kingdom; for the minas impose a claim "that must be acknowledged absolutely."[84] The fact that the promise of salvation is absolute makes the obligation absolute, not just formally but also in substance.

This correspondence between indicative and imperative is confirmed in a way by the parable of the two debtors (Luke 7:41ff.), which has been woven into the pericope of the sinful woman in the home of Simon the Pharisee. It is unimportant whether or not the evangelist actually composed the story by transforming the characters in the parable into historical figures. In my opinion, he probably did not.[85]

In this short parable, a creditor or moneylender has two debtors, one of whom owes him 50 denarii, the other 500. Since neither is able to pay, he makes both a gift of the sum owed. The parable ends with the question as to which of the two will love the creditor most, that is, be most grateful to him. Simon answers: "The one to whom he forgave most." This answer agrees with what v. 47 says about the prostitute who anoints Jesus with oil and his feet with ointment. The statement in v. 47 is not entirely clear; it may be paraphrased somewhat as follows: "God must have forgiven her sins, many as they are, because she shows so much gratitude [thankful love]; he who is forgiven little, his thankfulness [thankful love] is little."[86]

But it is also possible that Luke has already shifted the *tertium comparationis*, making the woman's display of love the basis (the real basis, not just the epistemological basis) on which Jesus forgives her sins (v. 47), in order to show that there is a mutual relationship between forgiveness and love.[87] Verses 41–43 and 47b show in any case that originally the relationship was the reverse: human love arises from God's love and imitates God's love, indeed "the measure of love corresponds to the measure of forgiveness."[88] Of course the emphasis is on love for God or for Jesus who represents him (especially in

84. Ibid., 205.

85. The parable is discussed by H. Drexler, "Die grosse Sünderin Lk. 7,36–50," *ZNW* 59 (1968): 159–73; Ulrich Wilckens, "Vergebung für die Sünderin (Lk. 7,36–50)," *Orientierung an Jesus* (Festschrift Josef Schmid), ed. P. Hoffmann, N. Brox, and U. Pesch (Freiburg: Herder, 1973), 394–422.

86. Jeremias, *Parables*, 127.

87. Heinz Schürmann, *Das Lukasevangelium*, HThK 3/1, 437–38.

88. Wilckens, "Vergebung," 405.

the present context). In the case of Jesus, however, this love cannot be separated from love for others.

So far this point has been made metaphorically, in parables. A final example expresses the same idea clearly and directly. The last antithesis of the Sermon on the Mount justifies the command to love one's enemies as follows: "Love your enemies and pray for those who persecute you, so that you may be sons of your Father who is in heaven; for he makes his sun rise on the evil and on the good, and sends rain on the just and on the unjust" (Matt. 5:44–45). Luke adds: "Be merciful, even as your Father is merciful" (Luke 6:36). Matthew has presumably changed this to: "You, therefore, must be perfect, as your heavenly Father is perfect" (Matt. 5:48).

God's undivided fatherly love for all creation, good and bad alike, is the motivation and guiding principle behind the command to love one's enemies. God sets no limits to his love, bringing even the wicked within its scope; we, too, should let our love benefit even our enemies. The "even as" of Luke 6:36 indicates both comparison and motivation. Closer examination, of course, shows the nature of the motivation or illustration to be problematic,[89] in that God's love is to be seen in the processes of nature, in the sunshine and rain bestowed on all alike.

It is not by chance that this "proof" based on elements of natural theology has parallels in Greco-Roman popular philosophy and in Judaism.[90] But the ancient world drew a variety of conclusions from the observation that sunshine and rain are given to all alike, including, for example, the position that the gods are indifferent to what befalls humanity (see the skepticism already found in Eccl. 9:2).

But Jesus' point is clear enough: even sinners live through God's love, because God proves to be a generous giver even to his disobedient creatures. That God responds to human injustice not with injustice or even with justice alone, but with love, is the heart and miracle of Jesus' words. For this very reason, however, the disciples are expected to show similar love and mercy. Such texts also as Luke 10:25ff., which call for mercy as well as sacrifice, can be understood only as reflecting God's radical love for sinners.

B. THE WILL OF GOD AND THE LAW

1. Repentance and Total Obedience

1.1 From what has been said, it should be clear that Jesus grounds human obligation on God's gift and that this indicative is the saving gift of God's eschatological kingdom, to which Jesus invites all in the name of God. But the invitation implies a responsibility and a demand. The new attitude demanded in response to God's offer of salvation is first of all a fundamental

89. See above, 32.
90. Seneca *De beneficiis* 4.26.1; Pesiqta 195a, cited by Strack-Billerbeck, *Kommentar* 1:374.

and comprehensive repentance and conversion, a change of course, a new orientation. The imperative "repent" is itself not so much a demand as a chance for a new beginning and a return to God (see Luke 15:11ff.). The nearness of the kingdom calls us to risk everything for it in a totally new way. To this extent it is hardly justified to eliminate the call to repentance from the message of Jesus, associating the nearness of the kingdom with Jesus and the call to repentance with John the Baptist; the difference between Jesus and John is not that one preaches repentance and the other proclaims the kingdom of God. It is probably correct to say, however, that John proclaims primarily the coming judgment of wrath, whereas Jesus proclaims the imminent kingdom of God as salvation.

But even if the kingdom of God were what distinguishes Jesus from John, this would in itself not justify eliminating the preaching of repentance for Jesus. Even if the term *metanoia* and its corresponding verb did not occur in his preaching (which would have to be proved: see Matt. 11:21–22//Luke 10:13; Matt. 12:41//Luke 11:32; Luke 13:3, 5; 15:10; 16:30), the central substance of Jesus' message is the call to repentance. Renunciation of self-righteousness (Luke 18:10ff.; cf. Mark 10:15), return to the father (Luke 15:11ff.), faith and "self-denial"—all are expressions of repentance. Although the coming of God's kingdom is the real motive for repentance, even Jesus can call to repentance in the context of threatened judgment, although the judgment is not so much the motive for repentance as the consequence of refusing to repent (in addition to Mark 13:1ff., see Matt. 11:20ff., the series of woes over the cities that did not repent). Both John and Jesus differ from apocalypticism in proclaiming this judgment not against the gentile world but against God's own people (Luke 3:7; Matthew 3:7 even mentions—secondarily—the Pharisees and Sadducees by name).

Becker, it is true, assumes that the call to repentance vanished from the core of Jesus' preaching along with the message of judgment, but proposes a distinction between a demand for repentance, which he restricts to the context of the message of judgment, and a "call to decision," for which he claims the promise of salvation is determinative.[91] He himself admits, however, that both contexts involve "an uncompromising, fundamental, and ultimate reorientation before God." Even here, then, judgment is an integral part of the message of salvation.[92]

1.2 But what does *metanoia* mean? Even in classical Greek the concept is not to be understood in a purely intellectual sense. It means not just a change

91. Jürgen Becker, "Busse, IV. NT," *TRE* 7:448.
92. See also Johannes Behm, "noeō (metanoeō)," *TDNT* 4:1000ff.; Herbert Braun, " 'Umkehr' in spätjüdisch-häretischer und in frühchristlicher Sicht," in *Gesammelte Studien zum NT und seiner Umwelt*, 3d ed. (Tübingen: Mohr, 1971), 70–85; for a different view, see Meinrad Limbeck, "Jesu Verkündigung und der Ruf zu Umkehr," in *Das Evangelium auf dem Weg zum Menschen* (Festschrift Heinrich Kahlefeld), ed. O. Knoch (Frankfurt: Knecht, 1973), 35–42.

of mind about something but also a change of attitude, of intention, of will, if not a total transformation of one's conduct and orientation.

Nor does the Old Testament as a whole provide the source for Jesus' preaching of repentance. In it we find penance and repentance side by side. Penance refers to cultic penitential rituals and practices (fasting, mourning garb, confession of sins, etc.). Repentance, however, as demanded by the prophets from Hosea to Jeremiah, means total devotion to God, return to the primal relationship with Yahweh, willingness to take the First Commandment seriously—unconditional trust and unconditional obedience (literarily, repentance appears primarily in proclamations of judgment, not in admonitions). In the postexilic period, the radical prophetic call to repentance did not continue to hold its place, as the increased emphasis on the law and increased moralizing show (e.g., Neh. 9:29).

This trend is accentuated in Judaism. Repentance is thought of increasingly as turning from disobedience to fulfillment of the law. The development is illustrated by the two recensions of the Eighteen Benedictions. In the Palestinian recension, the fifth petition still reads: "Brings us back to thee, O Yahweh, that we may repent." In the Babylonian recension, this petition reads: "Brings us back . . . to thy Torah and . . . make us repent with perfect penance."[93] Also characteristic is the phrase "perfect repentance," which arises from the importance of observing the law: it presupposes confession of sins, penitence, and sorrow, and involves not repeating conduct that is against the law, acts of renunciation, and the like.[94] "Penance and good works are like a shield against God's punishment" (Aboth 4:11).

At Qumran, too, *šûb* means turning to the Torah and, since the Torah is interpreted correctly only at Qumran, to the sect and its organization. The entering novice had to bind himself by oath "to repent and return to the law of Moses, according to all that he commanded" (1QS 5:8–9; cf. CD 16:1–2). One must repent and return to the Torah of Moses with all one's heart and with all one's soul (CD 15:12). Even here, however, the law is the central focus. Despite the radical nature, not lessened by any ritual, of the repentance preached at Qumran, and despite the eschatological focus of obedience to the Torah, this legalism distinguished it from the preaching of Jesus (not to mention the priestly and sectarian ideology of Qumran).

It would appear, therefore, that the substance of Jesus' message of repentance derives from Old Testament prophecy rather than from Judaism. Even though its terminology may be closer to that of the Apocrypha and Pseudepigrapha, in content at least it continues the line of Old Testament prophecy. In addition, penance is not prerequisite for salvation; salvation is prerequisite for penance.

Repentance, then, means total devotion to God, not legalistic penitential

93. Strack-Billerbeck, *Kommentar* 4:211.
94. Ibid. 1:170.

zeal. God's love means that everything can be expected from God (Mark 10:15). His kingdom reaches out for the whole person and therefore claims undivided obedience. God's love and God's claim to sovereignty, expressed also in the First Commandment, are absolute and radical; they spell the end to petty casuistry and superficial acts of penance, but also to the centrality of the law. Matt. 18:3 therefore speaks of repentance in parallelism with "becoming like children," and Luke with good reason sets return to the Father (Luke 15:11ff.) in the context of *metanoia* (15:[7], 10; cf. Matt. 18:13). Repentance is not just admission that we are sinners dependent on God's mercy (Luke 18:9ff.): it has consequences for the conduct of life (as in the preaching of John the Baptist: Luke 3:8, 10–12). The message of the kingdom of God goes forth unconditionally, without prerequisites, as God turns to us in love; we must repent and turn to him with equal openness and confidence. God does not want a share, this or that, some part of us; he wants us wholly.

1.3 This is the sense in which it is true to interpret Jesus' instructions as illustrating an ethics of intention, in which all individual demands are interpreted paradigmatically. Herrmann, for example, maintains[95] that all the concrete details merely illustrate one great fundamental principle, namely, that Christians must live their lives entirely on the basis of love. Herrmann also sees that Jesus requires absolute obedience, but he seeks to distinguish the considered obedience of those who are free from the dead obedience of those who are not. Jesus is concerned with total human autonomy. His words are an appeal to each person's conscience, not a model; they require people to judge and act according to their own consciences—without reservation or restriction, not half-heartedly but wholly.[96]

Others have taken similar positions: what matters is the human heart, the inward disposition or intention. Jesus' will is not fulfillment of this or that new commandment but a new attitude, a new heart, not a way of acting but a way of being, not works but character. Even someone like Dibelius, who considers "vague Christian idealism" a danger,[97] could say that what is required is not "that we *do* something, but that we *be* something,"[98] so that the crucial point is transformation of the individual.

This is no more than a brief summary of the interpretation of Jesus' ethics as an ethics of intention. In it true and false elements are intertwined. There can be no doubt that Jesus' purpose is to reshape human intentions and establish a new will, that he wants to claim for God not just the body but the heart, the whole person. "Where your treasure is, there will your heart be

---

95. Wilhelm Herrmann, *Die sittlichen Weisungen Jesu*, 3d ed. (Göttingen: Vandenhoeck & Ruprecht, 1921).
96. Soiron, *Bergpredigt*, 43ff.; Hendrik van Oyen, "Gesinnungsethik," *RGG*³ 2:1537–38.
97. *Sermon*, 143.
98. Ibid., 140.

also" (Matt. 6:21 par.). If the eye is sound, the whole body will be full of light (Matt. 6:22 par.). Only undivided obedience is possible; no one can serve two masters (Matt. 6:24 par.). Purity of heart (Matt. 5:8; cf. Matt. 5:28; Mark 7:15; Luke 11:41) is not only opposed to every kind of external ritual purity, it is also opposed to every kind of partial religiosity, practiced with hesitation and reservations. Any obedience that does not come from the heart, that does not touch and control the inmost center and the most profound depths of the individual, any obedience that plays hide-and-seek or wears a mask of devotion, is for Jesus no obedience at all. All functions of the will, the heart, or the intellect fundamentally represent the whole person. The "sound" eye (Matt. 6:22) is the "simple" eye (see also Matt. 10:16: "simple as doves"). The pure heart is the undivided heart. The implicit distinction between this attitude and adherence to the letter of the law, a casual or casuistic identification of trivia with major issues, will be discussed in detail later.

What is not correct is the low status accorded actual conduct by an ethics of intention. Beyond all doubt Jesus demanded not just a new attitude, a rethinking and an inward conversion, but concrete and specific obedience— not only in the form of a universal moral appeal to the human conscience, but in concrete injunctions. What Jesus requires is not the relationship of the soul to its God, not inward renewal, but the totality of the person, including concrete actions. A good tree brings forth good fruit (Luke 6:34ff.). A new being results in new conduct. A quantitative "less" can be a qualitative "more" (see the offering of the poor widow in Mark 12:41ff.), but this means that a material or financial contribution makes a real difference. This is shown not only by the particular commandments but by fundamental statements of principle.

1.4 The warning against coupling the enthusiastic acclamation "Lord, Lord" with a refusal to do God's will (Matt. 7:21ff. par.) is a product of the early church; the list of charismatic acts derives from post-Easter experience.[99] In its intention, however, this warning is quite in line with Jesus' message. At the judgment, the subject of investigation is not intention but acts of love (Matt. 25:31ff.). This is confirmed by other sayings of Jesus.

We may recall the parable of the two sons (Matt. 21:28ff.). Despite initial refusal, the first son obeys his father's command to work in the vineyard. The second son agrees to go, but does not keep his word and does not follow up his ready agreement with action. More is involved than just a warning against letting words suffice: the primary point is the change of a fundamental "no" into a "yes," and v. 31d (secondarily?) associates those who initially refused

99. See Gerhard Schneider, "Christusbekenntnis und christliches Handeln," in *Die Kirche des Anfangs* (Festschrift Heinz Schürmann), ed. R. Schnackenburg (Leipzig: St. Benno, 1979), 9–24; Heinz Geist, "Die Warnung vor den falschen Propheten," in *Biblische Randbemerkungen*, (Schüler-Festschrift Rudolph Schnackenburg), ed. H. Merklein and J. Lange (Würzburg: Echter, 1974), 139–49.

with tax collectors and harlots. It is now these very people who both say "Yes" to God and do his will.

The discrepancy between words and deeds is also the great theme of Matthew 23, in which Jesus settles accounts with the scribes and Pharisees, but extreme caution is advisable in using this chapter to reconstruct the message of Jesus. In any case, the concluding parable of the Sermon on the Mount/Plain confirms that deeds are what matter.[100]

The accusation of hypocrisy is probably historically accurate, although not in the broadcast form recorded in Matthew. It is imperative to warn against the common mistake of assuming that the typical Jew was a hypocrite, content with an outward religiosity that was both a self-deception and an attempt to deceive others. It is significant that Mark mentions the charge of hypocrisy only twice: Mark 7:6 and 12:15. The first passage deals with the discrepancy between the lips and the heart, but the words that follow have more to do with the contrast between the commandment of God and human tradition. This means that a hypocrite is not someone who battens on the discrepancy between theory and practice, but someone who sets more store by human tradition than by God's commandment. The evil of hypocrisy is not subjective unrighteousness but objective blindness (see Luke 13:15–16, which brands as hypocrisy the cruel paradox of allowing cattle to be watered on the Sabbath while not allowing a sick woman to be healed).[101]

This argument indicates that it is not just refusal to act that is attacked but also wrong actions; the contrast is not simply with a "practical Christianity" or activism. Jesus is well aware of the danger (expressed in Luke 11:39) of keeping the outside of cup and dish clean, while the inside is full of extortion and wickedness. This passage is aimed primarily at superficial obedience expressed in regulations governing ritual purity, but social actions as well as liturgical ritual can seek to capitalize on a false relationship with God. God's call can also be drowned out by an officious business in works of love (e.g., Luke 10:38ff.). The inside must not be played off against the outside or the outside against the inside, the social against the religious or the religious against the social. The point is always the doing of God's will, totally and radically.

This goal finds expression above all in certain antitheses in the Sermon on the Mount: what is evil is not just killing but anger, not just adultery but lust (Matt. 5:21ff.).[102] The radical totality of the response demanded is stated most clearly in Matt. 6:24: "No one can serve two masters; for either he will hate the one and love the other, or he will be devoted to the one and despise the other." The decision for God involves an either/or and thus an exclusive adherence to God. One cannot serve two masters with the same readiness and

100. See Jeremias, *Parables*, 193, as well as passages like Mark 3:35 par. and Luke 10:37.
101. See also Ulrich Wilckens, "hypokrinomai," *TDNT* 8:567.
102. See the further discussion below, 59–60.

devotion. To love God also, to serve God half-heartedly, means to hate him. The word "love" already suggests that repentance does not so much involve deadly seriousness, feelings of remorse and gestures of sorrow, as "the joy of penitence" (Schniewind), the joy of the prodigal son allowed to return to the house of a father who is already expecting him and running to meet him.

The statement in Luke 15:7 that there is more joy in heaven over one sinner who repents than over ninety-nine righteous persons must not be taken to mean that ninety-nine out of a hundred do not need to repent (as the verse means if taken literally). Nowhere do we read that only egregious sinners need to repent. Luke 13:3, 5, where Jesus is told of the victims of Pilate's violence and the fall of the tower in Siloam, therefore says: "Unless you repent, you will all likewise perish." Note also the image of the narrow door in Luke 13:24 par., which warns against trivializing the demand for effort, struggle, and sacrifice. The message of the kingdom is not preached to a restricted circle—Jesus does not espouse the concept, popular among his contemporaries, of a "sacred remnant"—nor is the call to *metanoia* addressed only to certain people. Everyone must turn totally in the direction of the coming kingdom of God; those who do not turn and repent fall victim to God's judgment.

1.5 We shall only mention in passing the fact that this criticism of interpreting Jesus' ethics as an ethics of intention has as its corollary a rejection of a position represented primarily by Lutheran orthodoxy. This view interprets Jesus' demands, like those in the Sermon on the Mount, primarily as *speculum peccati*, a mirror intended to reveal to sinners their sins.[103] According to this theory, Jesus deliberately made impossible demands in order to provoke human failure and reveal the need for salvation. But nowhere do we find the slightest hint that Jesus' demands lead to despair and are intended to reveal human impotence and guilt. It is undoubtedly true that this is in fact what they continually do, but there is no evidence that this is their purpose, not to mention their sole purpose. Jesus' demands, often shockingly radical, with their sharp contrast to normal behavior, are in fact meant to persuade the disciples not to follow the sinful praxis of the world but to practice a kind of alternative ethics.[104]

2. Discipleship

It is an undisputed fact that Jesus called people to follow him as his disciples. What is disputed is the meaning of this call. It is agreed that discipleship must not be confused with imitation, and that it involves a specific kind of adherence to Jesus and his cause. But what is its nature? Most writers describe discipleship at least in part after the analogy of the relationship between teacher and disciple in Judaism. Because such a comparison

103. A similar view is held by Kittel and others; cf. Soiron, *Bergpredigt*, 17, 23ff.
104. Cf. below, 62, 110.

is instructive in any case for understanding the sayings and episodes dealing with discipleship in the Synoptic Gospels, we shall give a preliminary survey of the situation in Judaism.

2.1 The New Testament uses the terms "following (after)" and "discipleship" almost interchangeably. In the Old Testament, "following" someone is an expression of subordination, as when soldiers follow the king (Judg. 9:49) or Elisha follows the prophet Elijah as his student (1 Kings 19:21). In the religious realm, the expression refers primarily to the relationship between Israel and foreign gods (Deut. 4:3; 6:14; 8:19; 11:28; 13:2; 28:14; Jer. 2:5; 7:6, 9; 9:14; 11:10; 13:10). More rarely it is used for following God; such usage does not refer to cultic processions but is meant figuratively (Hos. 11:10), despite the choice between following Yahweh and following Baal (1 Kings 18:21). "Following God" is used in parallelism with "obeying his commandments" (1 Kings 14:8; 2 Kings 23:3; Deut. 13:5, LXX).

In Judaism, "following" refers primarily to the way students of the Torah "follow" the teacher of the law at a respectful distance, walking behind him as his "disciples" when he goes out or goes on a journey. The implicit subordination also finds expression in other services rendered the teacher, with whom the students live a communal life. The purpose of rabbinic instruction was not solely the transmission of theoretical knowledge but also included its practical application, specifically the application of the Torah and Halakhah. In rabbinic Judaism, "disciples" are the rabbinic students who concern themselves theoretically and practically with Scripture and tradition.

2.2 Quite apart from the central importance of the law in this student/teacher relationship in Judaism, it seems highly questionable to interpret the discipleship involved in following Jesus after the analogy of rabbinic training. There is every reason to be skeptical about picturing Jesus as a rabbi, that is, as a member of the class of scribes who had gone through the formal educational process of the group and passed the appropriate examinations.[105] It is therefore all the more unlikely that the discipleship of following Jesus is to be understood from this perspective. It is not by chance that the exegetes who find here the closest parallel also note certain differences that break out of the framework of Judaism. In the call narratives, for example, it is noteworthy that Jesus usually takes the initiative (cf., however, Luke 9:57–58). Those whom Jesus calls do not become "disciples" by their own free will and choice, but by virtue of the word that evokes discipleship and calls others to itself. There are other unmistakable differences: women appear in the circle of Jesus' followers but not among the disciples of the rabbis; and social intercourse with sinners, harlots, and tax collectors would have been offensive if practiced by a rabbi.

In the case of Jesus, discipleship is not just a stage, which may be

105. For example, Bultmann, *Jesus*, 43.

interrupted by a change of teachers or come to an end when the disciple becomes a teacher.[106] Discipleship is rather adherence to Jesus and his cause based on the presence of the kingdom of God. The crucial point is that it represents the interests of the kingdom—not adherence to the law and its interpretation, not devotion to an idea or a tradition represented by a teacher, or respect for the teacher's wisdom and interpretive ability. Jesus' call to discipleship can be understood only on the basis of his unique authority to proclaim the kingdom of God. For this reason alone it takes precedence over all other earthly ties, traditions, and authorities.

Hengel has pointed out additional ways in which following Jesus differs from the rabbinic relationship between teacher and student:[107] the scholarly atmosphere of the school, engrossing study, concern for scholarly exegesis, formation of tradition, and so forth—all missing in the case of Jesus. Furthermore for orderly instruction the geographical stability of an established school was a fundamental necessity, while Jesus wandered through Galilee and the surrounding regions, addressing himself specifically to the uneducated and not engaging primarily in discussion with scholars or those who agreed with him.

Hengel[108] rightly emphasizes the charismatic and eschatological nature of Jesus' call. Even the disciples of John the Baptist (Mark 2:18 par.; Matt. 11:2; Luke 7:18) would seem out of place in the atmosphere of a school. More generally, it must be remembered that in the New Testament period the notion of discipleship involved not only the students of the rabbis but also the followers of apocalyptic prophets and the partisans of Zealot leaders.[109] As Hengel points out (while rightly stressing certain basic differences),[110] these latter circles recall other motifs in Jesus' teaching: separation from family and friends, encouragement of martyrdom, and eschatological motivation.

Especially important is the Elijah-Elisha relationship, at least in shaping the New Testament call narratives (cf. 1 Kings 19:19–21 with Mark 1:16ff. or 2:14ff.). If we compare the calls in the Synoptics, we note a clear similarity, down to such points as refusal to go away and the effectual word spoken by Jesus, which takes the place of the sign of the prophet's mantle. Encounter, a call in the midst of work, leaving family and possessions, service, and discipleship—all are brought together in these narratives.

The harsh and radical saying in Luke 9:59–60, however, that the dead are to be left to bury the dead, must have had a shocking and scandalous effect. It demands nothing less than a total break with piety and convention, spirituality and law. Funeral procession and burial are duties commanded by the

---

106. Bornkamm, *Jesus*, 146.
107. Hengel, *Leader*, 41ff.
108. Ibid., 50ff.
109. Merklein, *Gottesherrschaft*, 59–60.
110. *Leader*, 19ff., 57ff.

law; they even release people from studying the Torah and other duties. Conversely, denial of burial must be looked upon as unparalleled blasphemy. Jesus' challenging saying must therefore be grouped with his other sayings that demand freedom from all family ties on the grounds that the coming of the kingdom is imminent. The kingdom that comes with Jesus is therefore the crucial element in this "provocative prophetic sign,"[111] not the common reference to the Torah or its radical interpretation. It would in fact be better to speak of discipleship as criticizing and suspending the Torah, since the request "Let me go and bury my father" is based on the Fourth Commandment[112] (cf. also Mark 10:21 ["go, sell everything, and follow me"] after vv. 19–20 or Mark 3:21; Matt. 19:12).

2.3 Such uncommonly harsh sayings, which denigrate natural ties and family relationships, are uncompromisingly radical. Despite the exemplary nature of the call episodes (notice their parenetic interpretation in the Gospels), they obviously cannot simply apply as they stand to everyone in every situation. The same problem will arise when we discuss the question of giving up all possessions. The call to give up everything for the sake of the one precious pearl is addressed to all (Matt. 13:45–46), but the either/or and the break with familiar and customary rules of conduct, indeed the nature of adherence to the person and cause of Jesus and thus the presence of the kingdom of God, obviously take on different forms for different people. This may possibly reflect a "graduated ethics" in which "wandering charismatics" going about without home, possessions, or work are distinguished from "symphatisants" resident in the local congregations.[113] The earliest Jesus movement undoubtedly knew a variety of social manifestations, but these are more a consequence than a prerequisite of the call to discipleship, which is anything but a call addressed to a circle of sectarians with an ascetic ethos. The call contemplates instead a variety of "vocations" and specific responses.

This observation, however, cannot detract from the abruptness of the break described in the call narratives. It is obvious that in Mark 1:16ff. and 2:14 "following" means immediate personal discipleship in the sense of sharing Jesus' life and fate. The call to the tax collector Levi exemplifies the fact that Jesus does not call only those with unusual qualifications or attitudes. The disciples named here are called and leave their nets, their father, their jobs— without delay and without hesitation. Those who tie themselves to Jesus in this way will follow him through thick and thin, going "wherever he goes" (Matt. 8:19).

It would be wrong, however, to identify the disciples in this specific sense

111. Iris Bosold, *Pazifismus und prophetische Provokation*, SBS 90 (Stuttgart: Katholisches Bibelwerk, 1978), 84–85, 93. Bosold treats the command to salute no one (Luke 10:4) similarly.
112. Merklein, *Gottesherrschaft*, 61–62.
113. Theissen, "Wanderradikalismus," 83ff., esp. 86 (cited from *Studien*); cf. Schottroff and Stegemann, *Jesus*, 65ff.; Kuhn, "Nachfolge," 122–23.

with the Twelve, an interpretation fostered primarily by Matthew (cf. Matt. 8:21; 9:9; 16:24; 19:28). Whether or not the Twelve are a post-Easter institution, the circle of Jesus' disciples is not a closed group restricted to twelve males. It is characterized by its very openness. But it cannot be identified simply with all those who supported the Jesus movement. There is sufficient evidence that Jesus did not call everyone to this kind of discipleship, even though there is no clear distinction between various forms of discipleship. The boundaries are always fluid.

In Mark 5:18–20, Jesus explicitly forbids the healed demoniac to follow him as a disciple. This passage is obviously secondary and probably goes back to the situation of an age when it was no longer possible literally to "follow" Jesus as a disciple. It was then necessary to make it clear to Christians that faith does not necessarily mean living shoulder-to-shoulder with Jesus and giving up all social ties. Jesus sends the man back to his house, his everyday existence, to be a witness in that setting to the act of deliverance. There may also be overtones of legitimating a mission in the Decapolis.[114]

Even apart from such redactional interpretations, which document an extension of the concept of discipleship, what many exegetes observe is true: Jesus leaves others in their previous setting; although they do not give up home, job, and family, they are neither attacked for indecision and half-heartedness nor excluded from the kingdom of God.[115] Hengel[116] points out that there are no grounds for objecting that the idea of two kinds of discipleship is being developed here, because the crucial focus is not Jesus himself but "the absolute claim of the divine will in the light of the imminent coming of God's kingdom." Nor is it possible to support the distinction that an inner circle is called to discipleship and all others are called to imitation.[117]

The goal and center of Jesus' call to discipleship is therefore neither a double morality nor personal attachment to him, to his own person and authority, but rather participation in the coming of God's kingdom, whose representative he is. His demands relate functionally to this kingdom. In the final analysis, it is not Jesus who brings the kingdom but the kingdom that brings Jesus.[118] Those who follow Jesus are thereby "fit for the kingdom of God" (Luke 9:62). Admission to the inner circle of disciples is neither an indispensable condition of salvation nor an ascetic accomplishment for a religious elite. One can accept the message of the kingdom, repent, and

114. On Mark 5:18–20, see Rudolf Pesch, *Das Markusevangelium*, 4th ed. HThK 2; Kuhn, "Nachfolge," 192, 211.
115. Bornkamm, *Jesus*, 147–48; similarly Schweizer, *Lordship*, 20; Conzelmann, "Jesus Christus," 629; Kuhn, "Nachfolge," 106–7, 123–24.
116. *Leader*, 61ff.
117. Pace Raymond Thysman, "L'éthique de l'imitation du Christ dans le NT," *ETL* 42 (1966): 138–75, esp. 148.
118. Rudolf Otto, *Reich Gottes und Menschensohn*, 3d ed. (Munich: Beck, 1954), 75; cited with approval by other exegetes.

become an adherent of Jesus without entering into intimate association with him and walking the roads of Palestine with him. Of course those who are called cannot remain as they were; they cannot allow themselves to be held captive by the things of this world and hold on to them at all costs. Nor can they retreat into an inward attitude and disposition. Perhaps Jesus demanded courageous and irrevocable burning of bridges from those very people who were so entrapped that the only possible way out was a radical change and the total surrender of their previous way of life.[119] It is also possible, however, that a fitness on the part of some for accepting special obligations is the reason why Jesus does not call everyone away from house and home, even though this does not mean that these others are totally released from such obligations.[120]

2.4 For all, however, the call of Jesus implies readiness for self-denial and renunciation, for risk and suffering, even though the words of Mark 8:34 par. (cf. also the Q version in Matt. 10:38) are addressed primarily to those who follow Jesus in the narrower sense: "If any man would come after me, let him deny himself and take up his cross and follow me." These words, which were later interpreted in the light of the crucifixion, must not be understood as referring to the cross as a form of execution, as though Jesus were predicting his crucifixion. They do not present the cross as requiring an ethics of martyrdom in imitation of Jesus, specifically a readiness to die a martyr's death on the cross. Many scholars see in the saying about "taking up one's cross" a proverbial expression with roots in the Zealot movement.[121] Schneider[122] reviews the various theories and gives a plausible interpretation: we have here a graphic image depicting those who deny their own selves, with the most extreme possible consequence being readiness to lay down their lives. But even those who consider this saying secondary must admit that discipleship involves not only renunciation of the self but also readiness to suffer and take risks.

2.5 There is another essential point: those who are called to follow Jesus as his disciples not only have their lives totally changed but above all find themselves incorporated in Jesus' ministry. This is shown by the very first call narrative, where Jesus says to Andrew: "Follow me and I will make you become fishers of men" (Mark 1:17).

This much-debated saying, which may be authentic[123] but was used by the post-Easter community to justify its mission, does not refer to leading people by the nose or aggressive proselytizing, although the metaphor has occasion-

---

119. See the discussion of Mark 10:17ff. below, 103–4.

120. Rudolf Schnackenburg, *Christian Existence in the NT* (Notre Dame, Ind.: Univ. Notre Dame Press, 1968), 105–6, 107–8.

121. See Anton Fridrichsen, "Sich selbst verleugnen," *CN* 2 (1936): 1–8; Hengel, *Leader*, 58 n.76; Kuhn, "Nachfolge," 121.

122. Johannes Schneider, "stauros," *TDNT* 7:577–79.

123. Hengel, *Leader*, 77.

ally taken on such coarse and objectionable overtones. Hengel[124] suggests a provocatively paradoxical logion, as in the case of Matt. 8:21. In Mark the saying emerges from the situation. It is not by chance that it is preceded by the statement of Simon and Andrew's work ("for they were fishermen").[125]

The crucial element is inclusion in Jesus' ministry, so that call and sending coincide from the outset. Jesus does not call people to cultivate their own religiosity and inward spirituality, and certainly not to join a circle of the religious who withdraw from the world. People are called to be sent to others. People are called to the eschatological harvest (cf. Matt. 9:37–38 par.), to proclaim Jesus' message as his messengers and fellow-workers, and to share in his ministry of healing and helping. Therefore it is only logical that Luke 9:60b, "Go and proclaim the kingdom of God," should follow the call to discipleship in 9:57ff. Jesus' call comes to the disciples in the midst of everyday life, while they are catching fish, mending nets, or collecting taxes—not in the desert, in devout meditation, or in a vision. Similarly they are sent into this everyday world, not into a monastic community or a religious ghetto. Of course Peter and Andrew leave their nets, but not in order to flee a supposedly corrupt world, but in order to make themselves totally available for mission. Luke above all, by setting the call to discipleship of 9:57ff. in the framework of the missionary discourses (cf. 10:1ff.), emphasizes that discipleship involves being sent to preach the kingdom of God.

The missionary instructions in Mark 6, however, cannot be drawn upon in detail, since this chapter comprises mostly regulations for the post-Easter community. Nevertheless, even this section reflects the fact that Jesus connected commissioning for service with his call to follow him. This is confirmed by Q's missionary discourse in Matthew 10 and Luke 10. Here, too, many of the details reflect the missionary experience of the earliest Christians, but there is no reason to doubt that Jesus, too, gave his disciples a share in his ministry and authority and sent them out as messengers and agents of peace (cf. Luke 10:5).[126]

3. The Attitude of Judaism and Jesus to the Law

3.1 Although the ethics of Jesus cannot be derived from the Torah and the focus of his message is not the law but the kingdom of God, there can be no doubt that his ethical demands are connected with the Old Testament and its law. The only question is how strong this connection is. The central importance of the kingdom of God suggests that the fundamental break stated in Luke 16:16 ("the law and the prophets were until John; since then the good

124. Ibid., 78.

125. On Mark 1:17, see Pesch, *Markusevangelium*.

126. For discussion of the missionary discourses, see Ferdinand Hahn, *Mission in the NT* (London: SCM Press, 1965), 41ff.; Paul Hoffmann, *Studien zur Theologie der Logienquelle*, NTA 8 (Munster: Aschendorff, 1972), 236ff.; Schottroff and Stegemann, *Jesus*, 62ff.

news of the kingdom of God is proclaimed") also abrogates the law. The qualitatively new age marked by the coming of the kingdom, in which "old garments" and "old wineskins" are out of place (cf. also Mark 2:21–22), ranks the law with what is "old." The expression "good news of the kingdom of God" (Luke 16:16) is typically Lukan; probably the statement originally said that the kingdom of God, which supersedes the law and the prophets, is imminent (cf. the parallel in Matt. 11:12b).[127] In any case, there is a contrast between "the law and the prophets" on the one hand and the kingdom of God on the other. This eschatological caesura probably goes back to Jesus himself,[128] even though it usually appears in less absolute form, and the concept of the law does not even occur, for example, in the entire Gospel of Mark.

But if "the Sabbath was made for man, not man for the Sabbath" (Mark 2:27), the same judgment applies to the law as a whole,[129] and the purpose of the law can only be to establish the kingdom of love, not to fix the letter of God's will. This point is also confirmed by the observation that not only Jesus' praxis but also his words are often in conflict with conduct according to the law's demands. Healing on the Sabbath and table fellowship with tax collectors and sinners, touching of those who are unclean (Mark 1:41; 5:25ff.), and association with women repeatedly transcend, for the sake of God's limitless love that is integral to his kingdom, the ordinances of the law, especially its ritual prescriptions. Nevertheless the extent to which this represents a matter of principle as opposed to a response to the moment remains as open as the question whether the Torah and prophets find their end or their fulfillment in his words and actions, whether one should speak of transcendence or contradiction, radical reinterpretation or abrogation. To deal with this question we must first examine the understanding of the law in Jesus' time, remembering that this is not identical with the Old Testament.

3.2 The law underwent many changes in Israel, in its theological premises and implications as well as in its concrete substance. The original meaning of *tôrāh* is "(single) instruction"; only around 500 B.C.E. was the Pentateuch with its various legal codes put together and thought of as the one Torah. In the earlier historical works above all the law is clearly associated with the election and deliverance of Israel. It is based on the covenant and God's concomitant claim to sovereign authority, which places Israel under an obligation to be faithful to the covenant. The law is therefore not an independent entity but rather, like Israel's unmerited election, an act of grace, "the law of the God who saves."[130] The prophets above all recognize that fulfillment of the law can go hand in hand with refusal to obey and love God; they attack all attempts to glorify outward obedience. Cultic fulfillment of the law is the

127. See also Merklein, *Gottesherrschaft*, 81ff.
128. See Kümmel, *Promise*, 121ff.
129. See Collange, *Jésus* (B), 240.
130. Smend, in Luz and Smend, *Gesetz*, 15, with reference to the Decalogue.

focus of criticism (cf. Hos. 6:6; Isa. 1:10ff.; Jer. 7:22–23), but in other areas, too, outward legalism does not suffice (cf. Jer. 8:8). On the other hand, the long familiar law enshrining God's justice is assumed to be in force; indeed it is the basis of the prophetic message of judgment (Mic. 6:8).

I agree with Noth, Würthwein, and others[131] that a shift to the postexilic understanding of the law can already be observed in P, because there the revelation at Sinai is the fundamental fact of sacred history. Of course the law is an aid, a blessing, and a joy (as the psalms praising the law make clear), not a yoke and a burden, but it is now also a means of attaining God's favor and having God on one's side. The law increasingly becomes the determinative factor, autonomous and absolute. Everything depends on fulfillment of the law (see Neh. 1:9 and similar passages). The law becomes linked with the idea of merit and threatens to lose its foundation in the elective act of God.

3.3 This incipient legalism in the Old Testament continues in Judaism, albeit in different fashion. Undoubtedly the law is still associated intimately with the covenant and with grace, but its preeminence and dominance continue to increase.[132] Above all, the crisis of the second century B.C.E. caused the Torah to become increasingly fixed throughout the Jewish world.[133] The Torah is of central importance and is absolutely normative; its interweaving of law and parenesis makes it impossible to limit the application of the Torah to strictly legal cases.[134]

The rabbis distinguish the written Torah from oral Torah, understanding the latter as an interpretation and extension of the former, but also as a protection for it (a "fence about the Torah"). According to rabbinic theory, God gave Moses the content of the oral tradition on Sinai; it has since been handed down in an unbroken chain of tradition. But this notion is in conflict with the theory that the Halakhot are implicit in the Torah and can be determined by exegesis. In any case, the Pharisaic scribes of Jesus' day probably did not dispute the authority of the oral Torah. The devout Jew was normally "zealous for the traditions of the fathers," as Paul describes himself in Gal. 1:14. Sanhedrin 11.3 even says: "It is more culpable to teach what is contrary to the precepts of the scribes than to teach what is contrary to the Torah itself." Only the Sadducees clearly rejected the oral law.[135] Their position should be understood as increasing rather than reducing the burden of the law.

Although there were internal differences within Judaism as to the weight given oral tradition, the unique importance of the law for all of Jewish life is clear. One might almost say that the law is the representative of God. Syriac Baruch 48:22, 24 says: "We trust in thee, for thy law is with us. . . . And that

---

131. See Ernst Würthwein, "Gesetz, II. Im AT," *RGG*[3] 2:1515.
132. Banks, *Jesus*, 36.
133. This concentration on the Torah is discussed by Martin Hengel, *Judaism and Hellenism* (Philadelphia, Fortress Press, 1981), 1:308–9.
134. Luz and Smend, *Gesetz*, 53.
135. Josephus *Antiquities* 13.297; Rudolf Meyer, "Saddoukaios," *TDNT* 7:50–51.

law, which dwells among us, is our helper." The Torah becomes an "entity governing God himself."[136] It is eternally valid (cf. Baruch 4:1; Ethiopic Enoch 99:2): according to Jewish theology, the messiah does not bring a new Torah but interprets the Torah as it stands. It is also exclusive. It is the only revelation of God's will, the only way to life. The world, the human race, and Israel were created solely for the sake of the Torah.

In Hellenistic Judaism in particular the Torah takes on ontological and cosmological significance as the ground of all being and the basis of the created order (cf. the identification of the law with preexistent wisdom in Sirach 24). As an entity identified with nature or with the universal law and reason, the law is the plan of the cosmos, the essence of all order—both the order by which Israel lives and the order of creation.[137] In my opinion, however, this cosmic significance of the Torah does not play any role in the teaching of Jesus; it is neither affirmed nor denied. It is important above all to attack the still prevalent misunderstanding that the Jews perceived the law as an oppressive burden. The law is not a torment, a yoke, and an imposition but a source of joy and pride, the inalienable precious possession of Israel. The law is the vehicle, guarantee, and way of salvation. Fulfillment of the law brings life and righteousness and determines the fate of humanity. Even in apocalyptic literature obedience to the law is the only way to salvation and the world to come (4 Esd. 7:17; Test. of Joseph 11:1). The imminence of the eschaton makes the law more important, not less, as one may see at Qumran. Despite all sense of dependence on God's grace, there was never any doubt that the demands of the law were still equally stringent, if not more so.

Furthermore it would be wrong to conclude from the picture of Judaism sometimes painted by the Gospels that the Jews did not take their obligations under the law seriously. Commenting on Lev. 26:3, Symmachus says: "Those who learn the Torah without putting it into practice would have been better off not created." Unquestioning obedience is the rule. No one has the right to ask for a justification of the commandments. If anyone takes offense at the commandments, God replies: "It is I who established them, and you have no right to question them."[138] There is a much-quoted saying of Rabbi Johanan ben Zakkai to the effect that a corpse does not render anyone unclean and water does not make anyone clean. There is instead an ordinance of the "king of kings"; it must not be transgressed, and one must not ask to know its reasons.[139] The result was an atomistic and casuistic approach to God's demands, which will be discussed later. In any case, Jewish ethics rests fundamentally on the law and its interpretation.[140]

136. Luz and Smend, *Gesetz*, 40, citing bAboda Zara 3b.

137. Philo *Life of Moses* 2.48, 51–52; Limbeck, *Ohnmacht*, 17ff.

138. bYoma 67b.

139. Pesiqta 40a; cf. Strack-Billerbeck, *Kommentar* 4:524.

140. For further discussion of the Jewish understanding of the law, see Walter Gutbrod, "nomos," *TDNT* 4:1047–59; Eduard Lohse, "Gesetz, III. Im Judentum," *RGG*³ 2:1515–17; Meinrad Limbeck, *Die Ordnung des Heils* (Düsseldorf: Patmos, 1971); Luz and Smend, *Gesetz*, 45–57.

4. Acceptance, Interpretation, and Transcendence of the Law

It is not easy to distinguish Jesus' own attitude toward the law, since this very point is obscured by the variety of approaches to the law within the early Christian community and the argument over whether the law had been abrogated. One would expect a priori to find in Jesus neither a forerunner of Marcion nor a legal literalist. He probably neither rejected nor sanctioned the law as a whole. But further details are controversial.

4.1 It is relatively safe to say that for Jesus the law had a positive significance, however defined; his own ethics is therefore to be understood at least in part from this perspective. For Jesus, God's commandments can be a valid expression of God's will and a guideline for God's ethical demands.

Mark 10:17ff., for example, may be cited as an apt expression of Jesus' attitude.[141] The rich young man asks what he must do to inherit eternal life, and Jesus replies soberly and straightforwardly, "You know the commandments," and proceeds to list the second table of the Decalogue (Mark 10:19). This is basically a series of social duties, a form found above all in Philo and Josephus.[142] This is far from proving, however, that the pericope originated in the world of Hellenistic Judaism.[143]

It is correct to observe, however, that in both instances the Decalogue is interpreted primarily in social terms (cf. also Rom. 13:9; James 2:11). Nothing suggests that all God's commandments are absolutely valid; nor is the question of an individual path to salvation answered by reference to the ethical ABC's of a divine will known to all. Jesus cites the Torah, but not as a whole; he restricts himself to the commandments of the second table. In this sense, Matthew is right in interpreting Jesus' response by adding, "And you shall love your neighbor as yourself" (Matt. 19:19). What God in fact demands is love, not blind obedience to the entire Torah. Even the text of the Decalogue is not sacrosanct, as the list of commandments shows (the Fifth Commandment, for example, comes at the end; note also the double commandment of love, which combines two Old Testament commandments), but this change may go back to the early church. In any case, Jesus is quite capable of citing Old Testament commandments unhesitatingly as the criterion of proper conduct.

4.2 But Mark 10:17ff. also shows that one can speak of Jesus as reinterpreting the law. Matthew in particular emphasizes this point, describing Jesus as being in conflict with the interpretation of the law as practiced by the Pharisaic rabbis. But this view is not peculiar to Matthew. Jesus himself

---

141. Bultmann, *History*, 54.
142. Berger, *Gesetzesauslegung*, 362ff.
143. For a criticism of Berger's theory that the passage reflects hostility to the Torah in Hellenistic apocalyptic Judaism, see Hengel, "Jesus," 153; Hans Hübner, "Mk 7,1–23 und das 'jüdisch-hellenistische' Gesetzesverständnis," *NTS* 22 (1976): 319ff.

attacked certain interpretations of God's will. We see this happening, for example, when he finds the original "commandment of God" in conflict with tradition.

According to Mark 7:6–8, for instance, tradition (Halakhah) is a collection of human precepts, contrary to the commandment of God. It is true that probably only the basic thrust of this text goes back to Jesus. The specific dispute about washing hands should probably be considered a product of the Christian community, as the citation of the LXX suggests; the discrepancy between it and the Hebrew text in v. 7 is no minor matter, since the latter does not suggest any conflict between the commandment of God and human ordinances. The substance of the dispute is the charge that Jesus' disciples do not observe tradition; in particular, they do not wash their hands as the regulations governing ritual purity require.

These regulations were in fact very complex. The Jewish texts assembled by Billerbeck[144] are a classic example of the casuistry that regulated even the washing of hands. Nothing was irrelevant—not even such matters as the position of the hands, the quantity of water, or the vessels employed.

Verse 8, however, states that human tradition thus attempts to abrogate the commandment of God. The "tradition of the elders" (vv. 3, 5) is nothing more than a "human tradition" (v. 8), in no way comparable to the commandment of God. There is not even an echo of Matt. 23:23: "These you ought to have done, without neglecting the others"—in other words, you should keep God's commandment, but also continue to practice ritual ablutions. It is in fact assumed that the disciples no longer observe the ritual tradition. But this position does not square entirely with the quotation from Isaiah, which indicates that criticism of the cultic ordinances comes from other sources than Scripture. The real basis of the argument in Mark 7:1–8, which attacks Pharisaic teaching and practice on the basis of Scripture, is not entirely clear.

4.3 Although Mark 7:1–8 probably derives from the primitive Christian community, the early church is following the lead of its Lord in appealing to Scripture and downgrading tradition. This is shown by Mark 7:9–13 (of which only v. 9 and probably also the generalization in v. 13 go back to Mark), which likewise deals with the conflict between the commandment of God and human ordinances. Here we are given an example of how tradition can actually set aside God's command. The Fifth Commandment of the Decalogue is cited as an example of God's commandment: "Honor your father and your mother." In flagrant contradiction to this divine command, however, many rabbis—albeit not all—teach that one may say to one's parents, "What you would have received from me is an offering" (v. 11). By conveying (in fact or merely pro forma) a sacrificial offering to God or the temple, one might prevent the gift from being used by others, thus cheating one's parents, for

144. Strack-Billerbeck, *Kommentar* 1:691ff.

example, of the support owed them.[145] According to Billerbeck,[146] it was not even necessary to make an offering to the temple of one's parents' support; it was sufficient simply to state in the form of a vow that what was intended for one's parents was to be like an offering. It could then be retained, and nothing had to be given to the temple. In any case, under certain circumstances this "corban vow" could actually violate the Fifth Commandment, so that regulations governing oaths could circumvent a clear divine command. We merely note in passing that, since the Torah requires fulfillment of vows (Deut. 23:21), the passage is also an indirect attack on the Torah.[147]

Another example appears in Luke 11:42: "Woe to you Pharisees! for you tithe mint and rue and every herb, and neglect justice and the love of God." Of course the two things are not taken here as being mutually exclusive, as the continuation shows; once more, however, we see how tradition can conceal the original will of God.

4.4 The most familiar examples of Jesus' criticism of Halakhah, where we also have firm historical ground under our feet, are undoubtedly the conflicts over the Sabbath. In a sense they mark the point at which criticism of the law begins. They attack the Halakhah of the Sabbath, for which, however, appeal to the Torah plays only a secondary role. It is especially significant for the theme of ethics that the Sabbath can no longer be understood as a cultic vacuum, free from any duties to one's neighbor, in which one can, in the name of God, treat others neutrally or even withdraw from them.[148]

The significance of the conflicts provoked by Jesus can be judged only against the background of the enormous importance of the Sabbath as a sign of divine election and a symbol of Jewish faith, together with the intensity with which Judaism maintained the holiness of the Sabbath. Especially in the postexilic period, the Sabbath commandment increasingly became a central commandment of the law. At Qumran, for example, it was made more and more rigorous by detailed regulations (cf. CD 10:14ff.). In order not to profane the Sabbath, at the beginning of the Maccabean wars people allowed themselves to be killed without resisting the enemy (1 Macc. 2:32ff.). According to yBerakot 3c.13–14,[149] the Sabbath commandment is as important as all the other commandments put together. The casuistry surrounding the Sabbath produced a web of detailed regulations—interpreted, it is true, with varying degrees of rigor and not felt to be a burden. Something of their nature can be seen in the Mishnah tractate on the Sabbath. The general rule is

145. See Karl Heinz Rengstorf, "korban," *TDNT* 3:860ff.
146. Strack-Billerbeck, *Kommentar* 1:711ff.
147. See below, 60.
148. Christian Dietzfelbinger, "Vom Sinn der Sabbatheilungen Jesu," *EvTh* 38 (1978): 281–98, esp. 283; see also Eduard Lohse, "Jesu Worte über den Sabbat," in *Die Einheit des NT* (Göttingen: Vandenhoeck & Ruprecht, 1973), 62–72; Christoph Hinz, "Jesus und der Sabbat," *KuD* 19 (1973): 91–108; Maria Trautmann, "Zeichenhafte Handlungen Jesu," *FB* 37 (1980): 297–318.
149. Strack-Billerbeck, *Kommentar* 1:905.

that one must do only what is absolutely necessary. It is forbidden, for example, to pluck grain, since this is a subcategory of the thirty-nine prohibited kinds of labor. Nor is it permissible to heal diseases that are not immediately life threatening.[150]

Jesus, however, did or approved both (Mark 2:23ff.; 3:1ff. par.). Only in 2:23ff. is an attempt made to justify Jesus' action by reference to Scripture, namely the story of how David is said to have eaten the bread of the presence. But there is reason to assume that the scriptural reference in vv. 25–26 is a secondary interpolation. Furthermore, the Old Testament parallel is not convincing: (1) David was in mortal danger, while the disciples were not; (2) David was not violating the Sabbath (although the Midrash so states). Furthermore, Matthew shows that scriptural citations tend to be added during the process of transmission, for the Matthaean parallel includes additional Old Testament passages in the pericope.

The original reason for violating the Sabbath has nothing to do with the Old Testament. The hunger of the disciples is mentioned explicitly only by Matthew and presupposes legitimate violation of the Sabbath under exceptional circumstances. The real reason appears in Mark 2:27: "The Sabbath was made for man, not man for the Sabbath." The shock of this statement can be measured by looking at Matthew and Luke, who omit it, obviously because they found it too radical and liberal. But its very audacity and provocative freedom support its genuineness. It does not dispute the Sabbath in principle, but finds the measure and meaning of the sabbath in human life rather than cultic law. God did not create the Sabbath in order to impose intolerable burdens and restrict humanity by myriads of regulations but as an act of kindness. The Sabbath is not a yoke and a constraint but a gift and an opportunity. Jesus' Sabbath healings, which also have the nature of provocative signs,[151] interpret the Sabbath commandment so as to make clear the coming of eschatological salvation and the freedom it brings.

4.5 Criticism of tradition and violation of the Sabbath together with their explicit justification represent to some extent a new interpretation of God's will. This is especially true for the so-called antitheses in the Sermon on the Mount (Matt. 5:21–48 par.). Most commonly the first (5:21ff.), second (5:27ff.), and fourth (5:33ff.) are considered pre-Matthaean, since they make sense only in the context of their stated theses (the prohibition of swearing in James 5:12, which is not in the form of an antithesis, being a kind of

150. See, for example, CD 11:16–17 and Eduard Lohse, "sabbaton," *TDNT* 7:12–14, 23, 24–25.
151. Hinz, "Sabbat," 95.

counterexample for the fourth antithesis), and there is no reason to credit Matthew himself with the invention of the antithesis form.[152]

The first and second antitheses in their original epigrammatic form[153] are usually treated as tightening up, intensifying, and transcending the law; the commandments of the Torah are themselves cited apodictically and without distinctions (such as the difference between murder, homicide, involuntary manslaughter, etc.). It is much more significant, however, that Jesus does not support his own demands exegetically by interpreting or elaborating on the law of the Torah; even if he is addressing the intention of the Decalogue, it is not really correct to say that he is "tightening up" the Torah. Of course his thought moves in the direction established by the commandments, but he does not legitimize his conclusions by appealing to the authority of the Torah.

Much the same can be said of the fourth antithesis (5:33ff.), despite the fact that it does not cite the Decalogue. Jesus transcends the prohibition of perjury—although Exod. 20:7 and Lev. 19:12 merely forbid abuse of God's name for unworthy purposes[154]—and the requirement that vows must be performed. He goes beyond Judaism in cautioning against careless and thoughtless swearing, prohibiting swearing absolutely and demanding that "yes" be "yes" and "no" be "no." Absolute veracity makes oaths meaningless.

For Strecker,[155] the prohibition of swearing also exemplifies Jesus' readiness to "abrogate" particular commandments of the Torah, distancing himself from the Jewish practice and criticism of oaths. Dautzenberg[156] disputes that Jesus intends to criticize the Torah, on the grounds that there were no oaths prescribed by the Torah apart from the judicial system and Jesus did not concern himself with the modalities of criminal and civil law.[157] The parenetic prohibition of swearing, he maintains, represents an "intensification of the criticism of oaths and similar asseverations that is also found elsewhere in Judaism and the ancient world."[158]

4.6 These three examples illustrate what is often called an intensification or rigorization of the Torah, but is often hard to distinguish from abrogation of the Torah. Therefore many scholars speak in the case of the fourth antithesis of abrogation or criticism of the Old Testament law insofar as it deals with

152. See Dietzfelbinger, *Antithesen*, 7ff.; Hoffmann and Eid, *Jesus*, 37ff. For a different interpretation, see, for example, M. Jack Suggs, "The Antitheses as Redactional Products," in *Jesus Christus in Historie und Theologie* (Festschrift Hans Conzelmann), ed. G. Strecker (Tübingen: Mohr, 1975), 433–44; Ingo Broer, "Die Antithesen und der Evangelist Matthäus," *BZ* 19 (1975): 50–63. Most recently the question has been discussed by Georg Strecker, "Die Antithesen der Bergpredigt," *ZNW* 69 (1978): 36–72 (with bibliography).
153. For discussion of the interpolations, see below, 124.
154. Dietzfelbinger, *Antithesen*, 31.
155. "Antithesen," 70–71.
156. G. Dautzenberg, "Ist das Schwurverbot Mt. 5,33–37; Jak. 5,12 ein Beispiel für die Torakritik Jesu?" *BZ* 25 (1981): 47–66.
157. Ibid., 51.
158. Ibid., 52.

oaths. In no sense, however, are we dealing with a mere affirmation of the Torah.

A more rigorous interpretation, it is true, is sometimes supported by quotations from Scripture, as in the prohibition of swearing in Matt. 5:35, which cites Isa. 66:1 and Ps. 68:3 to the effect that heaven is God's throne. In other words, even the common practice of avoiding the name of God in oath formulas by using other terms ("by heaven," etc.) really involves God. This argument, of course, is probably secondary, since if swearing is forbidden absolutely there is no need for additional prohibitions of specific formulas.[159]

In most cases, however, there is no such appeal to Scripture, and never is such an appeal the *principium cognoscendi*. Nor does there seem to be any single guiding principle. Braun therefore speaks of "variability" and distinguishes Jesus' occasional "tightening up" of the Torah from the rigor found at Qumran.[160] It must be admitted that it is almost impossible to abstract a coherent theory from Jesus' treatment of the Torah. There is no single principle governing transcendence of the Torah—neither the contrast between outward and inward nor the sanctity of human life nor the importance of one's neighbor nor a simplification or intensification of the purpose enshrined in the commandments of the Old Testament.

It is certainly wrong to ascribe central importance to the "deep antagonism between the instinctual claims of each individual on the one hand and the limitation of these claims by the ethical norms imposed by human civilization."[161] There is more evidence to support "intelligent exaggeration," whose function is to "reorient us by disorienting us."[162]

The familiar hyperbole of admonitions like Matt. 5:29–30, 39–40, and Matt. 18:22 is discussed especially by Hoffmann and Eid. Citing the analogy of the parables, they speak of a deliberate attempt to alienate: the automatic response of normal human behavior and its reaction mechanisms is meant to be blocked by the startling command to do the very opposite of what is normal. The result is an openness (in others as well!) and increased room for love to operate.[163] But this applies more to the fifth antithesis, to be discussed below. Discussing the provocative words of Luke 9:59ff.,[164] Matt. 5:39ff.,[165] and similar passages, Eckert[166] speaks of "paradoxical extreme cases" that are not to be interpreted legalistically[167] but against the background of the

---

159. Dietzfelbinger, *Antithesen*, 32.

160. *Radikalismus II*, 7; cf. 14.

161. Hans-Richard Reuter, "Die Bergpredigt als Orientierung unseres Menschseins heute," *ZEE* 23 (1979): 84–105, esp. 93.

162. Ibid., 95.

163. Hoffmann and Eid, *Jesus*, 160; see also Hoffmann, "Eschatologie," 200.

164. See above, 48–49.

165. See below, 90, 111.

166. Jost Eckert, "Wesen und Funktionen der Radikalismen in der Botschaft Jesu," *MThZ* 24 (1973): 301–25.

167. Ibid., 312.

irrupting kingdom of God, which calls into question the values, relationships, and laws of the old eon.[168]

In formal terms, it is most reasonable to see here the demand for total
uncompromising obedience provoked by the salvation that comes with the
kingdom of God; at the same time, God's will also extends radical protection
to one's neighbor. Certain radical statements, it is true, seem not to take
account of the consequences for others and can sometimes lead to un-
charitableness (e.g., the prohibition against marrying a divorced woman in
Matt. 5:32; Luke 16:18). If we attempt to single out the central point of Jesus'
message, we might suggest that here too we are dealing with eschatological
signs (cf. Luke 9:57ff.).[169] But the law of love is also a candidate, especially in
light of the fifth antithesis and the preeminence of love elsewhere. Here, too,
the primary reference is probably to conduct reflecting God's unconditional
love rather than radical obedience.[170]

5. Jesus' Freedom from and Criticism of the Law

5.1 Sayings like Mark 2:27 already bear witness to Jesus' sovereign freedom. This is even more true of the sayings that deal not with how the Torah is
interpreted and put into practice, but with the Torah itself. They do not
introduce an enthusiastic lawlessness, but do downgrade the Torah as the
necessary and sufficient statement of God's will. This happens, for example,
when one passage from Scripture is played off against another. This is itself
unusual, but does have certain analogies.[171]

An instance of this use of the Torah itself to criticize the law is the debate
over divorce in Mark 10. Commenting on divorce as regulated by the law of
Moses, Jesus makes a statement (v. 5) that is usually translated: "For your
hardness of heart he [Moses] wrote you this commandment." This translation
suggests that Jesus sees in the Mosaic law governing divorce something like a
piece of emergency legislation or a concession to human weakness, an act of
leniency toward a man's weakness, infidelity, and lust. Because the human
race cannot engage in marriage according to the order established by God's
creation, an ordinance is given that takes this fact into account. But was Jesus
really saying that Moses was resigned to human weakness? In particular,
would this interpretation not require a causative link such as "on account of
your hardness of heart"?

Two proposals have been put forward to meet this difficulty, neither of
which has attracted much attention. Greeven[172] proposes to interpret the

168. Ibid., 318.
169. See Maria Trautmann, *Zeichenhafte Handlungen Jesu*, FzB 37 (Stuttgart: Katholisches
Bibelwerk, 1980); also below, 111.
170. See Limbeck, *Ohnmacht*, 75–76.
171. Bultmann, *History*, 49–52.
172. "Aussagen" (B2), 114–15.

saying as meaning that hardness of heart is the end result of the argument rather than the basis on which it is developed. The commandment, he maintains, does not concede anything to hardness of heart but attacks it. Verse 5 ("For your hardness of heart . . .") should be paraphrased: "to bear witness to your hardness of heart." Moses was not making concessions but was removing the veil of "secrecy and anonymity from sinful conduct and displaying it before God and the world." This would mean that the commandment's function is to convict people of sin and bring to light their radical separation from God. There are difficulties with this interpretation, however: the use of Greek *pros* to mean "as evidence of," and also the interpretation of the law as being meant to condemn *(usus elenchticus legis)*, which echoes the views of Paul and the reformers a little too patly (cf. Rom. 3:20).

A different suggestion comes from Taylor, who likewise prefers not to interpret the Mosaic law as a concession to a husband's hardness of heart, but to see it as God's intervention on behalf of the wife: "a merciful concession for the sake of the wife."[173] In this way the wife does in fact gain a modicum of legal protection and in the case of divorce the chance to remarry without coming into conflict with law and morality.

The intervention of the merciful God on behalf of the wronged wife would also agree with the Old Testament (cf. Exod. 21:20; 22:16; Deut. 21:14ff.). Above all, however, it would correspond better to Jesus' picture of God. This interpretation is also uncertain, but it would mean that Jesus shifted the original intent of the law further in favor of the wife—in this case explicitly criticizing the words and substance of the Torah.

In any case, it remains certain that Jesus here opposes the commandment of Moses, whatever its motivation, and makes clear that divorce, although sanctioned by the law (subject to the condition that there must be a certificate of divorce), is contrary to God's will.

In vv. 6–7, Jesus again cites Scripture against Scripture, impugning the authority of the passage cited by the Pharisees by citing a different passage: "But from the beginning of creation, 'God made them male and female.' 'For this reason a man shall leave his father and mother and be joined to his wife, and the two shall become one.'"

The question is whether Jesus really conducted a kind of exegetical debate. Undoubtedly his appeal to the initial act of creation is meant to impugn the authority of Deut. 24:1, the law of divorce: the Mosaic law is in conflict with the original will of the Creator. But the purpose of the Creator's will is itself expressed by passages from Scripture, namely Gen. 1:27 and 2:24. But do the two passages actually say what they are claimed to say? The two Genesis passages tell how God created man and woman and how they become "one flesh." But nothing is said of marriage. The sayings have no bearing for the

173. Vincent Taylor, *The Gospel According to St. Mark*, 2d ed. (London: Macmillan, 1974); see also Pesch, *Markusevangelium*, 4th ed. HThK 2.

Old Testament on either monogamy or the indissolubility of marriage. From the Old Testament perspective at least, Genesis 1 and 2 do not resolve the question of Deut. 24:1, and the appeal to the Genesis passages would probably not have convinced any Jew.

This shows that the real basis for rejecting divorce is not the Old Testament but the Lord's Word in v. 9, which is also the point and climax of the whole debate. In short, only the Lord's own Word lends weight to Genesis 1 and 2 against Deut. 24:1.

The third antithesis in the Sermon on the Mount (Matt. 5:31ff.) confirms this. Here without any reference to the Old Testament a saying of Jesus prohibiting divorce is cited against the law of Deut. 24:1. It was probably Matthew who introduced the conflict between Deut. 24:1 and Jesus' dictum, but it is clear in any case that the Lord's Word does not reinterpret the legal requirement of the Old Testament but rejects it.

5.2 Thus we come to the final and most critical example of Jesus' attitude toward the Torah: the law of the Old Testament is breached and abrogated by Jesus without any scriptural legitimation. Jesus does not, however, attack the law in principle, as the example of Mark 7 illustrates: the Fifth Commandment of the Decalogue is cited against the traditional practice of corban. On the other hand, Jesus' conflict with his family (cf. Mark 3:21ff.) shows that even a commandment of the Decalogue can be abrogated for the sake of the kingdom of God (cf. also Luke 14:26).

It would be quite wrong, however, to claim that those antitheses that criticize an Old Testament law are not to be taken as real antitheses. Goppelt[174] believes that Jesus thought the protases of the antitheses would continue in force as law as long as this world exists. "The law, which, for example, permits divorce, will remain in full effect so long as heaven and earth endure."[175] Jesus' real purpose, Goppelt maintains, is to withdraw everyday life from the jurisdiction of the law. Now it is true that Jesus interprets the Torah parenetically rather than juristically. He shows no interest in translating it into a practical code of law.[176] But a dichotomy between law on the one hand and ethics or parenesis on the other is alien to Jesus;[177] indeed, parenesis takes the place of law—paradoxically, in the form of legal dicta that underline its binding authority. It is by no means assumed that the disciples will continue to respect the law embodied in the protases, writing certificates of divorce and acting on the principle of "an eye for an eye."

For example, Matt. 5:38-39 abrogates the Old Testament *ius talionis*, the principle of equal retaliation, the precise correspondence of act and punish-

174. Leonhard Goppelt, *Die Bergpredigt und die Wirklichkeit dieser Welt* (Stuttgart: Calwer, 1968).

175. Leonhard Goppelt, "Die Herrschaft Christi und die Welt," in *Christologie und Ethik* (Göttingen: Vandenhoeck & Ruprecht, 1968), 102-36, quotation from 104.

176. Luz and Smend, *Gesetz*, 63.

177. Werner G. Kümmel, "Jesusforschung seit 1965, IV," *ThR* 43 (1978): 113.

ment or compensation (cf. Exod. 21:23ff.; Lev. 24:20; Deut. 19:21; but also already Gen. 9:6). It is not clear whether this principle was adhered to literally in Jesus' day when punishment was determined or whether it had in fact been replaced by indemnification; in any case, the repayment of damages was determined in fact by the law of the talion. Jesus' words are not directed against this or that specific practice or even any terrible abuses, but against the principle itself. The disciples of Jesus are not to insist on their rights but to renounce their rights. For them, the law of the talion is not in effect. Not even its Old Testament authority keeps Jesus from abrogating it. Since, however, the principle of equal retaliation was itself intended to put an end to uncontrolled vengeance, it is possible (as in the case of Mark 10) to speak of explicit criticism of the letter of the Torah simultaneous with an implicit transcending of the law's original intent.

The situation is similar with respect to the sixth antithesis in Matt. 5:43: "You have heard that it was said, 'You shall love your neighbor and hate your enemy.'" Only the first half of this quotation comes from the Old Testament, which never says directly that enemies are to be hated. According to Biller-beck,[178] we have here a "popular maxim," by which the "average Israelite" of the day lived.[179] Others assume that this refers to the hatred commanded at Qumran. In the Dead Sea Scrolls, the radical dichotomy between the children of light and the children of darkness leads to frequent admonitions to hate all who are not members of the semimonastic Qumran community. Since the other antitheses do not deal with any of the Qumran injunctions, it is equally possible that the statement simply follows from a radical interpretation of the law of love, because there is no middle ground between love and hate, and hatred is present wherever there is no love.

It is just possible, however, that certain passages of the Old Testament are alluded to, at least indirectly. Foerster,[180] for example, suggests that the Old Testament does indeed speak of a commandment to hate, for example, in the injunction to exterminate the Canaanites or in passages like Pss. 31:7; 139:21–22. Furthermore the concept of "hatred" should not be overworked or understood psychologically. From the perspective of Old Testament usage, "hate" is tantamount to "slight," "love less or not at all."[181]

Whether or not there is an explicit conflict with the Old Testament, it is clear that Jesus' commandment to love enemies implicitly runs absolutely counter to the imprecatory psalms of the Old Testament. Here, too, we see that Jesus' attitude to the Torah implies criticism, criticism—and this is what makes it fundamental and singular—with no exegetical basis in the Old

178. Strack-Billerbeck, *Kommentar* 1:353.
179. Cf. Dietzfelbinger, *Antithesen*, 47–48.
180. Werner Foerster, "Echthros," *TDNT* 2:813.
181. The fifth antithesis is also discussed by Hübner, *Gesetz*, 81ff.; Dietzfelbinger, *Antithesen*, 37ff.

Testament itself, which would have been a real possibility here in the light of such passages as Prov. 25:21–22.

5.3 It is precisely here that Jesus differs most clearly from all the rabbis; the difference is perfectly expressed in the words introducing each of the antitheses: "But I say to you." For Matthew, of course, this phrase merely cautions against erroneous interpretation of the law; he does not see a real conflict between Moses and Christ. In truth, however, we confront here a claim to authority equal—and sometimes contrary—to that of Moses, and on a plane with what has been "said" by God ("you have heard that it was said . . ."). Käsemann is therefore right in saying that whoever claims authority equal to that of Moses and contrary to Moses "declares himself in fact superior to Moses and ceases to be a rabbi, for the authority of the rabbis always derives from Moses alone."[182] Supposed rabbinic analogies must in fact be considered nothing more than formal parallels, because the antitheses of Jesus do not contradict another rabbi and that rabbi's interpretation of Scripture but Scripture itself and Moses himself. In Judaism we never find a doctrine proposed that is counter to the Torah.

Aboth 3.11, for example, even states: "Whoever interprets Scripture contrary to tradition has no share in the world to come." Various rabbis use expressions similar to "But I say to you . . ." to introduce an exegetical theory divergent from what is commonly accepted; they do not, however, imply a conflict with the law received by Israel at Sinai. Jesus' radical claim to authority in fact leads to "demolition of the Torah."[183]

Jesus neither opposes his interpretation to that of another scholar nor does he legitimate his words through exegesis of Scripture. He makes his demands contrary to "what was said" by God to "the men of old," namely, the Sinai generation, by virtue of his own *exousia*, without any support from the Torah, claiming the same authority.

5.4 Jesus' differences with Judaism and his criticism of the law are by no means limited to sayings introduced by: "But I say to you. . . ." Mark 7:15, for example, is a saying of unparalleled audacity, which must have struck any observant Jew like a blow in the face: "There is nothing outside a man which by going into him can defile him; but [only] the things which come out of a man are what defile him." This saying goes far beyond the prophetic criticism of the cult and the reinterpretation of ritual law in Hellenistic Judaism; no wonder that there are no parallels to it in Talmud or Midrash! It means nothing more nor less than the end of all cultic and ceremonial laws governing ritual purity. Whoever gives voice to such a revolutionary idea places himself

182. "Problem," 37; see already Gustav Dalman, *Die Worte Jesu* (1930), 258: "a claim to divine prerogatives."
183. Eduard Lohse, "'Ich aber sage euch,'" in *Einheit*, 73–87, quotation from 84; see also Dietzfelbinger, *Antithesen*, 10, and Luz and Smend, *Gesetz*, 68: "The Mosaic law is not the basis but the contrary of the antithesis."

in irreconcilable conflict with Judaism (cf. especially the spirituality of the Essenes and Pharisees), indeed with the Torah and Scripture itself.

"Whoever denies that uncleanness comes from without denies the presuppositions and clear words of the Torah as well as the authority of Moses. He also denies the presuppositions of the entire ancient cultic system with its sacrifices and acts of propitiation. In other words, he abolishes the distinction, fundamental for the entire ancient world, between the *temenos*, the sacred precincts, and the secular realm, and can therefore consort with sinners."[184] This quotation also suggests that we are not really dealing with a theoretical or even "enlightened" protest: Jesus transgresses the ritual laws "in the interests of the outcasts and those who suffer."[185]

Here we see once again with unmistakable clarity that Jesus engaged in de facto polemic against the Torah itself and came into conflict with it. It is undeniable that when this happened he could no longer appeal to the text of the Old Testament; his opponents in fact had the letter of the law on their side. Jesus' argument with Judaism is not merely over a better interpretation of the law. His criticism of the law's substance is based not on exegesis but on an authority that gives voice to the immediacy of God and of God's will. In a sense, Jesus stands in the line of the Old Testament prophets, but none of the prophets (with the exception of Ezek. 10:25) subjected the law itself to such radical criticism, simply laying aside, for example, the levitical legislation. As Mark 10 and the antitheses show, it would be wrong to suggest that this criticism affected only the ceremonial law and not the moral law as well.

5.5 Summary. The ambiguity of Jesus' attitude toward the law (cf. the analogous misunderstandings of whether the kingdom of God is present or future) of course does not reflect different stages in Jesus' ministry but a complex interrelationship. Beyond all doubt, Jesus denied the Torah the central position it had for Judaism. What matters in the light of the eschaton is not one's attitude toward the Torah but one's attitude toward Jesus' message of the kingdom of God and God's will. Not that God's will is no longer made known in the Torah, as though Jesus were attacking the Torah in principle. What is unique is his simultaneous "yes" and "no," not an anticipation of enlightened rationalism or even Marcionism. For Jesus, transgression of the law normally means disobedience to God and therefore sin. His assurance of forgiveness, for example, presupposes his recognition of the requirements laid down by the law, as does his response to the question of the standard for right conduct in Mark 10:19.

184. Käsemann, "Problem," 39. See also Matt. 23:25; Luke 11:39ff.; Hengel, "Jesus," 163–64; Bornkamm, *Jesus*, 97–98; Braun, *Jesus*, 54. For the contrary position, see Werner G. Kümmel, "Äussere und innere Reinheit des Menschen bei Jesus," in *Heilsgeschehen und Geschichte*, ed. E. Grässer and O. Merk (Marburg: Elwert, 1978), 2:117–29.

185. Luz and Smend, *Gesetz*, 60, goes so far as to say "always," citing Jesus' touching of lepers when healing them (Mark 1:41), his familiarity with unclean prostitutes (Luke 7:36ff.), his table fellowship with tax collectors and sinners, etc.

But the other side of Jesus' attitude toward the Torah is more apparent than continuity and affirmation; it brought him into conflict with the Jewish guardians of the law and with the hierarchy and resulted in his crucifixion. Had he merely polemicized against hypocrisy and pious pretense, he would hardly have been rejected and crucified. Even when Jesus abrogates the letter of the law, his primary concern is not saying "no" to the law but "yes" to God's will, which, however, has been partially obscured and rendered innocuous by law and tradition. The Torah does indeed continue to proclaim God's will, but the two are not identical. The criteria by which even the law must be judged are the kingdom of God and the double commandment of love.

C. THE DOUBLE COMMANDMENT OF LOVE

1. The Tradition in Mark 12:28–34 par.

As we have already seen in the preceding section, the *ius talionis* of the law was abrogated by Jesus and replaced with the commandment of love (see p. 65). That this demanded love is possible only in response to love already received is not stated as pointedly by Jesus as by Paul and John, but there can be no real doubt that for Jesus, too, love is grounded in being loved and has the nature of a response. We may recall God's unconditional love for all (Matt. 5:45), or what is sometimes rather pietistically called Jesus' love for sinners, that is, his friendship with outcasts and the lost, or sayings like Luke 7:47, which states that those who love little are forgiven little.

1.1 The best place to begin is the pericope of the greatest commandment (Mark 12:28ff.).[186] A scribe asks Jesus, "Which commandment is the first of all?" Jesus replies, "The first is, 'Hear, O Israel: The Lord our God, the Lord is one; and you shall love the Lord your God with all your heart, and with all your soul, and with all your mind, and with all your strength.' The second is this: 'You shall love your neighbor as yourself.'"

According to this tradition, Jesus responds to the scribe's question with a quotation combining two Old Testament passages: Deut. 6:5 and Lev. 19:18. The multiplicity of terms for "reason" within the pericope is striking, as is their anthropological variety (the text diverges from both the Hebrew and the LXX). In v. 33, the scribe's answer adds the term "intelligence," and his answer is called "intelligent." Scholars have concluded, probably correctly, that we have here a tradition deriving from Hellenistic Jewish Christianity. The explicit statement of v. 33 that love is superior to sacrifice and the quotation of the Shema, which stresses monotheism in contrast to Gentile polytheism, also point in the same direction.[187]

Some exegetes also state that there are Jewish analogs to the superiority of

---

186. Bornkamm, "Doppelgebot," 37ff.; Burchard, "Liebesgebot," 39ff.
187. Bornkamm, "Doppelgebot," 38–39.

the law of love. This question deserves examination. It must not be over-looked that a major feature of Jewish ethics is casuistry, the subdivision and categorization of God's will. According to Rabbi Meir (ca. 150), for example, there is no Israelite who does not fulfill at least one hundred commandments every day.[188] But there are occasional attempts to transcend the decomposition of the moral law. Rabbi Hillel's negative equivalent of the golden rule, for example, is well known. When a Gentile asks what the Torah says—with the condition that the answer should take no longer than the time one can stand on one leg—Hillel replies: "What is displeasing to you do not do to your neighbor. That is the substance of the Torah. All else is interpretation."[189] It would be wrong to attach too much weight to the negative form of this saying in contrast to its positive form in the Sermon on the Mount (Matt. 7:12), especially since the Letter of Aristeas (207) combines both, albeit not to summarize the Torah. In the Testaments of the Twelve Patriarchs in particular, which lay great stress on "singleness of heart," we read, for example: "Love the Lord and your neighbor" (Test. of Issachar 5:2). This commandment, however, appears in a series with such commandments as "Observe the law, and also acquire singleness of heart." In other words, it has no special weight.[190] But bYebamoth 79a can also emphasize love, saying: "Love of others is the beginning and end of the Torah," and Tosefta Pea 4.19 says: "Almsgiving and active love of one's neighbor outweigh all other commandments of the Torah."[191]

But all these attempts to transcend the plethora of legal details were ultimately unsuccessful. The words of the Mishnah remained decisive: "It pleased the Holy One—blessed be he—to vouchsafe Israel a reward; for he made the regulations of the Torah voluminous."[192] The genius of Jewish ethics does not lie in concentration but in the multiplication of detailed ethical demands, a process that never ends.[193] These casuistic efforts to comprehend the most trivial details in the law must not be caricatured, but the fact remains that Jewish ethics is not unified. By its very nature it could not achieve unity, but only a labyrinth of particular injunctions.

Much the same is true at Qumran. Obedience is interpreted more radically than among the rabbis, but according to Braun[194] the tendency to atomize is merely replaced by a tendency to summarize, which still gives equal weight to what is important and what is unimportant. There is no attempt at unity.

188. Wilhelm Bacher, *Die Agada der Tannaiten*, 2 vols. (Strassburg: Trübner, 1890–1903), 2:23.
189. bSabbat 31a; Strack-Billerbeck, *Kommentar* 1:460.
190. Cf. Nissen, *Gott*, 236: "two particular commandments among other particular commandments," which thus do not comprise the entirety of the Torah.
191. Strack-Billerbeck, *Kommentar* 1:357–58, 460.
192. b. Makkot 3.16; cf. also Josephus *Apion* 2.173–74: "Our lawgiver . . . did not leave anything, not the smallest detail, to the free choice of those for whom his law was decreed."
193. See Nissen, *Gott*, 416.
194. *Radikalismus* 1:28–29.

The heterogeneity of the hundreds upon hundreds of individual requirements reduces everything to the same level. There were occasional attempts
to make distinctions within the fundamental equality of all the commandments, but more typical is the statement of Rabbi Abba ben Kahana (ca.
310): "Scripture makes the smallest of the minor commandments equal to the
greatest of the major commandments."[195] In the face of this uniformity, the
scattered attempts to find a common denominator for the myriads of commandments were bound to fail. A commandment was a commandment, and
therefore the central commandments remain embedded in a wealth of regulations. Bornkamm states the situation clearly: "The Jewish understanding of
the law itself rejects and denies the question of a principle behind the law."
The rules laid down by Rabbi Hillel and others are to be understood merely
as "pedagogical devices, which are not meant to be taken in a fundamental or
exhaustive sense."[196] Even Jewish authors like Güdemann call the question of
the great commandment "un-Jewish and unrabbinic," because Mishnah and
Talmud, although they distinguish easy commandments and difficult commandments, do not distinguish major and minor commandments.[197]

1.2 In positive terms, then, the summary of the law in the double commandment of love is probably peculiar to the message of Jesus.[198] It must be
admitted then, that Hellenistic Judaism had laid the groundwork for such a
summary. Philo, for example, calls our duty toward God (devotion and
holiness) and our duty toward others (love and justice) "the two supreme
commandments."[199] This more systematic approach was probably widespread in Hellenistic Jewish Christianity. It is thus no wonder that Mark 12
should derive from these very circles, as has already been suggested by the
variety of terms meaning "reason."

But it is not necessary to go so far as to ascribe the entire tradition of the
law of love to primitive Hellenistic Jewish Christianity. Q, for example, has
preserved a similar tradition, as is shown by the points in this pericope at
which both Matthew and Luke differ from Mark 12, differences they are
most unlikely to have arrived at independently (e.g., the unusual expression
"a lawyer" instead of "a scribe").

The Lukan recension is especially revealing. Here the lawyer himself states
the law of love, probably because the question itself is shifted. In Mark, Jesus
asks what the most important commandment is and answers the question
himself. Luke has the lawyer attempt to trap Jesus by asking what life
requires ("What must I do . . . ?"). In this case the inquirer must also reply so
that the crucial answer can be left to Jesus: it depends on praxis.

195. Strack-Billerbeck, *Kommentar* 1:902; cf. also 4 Macc. 5:20.
196. "Doppelgebot," 38.
197. See Lindeskog, *Jesusfrage*, 227–28; also Nissen, *Gott*, 337ff.
198. Bornkamm, *"Doppelgebot,"* 38.
199. *De specialibus Legibus* 2.62.

In addition, the combination of quotations from Deut. 6:5 and Lev. 19:18 to summarize God's will is unique; it is not found in Jewish texts. Hengel therefore calls it "absolutely new," at odds with the Jewish thought of Palestine as well as the Diaspora.[200] It is therefore reasonable to assume that there was probably a tradition of the law of love free from Hellenistic influence, going back to Jesus himself. Even if this was not the case and Jesus did not speak in these fundamental terms, his teaching is in fact in harmony with the law of love. But what does this imply?

2. The Priority of the Law of Love

2.1 The priority of the law of love, as stated in Mark 12, means that love of God and of one's neighbor is no longer just one in a series of requirements demanded by the Torah: it is "greater" than the others (v. 31) and the "first" of all (v. 29). The law of love is thus something like a "canon within the canon," a hermeneutical principle and an ethical canon by which the Torah can be judged. In particular, it takes precedence over cultic regulations (cf. v. 33): "much more" than all whole burnt offerings and sacrifices. Even though this passage has been subject to redaction, it echoes Jesus' own thought and praxis, as attested by Jesus' criticism of corban (Mark 7:9ff.),[201] his table fellowship with tax collectors and sinners (where there can be no question of observing dietary laws and similar regulations governing what is clean and what is unclean), and his healings on the Sabbath. It is also confirmed by individual statements (cf. also Mark 7:15).

2.2 "So if you are offering your gift at the altar, and there remember that your brother has something against you, leave your gift there before the altar and go; first be reconciled to your brother, and then come and offer your gift" (Matt. 5:23–24). Unfortunately this passage cannot be claimed as historical evidence for the precedence of reconciliation over the cult in Jesus' teaching. It is a response to the Jewish-Christian interpretation of the first antithesis, and probably reflects a rule of the early Christian community.[202]

The passage does, however, reflect Jesus' own attitude, as we can see in Jesus' question in the pericope describing Jesus' healing on the Sabbath: "Is it lawful on the Sabbath to do good or to do harm, to save life or to kill?" (Mark 3:4). This question pulls the rug out from under all casuistry claiming to determine the lawfulness of healing on the Sabbath; it maintains the propriety of healing quite apart from the specific case in question and proclaims the fundamental precedence of good works and the saving of life over observance of the Sabbath. The real choice is not between cult and ethics

200. Hengel, "Jesus," 170; see also Jay B. Stern, "Jesus' Citation of Dt 6,5 and Lv 19,18 in the Light of Jewish Tradition," *CBQ* 28 (1966): 312–16. For a different view, see Burchard, "Liebesgebot," 55, 61; Berger, *Gesetzesauslegung*, 142–72.

201. See above, 57.

202. Joachim Jeremias, however, considers this an authentic saying of Jesus: "Lass all da deine Gabe," *ZNW* 36 (1937): 150ff.

but between death and life. Not to serve life is to serve death. When we recall that Jesus understands his healings and exorcisms as signs of the triumph of God's kingdom, this observation takes on added weight. It confirms that the law of love is also a sign of the presence of God's kingdom, which manifests God's love and makes all other ordinances and dicta secondary. Cultic questions, sacred times, "ecclesiastical" conventions and taboos—all must take a back seat to the elementary and fundamental requirement to act according to the divine sovereignty of God's love and preserve life. No Sabbath commandment may interfere with fulfillment of the law of love. The necessity of wresting life from the dominion of death takes absolute precedence.

If the decision reached here is to be given its proper weight, it will not do simply to say that moral law replaces cultic law. Jesus repeatedly attended synagogue and probably observed the Sabbath regularly (cf. also Matt. 23:23). The obligation to do good and to save life, however, is most likely given fundamental precedence over Sabbath observance, and the obligation to seek reconciliation over the offering of sacrifice.

Mark 3:4 and similar passages like Mark 7:15 do not simply espouse liberalism, substituting morality for cultic observance.[203] Matt. 5:24 says explicitly: "Leave your gift there," not: "It is no longer required." But reconciliation and mercy take precedence. Ritual purity and tithes are less important than justice, mercy, and faith (Matt. 23:23–24). By citing Hos. 6:6 ("I desire mercy and not sacrifice") twice (Matt. 9:13 and 12:7), Matthew emphasizes the primacy of love.

God will not accept any sacrifice from someone who is not open to reconciliation and is unwilling to practice love. Cult and sacrifice can neither replace nor limit love. Prayer can hope to be heard only when one's brother is forgiven (Mark 11:25). The priest and Levite who pass by the traveler who fell among thieves are not excused because they were on their way to some service in the temple. Love is not compensated or legitimized except by love. There is no such thing as a sacral sphere in which we deal with God alone alongside a secular sphere where our neighbor matters; in all areas of life we must be involved with both God and our neighbor.

2.3 It is wrong to cite Mark 14:3ff., the story of Jesus' anointing, to the contrary—a passage that is not among the most glorious pages of exegetical history, even in the New Testament itself. The scene has often been used to justify a church that disregards poverty to concentrate on cultic worship.[204]

Except for Matthew, who on the basis of chapter 25 shows more understanding for the criticism leveled against the woman's conduct (he omits the negative statements in Mark), the New Testament itself documents this

203. On the symbolic prophetic act of "cleansing" the temple, see below, 111.
204. See Rainer Storch, "'Was soll diese Verschwendung?'" in *Der Ruf Jesu und die Antwort der Gemeinde* (Festschrift Joachim Jeremias), ed. E. Lohse (Göttingen: Vandenhoeck & Ruprecht, 1970), 247–58.

development. John exhibits a "maximum of tendentious and subjective interpretation," placing the objection in the mouth of Judas, whom he also
disparages as a thief (John 12:6). This line of interpretation continued,
missing the point of the story: the presence of the Lord places all other duties
and concerns in abeyance. Jesus' answer expressly calls attention to the
uniqueness of the situation: "In fact it forbids making the woman's action the
norm of Christian conduct after Easter, or more precisely after Good Fri-
day."[205] The story does not enshrine a timeless principle to be cited in
downplaying social obligations in favor of emphasis on the cult.

The very naturalness of the objection in v. 5 suggests rather that wealth
should normally benefit the poor. In any case, there is no avoiding the fact
that for the earthly Jesus the priority and supremacy of the law of love are
absolute.

3. Love of Neighbors and Enemies

3.1 The classic example of love for one's neighbor is the story of the good
Samaritan (Luke 10:30–37), which answers the question "Who is my neighbor?" This question (v. 29) should not be thought of as a demonstration of
stupidity or evasiveness on the part of the questioner. In Jesus' day, "Who is
my neighbor?" was a matter of controversy.

In the Old Testament, the Hebrew term for "neighbor" (Lev. 19:18) refers
to members of the covenant community; the command "Love your neighbor"
refers accordingly to members of the people of Israel, even though there are
traces of an extension that takes into account strangers dwelling in the land.
The usage of this term in the Old Testament made it possible both to restrict
and to extend the scope of the commandment. Later Judaism understood an
explicit limitation of the law of love, making it apply only to Israelites and full
proselytes.[206] But there were also voices supporting the removal of limits.
The debate was clearly in full swing at the time of Jesus, although the earliest
evidence from the Talmud and Midrash cited by Billerbeck[207] favoring the
universal interpretation dates only from the second century C.E. It is clear
that in general the resident alien, the "stranger" in the Old Testament sense,
was no longer recognized as a "neighbor."

Certain Pharisees were even of the opinion that the *am ha-arets*, the
uneducated people who were ignorant of the law, should be excluded.[208] For
example, a rabbinic baraita discussing what to do when finding someone who
has fallen into a pit says: "A Gentile or herdsman should neither be helped out
nor pushed in; but those who are heretics or informers or apostates should be
pushed in and not helped out."[209] Leviticus 19:18 is restricted by the ruling:

205. Ibid., 247.
206. Johannes Fichtner, "plēsion," *TDNT* 6:312–15.
207. Strack-Billerbeck, *Kommentar* 1:354.
208. Ibid. 2:515ff.
209. bAboda Zara 26a.

"If he acts in accordance with the works of your people, love him; otherwise do not love him."[210] It would be wrong to generalize on the basis of such statements, but they illustrate the spectrum of interpretations given the law of love.

Jesus himself responds to the question "Who is my neighbor?" by telling the story of the good Samaritan. At least in its present form, the story is an exemplary narrative. There are no metaphors requiring specific applications. A single exemplary instance lets the subject speak for itself, and the subject is love: "Go and do likewise" (v. 37). Schlatter called the story "visualized ethics." Eichholz spoke of parenesis in which a particular case becomes a model.[211] Whether the story had this form from the outset is disputed. Zimmermann, for example, suggests a parable told by Jesus to justify his mercy toward a sinner, a parable in which he himself appears and in which he interprets his own ministry.[212] (See III.C.2.3 on Crossan's approach.)

3.2 We start with the question "Who is my neighbor?" This asks how far the obligation to love extends and what its limits are. The lawyer is therefore asking what can be demanded or required of him, but also when he can say with a clear conscience, "Thus far and no further." Jesus, however, tells the story from the perspective of the one who fell among thieves. Even if the framework of the story is Luke's, Jesus' purpose is to have the listener place himself in the situation of the victim, to identify with the one who needs help. This explains the shift in the question in Luke. In v. 29, the neighbor is the object of the lawyer's question ("Whom must I love?"); in Jesus' concluding answer in v. 36, "Which of these three proved neighbor to the man who fell among thieves?" the neighbor becomes the subject ("Who is the neighbor, i.e., to whom am I a neighbor?"). This may well be more than a "formal inconsistency" without deeper meaning,[213] even if it is redactional and the question in v. 29 together with its motivation (cf. 16:15) originate with Luke, and possibly also vv. 36–37 (cf. the similar construction in 22:24). In any case, the exemplary narrative shows that the obligation to love has no limits: love does not reach a boundary beyond which nothing is required. The unbounded character of love is illustrated by the fact that it is none other than a Samaritan who helps the victim lying half dead in the road, while a priest and a Levite pass by.

There have been many suggestions to account for their failure to act in

210. *ARM*, Version A, 64. Cf. Martin Hengel, "Jesus und die Tora," *ThB* 9 (1978): 162; Strack-Billerbeck, *Kommentar* 1:365; Fuchs, "What is Interpreted?" 3.
211. Eichholz, *Gleichnisse*, 149.
212. Heinrich Zimmermann, "Das Gleichnis vom barmherzigen Samariter," in *Die Zeit Jesu* (Festschrift Heinrich Schlier), ed. G. Bornkamm (Freiburg: Herder, 1970), 58–69, quotation from 67; see also Jüngel, *Paulus*, 169ff.; George Sellin, "Lukas als Gleichniserzähler," *ZNW* 65 (1974): 166–89; for a critical discussion, see Kümmel, "Jesusforschung, IV," 140–41.
213. Jeremias, *Parables*, 205; against this interpretation, cf. Bornkamm, *Jesus*, 112–13; Eichholz, *Gleichnisse*, 174.

love. The priest may have considered the victim lying there half dead to be a corpse and avoided contact because of the levitical regulations. Or he may have thought that there was no need to show an act of love to one of the *am ha-arets*. Or both may have been afraid of falling themselves into the hands of the robbers. There is nothing in the text, however, to support these or similar suggestions, and even if they were right they could not possibly provide an excuse. Who would not have had plenty of reasons handy to explain his lack of love and his decision to leave his neighbor lying in the road? The Samaritan could well have had similar reasons. If he is to be pictured as a man of some means—Jeremias[214] concludes from the mention of "his own beast" in v. 34 that the Samaritan was probably transporting his goods on a donkey or ass while riding on another—he had more to lose than the others.

Nor is it correct, at least in the first instance, to look for an anticlerical element in the mention of the priest and the Levite. Many exegetes maintain that it is not by chance that both of those who pass by are associated with the temple cult. Ernst, for example, maintains that the parable is meant to illustrate the blindness of the cultic officials to the present call of God in everyday life. Gewalt maintains that the narrative tension derives from two conflicts: a religio-ethical conflict and a religiosociological conflict between the temple personnel and the "laity."[215]

It is certainly tempting and undoubtedly topical to undertake an exegesis critical of theologians. Compare the passionately hostile interpretation of Ragaz, a religious socialist: "The *priest* is reading his breviary. It is his business to deal with theological and ecclesiastical problems. The man lying in the road—what does he matter in comparison to these concerns? Furthermore, he does not even know how to help him. He is not used to such situations, he does not understand them. And what matters is the spiritual life. The fact that a man is lying in the road half dead is the way the world is. The world, above all politics and economics, are, as God wills it, a 'law unto themselves.' "[216]

This reading is correct in its polemic against overvaluing the spiritual life. But the interpretation as a whole would be accurate only if the third person to arrive on the scene were also an Israelite, specifically a Jewish layperson. Instead a Samaritan appears—an even more shocking and offensive figure for Jews of the first century. Ever since its conquest by the Assyrians, the population of Samaria (the region between Judea and Galilee) was mixed with Gentiles. The Jews returning from the Babylonian exile did not recognize them as Jews and considered them unclean. They had their own cultic center

214. *Parables*, 204.
215. See Josef Ernst, *Das Evangelium nach Lukas*, RNT; Dietfried Gewalt, "Der 'Barm-herzige Samariter,'" *EvTh* 38 (1978): 403–17, esp. 416.
216. Leonhard Ragaz, *Die Gleichnisse Jesu* (Gütersloh: Mohn, 1944), 101–2; quoted also in Eichholz, *Gleichnisse*, 167–68.

on Mount Gerizim as well as their own Pentateuch.[217] Josephus[218] reports an incident in the first century C.E. that casts a clear light on the implacable hatred between Jews and Samaritans: during Passover, some Samaritans are said to have profaned the courtyard of the temple by littering it with human remains.

In short, the contrast between the heartless Jews and the merciful Samaritan is not accidental. Under normal circumstances, a Samaritan would have been the last person from whom the victim might expect help. Love does not follow the dictates of convention and prejudice but dares to ignore them, dares with sovereign freedom to surmount the barriers that separate people. A person who loves can see in anyone a neighbor in need.

3.3 This leads in Luke 6:35 and Matt. 5:44 to radical rejection of all limits on one's "neighbor": love is to embrace even enemies. These enemies include both personal enemies (the normal meaning of the word) and religious enemies, the enemies of God and of God's people. The emphasis on the latter meaning in Matt. 5:44 is shown by the parallelism between "enemies" and "persecutors." Luke 6:27–28 describes them as those who hate, curse, and abuse. While "neighbor" is in the singular, "enemies" are discussed in the plural; this very fact suggests that love of enemies is not limited to certain categories of enemies, for example, personal enemies. An enemy can be a legal adversary (cf. Matt. 5:25) or anyone "against whom one has anything" (Mark 11:25). But political and social enemies are also included.[219]

There are Old Testament precursors of the renunciation of vengeance that goes hand in hand with love of enemies (cf. Prov. 25:21, cited in Rom. 12:20; also Prov. 24:29; 1 Sam. 24:18). But these passages and others like Exod. 23:4–5 did not lead to a positive statement of a command to love one's enemies. The principle usually followed was: "Do not rejoice over the misfortune of your enemy and do not repay evil with evil."[220] This is not to deny that there were attempts to universalize the obligation to love so as to include enemies, especially within Hellenistic philosophy and Hellenistic Judaism, but their context and significance must always be kept in mind. Seneca,[221] for example, says that Stoics help support their enemies, but their real motive for doing so is to achieve inward peace and "apathy."[222] According to Dihle,[223] classical ethics, despite the phenomenon of altruism, had no appreciation for total self-surrender on behalf of one's neighbor.

In Hellenistic Judaism, we find numerous admonitions not to repay evil

217. See Joachim Jeremias, "Samareia," *TDNT* 7:88ff.
218. *Antiquities* 18.30.
219. Hoffmann and Eid, *Jesus,* 153–54; Schottroff, "Gewaltverzicht" (I.D); Theissen, "Gewaltverzicht," 174ff.
220. Strack-Billerbeck, *Kommentar* 1:368.
221. *De otio* 1.4.
222. See Piper, *Love,* and passim.
223. "Ethik" (B), 686.

with evil (e.g., Joseph and Aseneth 23:9; 28:5, 10, 14). Rabbinic Judaism speaks of intercession on behalf of sinners[224] and even of overcoming evil with good.[225] The Testaments of the Twelve Patriarchs above all contain admonitions comparable to Jesus' universal statement of the law of love so as to include enemies: Test. of Gad 6:7 urges forgiveness of one's enemy, and Test. of Joseph 18:2 reads: "If someone seeks to do you evil, pray for him by doing good; thus you will be delivered from all evil by the Lord." It is not clear, however, what kind of enemy is meant here. The wisdom passages refer only to personal enemies, not to the enemies of God and of God's people. There are also rhetorical elements (e.g., Test. of Joseph 18:2) and at times overtones of Stoicism. Furthermore, these statements stand alongside others calling it a good work to hate or even kill those who are wicked, following the example of the Lord (Test. of Issachar 4), a commonplace in other writings (e.g., 2 Macc. 15:16) on the basis of Ps. 139:21. These later passages thus neutralize the good beginnings. Above all, even here there is no direct positive admonition to love one's enemy.[226] There is nevertheless some similarity in content to Jesus' command to love enemies.

3.4 The commandment to love your enemies and persecutors, to do good to those who hate you, to bless those who curse you, and to pray for those who abuse you (Luke 6:27–28) shows that love cannot consist in discovering something lovable in the person to be loved. Instead love opens itself precisely to those whom we would naturally say are not worth loving. Here we are very close to the distinction between love as agape and love as eros, as desire, and instinctive attraction. The difference between eros, which desires, and agape, which gives, must not be exaggerated: it would surely be wrong to deny that there is an element of passionate desire in God's love, and furthermore those who disregard their own interests in loving, in the sense of agape, are themselves receivers. There is nevertheless a relative value in the distinction.[227]

Dihle calls Jesus' law of love "an ultimately unnatural demand, contrary to empirical human nature." He concludes that there is in principle an unbridgeable gulf between Greek ethics, "which culminates in the fulfillment of human nature, and Christian ethics, which teaches that human nature is to be transcended." Even for the disciples, love of enemies is clearly anything but natural: the sons of Zebedee ask if they may bid fire come down from heaven to destroy an inhospitable Samaritan village, and Jesus must rebuke them (Luke 9:51ff.).

The love of enemies is a supreme demonstration that love is not a matter of partiality (Kierkegaard), not a consideration of what will be most advan-

---

224. Cf. Strack-Billerbeck, *Kommentar* 1:370–71.
225. Nissen, *Gott*, 313–14.
226. Ibid., 316, etc.
227. See Bornkamm, *Jesus*, 111–12.

tageous (cf. Didache 1:3) or the principle of *do ut des* ("I give so that you might give"), as practiced by even the tax collectors and Gentiles (Matt. 5:46–47). Love that looks to receive love on the basis of mutuality—such love is not yet agape for Jesus. Agape loves without counting the cost or the reward, without worrying what can be kept in reserve, and without limitation to any particular group.

3.5 It is therefore not satisfactory to call love of one's neighbor the focus of Jesus' ethics, especially since there is a kind of tension between loving one's neighbor and loving one's enemy. Normally people love those who are like them (cf. Sirach 13:15). "The more unconditionally, boundlessly, unreservedly, and uncritically we love our neighbor, our family, our class, our nation, the easier it is to justify hating and killing their enemies."[228]

Identification with those with whom we share family ties, culture, religion, and so forth, is encouraged by the commandment to love our neighbors. The universalization of love in the concrete love of enemies demolishes this identification. The commandment to love our enemies censures love that is mere social solidarity. Jesus, for example, does not restrict his circle of disciples to those who are insiders in any sectarian or esoteric sense: as "the friend of tax collectors and sinners" (Matt. 11:19) he is available to the hated representatives of amorality and ignorance of the law. An important element in this openness is the comprehensive solidarity of love.

3.6 The story of the good Samaritan illustrates another feature of love. The Samaritan provides the specific form of aid needed by the victim to alleviate his distress, neither more nor less. He binds up his wounds, sets him on his beast, brings him to the nearest inn, and sees that he receives the food and treatment he needs by paying the cost of his future care. His actions make it unmistakably clear that love cannot be identified with feelings and emotions. Love means active and concrete involvement on behalf of those who suffer. Jesus does not preach an exorbitant heroism that easily provides the excuse that our limited means are overtaxed and a perfect world is an illusion in any case. The law of love addresses us where we are, in terms of what we have already received.

This does not mean that love can only be a personal transaction between an "I" and a "thou," even though Jesus would never have dreamed of "love through institutions" that is rightly a matter of concern today. It is often pointed out (anachronistically!) that Jesus did not try to make the roads safe between Jerusalem and Jericho. This should not be taken as scriptural proof that private acts of love are superior to involvement in social and structural reforms (the same argument could be cited against hospitals, for example). But patient labor to change the structures of society for the benefit of those

228. Noll, *Jesus*, 17.

who suffer can never excuse us from the specific demands of the present moment, which meet us unbidden.

Jesus' concern is not a vague love for the whole world, which can so easily become sentimental illusion. He realistically demands concrete involvement and personal action such as Matt. 25:31ff. illustrates in elementary terms. This does not reduce love to material assistance. In Matt. 5:44, for example, prayer for persecutors underlines and interprets the requirement of love. Love implies that we bring others with us before God. Of course the new relationship thus achieved does not dispense us from active charity (Luke 6:33) and corporal works of mercy. Those who present themselves before God in solidarity with their enemies receive new power for solidarity and self-lessness in everyday life.

If love is defined as self-surrender, it cannot be self-realization. This is where Jesus and the other New Testament authors part company with the Stoa: love is not a means to self-fulfillment.[229] The end and measure of all things is therefore not, as in Stoicism, one's own virtuous life, but the well-being of others. The phrase "as yourself" (Mark 12:31) is not a concession to self-love; it means "instead of yourself." It is assumed that we love ourselves; this assumption, however, is neither sanctioned nor merely restricted, but corrected (cf. also Luke 14:26; Matt. 10:37). Others or their needs are the measure. Like the "golden rule" (Luke 6:31; Matt. 7:12), the phrase "as yourself" is intended to awaken our own expectations and hopes so as to awaken in us an understanding of others.[230]

4. The Law of Love in Formal Ethics and Situation Ethics

4.1 We have seen that Mark 12 understands love as a fundamental, all-encompassing attitude and also as the quintessence of all the individual commandments. Does this mean that all specific applications are left to our own decision? Bultmann finds in the story of the good Samaritan a picture of a person who, "in contrast to the lawyer, realizes what is required of him in the given situation."[231] Jesus, according to Bultmann, never says anywhere *what* one should do or not do; this would see human existence as fundamentally guaranteed, so that we have control over the range of actions that can confront us. Jesus, however, sees human existence as totally without guarantees as to what may confront us.

This means that we cannot, in the moment of decision, appeal to any principles, any criteria based on the past or on universal experience. Every moment of decision is essentially new. Without deriving any specifics from the law of love, Jesus demands and expects that we will know what is good

229. Preisker, *Ethos* (B), 68ff.
230. Hoffmann, "Eschatologie," 206; cf. below, 149.
231. *Jesus*, 68.

and what is evil in any given situation requiring a decision. Therefore it is wrong to study Jesus in order to determine specific ethical requirements or themes.[232] According to Bultmann, Jesus says nothing specific about the concrete substance of the love he demands. Jesus can "only leave the decision to each individual in his concrete situation. . . . Anyone who truly loves knows what must be done."[233]

4.2 Now it is certainly true that love involves freedom, fantasy, and spontaneity. Love can never be prescribed in detail once for all. It cannot be reduced to convenient formulas or handy recipes. It cannot be defined casuistically, and its claims cannot be expressed in a list of specific imperatives. Anyone who thinks that love can rest content when it has forgiven seven times must be told: "I do not say to you seven times, but seventy times seven." This passage (Matt. 18:21–22) is therefore not meant to define a limit. And of course Jesus does not mean that anyone who finds a victim who has fallen among thieves must spend two denarii, like the Samaritan. One could also say that Jesus' concept of "neighbor" takes into account the present moment and thus "the existential demand of the gospel," as Dibelius puts it, "the sense of urgency that does not ask who is to be helped and who is not to be helped, but knows whom I, at this very moment and in these circumstances, am called upon to help, right here today—tomorrow the situation can be totally different."[234] My "neighbor" is not an abstraction but a concrete human being sent to me by God, for whom I am responsible.

But Bultmann's perspective is too one-sided. It exaggerates the element of the moment and scants the importance of specifics and above all the obligation they impose. Jesus' words cannot be understood as a system of legalistic casuistry. Nor, however, can they be taken as vague and colorless formal imperatives, whose content will be obvious at any given moment. The situation ethics of existential theology rejects all specifics, emphasizing exclusively the element of individual personal decision. This is not the ethics of Jesus.[235] Of course it is possible to call the concrete admonitions paradigms of love's total demand and call Luke 10:25ff. an exemplary narrative. But the primacy of love did not prevent Jesus from uttering specific binding instructions paradigmatically. It would be wrong to claim that such paradigmatic demands and individual commandments are not binding; if anything, they look to be extended. Of course it is not just the two terms of abuse cited in

232. Ibid., 63.
233. Ibid., 67; cf. also idem, *Theology*, 20–21. See also Hiers, *Jesus*, 79ff., 160ff.; Cyril S. Rodd, "Are the Ethics of Jesus Situation Ethics?" *ET* 79 (1968): 167–70; Heinz Eduard Tödt, *R. Bultmanns Ethik der Existenztheologie* (Gütersloh: Mohn, 1978), 85ff.
234. Martin Dibelius, "Das soziale Motiv im Neuen Testament," in *Botschaft und Geschichte*, 2 vols. (Tübingen: Mohr, 1953–56), 1:177–203, quotation from 197; cf. Heinrich Greeven, "plēsion," *TDNT* 6:317; Eichholz, *Bergpredigt*, 150.
235. See also Goppelt, *Theology* 1:107; Berner, *Bergpredigt*, 31–32; Flender, *Botschaft*, 53. See also n. 19 of the Introduction.

Matt. 5:22 that are forbidden (if indeed the original text did not contain only one) or the two denarii of Luke 10:35 that are required. The command to do "likewise" (Luke 10:37) is meant to encourage further thought, neither treating the specific example as arbitrary or irrelevant nor leaving everything to the situation.

Jesus' insight into the primacy of love did not lead him to declare all the other commandments null and void. The relative scarcity of texts citing the law of love in comparison to the wealth of specific commandments conveys a clear message. Jesus speaks of neighbors concretely as victims of robbers, tax collectors, people who are hungry or sick, just as he describes acts of love as first aid, table fellowship, healing, and so forth.[236] Even the Jewish authorities are not censured, for example, for collecting tithes on certain fruits or herbs, but for neglecting "the weightier matters of the law," justice, mercy, and faith (Matt. 23:23–24). "These you ought to have done, without neglecting the others"—so one might speak of the other commandments alongside the law of love; they are not meant to limit love but to reinforce it. Jesus says that no other commandment is "greater," not that there is no other commandment. He says that this is the "first" commandment, not that it is the only commandment.

Noll, I think, accurately states the dialectical relationship between the law of love and specific commandments.[237] According to him, the tension between the "general clause" and "case law," long a topic of legal theory, is ultimately irresolvable: "case law," as represented by individual commandments, is not simply abrogated and replaced by the "general clause." The latter, however, has superior authority, and particular norms must be tested against it. Both are mutually indispensable; neither can simply be ignored without impugning the other. This realization, it seems to me, rules out both the desire for an ethical blueprint and the schematic approach of situation ethics, which is vague, not particularly helpful, and all too easily confused with arbitrariness.

5. Love of Neighbors and Love of God

5.1 Finally we must return to the double commandment of love and discuss the relationship between its two requirements: love of God and love of our neighbor. We shall draw heavily upon the parable of the last judgment (Matt. 25:31ff.). In view of the great importance attached to the commandment to love our neighbor and our enemy, it seems appropriate to ask whether love of God cannot simply be equated with love of others. Is it not the command to love our neighbor rather than the double commandment of love that furnishes both the canon by which we can interpret the law and the fundamental criterion of human conduct? Does this not hold true even with

236. See Becker, "Feindesliebe," 6.
237. *Jesus*, 12ff.

respect to cultic regulations, which, we must remember, seek to govern our conduct toward God? When Luz states that a human being in distress is "like a textbook" from which we learn the will of God,[238] he is right insofar as we cannot love God without loving others and we demonstrate our love of God in loving our neighbors, so that we cannot avoid the human element. Our decision about God confronts us with our neighbor, and our encounter with our neighbor confronts us with a decision about God. It is therefore appropriate to call love of our neighbor the concrete manifestation[239] and proof[240] of our love of God.

5.2 But is it legitimate to go a step further and say that the right way to serve God is to serve others, that what the Samaritan does is "an act of love toward God," identifying a "trend" that would identify the two parts of the twofold law?[241] If so, it would mean that in a sense human beings are no longer directly accessible to the love of God and that God is no longer directly accessible to human love; both require human mediation. The more serious consequence is that God's love can come to human beings in this world only through the mediation of others. Here, however, our interest is focused on the latter suggestion, that love of God is identical with love of our neighbor. There is an unavoidable danger in this case that "God" will become nothing more than a codeword for "neighbor" or an ideological superstructure that can simply be dispensed with. The question of whether it is still of fundamental importance that Jesus speaks separately of loving God or whether this is not an element of objectively superfluous tradition is answered by Luz. He states that the commandment to love God establishes "that love of one's neighbor involves nothing less than the encounter with the God of the Old Testament."[242] Ultimately, however, God appears to be no more than a symbol actualizing or manifesting the gift I receive in others and the claim that others have upon me.

5.3 It is extremely unlikely, however, that Jesus thought God himself could be replaced as the subject or object of our love, either by the love manifested through or the love demanded by our neighbor. We begin with Matt. 25:31–46, a text that seems particularly open to the interpretation just outlined. In the description of the last judgment, we hear at the end: "As you did it to one of the least of these my brethren, you did it to me." The opposite is said of those who have not done the works of love described.

It is of course disputed whether and to what extent the parable goes back to Jesus himself.[243] It has certainly undergone editorial revision, which is re-

238. Ulrich Luz, EKKNT *Vorarbeiten Heft 2*, 125.

239. Conzelmann, "Jesus Christus," 639.

240. Bornkamm, *Jesus*, 111.

241. Braun, *Jesus*, 101, 95–96; cf. Dihle, "Ethik," in support of the identification.

242. Luz, EKKNT *Vorarbeiten Heft 2*, 126.

243. Ibid., Egon Brandenburger, *Das Recht des Weltenrichters*, SBS 99 (Stuttgart: Katholisches Bibelwerk, 1980); Ulrich Wilckens, "Gottes geringste Brüder," in *Jesus und Paulus* (Festschrift Werner G. Kümmel), ed. E. E. Ellis (Göttingen: Vandenhoeck & Ruprecht, 1975), 363–83.

sponsible, for example, for the introduction in v. 31a, a traditional apocalyptic topos that speaks of the coming of the Son of man with his angels (cf. Mark 8:38 par.; Matt. 16:27), and probably also for the Son's sitting on his glorious throne (v. 31b; cf. Matt. 19:18). But if v. 31 is not original, then it is not the Son of man but God who comes in judgment, and it is God himself who presides over the judgment and encounters us in the poor and lowly. (If the parable is genuine, vv. 32a, 34, and 41 must also be redactional.)

The major argument against the parable's authenticity is usually the existence of Jewish parallels listing works of love identical or similar to those listed in Matthew 25 (cf. Isa. 58:7; Test. of Joseph 1:5–6; Slavonic Enoch 9). In these passages it is primarily what is given to the poor that is counted as having been given to God. Luz, however, following Braun, points out that the parable goes beyond the Jewish parallels by identifying God with the least of the brethren.[244] Furthermore the universalization of the law of love corresponds best to the requirements stated by Jesus elsewhere, as does the absence of any reference to the law. It is thus quite likely that the parable derives in substance from Jesus.[245] In this context we shall not address the question of whether the expression "least of the brethren" refers to sufferers in general or to suffering Christians, and whether those interrogated about their acts of love at the last judgment are pagans or members of the Christian community.

When we examine the parable closely, we see that God himself is found in the least of the brethren. The eschatological division is determined on the basis of works of love vouchsafed to those who suffer and are oppressed. Those who have lovingly accepted these people in their want, their need, and their oppression are loved by God, who involves himself with everyday distress, who makes them his own. Those to be judged obviously expect that they will be judged on the basis of what they have done for God, but now their works of love toward those who suffer become the crucial standard, because God has identified himself with the poor, the hungry, the sick, and the prisoners.

When God appears in the form of a suffering human being, human charity is in fact the locus that decides the question of God and human salvation. But can we say, "The only locus"? Can we say "The neighbor in need is the only place where we find God in the world"?[246] In the light of Protestant theology and practice, it certainly requires an "unhappy courage" to protest against special emphasis on human charity. It is tempting to agree with Käsemann that it is better "to stand with those who have at least learned this much from Jesus and the Bible than with the fanatics who accept every dogma and have

244. But see Brandenburger, *Recht*, 75–76.
245. Friedrich "Gott und Bruder?"; pace Brandenburger, who finds a theology of Christ's preexistence in the background.
246. Luz, EKKNT *Vorarbeiten Heft 2*, 127.

nothing to say about the inhumanities tolerated and promoted by Christians, who rest on their orthodoxy and do not even hear the voice of Jesus asking: 'What have you done or not done unto me in my brother?' "[247] But even Käsemann is not content to see human charity as the quintessence of faith. There is, as it were, something in the divine that transcends human charity.

5.4 Even Matthew 25 raises the question whether God is found *only* in others: God appears here in twofold form and function. On the one hand, he is present although hidden in the form of the victim; on the other, he is yet to come and revealed as the judge of the world. We may agree with Luz that the God who appears in weakness in the present is the God of Jesus and the God manifest in the future is the God of tradition, and that in his identification with those who suffer the God of tradition comes to us in the present. But it would be an oversimplification to downgrade the element of the future here and elsewhere as simply the product of tradition. According to Jesus, it is the God of the future who shows that there is an enduring difference between God and the human race, and that it would be wrong to speak of simple identity. There are also other texts that caution us against ascribing absolute priority to Matthew 25. It would be wrong, for example, to postulate that Mark 10:28ff. incorporates the "second commandment" into the "first commandment" or that love of God and love of others are simply identical. It is obviously not by chance that both are mentioned independently.

Luke therefore follows the exemplary narrative of the good Samaritan with the story of Mary and Martha (Luke 10:38–42): in addition to an obligation to love others, there is an obligation to attend to the one thing needful, which the ancient church interpreted (not without reason) as combining the life of action with the life of contemplation (*vita activa*//*vita contemplativa*). The crucial point is not to evade Jesus and his demands, not even in our works of love on behalf of our neighbor.

Even Matthew, who unlike Mark affirms explicitly that the second commandment is equal to the first, does not say simply that both are identical (Matt. 22:39).

For Jesus himself, love of God and love of one's neighbor are certainly not identical, as though love of one's neighbor could simply replace love of God: "This would eliminate the boundary between God and humankind. Anyone who considers the two commandments identical in this sense knows nothing of God's sovereignty and quickly turns God into an empty expression that can easily be dispensed with."[248] We pray to God, not to our neighbor. We hope for the kingdom of God, not a human kingdom. Compare also Luke 11:42, which juxtaposes justice and "love of God," refusing to accept outward obedience. We may also recall many rigorous individual commandments based not on love of one's neighbor but (if they have any basis at all) on

247. *Freedom*, 35.
248. Bornkamm, *Jesus*, 110; see also Bultmann, *Jesus*, 80–81.

radical love of God and of God's kingdom (cf. 48 [renunciation of farewells] and 96–97 [renunciation of remarriage]).

Whoever considers love of God an obsolete mythological survival and seeks to replace it with love of others, thus reestablishing its true meaning, is welcome to do so, but such a proposal should not appeal to Jesus and the New Testament. The question will also soon arise as to why there is any need at all for love. Horkheimer states that "without any theological basis, there is no reason to claim that love is better than hate."[249] None of these comments, however, is meant to contest the fact that Jesus considered love of neighbors and enemies the crucial measure of human conduct. Jesus saw no love of God without love of neighbors and enemies.

Excursus:
Unique Features of Jesus' Ethics?

Before examining Jesus' approach to specific questions, we shall discuss briefly whether and how Jesus' ethics differs from the ethics of Judaism. Our purpose is not apologetic, to demonstrate Jesus' originality or "superiority," or to minimize his ties with Judaism. Of course even in his ethics Jesus is primarily a Jew; the relationship of his ethics to Judaism must not be ignored. In general terms, as many have pointed out with good reason, this relationship is manifest in the indissoluble bond between "religion" and ethics.[250] We also cite two instances of specific parallelism, one related to the first antithesis and the other to the central admonition of Luke 6:36 to reflect God's mercy. According to Rabbi Eliezer (ca. 90), hatred of one's neighbor is tantamount to murder.[251] Targum Yerushalmi I on Lev. 22:28 reads: "My people, children of Israel—said Moses—as our Father is merciful in heaven, so should you be merciful on earth."[252] On the other hand, it would also be wrong to gloss over all the unique features of Jesus' teaching that would be shocking or scandalous in the context of Judaism. In any case, it is clear that Jesus' ethics does not stand in splendid isolation, but has much in common with Jewish ethics.

Many scholars are of the opinion that "for almost every ethical statement of Jesus, taken by itself, a statement can be found somewhere in the universe of Jewish literature that is in its own way analogous."[253] Klausner, a Jewish scholar, goes even farther, maintaining that "there is not a single ethical teaching in any of the Gospels" that does not have a parallel in the Old Testament or in Jewish literature of Jesus' time.[254] Other Jewish scholars, too, often continue to come to the same conclusion—nothing new.[255]

Now this claim appears exaggerated. The radical contrast and conflict between

249. M. Horkheimer, *Verwaltete Welt?* (1970), 36–37; cf. H. Neumann, *The Death of God and the Problem of Altruism* (1969), 253–64.

250. Gerhard Kittel, "Die Bergpredigt und die Ethik des Judentums," *ZSTh* 2 (1925): 553–94; Robert T. Herford, *Talmud and Apocrypha* (New York: KTAV, 1971), 274.

251. Strack-Billerbeck, *Kommentar* 1:282.

252. Ibid. 2:159.

253. Kittel, "Bergpredigt," 561.

254. Joseph Klausner, *Jesus of Nazareth* (New York: Macmillan, 1925), 384.

255. See Lindeskog, *Jesusfrage*, 217; Schalom Ben Chorin, "Jesus und Paulus in jüdischer Sicht," *ASTI* 10 (1976): 17–29, esp. 23.

"old" and "new" and the fact that the eschatological age of salvation makes all things new (Mark 2:21–22 par.) suggest that the consequent discontinuities will not leave untouched the substance of what is required. We recall Mark 7:15 (already cited) or the truly unparalleled "But I say to you. . . ."[256] Specific examples from the ethical realm include the absolute prohibition of divorce, which conflicts with normative Jewish tradition, and the absolute prohibition of swearing, which, despite all calls to abstain from oaths (e.g., among the Essenes) and to beware of them, is not found in Philo or in any other texts antedating or contemporary with the New Testament.[257] The Jewish scholar C. G. Montefiore has determined that Jesus appears to "exhibit a revolutionary new attitude" toward children, women, and sinners; this means, for example, that he deals with women in a way that "is strange and offensive to rabbinic propriety," being "more merciful and compassionate."[258] His attitude toward family ties is not Jewish, especially his celibacy and lack of filial piety.[259] As we have seen above, 76–77, there are at most isolated parallels to the commandment to love enemies, which such Jewish scholars as Herford and Scheftelowitz, but also Braun and others consider contrary to Jewish thought. In contrast to Qumran and the Mishnah, it is striking how minor the theme of the law is for Jesus' ethics. Kümmel sees the revolutionary novelty of Jesus in his proclamation of God's will "without concern for correct or incorrect interpretation of the commandments of the Torah." Jewish voices, too, speaking of Jesus' "liberalism" and downgrading of the law, find no place for Jesus in Judaism.[260]

Unique features of Jesus' ethics are also accepted by Kittel and such Jewish scholars as Klausner, who often use such terms as "more," "intensification," or "concentration." Jesus, for example, is said to have applied the Sabbath commandment "more freely," to have given Judaism interiority and depth, to have reshaped or reoriented it.[261] According to Kittel, Jesus' uniqueness—apart from the fact of his person—lies in the force and concentration with which he consistently declares what is found in Jewish sources only at isolated high points and with many gradations.[262] In the Talmud, according to Jeremias, one must sift through much chaff to find the precious grain.[263] Even Jewish scholars like Klausner suggest that Jesus concentrated the ethical demands of Judaism so that they stand out much more vividly than in the Talmud and Midrash, "where they are submerged in discussions of Halakhah and debates over nonessentials."[264] Klausner also speaks, with less than complimentary intent, of Jesus' "extremely radical ethics," which necessarily leads to "degeneration of morality,"[265] because its exaggeration and absolutism at the expense of reality and

256. See above, 84.
257. See Werner G. Kümmel, "Jesus und die Rabbinen," in *Heilsgeschehen und Geschichte*, 2 vols. (Marburg: Elwert, 1965–1978), 1:1–14, esp. 3, 6; for discussion of the prohibition of swearing, see Strecker, "Antithesen," 80; and above, 60.
258. Lindeskog, *Jesusfrage*, 240.
259. Ibid., 144.
260. Kümmel, "Jesus und die Rabbinen," 8; cf. 12; and idem, "Jesusforschung, IV," 243–44.
261. Lindeskog, *Jesusfrage*, 223; cf. 230, 236, 238.
262. "Bergpredigt," 579–80.
263. *The Sermon on the Mount* (Philadelphia: Fortress Press, 1967), 5, citing Wellhausen's statement: "Everything that is to be found in the Sermon on the Mount is also to be found in the Talmud—and a great deal more." Jeremias finds the last phrase crucial.
264. *Jesus*, 389.
265. Ibid., 406.

practicality (not to mention its disregard for the ceremonial law) is un-Jewish and destructive of law and order. Others call it extravagant, impracticable, or monstrous.[266]

A further unique feature is largely identical with what was described above, 41–42, as Jesus' demand for radical obedience. Montefiore spoke of "exalted moral idealism" and "excess" in forbearance and forgiveness, giving and granting.[267] Lapide calls the Sermon on the Mount "the superhuman ideal ethics of a supermoralist."[268] It is probably more accurate, with Kittel, to speak of the "absolute intensity" of Jesus' ethics: "One might say that Jesus did not demand a minimum of love, a minimum of purity. Nor did he demand a maximum. His demand is simple and categorical: love; simple and direct: purity."[269]

These comments undoubtedly point to important differences. The list could be extended. We recall the double commandment of love in contrast to the casuistry and trivialization of God's will in Jewish ethics. We recall, finally, the difference in motivation and the relationship between indicative and imperative.

D. CONCRETE PRECEPTS

1. Fundamental Considerations

1.1 As we have seen, according to Jesus the eschaton does not render concrete human conduct unimportant but confronts it with a radical challenge. In addition, Jesus' message has implications for corporate ethics as well as for personal ethics. Does it also have social implications? Does it apply to the total reality of society within which people act? Of course for Jesus all institutions and structures of this world are provisional, and undoubtedly he does not think that salvation comes through them or by transforming them. It is significant, however, that he did not use this position simply to stabilize or sanction the existing order, as though the established order were from God and should therefore be defended or as though the present world were from the devil or totally ephemeral, so that all contact with it should be avoided. Nor, however, did he espouse an attitude of "neutrality" or indifference, an indifference that would in fact be tantamount to stabilizing the advantages of the privileged.

In case of conflict one must be prepared to leave father and mother as well as house and home, but this necessity did not lead Jesus to disdain life in this world or to espouse the life of ascetics and hermits. It is not by chance that the one who demanded this radical break with normality and what the world expects was also castigated as a glutton and a drunkard (Matt. 11:19 par.), a charge that shows at least that asceticism was not his program. It is not by chance that he maintained the doctrine of creation and used it, for example, to attack the practice of divorce and Sabbath casuistry, nor is it by chance that

266. See Lindeskog, *Jesusfrage*, 225, 243–44; Kümmel, "Jesus und die Rabbinen," 2–3.
267. Lindeskog, *Jesusfrage*, 234.
268. Pinchas Lapide, *Er predigte in ihren Synagogen* (Gütersloh: Mohn, 1980), 51.
269. "Bergpredigt," 581.

he broke through the customary discrimination against women to cite just two examples. Anyone who breaks down the boundary between clean and unclean (Mark 2:13ff.) is tampering with the social as well as the religious realm. Anyone who infringes on family obligations and property rights (cf. Matt. 8:22) does not in fact bring "peace" for the existing order but "a sword" (Matt. 10:34–35). Anyone who impugns the law attacks also the order imposed by the Romans, both religious and civil, which represents the law governing family, property, the state, for example.[270] Furthermore, even the preaching of the Baptist had political implications (Luke 3:19). All of this suggests that Jesus did not simply preach interiority and personal piety, considering the secular world nothing more than a foil for the totally other. Such a theory will not hold up even in the face of Jesus' healings and exorcisms, which are interpreted in Matt. 12:28 par. as symbolic anticipations of the reality of the kingdom of God.

Today we encounter both the error of spiritualizing and personalizing Jesus' ethics and the opposite error of making Jesus a representative of political messianism or Zealotism or maintaining that the real point of his message is to change the world. Now Jesus is anything but a defender of the status quo. And it is also true that his message has implications for the renewal of relationships between individuals and groups. But his promises are not fulfilled solely on the historical plane, and his eschatology cannot be reduced to the perspective of hope for the future of this world. The kingdom of God becomes reality not just when the hungry are filled and those who weep can laugh once more (Luke 6:21). The fullness of salvation therefore includes not only healing and bodily wholeness, but also the presence of God, which is preached to the poor (Matt. 11:4–5). According to Luke 12:13–14, Jesus refuses to mediate a dispute over an estate by saying, "Who made me a judge or divider over you?" This saying documents the fact that Jesus did not consider his true ministry to lie in the realm of social reform, even though we must remember that the primary point is refusal to become entangled in legal questions concerning an inheritance in order to help someone gain money and property (cf. vv. 15ff.).

1.2 On the other hand, it must be emphasized that the traditional Lutheran interpretation of the "two kingdoms" likewise fails to do justice to Jesus' message. As is well known, Luther distinguished between a spiritual and a secular kingdom, person and office, Christians as individuals and Christians in relation. Always, especially in interpreting the Sermon on the Mount and sayings concerning marriage, oaths, vengeance, and so forth, Luther seeks to show that the individual Christian is addressed simply as a Christian, not as a Christian "in the world," a Christian in a particular office, who cannot avoid the conditions of life in the old world in which he shares.

270. Hoffman, "Eschatologie," 219–20.

Such sayings as the prohibition against vengeance, according to this reading, cannot be applied to the civil authorities. They apply to the individual only as a person, not as an office holder; they do not apply to the secular order, which depends on the political use *(usus politicus)* of God's law, as found, for example, in Romans 13. "The person is indeed a Christian, but office or principate has nothing to do with his being a Christian."[271]

This is not the place to go into the background, pros and cons, presuppositions, and consequences of this theory—here grossly oversimplified—espoused by Luther and his interpreters. Our only purpose here is to contrast it in the form just outlined, which was to prove so fateful, with the preaching of Jesus. This is all the more necessary because many exegetes take an approach very much like that of Luther, limiting the application of Jesus' ethics de facto to the private sphere. We may cite as an example the fifth antithesis of the Sermon on the Mount (Matt. 5:38–42), the admonition to eschew violence in the name of justice. Several commentators read this admonition as bearing solely on how disciples should behave when they have to suffer injustice inflicted on them personally. As private individuals or Christians, they must act on the basis of Matthew 5. When acting officially and with public responsibility, however, they are obligated under certain circumstances to do the very opposite, answering evil with evil and force with force.[272]

1.3 This distinction between private and public responsibility, between a private sphere and a public sphere, however justified it may be in particular cases and however much it may emphasize the importance of individual conduct, will not suffice either historically or exegetically. The *lex talionis* (on which, see *ius talionis*, p. 64) is not suspended just for particular cases, for particular individuals, spheres, or areas of responsibility. The vignette of the legal adversary in Matt. 5:23–24, with its setting in secular law, shows that Jesus is addressing the realm of everyday life; he is not defining an internal ethics for the conduct of the disciples toward each other. The liberating power of the kingdom of God is meant to reach beyond the confines of the Jesus movement, penetrating the other areas and dependencies of life and effecting a change of attitude toward force and counterforce in all human relationships. It may be that Matthew himself understood the Old Testament requirement quoted in 5:38 as permitting some degree of private justice and countered it with the principle that in interpersonal encounter it is wrong to "resist one who is evil." In any case, however, Jesus' admonition impinges on the public realm, not only mentioning a slap in the face (v. 39) during an ordinary quarrel—Luke associates the act of violence (beating and robbery) more clearly with the everyday experience of the Palestinian countryside, whereas

271. WA 32:440; cf. also 11:255.
272. On Matth. 5:38–42, Michaelis, *Matthäus*, ZBK 1/1; and Schniewind, *Matthäus*, NTD [1937]; also Goppelt, *Bergpredigt*, 105; and others.

Matthew introduces the forensic situation—but going on in v. 40 to mention a lawsuit and in v. 41 the possibility of being conscripted for forced labor or for service in the military or the police.

In response to such two-tiered ethics, Schlatter[273] already maintained with good reason that "the distinction between public and individual ethics is out of place in the milieu of Jesus." Dietzfelbinger emphasized that such a dichotomy contradicts the point made by the antitheses, "which are particular examples from a human world addressed to the totality of a human world, a new mode of human society, which comprehends the total person, including all private and public relationships."[274] Bonhoeffer[275] and others cite the insoluble problem that in fact the various roles and realms overlap; everyone stands in relationship to others. This is even more true *mutatis mutandis* for the time of Jesus, when any "sharp distinction between private and public, religious and political, individual and social . . . would ignore the indissoluble solidarity joining the individual to society and vice versa."[276]

Certain precursors of a doctrine suggesting two types of divine sovereignty may be seen in the contrast between eschatology and protology, between the prophetic tradition and the wisdom tradition, and possibly also in the saying "Render to Caesar the things that are Caesar's and to God the things that are God's" (Mark 12:17), which will be discussed below.[277] But this never suggests a separation or isolation of an autonomous political and public sphere, as though the precepts of Jesus had no bearing on conduct in this part of the real world and should be limited to the private sphere, while the world is left to its own devices or the guidance of reason.

And is matrimony for Jesus really such an external and secular matter, governed only by reason, as Luther claims?[278] Does Jesus really have "nothing" to say about financial matters, but "leaves them to the dictates of reason"?[279] Jesus does not divide people into two halves or dimensions: they cannot take refuge in predefined roles, institutions, and structures or escape his demands by appealing to necessity.

Of course the admonition in Matt. 5:39b is not to be understood legalistically as a universal principle to be applied in each and every case. It is not by chance that Luke 6:29 subordinates this admonition to the commandment to love enemies (Luke 6:27). This means, however, that love is determinative even in the so-called public realm, and this love can manifest itself in a variety of specific ways. It does not mean that love is irrelevant here, that everything

273. Adolf Schlatter, *Der Evangelist Matthäus*, 7th ed. (Stuttgart: Calwer, 1982), 185.
274. *Antithesen*, 66; cf. also Hoffmann, "Eschatologie," 200; Lohfink and Pesch, *Weltgestaltung* (B5), 36, 63; Wendland, "Weltherrschaft" (B1), 85ff.; Mealand, *Poverty*, 83.
275. *Cost*, 124.
276. Hoffmann, "Eschatologie," 221–22.
277. See below, 112–13.
278. WA 32:378.
279. Ibid., 395.

is left to political and social expedience and "necessity," to reason, the legal system, natural law, and so forth.

In sum, although Jesus did not consider his true task to be reform of social and political structures, and one searches his teachings in vain for detailed concepts of a new political or social order, of new sexual roles or economic relationships, nevertheless the will of God that he preached impinges on these areas. If he does not annul legal institutions or the order of society, he does deny their autonomy and isolation from the concerns of God and neighbor, so that Luther may indeed rightly say: "Whatever does not benefit does harm."

2. Man and Wife/Marriage and Divorce

2.1 If we are to evaluate correctly what Jesus has to say about this aspect of life, we must briefly examine the context in which he taught. Only against this background can we see how much Jesus differs from the customary androcentric treatment of women, that is, discrimination against them.

Prejudice against women is in part a consequence of the ritual law (frequent "uncleanness" that excludes them from the cult), in part a consequence of conventional patriarchy. In any case, Jewish women at the time of Jesus ranked in many ways with slaves and children. Their status was inferior both socially and religiously. They could not read from the Torah, were not counted in determining whether the minimum congregation for synagogue worship was present, were not required to fulfill certain commandments and recite certain prayers, and so forth. They were segregated in worship: in the Herodian temple there was a separate courtyard for women, and in synagogues they were assigned to side rooms or galleries. Twice a day, devout Jewish males said: "Blessed art Thou who didst not make me a Gentile, who didst not make me a woman, who didst not make me ignorant [of rabbinic teaching, so the Tosefta; the Babylonian Talmud says 'who didst not make me a slave']." Rabbi Hillel says: "Lots of women, lots of magic; lots of girls, lots of lechery." A man should not spend much time with his own wife, and certainly not with another woman. Even the disciples were astonished that this was not Jesus' way (John 4:27). It was not Adam but Eve who brought sin and death into the world. Sirach 25:24 reads: "From a woman derives the beginning of sin, and on her account we all die." A woman's position was always burdened by religious and social discrimination. Josephus summarizes the situation accurately: "In every respect, women are subordinate to men."[280]

2.2 Viewed against this background, Jesus' words and actions appear downright revolutionary. Even though he did not pursue social reform in the strict sense, he undertook a reassessment whose effect could hardly be overestimated; in word and deed Jesus brought to an end the inferior status of women. Even if much of the evidence derives from the Christian community,

---

280. *Against Apion* 2.201. See also Leipoldt, *Frau* (B2), 69ff.; Schrage and Gerstenberger, *Frau* (B2), 106ff.; Leonard J. Swidler, *Women in Judaism* (Metuchen, N.J.: Scarecrow, 1976).

the attitude displayed is incomprehensible without Jesus' own initiative. He calls both men and women and associates with tax collectors and prostitutes, because the judgment and mercy of God cannot be separated. He addresses women without resentment or animosity. Luke 8:1–3 even speaks of women who follow him as disciples. Women appear in accounts of healings and serve as models of faith (cf. Matt. 15:28). None of this is easy or automatic.[281]

2.3 This basic attitude also lies behind the sayings about marriage and celibacy, adultery and divorce. Here Jesus' eschatological perspective cannot be missed. When he insists that marital companionship passes away with this world (Mark 12:25 par.), the point of his words is that the resurrection does not prolong the earthly situation but means something totally other. But it is also implied that marriage is not something absolute and definitive, but transitory and relative. Its provisional nature, which probably has nothing to do with the myth of an originally androgynous human being and does not consider sexual differentiation a sign of alienation,[282] is not destructive but liberating: it repudiates the absolutism and destructive force of sexuality and eros, of egoism and possession, of female helplessness and inferiority. For the sake of the kingdom of God, it is even possible to forgo marriage.

At the end of the pericope dealing with divorce, Matt. 19:12 says: "There are eunuchs who have been so from birth, and there are eunuchs who have been made so by men, and there are eunuchs who have made themselves so for the sake of the kingdom of heaven. He who is able to receive this, let him receive it." The meaning of this passage has been a matter of perpetual dispute. The primary question is whether "eunuchs" is to be taken literally or metaphorically, or perhaps literally in the first two clauses and metaphorically in the third. Most scholars have rightly concluded that celibacy is meant.[283] Verse 10 in the preceding section indicates that the saying about "eunuchs" does in fact refer to celibacy. The third group (those who have made themselves eunuchs) is the focus of attention; the reference can hardly be to self-castration. "Eunuch" instead stands for "someone who—voluntarily or involuntarily—lives a life of sexual asceticism."[284]

It is important to note that these words are a statement, not a command. Celibacy is not a general obligation. This observation is confirmed by the fact that Peter was married and remained so, as did Jesus' brothers (cf. Mark 1:30

281. See Johannes Leipoldt, *Jesus und die Frauen* (Leipzig: Quelle & Meyer, 1921); also idem, *Frau* (B2), 115ff.; Leonard J. Swidler, "Jesu Begegnung mit Frauen," in *Menschenrechte für die Frau*, ed. E. Moltmann-Wendel (Munich: Matthias-Grünewald, 1974), 130–46; Hanna Wolff, *Jesus, der Mann* (Stuttgart: Radius, 1975); Schrage and Gerstenberger, *Frau*, 114ff.
282. Pace Niederwimmer, *Askese* (B2), 53.
283. See Johannes Schneider, "euchomai," TDNT 2:765–68; Josef Blinzler, "Eisin eunouchos; zur Auslegung von Mt. 19:12," *ZNW* 48 (1957): 254–70; Jerome Kodell, "The Celibacy Logion in Mt. 19,12," *BTB* 8 (1977): 19–23; Francis J. Moloney, "Mt. 19,2–12 and Celibacy," *JSNT* 2 (1979): 42–60.
284. Greeven, "Ehe" (B2), 49–50.

par.). It is also assumed by 1 Cor. 9:5 that family ties were not severed and that Peter later took his wife with him on his missionary journeys.

It is probably reasonable to conclude that Matt. 19:12 represents Jesus as having decided to remain celibate for the sake of the kingdom. "Eunuch" has even been interpreted as a term of reproach, like "glutton and drunkard" (cf. also Matt. 10:25), applied to him by his opponents and then accepted with an apologetic twist.[285] The crucial point is that celibacy is not undertaken for ascetic or dualistic reasons, to gain merit. Its basis is eschatological: celibacy is meant to set people free for the gift and task implicit in the kingdom of God.[286] Here Jesus clearly parts company with rabbinic Judaism, for which marriage is a religious and moral duty. According to the rabbis, whoever is not married by the age of twenty transgresses a commandment of God.[287] It is true that Ben Azzai remained unmarried, but in the first place he is the only exception, and in the second he was sharply criticized for his celibacy.[288] There is a certain parallel in the celibacy practiced at Qumran,[289] the motives for which are not entirely clear.[290]

Thus Jesus did not understand celibacy as a universal requirement for entrance into the kingdom of God; in particular instances, however, or in cases of conflict, he demanded renunciation of the most intimate ties (Matt. 10:37–38; cf. Luke 14:26). Sexuality, marriage, and family must not have a priority or autonomy with respect to God. There cannot be any institutional or blood relationship that ignores the demands of God and the call of Jesus. Echoing Micah 7:6, Matt. 10:34 says that Jesus did not "come to bring peace on earth, but a sword" (Luke 12:51 reads the abstract "division" instead of "sword"). Dissolution of the most intimate relationships with relatives and family, especially the older generation that dominated the extended patriarchal family, is understood as an eschatological sign. Because natural family relationships must be secondary to doing the will of God (Mark 3:20–21, 31ff.; cf. Luke 9:59–60 par.), for the sake of his mission Jesus himself left his family, which obviously could not understand him, and led a life without home or family (Matt. 8:20; Luke 9:58).

2.4 Jesus' realization that his message dissolves family ties and sets an eschatological limit on marriage and sexuality did not lead him to condemn this whole realm in gnostic fashion or to view it as demonic. This is illustrated clearly by the justification in Mark 10 for the prohibition of divorce. God himself made male and female, as v. 6 says, echoing Gen. 1:27. For Jesus,

285. Greeven, "Ehe," 49–50; Moloney, "Mt. 19,2–12," 50–51.
286. See Schrage and Gerstenberger, *Frau*, 142ff.
287. See Strack-Billerbeck, *Kommentar* 2:372–73; 3:368, 373.
288. See bSota 4b; bKethubim 63a.
289. See Josephus *Antiquities* 18.21; Strack-Billerbeck, *Kommentar* 2:160–61.
290. See Hans Hübner, "Zölibat in Qumran," *NTS* 17 (1970–71): 153ff.; Niederwimmer, *Askese*, 57 n. 26; Schrage and Gerstenberger, *Frau*, 148–49.

too, a person must be either male or female, not simply a human being, and this sexual differentiation is based on the will of the Creator. Being male or female is not a secondary characteristic over and above being human, either superior or inferior; it is an essential aspect of humanity since creation. It is therefore impossible to make human sexuality either divine or diabolical. It is not a consequence of the Fall but a good arrangement from the Creator, part of the humanity of God's creatures and integral to the corporal and spiritual totality of each person.

It is quite natural, then, when speaking of marriage, to say that those who were created male and female by God become one in marriage: "For this reason a man shall leave his father and mother"—Matthew adds, "and be joined to his wife"—"and the two shall become one flesh. So they are no longer two but one flesh" (Mark 10:7–8 par.).[291] The claim that Mark 10:2–9 speaks the language of utopia and cites creation to communicate an element of hope[292] is exaggerated, but correctly points out that the real perspective here is eschatology, from which creation regains its meaning.

If God himself joins the couple (v. 9)—whether in the institution of marriage or in each specific instance is disputed—then marriage is not simply a private arrangement, a social convention, or a happy (or unhappy) accident. The Creator has a hand in it. The marriage bond that is willed by God is described in terms that echo the Old Testament: "one flesh" (Mark 10:8), "be joined to" (Matt. 19:5). This means an absolute personal unity, a total sharing and devotion, so strong that it severs even parental ties.

2.5 On the basis of this all-encompassing view of marriage, which includes reliability and permanence, divorce is rejected. The fact that this prohibition represents a transformation, indeed an abrogation, of the Old Testament law (cf. above, 63–64) and is totally un-Jewish is no longer quite clear in the first section of Mark 10.

For the Pharisees to ask Jesus whether divorce is lawful rather than what grounds are sufficient is anachronistic, since the Jews debated the grounds of divorce, not its legality. Deuteronomy 24:1 triggered the entire Jewish dispute over divorce: "When a man takes a wife and marries her, if then he finds something displeasing or indecent in her, and he writes her a bill of divorce . . ." The vague expression "something displeasing or indecent" can be interpreted in a wide range of categories, from moral to esthetic; it therefore became the focus of debate.

In the New Testament period, the primary conflict was between the schools of Hillel and Shammai. The latter interpreted the expression narrowly as referring to sins of unchastity. The more liberal followers of Hillel, however, interpreted the words far more broadly, finding an indecency sufficient to justify divorce even when the wife's offense involved nothing more than

291. See Baltensweiler, *Ehe* (B2), 54ff.
292. Schottroff, "Frauen" (B2), 104.

impropriety, for example, going out with her hair down or letting food burn.[293] Rabbi Akiba even allows divorce when a man meets a more beautiful woman to whom he is more attracted than to his own wife, on the grounds that Deut. 24:1 says: "If she finds no favor in his eyes."[294]

Despite their differences, the leaders of the schools and their disciples agree that Deut. 24:1 permits divorce. Besides the grounds based on Deut. 24:1, there is a whole series of other generally recognized grounds for divorce, some of which even make divorce obligatory, for example, if a woman gives her husband a bad name, shows him disrespect, fails to bear children, and so forth. We nevertheless hear occasional contrary voices (note already Sirach 7:26 and bGittin 89b: "God hates divorce . . ."), and it is clear that regulations governing personal property attempted to make divorce more difficult.[295] In addition, actual practice probably did not always follow what theory and jurisprudence allowed, especially among the lower classes.[296]

On the basis of considerable evidence, Billerbeck rightly concludes that "in the Mishnaic period there was no marriage among the Jewish people that could not legally be dissolved on the spot by a man's handing his wife a bill of divorce."[297] Against this background, Jesus' message stands out sharply and distinctly, even though many exegetes claim that he merely adopts the strict interpretation of the school of Shammai, fundamentally disapproving only the lax and frivolous approach of the school of Hillel. But this estimate is based on the mistaken assumption that the so-called "adultery clause" in Matt. 5:32 (cf. Matt. 19:9) is authentic (see the discussion of Matthew). In fact, however, Jesus does not attack laxity in divorce but divorce in general, because it calls into question the force and permanence of "togetherness."

While Mark 10:2–9 bases its prohibition of divorce on God's having joined husband and wife in marriage, the appended passage (vv. 10–11), originally independent, makes a point analogous to what we find in Q (Luke 16:18; Matt. 5:31): divorce is equivalent to adultery. This would be a provocative statement to a Jewish audience, because the Jewish notion of marriage, defined solely from the perspective of the husband, treats the wife as property and includes marriage under property law. A man's wife is his property, acquired through payment of the brideprice. Therefore a man's adultery cannot impugn his own marriage, but only the marrige of someone else. It has been rightly said that Jesus' words must have struck his contemporaries

---

293. bGittin 9.10.

294. For the exegetical debate between the two schools, see Strack-Billerbeck, *Kommentar* 1:313ff.; Niederwimmer, *Askese*, 21ff.

295. See Kurt Schubert, "Ehescheidung im Judentum zur Zeit Jesu," *ThQ* 151 (1971): 23–27.

296. For the situation at Qumran, see Ingo Broer, *Freiheit vom Gesetz und Radikalisierung des Gesetzes*, SBS 98 (Stuttgart: Katholisches Bibelwerk, 1960), 97–98. On Philo's condemnation of divorce, see Niederwimmer, *Askese*, 23.

297. Strack-Billerbeck, *Kommentar* 1:319–20.

as though someone had said: "Anyone who surrenders something he owns is a robber."[298] Above all, no Jew can consider divorce as conceded by the Torah to be a transgression of the Decalogue. According to Mark 10:10–11, however, anyone who divorces his wife and marries another is an adulterer and thus transgresses a fundamental commandment of God.

In the first place, Jesus forbids divorce and remarriage on the part of either a man or a woman. This inclusion of the wife is probably to be understood as a secondary accommodation to Roman law.

It is true that Jewish law also provides for rare cases in which a wife can sue for divorce, for example, impotence, nonsupport, or disfiguring disease. These, however, are relatively unimportant. The assignment of rights and obligations clearly favors the male. The statement of mYebamoth 14.1 is typical: "The man who releases [his wife by a bill of divorce] is not on the same plane as the woman who is released. For the woman is released whether or not she is willing, but the man releases his wife only of his own free will."[299] The second unique feature of Mark 10:10–11 is that it forbids only divorce followed by remarriage, which is interpreted as a transgression of the Seventh Commandment. Whether remarriage itself was prohibited is uncertain, but the emphasis clearly shifts in this direction over the course of time.

The Q tradition (Luke 16:18; Matt. 5:32) is rather different: it addresses only the man. First, he is forbidden to marry a divorced woman. On the second point, however, Matthew and Luke differ. Contrary to Luke 16:18— which, like Mark, prohibits divorce and remarriage (albeit only on the part of the husband)—Matt. 5:32 states that when a man divorces his wife and she enters into a new marriage with someone else after the divorce the result is adultery.

It is impossible to determine with certainty which is original: Luke 16:18 or Matt. 5:32. It has been claimed in support of the Matthaean version that it still presupposes the polygamous milieu of Judaism: since the husband by definition cannot commit adultery within his own marriage, his guilt rests in the new relationship of his wife with another man, which he has made possible by divorcing her.[300] In addition, the Matthaean passage forbids divorce per se, without mentioning remarriage, as do the other passages. Others think the Matthaean version represents a reversion to Judaism. Precisely because it was difficult for Jewish Christians to condemn a married man for adultery by ending his own marriage, they reshaped the tradition of Luke 16:18.[301] In any case, however, the texts concerned with prohibiting remarriage more than with prohibiting divorce must be considered post-Easter expansions or mitigations, which may have arisen because absolute prohibi-

298. See Greeven, *Ehe*, 66.
299. Cf. Strack-Billerbeck, *Kommentar* 2:23–24.
300. E.g., Greeven, *Ehe*, 67.
301. Schaller, "Die Sprüche."

tion of divorce must have appeared unacceptable to a community living in a Jewish environment.[302] Furthermore, calling remarriage after divorce adultery does not necessarily assume that the first marriage is still thought to exist in the eyes of God. Undoubtedly adultery "against her" (Mark 10:11) is more appropriate to the first wife than to the second; if originally remarriage was not mentioned, "against her" could refer only to the first wife, against whom a man commits adultery by divorce. To identify marriage to a divorced woman with adultery (Luke 16:18b) also appears to assume the continuance of the first marriage. It is possible, however, that the term "adultery" is to be understood simply as referring to the Decalogue, which Jesus here transcends. "Against her" (Mark 10:11) would then merely make it clear that, contrary to the teaching of Judaism, it is also possible to commit adultery against one's own wife and that it is she who suffers the burden of divorce. Divorce is not merely transgression of a divine command but also unfaithfulness toward one's spouse.

Furthermore, Jesus says, "Let no man put asunder," not, "No man can put asunder." It is clear that his words are not legalistic; he does not state a legal dictum to be enforced at all costs, if need be by the state. He transcends the legal sphere. It is probably wishful thinking to assume that failed marriages can be restored by insisting on the prohibition of divorce. But this observation does not impugn the validity of Jesus' prohibition of divorce.

Marriage in an institution ordained by the Creator for the benefit of humanity, just as the Sabbath was ordained for humanity, not the reverse. Jesus' prohibition of divorce stands in the service of the Creator's will for his creation; it is not meant to be the basis of legal casuistry, civil or ecclesiastical. Here, too, love is the crucial element and the final court of appeal. This is illustrated above all by the fact that the prohibition of divorce grants protection to the wife, who had virtually no legal standing; this protection goes far beyond the legal institution of divorce, which at least gives the woman the right to remarry. If the original prohibition of divorce was addressed only to the husband, Jesus was taking the side of the wife, who had no legal protection. Jesus' "strict interpretation of marriage" is therefore the "appropriate contemporary expression of the protection and respect proper to a woman, who had no standing in Jewish marital law."[303]

2.6 Jesus' rigorous stance finds expression above all in his harsh attack on adultery, as exemplified by the second antithesis of the Sermon on the Mount (Matt. 5:27–30).

In contrast to the prohibition of divorce, there are Jewish parallels to this rigorism, for example, Leviticus Rabbah 23: "You must not say that only he who commits physical adultery is called an adulterer; he who commits adultery with his eyes is also called an adulterer." And tractate Kallah 1 states:

302. Dietzfelbinger, *Bergpredigt*, 27.
303. Braun, *Jesus*, 103; cf. 98; for a different view, see Schottroff, "Frauen," 105.

"When a man looks on a woman with desire, it is as though he had slept with her."[304] Niederwimmer suggests that the extreme emphasis on sexual rigorism was due to "an internalization in the religious consciousness of political and social oppression."[305]

It must be noted that "woman" in Jesus' sayings and in the corresponding Jewish texts refers to a married woman, not to a woman in general, and certainly not to one's own wife, as Tolstoi suggested. Jesus did not preach the ideal of virginity or sexual continence within marriage, nor did he wish to provoke the fears of scrupulosity (see his astonishing freedom in allowing himself to be anointed by a prostitute in Luke 7:36ff.). The innumerable legal regulations governing this sphere of life in Judaism (e.g., the regulations governing sexual intercourse) clearly find no echo in Jesus' teaching.

Furthermore it is not "looking" that Jesus castigates, but "looking lustfully." What makes the difference is the lustful intention. The fact that fidelity is required specifically of the male reveals another facet of Jesus' uniqueness: rabbinic Judaism speak of adultery on the part of a man only when the wife or fiancée of another Jewish man is involved, not in the case of a woman who is a Gentile or unmarried—which does not mean that such conduct was thought to be lawful. Here again, Jesus breaks with the tradition that a man cannot commit adultery against his own wife. The double standard is abolished.

The crucial point in these passages is that Jesus breaks through all kinds of casuistry, returning to the simple and unambiguous commandment of God. God created marriage as a permanent union between a man and a woman. It is God's will to protect marriage as his own institution. Therefore Jesus takes a clear stand against autonomous sexuality, at the same time setting women free from their role as subservient objects of male desire. Marriage involves self-discipline and absolute commitment, but not the unbridled lust that follows the lead of innate passion and destroys the marriage.

The sayings that follow in Matt. 5:29–30 (about cutting off one's hand, etc.) were appended by Matthew to the prohibition of divorce with a consequent shift of emphasis. Originally these words applied radically to all temptations. The Matthaean context limits them to the sexual sphere. This change disguises the fact that everyone meets temptation as a whole human person. Sexuality is only one region of the entire battlefield, and should not be viewed in unnatural isolation.

3. Possessions/Poverty and Riches

3.1 The record of Jesus' attitude toward riches and possessions, toward voluntary or involuntary poverty, has been reshaped more extensively by

---

304. For even more extreme examples, see Strack-Billerbeck, *Kommentar* on Mark 10:2–9 (Luke 16:18; Matt. 5:31).

305. *Askese*, 28 n. 78; for further discussion, see Berger, *Gesetzesauslegung*, 326.

tradition than that of his attitude toward the relationship between man and woman, but its outlines are nonetheless clear. Here, too, a survey of the Old Testament and Judaism is needed.

At the time of Israel's earliest beginnings, when Israel still led a nomadic life, there were no pronounced social differences. The problem arose only after the settlement, especially after the economic prosperity of the monarchy. When social distinctions arose, the prophets above all took the side of the poor and inveighed passionately against the rich and powerful, their greed and excesses. After Amos (cf. 2:6ff.), it was primarily Isaiah who took offense at seeing property concentrated in the hands of the few and the rights of the poor infringed by the courts. Deuteronomic legislation (e.g., Deut. 24:19ff.; 15:1ff.; 12ff.; Lev. 25:8ff.) parallels in some ways the prophetic criticism, establishing a positive law to protect the poor and socially powerless (remission of debts, release of slaves, harvest rights, redistribution of land). Even if not much can be said about the practical effect of such legislation, the admonition of Deut. 15:11 is significant: "You shall open wide your hand to your brother, to the needy and to the poor, in the land" (cf. also Exod. 22:21ff.).

Of course we also find plentiful evidence, especially in wisdom literature, for example, the late sections of Proverbs and Sirach, that Israel considered poverty evil and wealth (employed with wisdom) good. Here poverty is sometimes viewed as the consequence of laziness (Prov. 6:6ff.), lack of discipline (Prov. 13:18), or hedonism (Prov. 21:17; 23:21). On the other hand, it is also wrong to pursue riches, since they easily tempt one into sin (Sirach 34: 5–6), and those who trust in their wealth are fools (cf. Sirach 5:1–2). Wealth is fleeting (Prov. 23:4–5). Sirach 11:18–19 (cf. also Eccl. 5:12ff.) is especially interesting in the light of Luke 12:16ff. Ultimately both wealth and poverty come from God (Prov. 22:2; Job 1:21). The proper stance toward the poor is to maintain their rights (Prov. 31:9) and treat them openhandedly (Prov. 31:20; Sirach 7:32), but there is little trace of social criticism like that of the prophets (cf., however, Sirach 13:9ff.; 34:24ff.). The situation in the Psalms is complex. Here "poor" is in the first instance a social category, but "poor" and "devout" are almost synonymous, and poverty is classed with humility and submission to God (Pss. 9:13, 19; 37:14; 132:15–16; 146:8–9).[306]

The lines of thought issuing from the Old Testament continued in Judaism. The rabbis usually consider poverty a disaster, reckoning the poor with the dead[307] but extolling the rich. Of course they inculcate generosity toward the poor, for charity and works of love outweigh all other commandments of the Torah.[308] Aboth 3:17 states that one should give to God from one's

---

306. See Friedrich Hauck and Wilhelm Kasch, "ploutos," *TDNT* 6:323–25; Ernst Bammel, "ptōchos," *TDNT* 6:888ff.
307. bNedarim 64b.
308. Tosefta Pea 4:19.

possessions, "for you and your possessions belong to him." The rabbis have an extremely effective and well-organized system of charity that is without parallel.[309]

Specific features important for the New Testament appear in apocalyptic literature, where the dichotomy "poor/rich" appears in eschatological contexts: promises are addressed to the poor, accusations and woes to the rich. This second perspective continues the prophetic line of social criticism (cf. Ethiopic Enoch 94:7–8; 96:4ff.; 97:8ff.; as well as James 5:1ff., which draws upon the same tradition): it is not so much wealth per se that is condemned but oppression and exploitation of the poor. We also find eschatological promises, which appear in many forms. On the one hand, it is expected that the wealthy will support the poor with their utmost ability (e.g., *Sib. Or.* 3:241ff.); on the other, reversal of the present relationship between rich and poor is a favorite topos (cf. 1QpPs37 3:3–4, 10–11; as well as the Magnificat [Luke 1:52–53], which recalls Jewish eschatological hymns).

Qumran deserves special attention. Here the line of devotion found in the Psalms is continued, especially in the Thanksgiving Hymns (cf. 5:18; 2:32ff.). The Qumran community calls itself "the community of the poor" (1QpPs37). Here "poor" is not primarily a social category but an expression of religious humility or eschatological dignity, coupled with a sense of dependence on God. But there is also a social dimension. Especially noteworthy is the institution of a fund to support orphans, the poor, and so forth (CD 14:12ff.), and (in the Community Rule) the renunciation of private property in favor of communal possessions. The motives are not clear. Bammel suggests that communal property at Qumran should be understood as "reflecting the form of life . . . that God will establish in the age to come."[310] This recalls the hope expressed in the *Sibylline Oracles:* "Life and wealth will be shared in common by all" (*Sib. Or.* 8:208; cf. 3:247).

In any case, it would be wrong simply to spiritualize the concepts "poor" and "rich" in the New Testament period. We must also note the attitude of the Zealots, whose struggle for freedom involved social goals. When they captured the upper city of Jerusalem in 66 C.E., their first act was to set fire to the city archives "to destroy the promissory notes of the moneylenders and to make collection of debts impossible."[311] Jesus' parables also paint a vivid picture of the conflicts among large landowners, peasants, and tax collectors.

3.2 If we look at the message of Jesus against this background, we find many similarities, above all in Jesus' preferential option for the poor. Jesus criticizes wealth radically, promises the kingdom of God to the marginal poor,

309. See Strack-Billerbeck, *Kommentar* 1:818ff.; 4:536ff.
310. Bammel, "ptōchos," 898; for a different view, see, for example, Braun, *Radikalismus* 2:36–37.
311. Josephus *Jewish War* 2.427; cf. Hengel, *Property* (B3), 24; see 23ff. for a discussion of the social tensions in the feudalism of Palestine.

and asserts their rights. Poverty can denote both penury and misery as well as submission to God. It would be wrong simply to identify these two aspects, but it would also be wrong to overlook the parallelism and affinity between them. The beatitude addressed to the poor (Luke 6:20) has in mind both social and religious status. In Luke 6:20, however, the parallel beatitudes addressed to those who hunger and weep (v. 21) make it quite clear that the "poor" are really suffering material poverty (cf. Isa. 6:1). They are obviously called blessed because they are open to the salvation that comes with the kingdom; they have no worldly props or diversions to distract them from the promise and the call to repent. Because possessions can only alienate people from God, they cease to be a sign and guarantee of God's blessing. Salvation is promised instead to the poor. Because God is on their side, Jesus declared his solidarity with them in word and deed. On the other hand, Matthew's addition ("poor in spirit"; Matt. 5:3) maintains the truth that the poor are not blessed simply because they are poor: poverty implies dependence on God. Jesus was sober and realistic enough to realize that need can teach people to curse as well as to pray and that poverty is not simply identical with submission to God.

This is not to dispute the fact that, according to Jesus, God takes the part of those who especially need him and are also especially impoverished materially. One who stands before God as a beggar stands also in the world with empty hands, with nothing to depend on in this world—including outward and material dependence.

This position cannot be countered by the observation that Jesus also turned to the tax collectors and admitted them to the kingdom of God (Mark 2:13ff.; Matt. 21:31). It is uncertain whether we should maintain a general distinction between "tax contractors" and their minor employees,[312] for the "contractors" also have factors who, like the contractors, try to collect more than the sum actually owed so as to gain a profit. It is true, however, that tax collectors are not *eo ipso* well-to-do people. What puts them beyond the pale for Judaism, however, is their transgression of God's law, and this is clearly not just the verdict of the educated upper classes. Herrenbrück[313] does not consider the tax collectors to be associated with the Roman tax system, either as employees of a tax-collecting association or as large-scale tax contractors, but as Hellenistic tax factors, members of the upper middle class.

On the contrary, despite the love Jesus shows toward the often exploitative tax collectors, he warns unmistakably that earthly riches imperil salvation (Matt. 6:19–21). What matters is where one's heart is fixed (v. 21). It is impossible to be divided as to purpose and support. One cannot set one's heart on both earthly and heavenly treasures; one cannot serve both God and mammon (Matt. 6:24).

312. Schottroff and Stegemann, *Jesus*, 16ff.
313. Fritz Herrenbrück, "Wer waren die 'Zöllner'?" *ZNW* 72 (1981): 178–94.

The etymology of "mammon"[314] is uncertain. Here, as in rabbinic usage, it means not just money in the narrow sense but all one's possessions, everything of monetary value, one's total resources. It is not limited to especially great wealth, but refers to possessions of all kinds without regard for quantity and value. There is no evidence to identify mammon with Satan, but in practice mammon plays the role of God's opponent or rival when it engrosses people and wins their trust. (On the dichotomy between love of God and love of wealth or the world, see Eth. En. 108:8; James 4:4; 1 John 2:15).

The fact that one can have only a single master reinforces the clear either/or of Matt. 6:24. But the use of the word "serve" and the contrast between "love" and "hate" show clearly that it makes all the difference who the master is, whom one serves and whom one loves. Besides Luke 12:15, we may note also the exemplary story of the rich farmer who deceives himself into making great plans for the future so as to enjoy his wealth, but fails to take into account either his own death or the possibility of using his wealth for others. Reliance on worldly goods does not give meaning to life. Abundance (v. 15) and full barns (v. 18) get in the way of living.

Because of its individualistic eschatology, Luke 12:16–21 may not be authentic Jesus material.[315] According to Schottroff and Stegemann,[316] the passage is aimed at an "economic crime" that damages society, because the farmer wants to hoard the record harvest so as to sell it for a higher price in poorer times. But the primary point of the story is undoubtedly to warn against false confidence in earthly riches (cf. Sirach 11:18–19; Ethiopic Enoch 94:7).

Jesus does not say how much wealth it takes to turn possessions into "love" of possessions or when possessions take control. But he does state clearly that property must not become an idol, and that even someone who gains the whole world can lose or forfeit his very self (Luke 9:25 par.).

3.3 This does not mean that only the inward attitude of the wealthy matters or the psychological danger to which they are exposed. Jesus considers wealth irreconcilable with the kingdom of God. This is clear in Mark 10:23: "How hard it will be for those who have riches to enter the kingdom of God!" "It is easier for a camel to go through the eye of a needle than for a rich man to enter the kingdom of God" (Mark 10:25). These extreme words may have been attached to the pericope of the rich young man (vv. 17–22) even before Mark (cf. the discussion of Mark below). It is disputed whether they go back to Jesus himself, but their very radicalism argues for authenticity,[317] as does the paradoxical and exaggerated tone of v. 25.

314. Friedrich Hauck, "mamōnas," *TDNT* 4:389; also 1QS 6:2; CD 14:20.
315. See, however, Egbert W. Seng, "Der reiche Tor," *NT* 20 (1978): 136–55, esp. 141, 145–46; also J. Duncan M. Derret, "The Rich Fool," *HeyJ* 18 (1977): 131–51; Mealand, *Poverty*, 52–53.
316. *Jesus*, 125–26.
317. See Braun, *Jesus*, 106; idem, *Radikalismus* 2:77 n. 1; Huuhtanen, "Pericope," 88–89.

Their meaning is that riches and participation in the kingdom of God are, as a rule, mutually exclusive. On the basis of the passages already discussed, we have to say that wealth normally so takes possession of people's hearts that it becomes their real treasure. This does not mean that Jesus demanded universal renunciation of possessions,[318] but neither does it imply indifference toward wealth and possessions. This brings us to the story of the rich man and Lazarus (Luke 16:19–31), which has a double climax in its present form.

In vv. 19–26, the point is the reversal in the next world of the earthly fates of the two men: the beggar Lazarus is well off in the next world, while the rich man suffers. Verses 27–31, on the other hand, point out how senseless it is to raise someone from the dead so that the rich, unrepentant even though warned by the law and the prophets, might be brought to repentance by the miracle.

Jeremias is of the opinion that this section does not even deal with the question of rich and poor. The point is to warn those who are like the rich man's brothers of the fate in store for them. He bases this conclusion on his claim that the first part of the parable is a traditional Jewish narrative that taught the reversal of fortunes in the next world, so that the emphasis is on the new material added by Jesus.[319] This explanation, however, does not account for the circumstantial detail of vv. 19–26, if the only point is rejection of the demand for a sign. But Jeremias is probably right that nowhere else does Jesus represent the view that wealth by its very nature entails hell and poverty paradise.[320] It remains an open question why there is not more emphasis on the guilt of the rich man. We are told only that he feasted sumptuously every day and dressed in fine garments. It is not even made clear that he did so at the expense of the poor.

Possibly the rich man's guilt is not made clearer because Jesus is borrowing familiar material. But possibly Luke 16:19–31 does not even derive from Jesus (notice the descriptions of the torments, the emphasis on individual death, etc.) and, like the woes against the rich, reflects the tension between poor and rich Christians. Probably the story is intended, like Luke 1:53, to express "the hope of the poor in the God of justice," without any indictments or yearning for revenge.[321] If the story were also addressed to the rich, it could be accepted as embodying Jesus' principles only if the rich man is guilty of being so engrossed in his luxurious living that he does not even notice poor Lazarus at his door, not as meaning that possessions are *eo ipso* wicked and must therefore be surrendered.

It is probably also wrong to interpret the story of the rich young man

318. See the discussion of disciples in section B.2 above.
319. *Parables*, 184–85.
320. Ibid., 184.
321. Schottroff and Stegemann, *Jesus*, 41; cf. also Mealand, *Poverty*, 32.

(Mark 10:17–22) in this sense. He asks Jesus about the way to eternal life. Jesus replies by citing the commandments of God. The young man insists that he has observed them all from his youth. Jesus does not dispute his claim or condemn it as hypocrisy; indeed, Jesus is drawn to him. Then, however, comes the crucial statement: "You lack one thing; go, sell what you have, and give to the poor, and you will have treasure in heaven; and come, follow me" (v. 21). If we take the beginning of the story seriously, this requirement can hardly be viewed as an additional commandment surpassing all the others, a kind of eleventh commandment requiring a supreme act of asceticism. What the inquirer lacks is not one final step or a little bit more, but the one thing that is absolutely necessary. Only in Matthew do we find the question, "What do I *still* lack?" Here "absolute lack becomes merely an additional requirement."[322] Jesus' words in fact only make the test of the young man's recognition of the First Commandment more precise by diverting his attention from himself to the poor. His words demand a concrete response in the form of discipleship to the radical implications of the double law of love (cf. also Mark 10:28). What is supremely important is this call to discipleship. It is what gives meaning to the surrender of possessions (cf. Mark 1:16ff.).

It is therefore inappropriate to belabor either the analogy of giving away of all possessions in a holy war (1 Macc. 2:28; 2 Macc. 8:14) or the obligation of novices at Qumran to hand over all their property to the order (community of goods is discussed below, 126–28). Nor are the words addressed to proselytes "Go and sell all that you have, then come and be proselytes"[323] critical of wealth; they are motivated by questions of ritual purity.[324]

The rich man of Mark 10 is not said to be especially attached to his wealth so that, unlike other rich people, he had to part with his possessions. In this sense it is misleading for many exegetes to state that Jesus' absolute demand is "pedagogical," singling out the inquirer's most vulnerable point, at which he needs help.[325] Matthew 5:40 and 42, for example, are formulated in quite general terms. If we ask what might have caused Jesus to confront this particular rich man with the demand to give up his possessions, we can also point to the remarkable conclusion to the string of prohibitions in v. 19, "Do not defraud," which can be understood as referring to keeping sustenance from the poor (cf. Sirach 4:1) or keeping back wages (cf. James 5:4).[326]

3.4 The absence of a universal renunciation of possessions is confirmed by a series of observations. Without any reservations, Mark 1:29 speaks of the house of Simon and Andrew; it was not sold, but provided the center of Jesus' ministry in Capernaum. In the context of the generalization in Mark 10:28,

322. Ulrich Wilckens, "hysteros," *TDNT* 8:595.
323. bAboda Zara 64a.
324. Mealand, *Poverty*, 71.
325. Cf. Braun, *Jesus*, 107.
326. Cf. Schnackenburg, *Existenz*, 96.

"we have left everything" therefore means primarily "we have placed every-thing in the service of the Jesus movement," not "we have given everything away." For Levi, too, whose house is mentioned in Mark 2:14ff., discipleship clearly does not imply renunciation of possessions: he leaves his place of business at the tax office, but the passage suggests he does so only to invite Jesus and his disciples to a feast, even though vv. 13–14 and vv. 15ff. were probably originally independent (but cf. the mention of Martha's house in Luke 10:38). Quite generally, the invitations to dine addressed to Jesus by tax collectors and the charge that Jesus is a glutton and drunkard, the friend of tax collectors and sinners (Matt. 11:19 par.), shows how wrong it is to understand him simply as a rigorous opponent of conspicuous consumption, motivated by the ideals of asceticism or social revolution.[327] Of course it is also wrong to claim his support for the fetish of property rights that holds sacred the existing distribution of wealth or for the consumption mania of liberalistic capitalism. That anyone should have an unrestricted right to private property would never have entered Jesus' head.

What Mark 1:29 implies and Mark 10:21 states explicitly ("give to the poor") is confirmed by other texts: possessions should be used either to help one's neighbor or to advance the cause of Jesus. The latter use appears in positive terms in Luke 8:3, which describes the women as providing for Jesus and his disciples out of their means. This implies frugality on the part of Jesus' followers, as the missionary instructions show: the disciples are told to go forth without money (Mark 6:8–9), and Q even goes beyond Mark, forbidding the possession, conceded by Mark, of a staff and sandals.

It is true, of course, that these instructions probably do not go back to Jesus himself, but derive from the mission of the post-Easter community. But there can be no doubt that this utter disregard for the necessities of life, which matches that of the Cynics, is thoroughly in the spirit of Jesus.[328] The disciples are to trust solely in God to provide, which means that they must rely on what is given them by others. These instructions probably date from the period of the earliest community, when its mission still lived by im-provisation and was not being carried on throughout the world, which required planning and organization.[329]

Apart from Mark 10:21, the principle that possessions should be used for the benefit of neighbors is also illustrated by the parable of the Good Sa-maritan. His exemplary conduct does not consist in surrendering all he has but in using his financial means to help the victim recover and guarantee his support for a limited period. Other statements, too, presuppose possession of some resources: for example, one should help those in need (Matt. 25:40), support one's parents (Mark 7:9ff.), lend money freely without expecting

327. Cf. Hengel, *Revolutionist*, 19.
328. Mealand, *Poverty*, 65ff.
329. See n. 126 above for bibliography on the missionary discourses.

repayment (Luke 6:34–35), or invite the poor to feasts (Luke 14:12–13).[330] Perhaps Luke 16:9 may also be cited in this connection: "Make friends for yourselves by means of unrighteous mammon, so that when it fails God may receive you into the eternal habitations." It is clear that this was not the original point made by the difficult parable of the unjust steward.

The question is whether v. 9, considered as an isolated logion, derives from Jesus himself. Jeremias assumes that it referred originally to the clever use of unjustly acquired wealth and was probably addressed to tax collectors and others considered deceitful.[331] In my opinion, however, "mammon of unrighteousness" is neither unjustly acquired wealth (the address to tax collectors is purely hypothetical) nor is it characterized as evil in principle.[332] The genitive should probably be interpreted as meaning "wealth that is untrustworthy, deceitful, undependable."[333] See also Mark 4:19, "deceitfulness of riches," and the expression "when it fails." See also the discussion of Luke below.

Since meaning depends on context, we cannot be sure what the saying meant originally, if in fact it was current at first as an isolated saying. In any case, what matters is proper and unselfish use. Mammon, however characterized, is to be used to make friends, not for its own sake. Here, too, interpretations differ. Grundmann suggests that the "friends" are the angels of God, who receive people into the eternal habitations, as well as works of charity and almsgiving; they are considered intercessors in Jewish texts.[334] According to Stählin,[335] whatever life offers in this wicked world is to be used in agape toward God and toward one's neighbors so as to gain the friendship of God, although it is difficult to make the plural "friends" include God. Most likely the reference is to other human beings.

The crucial point is to use earthly possessions in the service of love. For Jesus, therefore, the problem of property is primarily a problem of social rather than individual ethics, as in the Stoa.[336] There is no hint that such charity might degrade those who receive alms. The concern is rather that enough might not be offered. One may also cite the contribution of the poor widow (Mark 12:41ff.), who puts money in the treasury not out of her abundance but out of her poverty, doing qualitatively more with her quantitatively less. It is not just what one gives that matters, but what one keeps. Here as elsewhere the law of love is the absolute norm, to which all other considerations are secondary. This love knows nothing of inviolable property

330. Werner G. Kümmel, "Der Begriff des Eigentums in NT," in *Heilsgeschehen* 1:273.

331. *Parables*, 46; see also Gottlob Schrenk, "adikia," *TDNT* 1:157; Hauck, "mamōnas," 389.

332. Braun, *Radikalismus*, 2:74; for the contrary view, see Schrenk, "adikia."

333. This is also Schrenk's interpretation.

334. On Luke 16:9, see Walter Grundmann, *Das Evangelium nach Lukas*, ThHK 1.

335. Gustav Stählin, "philos," *TDNT* 9:163–64.

336. Kümmel, "Eigentum," 274.

rights and distribution of wealth, but controls and restricts the use of possessions lest they become a source of idolatrous dependence.

4. The State and Violence

4.1 Since the statements of Jesus and the other New Testament authors are based in large measure on the environment of the Old Testament and Judaism, we begin once again with a sketch of this traditional background. These roots are of most critical importance for Romans 13 and Revelation 13, but Jesus himself does not stand apart from this stream of tradition; there have recently even been (surely misguided!) attempts to turn Jesus into a Zealot and thus place him in the company of the Jewish freedom fighters against Rome. The Old Testament itself contains various approaches. Certain Old Testament prophets even saw the powers oppressing Israel as instruments in the hand of Yahweh (Jer. 25:9; 27:5–6, 12–13; 43:10; Isa. 45:1ff.; 42:2ff.).

Of course this perspective is not reduced to a single systematic statement about God's commissioning these rulers. Distinctions are made between particular rulers and powers, who are called in specific situations to bring Israel into subjection in order to make known God's will. None of these powers is even recognized as God's instrument by all the prophets. Micah, for example, looks on Assyria as God's enemy. In addition, Haggai and especially Zechariah stand in total contradiction to the line of development from Isaiah through Jeremiah to Deutero-Isaiah, in that both consider the fall of the Persian Empire necessary for the resurgence of the Davidic kingdom.[337] The focus, it should be noted, is almost always on the punitive action of these powers against Israel, not on any positive action of maintaining righteousness and justice, as well as on the relationship between the entire nation of Israel and the powers in question.

The situation is not much different in the apocalyptic literature of the Old Testament and Judaism, except that God is generally described as "the one who deposes and appoints kings" and gives the kingship to whom he will (Dan. 2:21; 4:14; cf. 4:29). This agrees with statements from later Jewish apocalyptic texts such as Ps. of Sol. 2:28ff.; Ethiopic Enoch 46:5. In Daniel we also find for the first time the conflict that arises when a ruler issues edicts contrary to God's will (Dan. 3:1ff.; 3:17–18). A famous instance of such conflict is the blasphemy of Antiochus IV Epiphanes, who invaded and plundered the Jerusalem sanctuary in 170 B.C.E. and in 168 B.C.E. even set up "the abomination of desolation" (Dan. 9:27) upon the altar by establishing the Hellenistic cult of Zeus Olympios in the Jerusalem temple and prohibiting observance of the Jewish religion and law. His act led to guerrilla actions and the so-called wars of the Maccabees.

In the New Testament period, it was primarily the militant Zealots who

337. Leonhard Rost, "Das Problem der Weltmacht in der Prophetie," *ThLZ* 90 (1965): 241–50.

carried on the Jews' fight for freedom against their Roman overlords.[338] Their resistance was total and radical. This is all the more surprising in that the Romans generally treated the Jewish religion as legal (*religio licita*). The Zealots therefore did not, like the rest of the Jews, merely defend themselves passionately against infringements on the part of the Roman state, but waged an uncompromising holy war against any political dependence on Rome. Because they thought Roman rule impugned the sole sovereignty of God, they expected the messianic age to come only after or through violent removal of the blasphemous power of Rome. In any case, the Zealots considered simultaneous subjection to both God and Rome impossible. Here faith and politics are identical. Eleazar, the commander of Masada, for example, preached that "one must not be subject to the Romans or to any other human beings, but to God alone.[339] Judas, the founder of the Zealot movement, castigated the Jews who "submitted not only to God but also to the Romans."[340]

The Zealots attempted to achieve their theocratic ideal by force, while on the other side certain Jewish circles collaborated more or less freely. These Jewish collaborators included the tax collectors working for Rome and probably also the Sadducees.[341] The Pharisees, representing rabbinic Judaism, generally attempted to remain loyal while continuing to observe certain Old Testament traditions, seeking a modus vivendi with the Romans. It is reasonable to assume that at least some of the Pharisees were closer to the Zealots than later rabbinic tradition would have it.[342] They longed for an end to foreign domination, reciting, for example, the twelfth of the Eighteen Benedictions: "Mayest Thou bring to a speedy end the impudent regime [Rome]." Many expressions of criticism and intellectual resistance show that the attitude toward Rome was anything but friendly. Rabbi Gamaliel II, for example, is credited with saying: "This regime gnaws at us with four things: its taxes, baths, theaters, and payments in kind."[343] When the faith and its observance appeared to be in fundamental danger, the rabbis, too, participated in bloody revolts. Much more typical, however, despite all silent resistance, was a realistic search for a viable relationship with Rome, indeed a positive estimate even of foreign rule inspired by the Old Testament tradition. The following saying is attributed to Hananiah, the last high priest, shortly before the outbreak of the Jewish War: "Pray for the good of the authorities [Rome], for if there were no fear of them we should have devoured each other long ago."[344]

338. Martin Hengel, *Die Zeloten*, 2d ed. (Leiden: Brill, 1976), 176ff.
339. Josephus *Jewish War* 7.323.
340. Ibid. 2.433; cf. 2.118; idem. *Antiquities* 18.23; Acts 5:37.
341. Ernst L. Dietrich, "Sadduzäer," *RGG*[3] 5:1278; Schrage, *Staat* (B5), 21 n. 29.
342. Hengel, *Zeloten*, 91.
343. For additional material see Schrage, *Staat*, 22–23.
344. Aboth 3:2.

We find an even closer approximation to the Pauline view of the state and its power in Hellenistic Judaism, which drew on the traditions of Old Testament wisdom literature, where we already meet the assumption that all authority is from God (cf. Sirach 17:17). The New Testament also alludes to Prov. 24:21. In a similar vein, the kings were later told that power had been granted them by the Lord and dominion by the Most High, so that rulers could also be called "servants of His Lordship" (Wisd. of Sol. 6:3–4). Even though there is no room for glorification of the ruler or acceptance of his absolute sovereignty, not to mention a cult surrounding his person, it is nevertheless God who bestows sovereignty (*Letter of Aristeas* 219; cf. 4 Macc. 12:11) and kingship is "God's gift" (*Letter of Aristeas* 224).

4.2 Now to Jesus. Eisler maintained that Jesus was a revolutionist, executed on account of a revolt. In recent years this theory has been revived. This view has lately enjoyed enormous popularity, combining uncritical exegesis with uncritical fantasy. Jesus, freed from ecclesiastical revisionism and pacifistic retouching, is reputed to have been a nationalistic prophet seeking to establish the kingdom of God through a massive revolt against the power of Rome and its eastern vassals.[345]

This approach turns Jesus' entrance into Jerusalem into a carefully calculated demonstration of his messianic office, the cleansing of the temple into an act of provocation against the Romans with robbery and bloodshed, and Peter's sword stroke in Gethsemane into an act of armed rebellion. Cullmann and Hengel criticize these reinterpretations of the texts to reflect the Zealot movement, although they place too much emphasis on the question of nonviolence and the choice between armed insurrection and inwardly free individual alleviation of suffering.[346]

There is evidence enough that Jesus was not a political revolutionary or a Zealot. Whether he was ever tempted to be one is dubious. The story of the tribute money (Mark 12:13ff.), for example, is not concerned about resisting attempts to represent the messianic savior as a military hero who would deliver Israel from the Roman yoke. The later temptation narrative may reflect Jesus' rejection of a chance to exercise political power in an anti-Roman freedom movement (cf. John 6:15 as well as Matt. 4:1ff. par.). It is doubtful, however, whether a specifically messianic temptation is involved. Above all, Mark 12 is not concerned with the question of the Messiah in the context of national liberation but with Jesus' attitude toward the tax and the Roman Empire. Implicitly, of course, Mark 12 is also a rejection of the Zealot resistance movement.

This is probably not by chance. Jesus, although he did not himself belong

---

345. Joel Carmichael, *The Death of Jesus* (New York: Macmillan, 1962); similarly S. G. F. Brandon, *Jesus and the Zealots* (Manchester: Manchester Univ. Press, 1967); cf. also Pinchas Lapide, *Der Rabbi von Nazareth* (Trier: Spee, 1974).
346. Hengel, *Revolutionist*, 17.

to the Zealot movement or take part in armed uprisings, must have come in some kind of contact with the Zealots. It is noteworthy, for instance, that he was crucified between two men who appear to have been Zealot rebels (Mark 15:27). It is equally noteworthy that his trial is associated with Barabbas, who Mark 15:7 says was "among the rebels in prison, who had committed murder in the insurrection" and therefore probably was connected with the Zealot movement. Furthermore even without a sword in his hand Jesus himself must have had some attraction for Zealots, for there were former Zealots among his intimate circle of disciples: Simon the Zealot (Luke 6:15; Acts 1:13, probably identical with Simon the Cananaean of Mark 3:18 par., the Aramaic equivalent of "Zealot"), and perhaps also Judas Iscariot.

The name "Iscariot" is sometimes connected with the Latin *sicarius*, "assassin, cutthroat" (from *sica*, "dagger"), which also appears as a loanword in Greek (Acts 21:38). Josephus, too, speaks of a group of radical Zealot freedom fighters so named. We may also note the reading of the Old Latin text of Matt. 10:3: Judas Zelotes. The suggestion that Peter was originally a Zealot is completely hypothetical.[347] In any case, the disciples certainly included former Zealots.

Certain points of contact between the message of Jesus and the Zealot movement cannot be denied: the social dimension, the demand for absolute commitment even at the expense of family ties and readiness for martyrdom, the eschatological perspective, and the requirement of radical obedience. It is nevertheless beyond doubt that Jesus rejected Zealot extremism. Luke 22:36–38 calls on him without a sword to sell his mantle and buy one and has Jesus reply, "It is enough," when told that two swords are available. But even this text does not preach establishment of the kingdom of God by force, especially in the light of vv. 49–51, where Jesus orders the disciples to put up their swords. Whether Luke 22:36–38 symbolizes the daily battle with temptation and the seriousness of the situation or refers to personal defense is uncertain.[348]

Matthew 26:52 also contains an indirect attack on the Zealot movement: "Put your sword back into its place; for all who take the sword will perish by the sword." This can hardly be just a warning against using the sword at the moment of Jesus' arrest on the grounds that to do so would not defend or promote God's cause. As the motivating clause shows, this is a general prohibition against the use of armed force, at least by private individuals. The verse itself, of course, can hardly go back to Jesus. Verse 52b not only states that one act of violence begets another, demanding nonviolence, but assumes

347. Cullmann, *State* (B5), 16, sees a hint of this possibility in the epithet "Bar-Jona" of Matt. 16:17.

348. See Hans W. Bartsch, "Jesu Schwertwort Lukas XXII 35–38," *NTS* 20 (1973–74): 190–203; Mealand, *Poverty*, 69–70.

the operation of *lex talionis* (see p. 64), in contradiction to the Sermon on the Mount.

It is in fact the exhortation of the Sermon on the Mount to love enemies and turn the other cheek that signalizes Jesus' distance from the Zealot use of force and violence. Although the extreme words "Do not resist one who is evil" probably derive from Matthew and have a forensic setting (cf. Deut. 19:18, LXX), Jesus' own perspective appears more clearly in the following passage, where he advocates not passive surrender but paradoxical activity. In specific instances, this may imply renouncing one's rights and refraining from the use of force in order to break the vicious circle of violence and the chain reaction leading to new wrongs. Such renunciation of force is not resignation or weakness but an expression of freedom and strength, which would rather suffer than add to suffering. The exemplary illustrations are in part hyperbolic and intended to shock, barring the normal response and emphasizing the contrast to what is usual and expected (cf. above, 62). They refuse to let anyone answer, with a clear conscience, violence with violence and are therefore irreconcilable with the Zealot program, even though they do not imply support of Rome or fundamental nonviolence.

The Cleansing of the Temple (Mark 11:15–17) has often been interpreted as evidence for Jesus' use of force. Its historical background, however, is unclear. Matthew and John show that the incident has been exaggerated by tradition: Matthew adds "all" in 21:12; John 2:14ff. adds "oxen and sheep" and quotes Ps. 69:10, "Zeal for thy house will consume me." John, however, speaking of the destruction of the temple, may indicate the original meaning of the symbolic action: not open violent rebellion but a prediction of the eschatological end of the temple and its cult or a campaign for its eschatological purity. A truly revolutionary action, which would also have attacked the prevailing economic system because the money-changers of the temple were also bankers, would certainly have provoked the intervention of the temple police and the Roman garrison. Our inability to achieve total clarity does not give us grounds to mitigate Jesus' "No!" to the political action preached by the Zealots, but it also cautions us against emphasizing nonviolence as a principle or program.[349]

But rejection of the Zealot option is not the same thing as introversion or uninvolvement. Several sayings reverse the common priorities and power structures, calling on Jesus' followers to become servants or slaves of others (Mark 9:35; 10:41ff.), distinguishing not coincidentally the disciples' conduct from that of those holding political power. The disciples are not to take for their model the existing pattern of social and political power and authority, but are instead to renounce domination in a community of equals engaged in love and service (cf. also Matt. 23:8–9). This demand is not limited to private

349. For discussion of the incident, see Cullmann, *Jesus*, 16–21; Hengel, *Revolutionist*, 15–18, 28, 33–34.

relationships, nor is it without visible and social consequences. Mark 9:35 is rather an attempt "to translate the expected eschatological reversal of the secular order into present conduct."[350]

This is the context in which peacemakers are called blessed (Matt. 5:9). The "peace" referred to is of course not "peace of mind" but, as in passages like Rom. 12:18, peace between individuals. The dynamism and creative power of God's peace that comes with the kingdom, which the disciples hand on as "messengers of peace" (Luke 10:5, 16), seek to be incarnate on earth in the peacemaking of the disciples. They do not utter threats. With mercy, not violence, they will attempt to take the battle lines and trenches of this world and to surmount the walls of hostility, enmity, and distrust. That peacemaking cannot be limited to the private sphere is shown by the final macarism of the persecuted in Matthew (5:10–11).[351]

4.3 This is also the general context in which we may place the short scene preserved in Mark 12:13–17, which culminates in the famous words: "Render to Caesar the things that are Caesar's, and to God the things that are God's" (v. 17).

As is true of most debates in the Gospels, we may well have an "idealized scene," the climactic saying of which usually goes back to Jesus himself.[352] Petzke has recently expressed certain reservations. He considers it more likely that the dialogue has been historicized than v. 17,[353] although in my opinion he overdramatizes the purported conflict with Matt. 6:24. On the other hand, he rightly rejects attempts to make the unpolitical Jesus out to be the "real" Jesus.[354] In any case, it is not clear that the climactic saying in v. 17 was addressed from the outset to opponents rather than to Jesus' disciples; the Christian community to this very day understands the saying as applying to itself, the more so because Mark 3:6, where Pharisees and Herodians again appear together, is also redactional.

In order to understand the importance of the question of whether the imperial tax was right or wrong, it is necessary to recall the dispute within Judaism, mentioned above, concerning taxation by the Romans. Apart from the general unpopularity of taxes and widespread discontent over the violent means employed to collect them and the economic exploitation of the land, the head tax in particular was felt to be an oppressive reminder of dependence on the Roman state. The trick question of the Pharisees and Herodians is clearly meant to trap Jesus into making an incautious statement on one side or

350. Hoffmann and Eid, *Jesus*, 202; cf. 186ff.; John H. Yoder, *The Politics of Jesus*, 4th ed. (Grand Rapids: Eerdmans, 1974), 46–47.

351. See Friedrich A. Strobel, "Die Friedenshaltung Jesu im Zeugnis der Evangelien," *ZEE* 17 (1973): 97–106, esp. 103.

352. Schrage, *Staat*, 26–27.

353. Gerd Petzke, "Der historische Jesus in sozialethische Diskussion," in *Historie*, 223–35.

354. Ibid., 224–25 and n. 29.

the other. In any case, the question touches on a central concern of political ethics in that period.

Jesus asks for a denarius, a Roman silver coin, a visible symbol of Roman power and sovereignty. Its obverse depicted the emperor with a laurel wreath symbolizing his divinity; the reverse depicted his mother seated on a divine throne as the earthly incarnation of heavenly peace. The reference to the emperor's apotheosis in the inscription made it no less offensive than the portrait: the obverse read "Emperor Tiberius, venerated son of the venerated God," and the reverse "High Priest."[355]

But what is the point of this scene with the coin? It should probably be understood as reflecting the de facto sovereignty of the emperor, to which the questioners clearly submit without a qualm by making casual use of Roman coinage. It does not mean, however, that Jesus argues from this de facto sovereignty that the emperor is commissioned by God or has the right to impose taxes. The scene is in fact intended to make the questioners reflect and provide their own answer. They have reached their decision long since, and must learn to live with it.[356]

The climax and point of the entire pericope is the familiar saying, obscure in its clarity: "Render to Caesar the things that are Caesar's, and to God the things that are God's." The context suggests that the "things that are Caesar's" include first and foremost payment of the tax, which is not only "lawful" (v. 14) but obligatory. But even if these words were not originally an isolated saying later placed in a narrative setting, this interpretation, based solely on the question in v. 14, is too narrow. The principle is stated in universal terms. Verse 17 certainly may be applied concretely to the tax, but it can also be interpreted paradigmatically.

Earlier periods found in v. 17 a text to support the alliance of throne and altar and deduced a demand for equal obedience to both God and the emperor. This reading was certainly just as mistaken as the theory that the verse proclaims the independence and autonomy of the emperor's sphere or demands unconditional obedience to the authority of the state on the part of its subjects. The two realms are not conceived as totally separate, the emperor having absolute and autonomous authority within his own realm; nor are they identified (as in a theocracy or a national church) or even placed on the same plane. The incontestable parallelism in v. 17 does not imply that both elements are equal or equivalent. Several scholars therefore describe the saying as an "ironic parallelism" or even an antithesis.[357] Throughout the ancient world, there was a total interpenetration of religious and political life. Seen against this background, Jesus' saying effectively secularizes civil authority and removes it from the realm of ideology. Of course Jesus does not

355. Ethelbert Stauffer, *Christ and the Caesars* (London: SCM Press, 1955), 133–34, 135–36.
356. Cf. Bornkamm, *Jesus*, 121–22.
357. Schrage, *Staat*, 37.

contest the power and legitimacy of the state—although unlike Paul he does not say that the emperor has been appointed by God—nor does he denigrate the things that are Caesar's. But he puts them in their proper place and rules out any religious exaltation of the state.

This downgrading of the emperor finds expression primarily in the second half of the logion. The centrality of these words can be seen from the very fact that Jesus adds them unbidden. Obedience to God has absolute priority. It defines and delimits what is Caesar's. It is not the emperor who determines what is his, or even what is God's, but God; v. 14 already asks what the law of God allows. It is impossible to define once for all the extent and limits of what is Caesar's so as to provide practical guidelines in particular cases. These limits must be constantly explored. It is nevertheless totally clear that we are not dealing here with peaceful coexistence of separate and distinct spheres of competence and authority, leaving God content with our private spiritual lives or a spiritual and religious realm. Just as the coin belongs to Caesar, so each human being belongs totally to God. In the light of what God requires, the demands of the state can have only limited authority and relative importance. Jesus' words take a mediating position between the extremes of rebellion and revolution on the one hand and the apotheosis and glorification of Caesar and the empire on the other, but they leave the emperor no room for aspirations to divinity.

4.4 Jesus was not a Zealot revolutionist, nor did he reject the emperor in principle. This does not mean, however, that he accepted the emperor uncritically or was naive enough to think that the emperor and his agencies could not abuse their power. The extant texts presuppose the emperor as a given and therefore indicate no fundamental rejection. The texts show, however, that there can be no question of Jesus' affirming the Roman state without reservations. The Baptist is said to have accused Herod Antipas not only of an illegal marriage but of all kinds of "evil things" (Luke 3:19; cf. also Mark 8:15). Mark 10:42 speaks quite openly of the way earthly rulers lord it over their subject peoples, which has rightly been seen as implying a degree of criticism and implicit opposition. In Luke 13:32, Jesus refers scornfully to Herod Antipas, the local governor, as a "fox," although the term probably refers to cunning and deceit rather than violence and bloodthirsty brutality. Luke 22:25 can also be taken as criticism or ironic sarcasm directed against the common desire of rulers to be called "Benefactors."

Above all, however, Jesus' own passion and death show that he came into conflict with the Roman Empire. It was the Roman procurator who had the man from Nazareth condemned and crucified. Even if the Jewish hierarchy probably handed Jesus over to the Romans, charged with having political aspirations as a Zealot and being a revolutionary pretender to the role of messiah, as the inscription "king of the Jews" suggests, there must have been concrete elements in his life that made the authorities consider him dangerous. His death on the cross also confirms that any "Yes!" to the structures and institutions of the world is always accompanied by a "No!" a critical distance and an inner freedom.

ETHICAL BEGINNINGS
IN THE
EARLIEST CONGREGATIONS

BIBLIOGRAPHY

Dibelius, Martin. *Die Formgeschichte des Evangeliums*. 4th ed. Tübingen: Mohr, 1961. Eng. trans. of 2d ed.: *From Tradition to Gospel*. New York: Charles Scribner's Sons; London: Nicholson & Watson, 1934.

Hoffmann, Paul. *Studien zur Theologie der Logienquelle*. 3d ed. NTA, N. S., 8. Münster: Aschendorff, 1982.

Schnackenburg, Rudolf. *Botschaft* (B). Pp. 131ff.

Wendland, Heinz-Dieter. *Ethik* (B). Pp. 33–48.

Wilckens, Ulrich. "Urchristlicher Kommunismus." In *Christentum und Gesellschaft*, ed. W. Lohff and B. Lohse, 129–44. Göttingen: Vandenhoeck & Ruprecht, 1969.

This chapter is the most problematic, because, lacking direct sources from this period, we must rely on indirect arguments based in part on the idealized description of the early church in Acts, in part on the reconstruction of pre-Pauline traditions in the Pauline and deutero-Pauline Epistles, and in part on the traces of the early communities in the Gospels, above all in Q.

Although we can make out certain features of the ethics of this period, we must always note that we do not have a coherent picture and much must remain hypothetical. In the last analysis, all we can do here is list a few observations giving us an idea of the variety found in earliest Christianity before Paul. New Testament scholarship has made it increasingly clear that it is not enough simply to postulate an original Palestinian Christian community and a pre-Pauline gentile Christianity between Jesus and Paul. Jewish Christianity itself must have been a very complex phenomenon. It is unfortunately true, however, that the necessary traditio-historical distinctions are even more difficult in the case of ethics than elsewhere. This may be due to the reduction of ethical teachings to more elementary and universal principles in earliest Christianity, but it may also be due to the general fluidity of the situation.

A. PRESUPPOSITIONS AND INFLUENCES

1. The basic presupposition and motive force behind all post-Easter ethics is the event of the crucifixion and Easter. The Jesus who proclaimed the good news and was crucified is himself proclaimed as the present and expected Christ: his resurrection is believed and proclaimed as the dawning of the eschatological kingdom. This sudden change must be considered a fundamental new beginning, altering everything. We may assume a priori that it also entailed significant ethical consequences. Easter was understood as an absolute miracle of God, not something brought about by the activity of the disciples themselves or the fruitfulness of their faith. The resurrection of Jesus was also not looked upon as a singular fact involving Jesus alone. It was closely related to the imminently expected resurrection of the dead (cf. 1 Cor. 6:14; 2 Cor. 4:14). The result, however, was not simply patient waiting. The sending forth of the disciples on their mission is a constitutive element of the Easter stories themselves. Paul did not originate the association of mission with christophany.

2. It is important for ethics that there is never any doubt that the risen Jesus is identical with the earthly Jesus. Even if Easter cannot be reduced to the statement that the movement begun by Jesus continues, the resurrection remains God's "Yes!" to the person, message, and ministry of Jesus. As a result, for example, Q exhibits a great interest in the ongoing proclamation of Jesus' message. This does not mean that there is no new content to the Easter faith, but it does mean that Easter, far from departing from the ethical substance of Jesus' preaching, gives it new vigor. The evidence is found both within and outside the gospel tradition.

The tradition of the Gospels and that of the earliest Christian confessions of faith and kerygmatic formulas appear in large measure to go their own separate ways. It would nevertheless be wrong simply to assign them to different schools of tradition, and it would certainly be mistaken to maintain that the christology of the kerygmatic and confessional traditions, whether titular or not, is an ethically irrelevant alternative to the Jesus tradition. The interpretation of Jesus' death in the confessions, for example, is not without echoes of Jesus' words and ministry. In the same way, certain titles ascribed to the risen Lord by earliest Christianity reflect the stated program of the earthly Jesus, including his ethics.

To cite only a few illustrations: in its primal Christian setting, the title "Christ," for example, although primarily defined by the cross and resurrection and devoid of its nationalistic political overtones, must not be understood simply as an antithesis to political messianism or even all ethical activism. He who was crucified for his objectionable preaching and way of life and died under the title "king of the Jews" was vindicated by God through the resurrection and made Christ. From this observation we may conclude that, in spite of the "messianic secret" in the earthly life of Jesus, his own words and deeds played a role in his being called Messiah (cf. Matt. 11:2). Above all, the title "Kyrios" has overtones suggesting that Jesus is not just the Lord who will return on the "day of the Lord," and certainly not just the cultic Lord present in the cult, but also the Lord whose word is to be done here and now (cf. Luke 6:46: "Why do you call me 'Lord, Lord,' and not do what I tell you?"). Even the title "son of Man" in passages that exhibit the paradox of humility and majesty has parenetic implications (cf. Luke 9:58 with 10:2ff.; or Mark 2:10 with Matt. 9:8), and the fact that the son of Man functions as judge is also ethically significant (cf. Matt. 25:31; Luke 18:8; 21:36).

3. Easter heightened eschatological expectations, and as hope for the Parousia of the coming son of Man and Lord provided the driving force for the life of the early Christians, therefore eschatology is significant for early Christian ethics. Not that the earliest community accepted what Jesus rejected (cf. above, 30–31), making Christian ethics simply an "interim ethics." But above all the call to watch and be ready played an important role, since the first Christians lived undeniably in expectation that the eschaton was imminent.

The community was also led by prophets through whom the heavenly Lord or the Spirit comforted and admonished it in the present. The admonitions of early Christian prophets threaten judgment upon those who (only) eat and drink, buy and sell, plant and build (Luke 17:26ff.; cf. Matt. 24:37ff.). This criticism of the indifference displayed by the last generation, who will not allow the message of the end to unsettle their daily routine, is an important element of Q in particular.[1]

1. Hoffman, *Studien*, 49.

Eschatology is not an independent theme; it has a functional purpose that has less to do with comfort (as in 1 Thess. 4:15ff.) than with parenesis. In 1 Cor. 7:29–31, for example, earlier material incorporated by Paul argues, on the grounds that this world is already passing away, not for mere passivity but for critical distance from the world.[2] At a moment when the world is clearly recognized to be transitory, it would be strangely anachronistic to reckon with its permanence. Even when Christians had to come to terms with the delay of the Parousia—albeit without ever giving up hope for it entirely (cf. Matt. 25:1ff., for example)—eschatological expectation remained a mainstay of early Christian ethics (cf. the Pauline expression "not inherit the kingdom of God" in the context of catalogues of vices such as 1 Cor. 6:10 and Gal. 5:21).

Even the Christians' use of the term "saints" for themselves (cf. Rom. 15:25–26, 31; Acts 9:13; 26:10; etc.) shows that they felt totally claimed by God as his eschatological people. This view may help account for the punishment of Ananias and Sapphira (Acts 5:1ff.). Whether we should think in terms of a "divine judgment" through which God himself maintains the purity of the community or of ecclesiastical efforts to define clearly the acceptable limits within the community, dishonesty toward the apostles or the community is a "lie against the Holy Spirit."[3] The result is not the conventicle ethics of a sect retreating into a ghetto (note the absence of any terms of sectarian self-identification), and certainly not an ethics based on official status, as though only the apostles could deal with the Spirit and had to determine the proper course for the community. This impression first appears in Luke, who presupposes an ecclesiastical structure for the church even in its earliest beginnings. There can be no doubt of the apostles' authority, but there can also be no doubt that the entire community played a prophetic role (cf. Matt. 5:12; 10:40; Luke 11:49).

4. The role played by prophecy also illustrates the great importance of the post-Easter experience of the Spirit for the ethics of the early Christian communities. Baptism, which incorporates the baptized into the eschatological company of the redeemed and binds them ("in the name of Jesus") to Jesus, bestows the Spirit. The popular view of the Spirit current in the pre-Pauline communities sees it primarily as a supernatural mystery in which miraculous divine power is manifest. Pneumatic phenomena therefore include above all such extraordinary manifestations of the Spirit as glossolalia and ecstasy, demonstrations of power and miracles (cf. Acts 2:4; 10:38, 46; also the numerous pre-Markan miracle stories, some of which encourage members of the community to perform miracles), but the Spirit is also closely

2. Wolfgang Schrage, "Die Stellung zur Welt bei Paulus, Epiktet und in der Apokalyptik," *ZThK* 61 (1964): 125ff.; Schulz, "Evangelium" (B), 486–87.

3. Kümmel, "Sittlichkeit" (B), 74; according to G. Schneider (on Acts 5:1ff. see, *Die Apostelgeschichte*, HThK), this view draws on such passages as Deut. 13:6; cf. 1 Cor. 5:13.

associated with prophecy (cf. Acts 2:11ff.; 21:11). The work of the Spirit is not, however, limited to ecstatic and prophetic utterance (cf. Mark 13:11; Matt. 12:28). It is possible that Paul was not the first to note the ethical implications of the Spirit, a familiar theme of Judaism.

It may well have been the common belief of Christians that the Spirit intervened in critical situations and decisions, guiding them and giving them specific instructions (cf. Acts 8:29; 10:19, 44; 11:28; 13:2, 4; 16:66–67). This view did not, however, extend to ethics. Whether by chance or not, the fact that the Spirit follows the pattern of Christ meant that ethical dicta could not be produced at will.[4] To what extent the ethical implications of the Spirit were realized before Paul must remain an open question, but baptism was certainly cited as a basis for ethics: Romans 6, for example, is unthinkable apart from a pre-Pauline tradition. It is hardly possible, however, to reconstruct precisely what might be called the post-Easter foundation of ethics. Above all, the details of how ethics was erected on this foundation remain obscure. We must therefore be content with these few observations, especially in the absence of much more detailed analysis.

B. THE SAYINGS OF JESUS AND
THE LAW

1. This topic is of primary importance for the theme of early Christian ethics. What was mentioned briefly above in our discussion of Q must be reiterated with emphasis: the words of the earthly Jesus were obviously collected because they were felt to provide binding guidelines for Christian living. Of course the Gospels also indicate that the voice of the exalted Lord is heard not just in the words of the earthly Jesus, but also, for example, through the mouths of prophets (Luke 10:16). But there were collections of Jesus' sayings at a very early date. This is documented above all by the Q source used by Matthew and Luke, which represents a collection of sayings and saying complexes.

Q probably presupposes a charismatic-prophetic missionary movement.[5] Even after Easter it exhibits "the hard rootless life of wandering homeless charismatics, who travel through the countryside without personal property or employment,"[6] a life guided entirely by Jesus. Of course this can hardly hold true for Q as a whole, since Q itself grew by accretion and contains various strata. This is not the place, however, to discuss the differentiation of individual stages proposed by Schulz.[7]

It is doubtful that the prophetic and wisdom sayings of Jesus were collected solely for parenetic purposes, so that Christians might have rules for guid-

---

4. Wendland, *Ethik* (B), 37.

5. Hoffmann, *Studien*, 332.

6. Gerd Theissen, "Wanderradikalismus," *ZThK* 70 (1973): 251.

7. Cf. Hans Conzelmann, "Literaturbericht zu den synoptischen Evangelien," *ThR* 43 (1978): 16–18.

ance,[8] but it is indisputable that parenesis was an important element. The crucial element is the eschatological motivation of the sayings. Since Q is concerned primarily to continue preaching the eschatological message of Jesus (although marked from beginning—cf. Luke 3:16–17—to end with a stronger element of judgment), people were "convinced that Jesus' message of the coming of the kingdom was not irrelevant to the post-Easter situation, but had to be proclaimed anew."[9] This context also gave rise to parenesis, which is intended to provide instruction in the conduct of life.

It has been suggested that, since the supernatural world has already come with the death and resurrection of Christ, the new age rules out any appeal to the words of Jesus; all who would continue "simply to preach ethics by appealing to the words of the historical Jesus" commit "an unpardonable anachronism."[10] But both Q and Paul prove the contrary. The fact that the Christian way of life, standing in the sign of the eschaton, derives its vitality and impetus from the new post-Easter world has not abolished eschatology. This way of life bases itself on criteria that are equally valid both before and after Easter, the more so because Easter, God's affirmation of Jesus, also vouches for the truth of Jesus' ethics. This is not to deny that the passage of time led in individual instances to a sense of distance and a different standard of conduct (in Mark 2:19, e.g., a new discipline of fasting supersedes refusal to fast).

2. It is true in any event that the early church did not adhere slavishly to the words spoken by Jesus, but adapted them constructively for the conduct of life in new situations. There are many examples in the Synoptic tradition. Jeremias, for example, has shown that the parables were not only elaborated, provided with new illustrations, and reshaped under the influence of popular narrative themes, but above all were substantially influenced by their use in parenesis.

The eschatological parable of appearance before the judge (Luke 12:58–59), for example, becomes an exhortation urging reconciliation (Matt. 5:25–26). A similar shift toward parenesis is also apparent in the parable of the great supper, which Luke interprets as an exemplary story calling for an open invitation to the poor, the maimed, and the blind (Luke 14:22ff.; cf. also the parenetic reworking of Luke 12:39–40, 42ff.; and the parenetic interpretation of Mark 4:1ff. in 4:13ff.). This reshaping continued, as we see, for example in the parable of the unjust steward (Luke 16:1ff.), which has undergone three (or even four) parenetic reinterpretations.[11]

Even within the parables themselves we find such parenetic adaptations of

8. Dibelius, *Tradition*, 233–34.
9. Heinz Eduard Tödt, *The Son of Man in the Synoptic Tradition* (Philadelphia: Westminster Press; London: SCM Press, 1965), 249.
10. Albert Schweitzer, *The Mysticism of Paul the Apostle* (New York: Seabury Press, 1968), 297.
11. Jeremias, *Parables*, 45ff.; cf. Dibelius, *Tradition*, 248ff.

Jesus' words. The sayings about salt and light, for example, are still metaphors in Mark (4:21 and 9:50) and Luke (14:34; 11:33; 8:16). In Matthew,
however, the sayings have become an appeal to the disciples to be aware of
their function and responsibility. The disciples are the light of the world only
insofar as the light shed by their good works illuminates the world (Matt.
5:13–16). Here and elsewhere we find a clear tendency on the part of the
communities to find as much parenesis as possible in the words of Jesus.[12] It
is therefore natural that the parables were reshaped and amplified. Sayings of
Jesus that belonged originally only to a Jewish environment and reflected
specific Jewish situations were extended to new contexts and applied to
different situations. The prohibition against divorce, for example, was now
extended. Originally it had addressed only the husband, because it was
almost unheard of in Judaism for a wife to divorce or be able to divorce her
husband. When Christianity entered territories governed by Hellenistic Roman law, the Lord's words were applied to wives (Mark 10:12; 1 Cor. 7:10).
Cultural and socioeconomic factors also played a role in this transposition;
urban congregations, for example, had other needs than those living in a rural
agrarian milieu.

It was of course possible for these changes either to preserve Jesus' intentions or to falsify them. There were legitimate extensions and restatements of
Jesus' words, but there were also tendencies to mitigate their force. It is not
always possible to decide which process was at work.

We may recall the examples in which the prohibition of oaths in Matt. 5:37,
originally associated with the requirement of absolute truthfulness, became
itself a simple oath formula (cf. the different development in James 5:12).
Repetition of "Yes" or "No" is probably a concession to contemporary oath
practice (cf. Slavonic Enoch 49:1), even though people probably thought they
were not transgressing the prohibition. Another example is Jesus' radical
prohibition of anger, which abolishes the distinction between feelings,
thoughts, and inclinations on the one hand and actions on the other. Matthew
5:22 turns this prohibition back into a casuistic list and trivializing classifica-
tion of prohibited insults, with corresponding emphasis on sanctions and
punishments: if you call someone a blockhead, you are liable to the council; if
you call someone an idiot, you are liable to the fires of hell. This process often
resulted in superficial moralizing and continued on in the manuscript tradition. In the same v. 22a, for example, many manuscripts interpolate the
phrase "without cause," thus prohibiting only groundless and unmotivated
anger. Of course this change guts Jesus' own words, which are specifically
intended to abolish such distinctions between justified and unjustified anger.

Such misunderstandings and misinterpretations were not simply the rule.
The fact that it is often very difficult to decide which are Jesus' own words

12. Dibelius, *Tradition*, 257.

and which are the product of the community is a sign that earliest Christianity tried to keep within the guidelines set by Jesus. This is true of the eschatological motivation, but it is also true in concrete applications. Mark 9:41 provides an example of both: "For truly, I say to you, whoever gives you a cup of water to drink because you bear the name of Christ, will by no means lose his reward." In addition, it is often difficult in individual cases to localize and date the extensions of Jesus' sayings.

3. We are on firmer ground when we examine the status of the law. Here we can make clearer distinctions as to both locus and date, since the extant texts reflect a conflict within the primitive community. It was never a matter of debate whether the words of the Lord laid down guidelines for Christian living; there were only differences of interpretation. The situation with the law was different. Even if the early Christian communities did not constitute themselves a special group distinct from Israel, there was controversy over the status of the law. Matthew 5:18 and Luke 16:17 defend the obligations imposed by the law to the last detail. It would be impossible to make a more fundamental claim for the continued validity of the law in all its demands.[13] After all we have said about Jesus' attitude toward the law, it is immediately clear that this does not reflect the position of Jesus. The same is true of Matt. 5:19, which states that whoever relaxes one of the least of the commandments and so teaches will be least in the kingdom of heaven. Matthew 5:19 thus presupposes that there were people who not only abrogated the law in practice but taught others to do so.

Some scholars find here a reference to Paul, his followers, or ultra-Paulinists. Others suggest Hellenistic antinomians or libertines. The most likely target is the so-called "Hellenists," the circle about Stephen (cf. Acts 6:1ff.). They represent the more liberal faction of the earliest Jewish Christians: they did not preach that the Torah had been abrogated in principle, but found their identity now in the message of the eschatological Christ event rather than in the law of Moses and observance of the Torah.[14] The conviction that the law was no longer in force and the beginning of a gentile mission with no reference to the law immediately resulted in bloody persecutions of these Hellenistic Jewish Christians on the part of the Jews (Acts 8:1).

The subsequent compromise of the "apostolic decree" (Acts 15:20, 28–29) attempted to reach a minimal consensus that would make it possible for Jewish and gentile Christians to live together in a mixed community. It dates from a later period and was obviously unknown to Paul. In any case it is not a document of the earliest period, even though it would be wrong to underestimate the desire for mutuality that was present from the beginning (cf. the Apostolic Council). The nature of the modus vivendi depends on whether the

13. See the numerous Jewish parallels in Strack-Billerbeck, *Kommentar* 1:244.
14. See Martin Hengel, "Zwischen Jesus und Paulus," *ZThK* 72 (1975): 151–206, esp. 191–92; cf. Ulrich Luz and Rudolf Smend, *Gesetz* (Stuttgart: Kohlhammer, 1981), 86ff.

moral wording or the cultic wording reflects the original form of the text. The cultic version, which is probably earlier, deals with questions of ritual slaughtering and food that is levitically pure. It was intended to put an end to the practices that the Jewish Christians obedient to the law found most offensive.

Contrary to the picture painted by Acts 6, New Testament scholars are generally agreed that the charges of attacking the law and the temple brought against Stephen, which Luke claims were false, were in fact true, and that the "seven," representing the leadership of the Stephen faction, probably did not exercise diaconal functions but served as community leaders and initiated the gentile mission. The conservative faction of the community remained true to the law, retaining the Sabbath, circumcision, and other observances, and therefore did not suffer persecution and martyrdom. The Stephen faction, giving up these practices, led a freer life. It is probably this group that preserved the tradition of Jesus' own free way of life.

C. COMMUNITY OF GOODS

1. This community of Hellenistic Jewish Christians appears also to be the source of what little we know about the specific ethics of the early community, what people since Troeltsch have called the "communism of love" of the early church. In Acts 2 and 4, Luke provides two summaries describing the early Christian community of goods. In Acts 4:32ff. (cf. also 2:44ff.) we read:

> Now the company of those who believed were of one heart and soul, and no one said that any of the things which he possessed was his own, but they had everything in common. . . . There was not a needy person among them, for as many as were possessors of lands or houses sold them, and brought the proceeds of what was sold and laid it at the apostles' feet; and distribution was made to each as any had need. Thus Joseph who was surnamed by the apostle Barnabas (which means, son of encouragement), a Levite, a native of Cyprus, sold a field which belonged to him, and brought the money and laid it at the apostles' feet.

This picture of the community is surely not historically accurate. There is obvious conflict between the general statement of the summary and the concluding account of Barnabas's donation. The question arises at once why Barnabas's sale of his field is mentioned at all if it was the general practice. The story of Ananias and Sapphira in 5:1ff. also presupposes that donation of all one's property was not the rule; in v. 4, Peter says explicitly that they could have kept what they owned. This is confirmed by Acts 12:12, which mentions a house belonging to Mary, obviously still in her possession. There is also a certain tension in the summary statement of 2:44–45: we are told that property was held in common, which implies that it was not alienated, but also that real estate and other property was sold (vv. 44 and 45). Acts 4:32ff. also presupposes that possessions were sold from time to time, as necessity arose (this is underlined by the use of the imperfect tense). This evidence has with good reason led scholars to conclude that in the summaries Luke has generalized individual cases. Possibly his idealized picture was inspired by Jesus' own words about wealth as well as by ancient expectations and models. Qumran, for example, practiced community of goods, and similar ideals appear in Greece (Pythagoras, Plato).[15]

2. More significant than this generalization is the fact that the new reality of the Spirit and human transformation extends concretely into the economic sphere (cf. also Mark 12:30). It is wrong, of course, to speak of "communism," with or without love. There is no socialized ownership of property or the means of production. Kautzky already pointed out that consumption was shared, not production (e.g., Qumran).[16] Nor is there any notion of revolutionary violence or a universal social system. But neither—again in contrast to Qumran—are we dealing with a monastic ideal to be realized in a cloistered environment, isolated from the impurity of the world (the members of the Qumran community were required to surrender all their property when they joined the order). The transformation affects instead the economic relationships of property ownership in the world of everyday society.

This fundamentally positive estimate is at variance with the history of interpretation outlined by Kraus,[17] which emphasizes the utopian and unrealistic nature of primitive Christian "communism" and appears almost to delight in observing that Paul referred to the Jerusalem Christians as "the poor," suggesting that property is a curse resulting from wicked behavior[18]— a valid exegetical point.

Kraus shows that according to Bonhoeffer,[19] the "new creature" is also manifested as a "new society," and that Barth interpreted Acts 2 as a notable experiment and invitation, an experiment that must be repeated whenever the gospel is heard.[20] Both he and Iwand have protested against simply assuming that we are dealing here with unrealistic fanaticism, as though radical eschatological transformation could not affect economic reality. But they have also warned against turning liberty into law and the gifts of the Spirit into a program for reshaping the world. The passages deal in fact with a community of fellowship, not a world order.

3. We may also note parenthetically that Luke not only generalized individual instances of donation but also clearly associated the donors with the wrong groups. He knew that Barnabas had sold a field and later held a position of leadership at Antioch (Acts 13:1). He therefore concluded (wrongly) that Barnabas was a highly respected member of the community, who was sent to Antioch on an official mission as the representative of

15. Friedrich Hauck, "koinos," *TDNT* 3:791ff.; Hengel, *Property* (B3), 19, 42–46.
16. Wilckens, "Kommunismus," 130.
17. Hans J. Kraus, "Aktualität des 'Urchristlichen Kommunismus'?" in *Freispruch und Freiheit* (Festschrift Walter Kreck), ed. H. G. Geyer (Munich: Kaiser, 1973) 306–27.
18. The true situation is discussed by Mealand, *Poverty and Expectation in the Gospels*, 38ff.
19. Dietrich Bonhoeffer, *The Communion of Saints* (New York: Harper & Row, 1963), 135–36.
20. Karl Barth, *Church Dogmatics*, 4 vols. (Edinburgh: T. & T. Clark, 1936–77), 4/2:174.

Jerusalem.[21] In fact Barnabas was most likely among those expelled from Jerusalem who initiated the gentile mission.

In this case, the Hellenists constituted the group that not only in the freedom of the Spirit practiced freedom from the law but also practiced freedom from possessions. The Hellenists were indeed charismatic enthusiasts, but far from contenting themselves with prophecies, exorcisms, and miraculous cures (as the polemic in Matt. 7:22 against those who say "Lord, Lord" might be understood to suggest) they were well aware of the importance of concrete ethics and specific change.

D. CRITICAL RECEPTION OF
TRADITIONAL PRINCIPLES

Even in the pre-Pauline communities, certain principles of traditional ethics were borrowed selectively; here again, the Hellenists were the most likely initiators. Such borrowing was necessary, if only because the extant sayings of the Lord no longer sufficed for guidance in the new situation and the larger environment. Less important was the waning of eschatological expectation. Even in Paul we still find both side by side: strong eschatological hope or expectation and acceptance of traditional ethics (see below, IV. A.5. and IV. C).

Dibelius sees the situation differently: "The primitive Christian communities concentrated on the passing away of this world, not on living within it; they were therefore totally unequipped for the need to provide parenetic solutions to everyday problems."[22] But the collection of the Lord's sayings in Q, which Dibelius puts under the heading of parenesis, exhibits a clear eschatological perspective. Of course it also shows traces of concern with the delay of the Parousia (Luke 12:39–40, 42ff.), but Lührmann can speak of a return to apocalyptic.[23] In any case, there can be no doubt of Q's eschatological tone. This means, however, that the concern for parenesis, which led to incorporation of non-Christian ethics, was not made possible and stimulated by an uneschatological attitude. In addition, the borrowed parenetic forms often have an eschatological foundation, as in the lists in 1 Cor. 6:9–10 and Gal. 5:21, which threaten explicitly that those who practice these vices "will not inherit the [eschatological] kingdom of God" (also evidence that Paul has borrowed these catalogues, since the expression is un-Pauline).

1. When we turn to examine the borrowed material in detail, we come first to the so-called catalogues of virtues and vices. In them a common schema of ancient ethics was incorporated, linguistically and stylistically distinctive. They are characterized by a free listing of terms without clear sequence,

---

21. On Acts 13:1, see Ernst Haenchen, *The Acts of the Apostles* (Philadelphia: Westminster Press; Oxford: Basil Blackwell, 1971).

22. *Tradition*, 240.

23. Dieter Lührmann, *Die Redaktion der Logienquelle*, WMANT 33 (Neukirchen: Neukirchener Verlag, 1969).

system, or logical organization. It is also significant that this form is broadly distributed through the entire New Testament, which makes its origin hard to pin down.

1.1 Earlier scholars often assumed that these catalogues were borrowed from the Cynic or Stoic diatribe and popular philosophy. Wibbing, however, citing primarily the Dead Sea Scrolls, points out their dualistic background and the Jewish schema of the two ways. Galatians 5 in particular, with its dualism of flesh and spirit paralleling antithetical catalogues of virtues and vices, can doubtless be interpreted from this perspective, but it would be wrong to generalize from this chapter. Both the New Testament examples and the extraordinarily wide distribution of such catalogues outside the New Testament caution against such a one-sided interpretation. Even Wibbing does not propose to derive the catalogue form in the New Testament from Judaism alone, but sees it as a clear illustration that the New Testament draws on a variety of traditions.[24] Popular philosophers and itinerant rhetoricians used it in their lectures; orators used it in their panegyrics and eulogies; and astrologers used it in their horoscopes. The Hellenistic strain is illustrated quite clearly, for example, by the use of such rhetorical devices as parechesis and paronomasia (cf. Rom. 1:29, 31). The elements of the lists are themselves mostly traditional. Even though the individual terms may vary and the catalogues of virtues in particular often exhibit Christian overtones, the content consists mostly of commonplaces from contemporary ethics.

1.2 The purpose of these lists of virtues and vices is probably to remind Christians that they are not dispensed from responsibility in their concrete actions and to illustrate paradigmatically what should and should not be done. A right or wrong attitude manifests itself in particular right or wrong actions. Sin and righteousness are not ideas or abstractions but concrete reality. Vices are not petty offenses but signs of human sinfulness; the so-called "virtues" describe obedience as concrete action, not merely an attitude. The appearance of these catalogues should not be treated as a dubious symptom of moralism but as an attempt to resist abstraction and give specific decisions and actions their due, even though the dangers involved are undeniable. The listing of various "vices" and "virtues" can lead to atomization of obedience, but the real danger lies not in specification as such but in an illegitimate tendency to treat everything alike. It must be noted, furthermore, that these lists were not simply drawn uncritically from the broad stream of ancient ethics. The four cardinal virtues heading the Stoic list never appear, for example, and under certain circumstances traditional words and values can take on a totally different meaning than in pre-Christian usage (cf. below, IV.D.1). These traditions were received not only selectively but critically.

2. After the catalogues of virtues and vices, we turn for our second

---

24. Wibbing, *Tugend- und Lasterkataloge* (B7), 78.

example of traditional parenesis to the so-called *Haustafeln* lists of domestic duties. This may seem odd: they are generally (and rightly) associated with the late phase of New Testament ethics, because the first *Haustafeln* appear in the deutero-Pauline corpus (cf. Col. 3:16ff.; 1 Pet. 2:13ff.). But the relationship between 1 Pet. 2:13ff. and Rom. 13:1ff., which are based on a common tradition, shows that even before Paul the Christian community was using admonitions like those in the *Haustafeln*. This indicates a need to go beyond regulating internal community problems and deal with conduct within the social structures of the world. A similar need appears in 1 Cor. 7:17ff., where the context is dominated by eschatological expectation. The discussion of mixed marriages in 1 Cor. 7:12ff. also exemplifies the personal involvement of community members outside the structures of the community itself. Here, too, there is no hint of any need to avoid contact with the outside world. Goppelt even suggests that this whole section derives indirectly from authentic Jesus traditions.[25]

The texts in question are parenetic passages that attempt to regulate relationships among various members of the same household. Their internal unity and organization distinguish them formally from other, more haphazard, series of admonitions. Besides the New Testament examples (Col. 3:16ff.; Eph. 5:22ff.; cf. 1 Pet. 2:13ff.), there are some from the Apostolic Fathers, which confirm in their own way that the schema is not a product of the deutero-Pauline corpus. We are dealing with a commonplace of early Christian parenesis, but not one created out of whole cloth by the community. The traditional background also explains why the passages are not as a whole formulated ad hoc and adapted to specific situations. On the other hand, comparison of the various examples shows that we are not dealing with a fixed schema; the form admitted substantial variation.

2.1 Here, too, it is clear that diaspora Judaism with its religious propaganda in the Hellenistic world paved the way for early Christianity. Of course Hellenistic Judaism need not have been the source; it may only have been a channel. The so-called Hierocles fragment is often cited as a non-Jewish example; here the various sets of duties and obligations are assembled in a catalogue. The schema of the Stoic catalogue is clearest in Epictetus, where it is limited essentially to listing the classes to which deference is owed, suggested by a sequence of isolated terms.[26] If we examine the particular statements of Epictetus more closely, we can also see fundamental differences, which we can only summarize by citing the characteristic features of Stoic ethics: intellectualism and optimism, eudaemonism and pantheism. The

---

25. Leonhard Goppelt, "Jesus und die 'Haustafel'-Tradition," in *Orientierung an Jesus* (Festschrift Josef Schmid), ed. P. Hoffman, N. Brox, and W. Pesch (Freiburg: Herder, 1973), 93–106.

26. Epictetus *Dissertationes* 2.17.31; 4.6.26.

Stoic admonitions, furthermore, are not mutual. They are addressed to the individual, whose fundamental stance of ataraxia is all-important.

A famous example from Hellenistic Judaism is the so-called Admonitions of Phocylides (175–230), which discusses relationships between husband and wife, parents and children, friends and relatives, masters and slaves, and so forth. Here we find warnings against celibacy, regulations governing sexual conduct, advice about marrying for money and polygamy, and questions of inheritance and friendship. We may also cite Philo and Josephus, who give admonitions of this type within the context of interpreting the law. In discussing the Decalogue (*De decalogo* 165–67), Philo, for example, uses legal parenesis treating each primary commandment as governing a variety of individual commandments. He exegetes the Fifth Commandment as implying all the laws affecting the relationship between parents and children, young people and the elderly, rulers and subjects, slaves and masters. There are many points of agreement: subjects must obey authority, slaves must serve with love, and masters must treat their slaves kindly.[27] This emphasis on the household (cf. however 1 Pet. 2:13ff.) with its three groups, as well as the greater stress on mutuality and the concern for obedience, leads scholars such as Lührmann and Thraede[28] to cite as a parallel the classical tradition of *oeconomia*.[29] In my opinion, however, there are no clear distinctions to be made.

2.2 Whether or not earliest Christianity borrowed the *Haustafel* schema from the legal parenesis of diaspora Judaism, it is not a form that originated in the Christian community. This observation is confirmed by the content of the *Haustafeln*, which stays within the framework of normal expectations. Their purpose was obviously more to demonstrate agreement with contemporary moral convention than to establish points of difference and to show that Christians were not dispensed from their existing duties. Despite the outbursts of enthusiasm, the primitive communities maintained their life of service in the world.

What the secular world considered right and proper, however, now takes on a new dimension in relationship to the Lord. Therefore respect for the order of the "household" and the borrowing of the *Haustafeln* that inculcate this order were not uncritical and absolute. It is illuminating merely to record what was not borrowed from the extensive parenetic material of the *Haustafel* tradition, above all the commonplaces of self-realization and worship of the gods. The major formal departure from the Stoic lists of obligations is the arrangement of the duties in pairs, which reflects the mutual relationship

27. Cf. also Philo's treatment of Cain's descendants (*De decalogo* 181). See also Crouch, *Origin and Intention of the Corinthian Haustafel*; Schroeder, "Die Haustafeln"; commentaries on Col. 3:16ff.; and below, 252ff.).

28. Dieter Lührmann, "Wo man nicht mehr Sklave oder Freier ist," *WuD* 13 (1975): 53ff.; idem, "Neutestamentliche Haustafeln und antike Ökonomie," *NTS* 27 (1980–81): 83ff.

29. Cf. Seneca *Epistulae* 94.1.

existing between the various classes or partners in the *Haustafeln*. Even though they do not automatically address subordinates independently as responsible ethical subjects, the Christian *Haustafeln* think more in terms of mutual relationships and less in terms of the status of individual members. We should also note new emphases in substance, especially the exhortation to agape. The purpose of the *Haustafeln* was anything but social reform, and there was danger from the outset that the existing class structures would be accepted and approved uncritically (notice the greater detail of the admonitions addressed to the underprivileged). But the shift of focus to the Lord at least incipiently made interpersonal relationships and social structures less self-serving and autonomous and put them in the service of love (see the discussion below of the deutero-Pauline material).

3.1 Certain ethical exhortations that go beyond the ethics of Jesus in form and content are therefore pre-Pauline. This is true also of the material Paul incorporates in the parenetic chapters of his epistles (Rom. 12:12ff.; 1 Thess. 4:1ff.; Gal. 5:16ff.; cf. also the deutero-Paulines), but the individual cases are hard to analyze. Specific admonitions are generally brought together without system or logical order; they are usually general in scope and appropriate to most ways of life. The content of the tradition and teaching borrowed by Paul was therefore itself undoubtedly parenetic. A comparison of Rom. 12:10ff. with 1 Pet. 3:8ff., for example, shows clearly that both drew on a common tradition. Various scholars have even claimed that borrowing of the Jewish form of teaching by the early Christian community has implications for what was taught: "not primarily facts of salvation, but exegesis and parenesis."[30] This statement is too one-sided when applied to Paul (cf. 1 Cor. 11:23ff.; 15:3ff.). It is therefore impossible to maintain the strict distinction, proposed above all by Dodd,[31] between kerygma and didache (in the sense of instruction in ethical obligations). Nor is a temporal sequence very likely, in the sense that ethical instruction followed after conversion: it appears to have been an integral part of missionary preaching from the beginning (cf. Gal. 5:21; 1 Thess. 4:6). The intertwining is quite clear above all in 1 Thessalonians, with its various echoes of missionary preaching.

It is therefore wrong to restrict didache to Halakhah, as the example of Judaism might suggest. It is equally true that the didache of the pre-Pauline communities included catechetical and parenetic material. Paul was not the first to teach "how you ought to live" (1 Thess. 4:1; cf. later also 2 Thess. 2:15 and 3:6). Elsewhere, too, we hear echoes of traditional parenesis where Paul builds on existing material—not just the Old Testament and sayings of the Lord, but also early Christian parenesis.

3.2 It is undeniable that even before Paul there were Christian rules and principles, forms and teachings, current in the community. It is much less

30. Karl H. Rengstorf, "didaskō," *TDNT* 2:145.
31. *Gospel* (B), 11–12.

certain, and in fact not even probable, that there was any such thing as an early Christian catechism. The many attempts since the time of Seeberg to reconstruct such a catechism—even just an ethical catechism—have rightly found little support.

Seeberg's work has been criticized above all for going beyond the realm of parenesis. In fact development of credal statements based on the Christ event followed a different course from that taken by parenesis, which drew in part on Jewish and Hellenistic traditions. But attempts to reconstruct an ethical catechism have been no more successful than attempts to recreate a theological catechism.[32]

Even the theory that there was a catechism for Jewish proselytes, which might have served as a model for the first Christian community, is anything but certain. The schema of the two ways by itself does not constitute evidence. Michaelis[33] points out that such a catechism would most likely have left traces in rabbinic literature, which is not the case. It is not even possible to speak of a fixed and universal two-ways schema. However that may be, there is unlikely to have been a similar catechism in early Christianity, which would have derived such a teaching tool from Jewish practice. There is no even reasonably certain evidence that parenetic exhortations were fixed in anything like a catechism, either before Paul or later by Paul himself.

The most recent attempt to demonstrate the existence of such a catechism, after Daube and Selwyn,[34] is that of Dodd.[35] Dodd tries to prove that even before Paul there was an ethical catechism for Christian converts, with something like the following schema: first a call to renounce pagan vices, then a list of typical virtues, then duties toward the Christian community, then relationship toward neighbors, the state, and so forth, and finally an eschatological conclusion. The reconstruction is highly uncertain in detail, but Dodd's basic error is to assume that parenetic traditions were issued as portions of an early Christian ethical catechism, whose structure is then recovered.[36]

We conclude, therefore, that even before and alongside Paul there were many beginnings in early Christianity on which Paul himself as well as the Gospels could build.

32. Martin Dibelius, "Zur Formgeschichte des NT," *ThR* 3 (1931): 212–13.
33. Wilhelm Michaelis, "hodos," *TDNT* 5:58.
34. D. Daube and E. G. Selwyn, *The First Epistle of St. Peter* (Grand Rapids: Baker, 1981 repr.), 467–88.
35. *Gospel*, chap. 1.
36. Cf. Wolfgang Schrage, *Die konkreten Einzelgebote in der paulinischen Paränese* (Gütersloh: Mohn, 1961), 131ff.; Franz Laub, "Eschatologische Verkündigung und Lebensgestaltung nach Paulus," *BU* 10 (1973): 2ff.; Ferdinand Hahn, introduction to Alfred Seeberg, *Der Katechismus der Urchristenheit* (reprint, Munich: Kaiser, 1966), xxi–xxviii.

III

ETHICAL ACCENTS
IN THE SYNOPTIC GOSPELS

BIBLIOGRAPHY

General

Sanders, Jack T. *Ethics* (B), 31–46.

———. "Ethics in the Synoptic Gospels." *BR* 14 (1969): 19–32.

Schulz, Siegfried. *Die Stunde der Botschaft*. 2d ed. Hamburg: Furche, 1970. Cited here from 1st ed. (1967).

Vielhauer, Philipp. *Geschichte der urchristlichen Literatur*. Berlin: de Gruyter, 1975. Pp. 329–409.

A. Discipleship in Mark (pp. 138–43)

Ambrozic, Aloysius M. *The Hidden Kingdom*. CBQ.M 2. Washington, D.C.: Catholic Univ. America, 1972. Pp. 136–82.

Kee, Howard Clark. *Community of the New Age*. Philadelphia: Westminster Press; London: SCM Press, 1977.

Reploh, Karl-Georg. *Markus—Lehrer der Gemeinde*. Stuttgart: Katholisches Bibelwerk, 1969.

B. The "Better Righteousness" in Matthew (pp. 143–52)

Barth, Gerhard. "Das Gesetzesverständnis des Evangelisten Matthäus." In Günther Bornkamm, Gerhard Barth, and Heinz Joachim Held, *Überlieferung und Auslegung im Matthäus-Evangelium*, 54–154. 5th ed. WMANT 1. Tübingen: Mohr, 1968. English: "Matthew's Understanding of the Law." In Bornkamm, Barth, and Held, *Tradition and Interpretation in Matthew*, 58–164. Philadelphia: Westminster Press; London: SCM Press, 1963.

Broer, Ingo. *Freiheit vom Gesetz und Radikalisierung des Gesetzes*. SBS 98. Stuttgart: Katholisches Bibelwerk, 1980.

Hummel, Reinhart. *Die Auseinandersetzung zwischen Kirche und Judentum im Matthäusevangelium*. 2d ed. BEvTh 33. Munich: Kaiser, 1966. Cited here from 1st ed. (1963).

Kretzer, Armin. *Die Herrschaft der Himmel und die Söhne des Rechts*. SBM 10. Stuttgart: Katholisches Bibelwerk, 1971.

Simonsen, Hejne. "Die Auffassung vom Gesetz im Matthäusevangelium." In *Theologie aus dem Norden* (ID), 44–67.

Strecker, Georg. *Glaube* (B). Pp. 36–45.

———. *Der Weg der Gerechtigkeit*. 3d ed. FRLANT 82. Göttingen: Vandenhoeck & Ruprecht, 1971.

Thysman, Raymond. *Communauté et directives éthiques*. Gembloux: Duculot, 1974.

Trilling, Wolfgang. *Das wahre Israel*. 3d ed. StANT 10. Munich: Kösel, 1964.

Zumstein, Jean. *La condition du croyant dans l'évangile selon Matthieu*. Orbis biblicus et orientalis 16. Fribourg: Éditions universitaires, 1977.

C. The Christian Life in Luke (pp. 152–61)

Barraclough, Ray. "A Re-Assessment of Luke's Political Perspective." *RTR* 38 (1979): 10–18.

Cadbury, Henry Joel. *The Making of Luke-Acts*. 2d ed. London: SPCK, 1958.

Conzelmann, Hans. *Die Mitte der Zeit*. 6th ed. BHTh 17. Tübingen: Mohr, 1977. English: *The Theology of St. Luke* (1961). Philadelphia: Fortress Press, 1982 repr.

Degenhardt, Hans Joachim. *Lukas—Evangelist der Armen*. Stuttgart: Katholisches Bibelwerk, 1965.

Huuhtanen, Pauli. "Die Perikope vom 'Reichen Jüngling'" (ID). Pp. 79–98.

Nickelsburg, George W. E. "Riches, the Rich, and God's Judgment in 1 Enoch 92–105 and the Gospel According to Luke." *NTS* 25 (1979): 324–44.

O'Hanlon, John. "The Story of Zacchaeus and the Lucan Ethic." *JSNT* 12 (1981): 2–26.

Schmithals, Walter. "Lukas—Evangelist der Armen." *ThViat* 12 (1973–74): 153–67.

Schottroff and Stegemann. *Jesus* (I). Pp. 89–153.

Thériault, J.-Y. "Les dimensions sociales, économiques et politiques dans l'oeuvre de Luc." *ScEs* 16 (1974): 205–31.

A. DISCIPLESHIP IN MARK

1. Mark was the first to write a Gospel, a step beyond collections of disputes, miracle stories, and parables or the traditional complex of the passion narrative. In his account of Jesus' life and death, he laid an unexcelled foundation for the preaching of the church. As his programmatic title ("Beginning": 1:1) suggests, his purpose in including the tradition of the earthly Jesus is not simply to preserve historical memories and describe the ministry of Jesus as an event of the past. Mark wants to make Jesus' ministry transparent for the present. Of course it would be wrong to overlook the historical and narrative dimension and subsume everything under the heading of kerygma. In 2:19–20, for example, Mark distinguishes the pre-Easter period of messianic salvation, when fasting is inappropriate, from the period when the bridegroom is taken away and the disciples will fast. It would be wrong, however, to generalize by finding here a sharp distinction between the time of Jesus and the time of the church.[1] In many other respects, Mark's presentation of Jesus' life and ministry is guided by kerygmatic interests or at least is not shaped by mere historicism.

Mark describes the life of Jesus from the outset in the shadow of the cross (cf. the references to the Passion, beginning with 1:14; 2:20; and 3:6), up to which the entire narrative leads. This is also the real explanation for the paradox of revelation and concealment, reflected in the so-called "messianic secret," which pervades the Gospel. Together with the proportion of the entire Gospel devoted to the Passion narrative, this has led to Kähler's frequently quoted description of Mark as a Passion narrative with an extended introduction. This perspective also explains the critical and restrictive interpretation of the miracle tradition. Although miracles usually occasion misunderstanding and resistance (3:22; 6:6, 52; 8:17–18), Mark leaves no doubt of Jesus' victory in his struggle with the demonic powers: the miracles and healings are to be understood as signs that the kingdom of God is dawning, and not only in the past. Discipleship and service can also be grounded in this experience of salvation, illustrated by Jesus' sovereignty over sickness and hunger, wind and waves (cf. 1:31; 10:52).

At the center of Jesus' preaching as described by Mark stands the summary in 1:14–15. Here the fulfillment of time and the presence of the kingdom of God interpret each other mutually. This accentuates the present actuality of the kingdom, which is the basis for the call to repent. The crucial turning point has come (perfect tense); time cannot be turned back. But fulfillment and the kingdom are linked with Jesus (cf. 4:11 and 10:15; on the association of the kingdom of God with christology, cf. 8:38 and 9:1; but also 11:9–10). At the same time, however, Mark consciously associates the Son of man who suffered and rose with the Son of man who is to come (8:31, 38). Those who

---

1. Kee, *Community,* 145.

follow Jesus as his disciples—discipleship and conformity to Jesus' way are
the central features of Markan ethics—are under the sway of Jesus' death and
resurrection on the one hand and the Parousia on the other. The Gospel
reveals traces of a delayed Parousia and does not expect an imminent eschaton
(cf. 13:10). The Markan community therefore cannot be understood as an
apocalyptic sect with a sectarian ethics. Mark was well aware, nevertheless,
that neither a theology of the cross (*theologia crucis*) nor a Christian life
following in the footsteps of the crucified Jesus can be maintained without
hope for an ultimate consummation. Ethical statements (e.g., 9:41), however,
do not often include an eschatological motif (e.g., eschatological reward).
There is no reason to speak of apocalyptic parenesis[2] or, on the other hand, of
gnostic tendencies.[3]

2. The centrality of the discipleship theme for Mark can be seen from the
fact that it was probably Mark who turned the healing narrative of 10:46ff.
into a discipleship narrative by adding v. 52.[4] At the very beginning of the
Gospel, the programmatic summary of 1:14–15 is followed by the first call
narratives. In Mark, Jesus is surrounded by disciples from the very outset. It
may well be no accident that the story begins, not with an individual call like
that of Levi (2:13ff.) or that of the rich young man (10:17–18), but with the
simultaneous call of four men, a call that establishes a social group into which
Jesus' followers are incorporated. It is made clear to the community at the
same time that these men, bearing witness to the tradition, guarantee the
continuity between the earthly Jesus and the continued ministry of the
community in his spirit. This is also the background against which we must
understand the words of v. 17, which point to the future: "I will make you
become fishers of men."

Although the relationship between the Twelve and the disciples as a group
is not entirely clear, what is said of the Twelve probably applies to the rest as
well: Jesus appointed them "to be with him" (3:14b). The emphasis is on
their sharing in Jesus' ministry, as the continuation in vv. 14c–15 explains and
above all as the missionary charge in 6:6ff. confirms: they are to preach and
teach like Jesus, to drive out demons and heal like Jesus, to receive authority
like Jesus (cf. 1:38 with 6:12; 1:21 with 6:30; 1:27 with 6:7; 1:23 with 6:13).
It is characteristic of all three discipleship pericopes that the statements about
Jesus also for the most part apply to the disciples or the Twelve, so that they
are included in the ministry of the earthly Jesus. In each case, however, his
initiative is strongly emphasized: it is he who appoints the Twelve, he who
sends them forth, he who grants authority and imposes duties. Mark describes the disciples' weakness and incomprehension, even emphasizing the

2. Sanders, *Ethics* (B), 33.
3. Pace Houlden, *Ethics* (B), 41–42, who is nevertheless right to maintain that the focus of the
ethical sections is on the person of Jesus and the kingdom of God (43–44).
4. Cf. Reploh, *Markus*, 222–23.

contrast between them and Jesus (especially in the passion narrative), but he is also concerned to emphasize their "being with Jesus," at Jesus' own behest, as the mark of discipleship both before and after Easter.[5]

3. The crucial turning point in the Gospel is Peter's confession (8:27–30). From this moment on, the emphasis is on instructions to the disciples that have following Jesus as their theme. Here the disciples appear as representatives of the community (especially 8:27—10:52). In the texts so far discussed, one might think of the Twelve or the disciples more as models of a collegial group with special functions and special authority than of the church as a whole, but this is impossible in such discipleship sayings as 8:34ff. Here the disciples appear neither as representatives of an opposition group or of a false christology picturing Christ as a miracle worker, nor (pace Kee[6]) are they specifically prototypes of wandering charismatics. Here discipleship in suffering is clearly a mark of the church as a whole. Furthermore, it is not limited to the period before Easter (cf. the sufferings of the community described in chap. 13). This is already clear from the words ("and he called to him the multitude with his disciples and spoke to them": 8:34) that introduce the familiar sayings about suffering and taking up one's cross. For Mark there is no following after Jesus, no discipleship, without self-denial and the cross and therefore without relationship to the crucified Jesus.

Mark accordingly concludes the second prophecy of the Passion with the pericope of the disciples' quarrel over their own status, to which Jesus responds by saying, "If anyone would be first, he must be last of all and servant of all" (9:35). The final phrase is probably Mark's own, because it goes beyond the basic antithesis.[7] In other words, Mark is concerned primarily with the notion of service. The importance of this logion to Mark is shown by its variation in 10:43, concretely illustrated in 9:37 by the example of receiving children in need: whoever receives such a child receives Jesus himself, who—as in Matthew 25—identifies himself with this child. It is significant once more that the disciples' dispute over status stands in contrast, not in correspondence, to the way of the cross taken by Jesus. Because Jesus took this way, it is also the way of the disciples.

The third announcement of the Passion also does not stand in isolation but appears in the context of sayings about discipleship. It follows the request of the sons of Zebedee to have places of honor reserved for them (10:35ff.). Jesus' immediate answer is that they do not know what they are asking (v. 38). Verse 40 would make an appropriate continuation: it is not up to Jesus to assign such places of honor. Mark has obviously interpolated vv. 38b–39, which announce that the disciples will have to travel the same way of suffering

5. See Klemens Stock, *Boten aus dem Mit-Ihm-Sein*, AnBib 70 (Rome: Biblical Institute Press, 1975); Günther Schmahl, *Die Zwölf im Markusevangelium*, TThSt 30 (Trier: Paulinus, 1974).

6. *Community*, 87ff.

7. Ambrozic, *Kingdom*, 155.

that Jesus himself had to travel: "The cup that I drink you will drink; and with the baptism with which I am baptized, you will be baptized" (v. 39). The disciples will experience the same fate as Jesus: both images—the cup and baptism—suggest suffering. The evangelist is not interested solely in the particular fate of the two sons of Zebedee. The pericope is meant to remind the community as a whole of the consequences resulting from Jesus' own fate. The disciples are not to share his glory, with places of honor and positions of power beside his throne, but to share his suffering.

Mark has also added vv. 42–45 to the story of the sons of Zebedee (Luke 22:24ff. confirms that this passage was not associated originally with their request). In this tradition incorporated by Mark, the way of the world is contrasted to that of the community: in the world, greatness is based on power and its abuse, on "subjugation" and "violence." Within the Christian community, however, power does not derive from the powerlessness of others; to be great means to serve. This conclusion is based on the work of the Son of man, who also came to serve. The statement of correspondence in conduct (v. 45b) has itself been augmented by the saying about ransom. Possibly Mark appended this passage here because his community was already experiencing the desire to gain positions of respect and authority instead of following in the footsteps of the crucified Jesus.

4.1 Another text that illuminates Mark's view of discipleship is 10:1–13. It focuses on ethical conduct rather than suffering. Mark is clearly responsible for the quotation in vv. 11–12 (cf. the characteristic "again" and the house motif). Since vv. 2–9 culminate in the statement that the union of man and woman ordained by God must not be broken by human agency, Mark sees in God's "joining" (v. 9) the reason why any dissolution of this marital union is contrary to God's will, not merely a divorce initiated by the husband as in vv. 2–9.

4.2 The situation is more complex when we come to the blessing of children that follows. According to v. 14, the kingdom of God belongs to them. It is generally agreed that v. 15, which states that the disciples must receive the kingdom like children, was originally an independent logion, introduced secondarily into the pericope. Mark's special interest in this saying is clear from the admonition in 9:35, cited above, which is also followed by a scene with a child (v. 36). To receive a child is a concrete instance of diakonia (v. 37). Receiving the kingdom of God like a child (10:15) could then mean for Mark both a gift and a chance for service at once.[8] In any case, Mark is concerned with the proper attitude toward children. They are members of the community. On the other hand, Mark did not evade the breaking of family ties. In 3:31ff., for example, he relativized

---

8. Ibid., 157.

the traditional understanding of the family, although it is replaced by incorporation into the new community (3:35).[9]

4.3 Especially instructive is Mark's attitude toward riches and possessions in 10:17ff., where he combines two originally independent passages: the story of the rich young man (vv. 17–20) and Jesus' instructions to his disciples (vv. 23–27).[10] While the first section is relatively unified, the second has probably undergone substantial redaction (cf. the typically Markan expressions "again," "exceedingly," "amazed," "astonished," "can be saved"). The tradition probably included only the saying that it is difficult for a rich man to enter the kingdom of heaven, which Mark appended to the preceding passage by means of a typical transitional formula (v. 23a), and the saying about the camel and the eye of the needle (v. 25). Each is followed by the disciples' reaction: amazement and astonishment. Even this is anachronistic, for to the best of our knowledge the disciples were not especially wealthy. It makes more sense if they here represent a later period, when there was an influx of wealthy members into the community for whom what Jesus said about riches presented a problem.

It is usually claimed[11] that Mark here evades the central problem: while v. 23b emphasizes that it is difficult for the rich to enter into the kingdom of God, v. 24b emphasizes that it is difficult for everyone. But the only reason why the doublet in v. 24b omits the specific reference to riches is probably due to the following saying about the camel and the eye of the needle which refers explicitly to the rich (cf. also 4:18–19, on the deceptive temptations of riches, which together with the cares of the world choke the Word of God).

We also must note that Mark adds vv. 28(29)–30, stating that the disciples have left everything and establishing a contrast to the rich man, who is unwilling to follow Jesus.[12] These verses emphasize also that renunciation and sacrifice are not undertaken for ascetic reasons or in hope of eschatological reward. They will be repaid in this age with concrete material and personal reward within the community as the family of God (*familia dei*).

For Mark, however, the crucial answer is in v. 27: impossible with men, but not with God. Nothing already said is taken back, nor is the concrete problem evaded. There are no generalities about total insecurity or the universal impossibility of achieving one's own salvation. But v. 27 lends everything already stated in apparently absolute terms a dimension of openness. It rejects any guaranteed condemnation as well as any false security

9. Cf. Hans-Hartmut Schroeder, *Eltern und Kinder in der Verkündigung Jesu*, ThF 53 (Hamburg: Reich, 1972), 110ff.
10. See Nikolaus Walter, "Zur Analyse von Mk. 10,17–31," *ZNW* 53 (1962): 206–18; Wolfgang Harnisch, "Die Berufung des Reichen," in *Festschrift für Ernst Fuchs*, ed. G. Ebeling, E. Jüngel, and G. Schunack (Tübingen: Mohr, 1973), 161–76.
11. Ibid.
12. Ibid., 164, 170.

based on inclusion or exclusion.[13] On the one hand, Mark repeats, simply and directly, Jesus' critical words concerning the rich. On the other hand, he criticizes an attitude that would interpret them as an assurance of one's own salvation while seeing only condemnation for the rich. He points to the basic human situation: everything comes from God alone. Since the pericope appears in the context of sayings concerning discipleship, it shows clearly that riches make it very difficult to follow Jesus. True discipleship, however, is not a meritorious achievement but the work and gift of God.

5. It would be possible to suggest many additional theories about details of Mark's ethics, but his redactional hand is always highly hypothetical. For example, the pericopes dealing with the law contain very few specifically Markan features. Mark 7:9 is probably Markan (cf. the new introduction): "You have a fine way of rejecting the commandment of God, in order to keep your tradition!" By using the stronger term "annul" (instead of "leave," as in v. 8), Mark makes the rejection of cultic regulations more vehement. By their "human traditions," the Jewish authorities are abrogating the law of God (cf. also v. 13). It is dubious, however, to speak of an attack by Jesus on the Mosaic law in Mark.[14] God's commandment is cited to reject tradition. The authority of the Decalogue is also accepted without reservation (10:19).

It is uncertain how Mark understands the summary of the law in the law of love (12:28ff.). Many scholars think that the pericope in its Markan context is intended only to show that Jesus is the better interpreter of the Old Testament.[15] Whether it is legitimate to say that in the Markan community "only the requirement to love God and show compassion was recognized as enduring"[16] is also dubious, at least with respect to the "only." We must note, of course, that Mark is greatly concerned with compassion.

B. THE "BETTER RIGHTEOUSNESS"
IN MATTHEW

For Matthew the ethical theme is much more central than for Mark: he sees the Christian life as fulfilling the demands of the "better righteousness" taught authoritatively by Jesus. Matthew's guiding principle is strongly parenetic.[17] He sees Jesus' teaching and ministry as a whole in continuity with the Old Testament and interprets the Christ event as fulfillment of the promise. The Torah above all is the link connecting Israel and the church. Its proper interpretation is therefore Matthew's central problem, above all in the conflict with Judaism. Jesus' instruction concerning the will of God—summarized by Matthew almost in the form of a catechism (cf. 6:1ff.)—is expressly reaffirmed at Easter, as we see from the reference in the missionary

13. Reploh, *Markus*, 198–99.
14. Schulz, *Stunde*, 147.
15. Sanders, *Ethics*, 32; idem, "Ethics," 20.
16. Schulz, *Stunde*, 148.
17. Kretzer, *Herrschaft*, 303.

commission of the risen Lord to Jesus' earthly ministry and especially his "commanding": "teaching them to observe all that I have commanded you" (28:20). This verse documents Matthew's efforts to define "a program of Christian ethics for the church of all ages."[18]

1.1 Fundamental for Matthew's ethics is its foundation in the person and work of Jesus. The Matthaean Jesus is not merely the messianic interpreter of the Old Testament, who calls for a "better righteousness" (5:20), but also the one who fulfills this righteousness in word and deed (3:15). He is "Emmanuel" (1:15; cf. also 28:20), the humble (21:5) and obedient one who willingly accepts his Passion (cf. 26:2) and dies for others (cf. the addition to the words of the Lord's Supper: "for the forgiveness of sins"). In his healings he comes to the aid of the helpless. He is "Lord" in a special sense (cf. 8:25; 24:42), risen from the dead, who promises to be present with his own (18:20; 28:20). Above all, however, he is the authoritative teacher who shows the disciples the way of the "better righteousness" (5:1) and makes it possible for them to follow him in doing the will of God as he taught and lived it. Because he is the risen Lord, all power in heaven and earth is given to him (28:18); therefore the witnesses to the resurrection are to go forth on a universal mission and call others to discipleship even after Easter (cf. 28:19; the only real difference between the pre-Easter and post-Easter mission is that the mission to Israel in 10:5–6, 23 becomes a mission to the nations).

In speaking of the disciples, Matthew prefers to restrict the term to the circle of the Twelve (cf. 10:1; 11:1; 26:20). What stands out, however, is not the historical distance between Jesus and the present, but the prefiguration of the church in the group of disciples (cf. not only 28:19; but also 23:52 and 27:57).[19] To be a Christian is to be a disciple. The sign par excellence of this discipleship is following Jesus—doing the will of God and sharing in Jesus' mission (cf. 8:23; 9:37ff.; 12:49). It is not by accident that the first of the five great discourses is the Sermon on the Mount.

1.2 Despite the delay of the Parousia (cf. 25:1ff.; 24:48), eschatological expectation has special importance for Matthew, especially with respect to the church, which awaits the judgment as *corpus mixtum*, in which weeds are still found among the grain (13:31ff., 47ff.). It is therefore not surprising that sections like the Sermon on the Mount have a strong eschatological focus. The kingdom of God (despite 12:28) or of heaven does appear to lie in the future and to be distinct from the present kingdom of the Son of man (cf. 13:36ff.), but this preserves its dynamism (cf. 13:11, 18a)[20] and makes it a central motif of ethics (cf. 5:8ff.; 13:43; 21:43). True fruits are "fruits of the

18. Martin Dibelius, *The Sermon on the Mount* (New York: Charles Scribners Sons, 1940), 102.
19. See Ulrich Luz, "Die Jünger im Matthäusevangelium," *ZNW* 62 (1971): 141–71; for a different view, see Strecker, *Weg*, 191ff.
20. Kretzer, *Herrschaft*, 93ff., 225ff.

kingdom of God" (21:43), brought forth by the kingdom itself or the "sons of the kingdom" (13:38). The notion of eschatological judgment and reward is emphasized repeatedly (5:46; 6:1ff.; 7:21ff.; 13:41ff.; 22:11ff.; 24:45ff.; 25:14ff.) in order to inculcate "endurance to the end" (24:13),[21] fidelity (25:21), and working with the talents that one has in trust (25:16), but above all because the Son of man will "repay every man for what he has done" (16:27) and will ask about solidarity with "the least" (25:31ff.).

1.3 Matthew does not, however, ignore the indicative statement of salvation, as we see from the incorporation of the Sermon on the Mount into the story of Jesus' life (cf. 4:12ff., 23ff.; 8—9) and its setting in the context of divine history (cf. 4:15–16). We also note the reference to baptism in 28:19, which Matthew sees as establishing a state of salvation. It is especially true for Matthew that the indicatives are also parenetic in character, while the imperatives can be a form of grace.[22] He therefore senses no contradiction in the notion that human forgiveness is sometimes the prerequisite for God's forgiveness (6:14–15), sometimes its consequence (18:23ff.). In this intertwined complex of indicative and imperative, however, the stress is not on the declaration of salvation but on the imperative, itself understood as an act of divine grace. In any event, Matthew's goal is concrete, visible, effective obedience, realized in discipleship and recognizable in "good works" (5:16) and "fruits" (7:16, 20). This obedience also has missionary implications.[23]

2. Discipleship is more than obedience to the law: it includes distress (8:23ff.), acceptance of suffering (10:17ff.), humility (18:1ff.), service (20:20ff.), works of love (25:31ff.), and general willingness to share Jesus' fate, but Matthew is undeniably concerned above all with fulfillment of the law as expounded authoritatively by Jesus. He states programmatically in 5:17 that Jesus did not come to abolish the law and the prophets but to fulfill them.

Since this verse exhibits many characteristic features of Matthew's language, it is usually understood (correctly) as his introduction to the central section of the Sermon on the Mount, which follows (cf. "think not," with 10:34; "law or prophets," with 7:12 and 22:14; "fulfill," which occurs sixteen times in Matthew).[24] It is unlikely, however, that Matthew means to assert the absolute and unqualified authority of the law down to its last jot and tittle, as v. 18 seems to say. Matthew himself cannot have thought of v. 18 as establishing the authority and eternity of each and every letter, as we can see from his

---

21. See Rudolph Pesch, "Eschatologie und Ethik," *BiLe* 11 (1970): 223-38.
22. Zumstein, *La condition*, 303.
23. See Christoph Burchard, "Versuch, das Thema der Bergpredigt zu finden," in *Jesus Christus in Historie und Theologie* (Festschrift Hans Conzelmann), ed. G. Strecker (Tübingen: Mohr, 1975), 409–32, esp. 420.
24. See Eduard Schweizer, "Anmerkungen zum Gesetzesverständnis des Matthäus," *ThLZ* 77 (1952): 479ff.; Trilling, *Israel*, 165ff.; Thysman, *Communauté*, 36ff.

limitation of the law to this eon[25] and the reservations he expresses elsewhere concerning the cultic and ceremonial law. The same holds true for v. 19, which says that anyone who relaxes one of the least commandments, although not excommunicated, must be content to be least in the kingdom of heaven. In fact Matthew here condemns himself, because he distinguishes de facto between moral and cultic laws. He was able to appropriate the rigorous legal position of Jewish Christianity, the source of vv. 18 and 19, only by reinterpreting it. The reader should not be deceived by these verses.

Matthew protests against relaxing the law, not to mention abolishing it (cf. his restatement of the Q tradition from Luke 16:16a) but for him to "fulfill" the law does not mean to exhaust its requirements but to act so as to fulfill it, to realize it and carry out its intent. Jesus himself personifies this fulfillment (cf. 3:15 and the quotations he applies to himself).[26] Above all it means to establish its true meaning with authority and bring it to fulfillment by correct interpretation. Matthew's primary aim is a different interpretation of the law, an interpretation that precludes all Christian forms of antinomianism and freedom from the law (cf. 7:21ff. and 13:41), but especially Pharisaic misinterpretations of the law, "the blind leading the blind" (15:14; cf. 23:24). The antitheses in vv. 21–48 show that v. 17 is concerned less with carrying out the law's requirements than with correct interpretation of the part of Jesus.[27]

3.1 This double attack is especially clear in 5:20: righteousness must be superior to that of the scribes and Pharisees. The "more" that is required is in the first instance effectual realization of righteousness (cf. also v. 19) and overcoming of "hypocrisy" (cf. 6:1ff. and 23:25ff.) or the discrepancy between words and actions (cf. 7:21ff. and 23:3–4). In v. 20, then, "righteousness" is the righteousness that acts according to the will of God, righteous conduct in practice. Only in this sense can one speak of it quantitatively and comparatively ("better"). Those who lag behind in the practice of righteousness, unlike the false teachers of v. 19, are not accorded a modest place in the kingdom of God but are excluded entirely. For Matthew, criticism of "hypocrisy" includes criticism of religiosity for show. In chapter 6 in particular he pillories all ostentatious forms of devotion: "sounding trumpets" when giving alms, fasting for show, prayer in public in synagogues and on the street (cf. also 23:5–6). The "more" here consists in concealment of devotion and love from one's own eyes and from the eyes of others. The ideal is of course not a purely inward spirituality but an absence of ulterior motives and self-interest.

3.2 Just as important as Matthew's attack on religious show and masquerade—aimed primarily at the Pharisaism of his own day, which he car-

25. Simonsen, "Auffassung," 51.
26. See also Ulrich Luz, "Die Erfüllung des Gesetzes bei Matthäus," *ZThK* 75 (1978): 398–435, esp. 413ff.; Strecker, *Weg*, 147, 149.
27. See Barth, "Understanding," 67ff., 147.

icatures (the criticism in chap. 23 is less sharply focused)[28]—is his similar internal warning to the community, criticizing of the "enthusiastic" Christianity of the charismatics and those who say "Lord, Lord." Therefore Matthew incorporates in 7:19 a statement from the preaching of the Baptist in 3:10, now turned against the Christians: a tree that does not bear fruit is cut down and thrown into the fire. The remark about those who say "Lord, Lord" (7:21) refers to more than cultic piety. In contrast to the situation in Luke, these people appear to perform charismatic acts (prophecy, exorcism, mighty works: v. 22), which Matthew does not reject in principle (see, e.g., the series of miracles described in 10:8 and the significance of prophecy in 5:12; 10:41; 23:34). But for Matthew doing the will of God in righteousness and love is itself a charismatic act and the criterion by which even prophecy is judged.

3.3 The real opposite of doing the will of God is not doing charismatic acts but merely hearing, as the conclusion to the Sermon on the Mount stresses. For Matthew, obedience and action are the crucial requirements to avoid condemnation at the judgment. The guests without "wedding garments," who have not responded to their call with the "better righteousness," are condemned (22:11–14). The kingdom of God is taken from a nation that bears no fruit and given to a nation that produces "the fruits of the kingdom" (21:43).[29] Matthew is therefore more interested in the relationship between hearing and doing than in that between hearing and understanding. Understanding is important because it is required for responsible action (cf. Matthew's omission of the disciples' incomprehension described in Mark 6:52; 8:17; or the positive statement in Matt. 13:51), but hearing and understanding must result in bearing fruit (13:23). The Sermon on the Mount in particular is not concerned with ideas or attitudes but with action. It is the disciples' good works that make them the "salt of the earth" and the "light of the world" (5:13–16). The guidelines for these actions, according to 7:24, 26; 28:20, are provided by Jesus' deeds as well as his words, which are congruent with each other (cf., e.g., 5:4 with 11:29; 5:39 with 26:52; 6:10 with 26:42–43). This brings us once more to the question of how these guidelines are related to the law and particularly to the Jewish interpretation of the law.

3.4 As we have already suggested, the "more" of 5:20 refers not only to the community's practice of what Pharisaism only teaches, but also to what is taught. This "more" implies a messianic corrective to the Jewish law as interpreted by the scribes and Pharisees (on the position of the Sadducees, cf. 16:12). Of course the will of God must be done under all circumstances. For Matthew as for Jesus, what God's will requires is no longer simply identical with Halakhah as taught by the Pharisees (despite 23:3). This is shown by the great value set on the teaching of the community (cf. 5:19; also 5:2; 7:29;

28. See Hummel, *Auseinandersetzung*, 12ff.
29. Trilling, *Israel*, 58ff.

18:20) and its difference from the teaching of the Pharisees (16:2; cf. also 15:12–14). Above all it is shown by the so-called antitheses in 5:21–48 (cf. above, 66ff.). For Matthew Jesus' "but I say to you" is the Messiah's protest against a mistaken interpretation of the law given at Sinai, but not against the law itself. Matthew does not gloss over the fact that Jesus' protest does affect the words of the Torah themselves (see the third, fifth, and sixth antitheses; also 19:8). He understands Jesus' words, however, not as abrogating the law but as reinterpreting it fundamentally so as to reveal its true intention.[30]

Elsewhere, too, Matthew mitigates the abrogation of the law. This is especially clear where we find Jesus not abrogating the law but radicalizing it. We may cite the reinterpretation of the first antithesis, where a scale of derogatory terms appears alongside anger. Matthew probably understood this addition as a concrete illustration, and also expanded the admonition positively by adding the demand for reconciliation (cf. 18:21–22). The fourth antithesis similarly appears to tolerate a minor oath formula or its equivalent, although still prohibiting an actual oath. In both cases it is not clear whether the changes stem from Matthew or the tradition on which he drew. In 5:32, the addition of "unchastity" (probably marital infidelity on the part of the wife) as grounds for divorce is more likely to derive from the evangelist himself. The same concession (albeit differently worded) appears in 19:9. The effect, however, is not to permit divorce in general but to limit it to a marriage that has been destroyed by a wife's adultery.

Although this casuistry sometimes contradicts Jewish interpretation of the law, it also represents conscious or unconscious assimilation. It remains an open question whether "accommodation" is the proper term,[31] but it is also uncertain whether all the antitheses are meant in fact as concrete applications of the law of love.[32] It is certainly true that for Matthew they unfold the meaning of the Torah, which culminates in the law of love.

4. For Matthew, as for Jesus, the real standard for correctly interpreting the law is the law of love. Therefore in borrowing the commandments of the Decalogue from Mark, he has them culminate in the law of love (19:19); the sixth antithesis similarly climaxes the series of antitheses. Antinomianism also can make love grow cold. Perfection, however, comes not through the law but through love. In 5:48, citing the commandment to love enemies, Matthew also incorporates the idea of imitating the Father, but changes its substance. In the original form of these words in Luke 6:36, the Father's mercy is to be imitated. Matthew reads instead: "Be perfect, as your heavenly Father is perfect." In 19:21, too, the notion of "perfection" has been introduced redactionally into the pericope of the rich young man.

---

30. Christian Dietzfelbinger, "Die Antithesen der Bergpredigt im Verständnis des Matthäus," *ZNW* 70 (1979): 1–15; Thysman, *Communauté*, 35ff.

31. Cf. Thysman, *Communauté*, 55: "une concession pastorale."

32. Dietzfelbinger, "Antithesen," 14.

Much ink has been spilled over this notion of perfection. It does not mean painstaking fulfillment of the law as in pietistic perfectionism (cf. the importance of humility and lowliness for the disciples: 11:25ff.; 18:3–4), nor does it refer to an elitist double standard. It should be interpreted in the sense of Hebrew *tamin* and *shalim* as meaning "whole, without division." It refers either to all the instructions of Jesus or—as its position immediately following the last antithesis suggests—intensive or extensive perfection of love.[33]

There is much additional evidence that Matthew considers the law of love as the true standard for interpreting the law. Just as it occupies a climactic position concluding the series of antitheses, so the golden rule is restated in 7:12 as the sum and quintessence of the "law and the prophets." For Matthew, too, it is more than a plausible rule of intelligent self-interest; it is, as it were, a commentary on the "as yourself" of 22:39 and above all a summary restatement of the law and the prophets. Finally, Matthew addresses the tradition of the law of love in his own fashion. Whereas Mark states that the law of love is the "second" commandment after the commandment to love God (Mark 12:31), Matthew states that it is "like" the first and greatest commandment (Matt. 22:38), thus explicitly emphasizing that love of others is equal with love of God. In addition he goes on to say that all the law and the prophets depend on these two commandments (22:40), on which they agree.[34]

However Matthew emphasizes the commandment to love enemies (5:43ff.), for him the law of love applies above all to the internal life of the community and even the details of its organization. In chapter 18, for example, he emphasizes the responsibility of the community toward its members who have gone astray (18:12–14); in his outline of church discipline, despite the final recourse of exclusion from the community (18:17), he assigns the climactic position to unlimited readiness to forgive.

That Matthew sees the law of love as the criterion by which, for example, cultic and ceremonial regulations are to be judged is shown by the obvious importance he attaches to Hos. 6:6, "I desire mercy, and not sacrifice," which he incorporates twice into his tradition (9:13; 12:7).

5. In each case the context of the interpolation is a conflict over ceremonial legalism. Citation of Hos. 6:6 in 9:13 serves to support and legitimize table fellowship with tax collectors and sinners, to which the Pharisees objected because it abrogates the Jewish laws governing ritual purity. In 21:14, similarly, Jesus heals the blind and the lame in the temple, although 2 Sam. 5:8 forbids them to enter the house of God (similarly at Qumran). In 12:7, the quotation from Hosea appears in the context of the pericope describing the disciples' plucking of grain on the Sabbath. Since Matthew explicitly introduces into the Markan text a reference to the disciples' hunger (12:1),

---

33. Gerhard Delling, "teleios," *TDNT* 8:73–74.
34. Barth, "Understanding," 75ff.

transgression of the Sabbath commandment for humanitarian reasons is permitted (cf. 12:12). The law of love takes precedence over the Sabbath, even though 24:20 probably indicates that Matthew's community generally observed the Sabbath. Nowhere, in fact, do we find an attack on the ceremonial law in principle.

In 5:23–24, similarly, the necessity of reconciliation takes precedence over cultic obligations without suspending them in principle. If we interpret the passage from the perspective of Matthew's purpose, we see that here, too, everything depends on love as the critical principle governing choice and interpretation. Therefore 23:23 declares woe upon the scribes and Pharisees: "Woe . . . to you hypocrites, for you tithe mint and dill and cumin, and have neglected the weightier matters of the law, justice and mercy and faith." The "weightier matters" are not the requirements that are harder to fulfill, but the more important matters. The comparative is important. Mercy takes precedence over cultic considerations. But Matthew adds explicitly: "These you ought to have done, without neglecting the others" (v. 24).

Apart from these instances of conflict, Matthew exhibits a conservative attitude toward the temple and the sacrificial cult.[35] It is true that the temple has lost the central position it has in Judaism. Indeed, the destruction of Jerusalem and the temple is probably understood as punishment for rejecting the prophets and crucifying Jesus (cf. 27:24–25, 51; 22:7; it is no accident that the destruction of the temple is predicted in 24:2, immediately after the attack on the Pharisees in chap. 23, especially 23:38). This does not alter the fact, however, that Matthew never spiritualizes the temple, nor does he treat it with an attitude of indifference, skepticism, or enlightenment. It is done away with because of something greater (cf. 12:6: "Something greater than the temple is here"). The temple is surpassed, not discredited.

6.1 Many scholars have stated that Matthew saw in Jesus the bringer of a new law. This does not mean, of course, that he promulgated a new law either analogous or antithetical to the law of Moses. Matthew so insists on the identity of this law with the law of Sinai that the Sermon on the Mount does not seek to promulgate a new or better law, but the law of Moses newly interpreted and revealed in its true meaning by the Messiah. The Moses typology of the infancy narratives and the mountain recalling Sinai in 5:1 suggest that Jesus rightly understands and interprets Moses.[36]

The question that arises with respect to both Jesus and Paul is whether Matthew's vehement opposition to antinomianism is not itself legalistic, threatening to drown out the message of Jesus. Although the attack on antinomian and libertinistic tendencies and the insistence on works are justified, there is a problem: the works themselves are not unambiguous and

---

35. Simonsen, "Auffassung," 58, 60; Hummel, *Auseinandersetzung*, 76ff.; for a different view, see Strecker, *Weg*, 32–33, 135.
36. Barth, "Understanding," 153ff.

may hide a wolf in sheep's clothing. Paul, for example, saw this danger more clearly. It is therefore unnecessary to brand Matthew a precursor of early Catholicism.[37] It is necessary, however, to insist even more absolutely than Matthew on the centrality of love as the standard by which all else is judged if the substance of the "better righteousness" is to avoid the temptation of legalism.

6.2 As we have already seen, it would be wrong to interpret Matthew simply as an exponent of a spirituality based on merit. Further evidence appears in the Beatitudes and perhaps also in 7:7–12.[38] In his commentary, Grundmann has suggested that 7:7–12 is meant to summarize all that has gone before. If so, the thrust of the passage would be that what Jesus reveals as the Father's will in the Sermon on the Mount cannot be fulfilled without prayer. This would make it clear: "The better righteousness is ultimately the gift of God, vouchsafed to those who ask."[39]

It would be wrong in any case to say that Matthew reduces the gospel to ethical terms. Even Walter's claim that the Beatitudes in 5:3ff. illustrate the two tablets of the Decalogue or the double law of love is open to question. In my opinion, they do not function simply as "entrance requirements" or a "list of eschatological virtues," but also as a recollection of the promise, intended to comfort and encourage the community.[40] This is true even though Matthew includes ethical elements, establishing an intimate connection between promise and requirement, indeed to the point that the ethical requirement predominates.

The Matthaean additions to the tradition of the Beatitudes are highly characteristic and make it difficult to call the latter a catalogue of virtues. The first addition, "in spirit" in 5:3, singles out the spiritually poor (not those who freely accept material poverty), who stand before God as beggars and let him fill their empty hands (cf. Isa. 61:1–2; 57:15). This jibes with the description of the disciples as "little," that is, lowly, weak, and helpless (see their appeal for help in 8:25 and 14:30), and with the call to become children, that is, dependent. The third Beatitude also refers to the meek and lowly, who must rely on God.[41]

6.3 The second addition, "and thirst after righteousness" in v. 6, does not refer, I think, to moral probity or any ethical quality; it is addressed to those who are driven by a thirst for the righteousness of God, which will not be

37. As is done by Schulz, *Stunde*, 191.

38. For the Beatitudes, see Nikolaus Walter, "Die Bearbeitung der Seligpreisungen durch Matthäus," *StEv* 4 (TU 102) (1968): 246–58; Hubert Frankemölle, "Die Makarismen (Mt. 5,1–12; Lk. 6,20–23," *BZ* 15 (1971): 52–75; Georg Strecker, "Die Makarismen der Bergpredigt," *NTS* 17 (1970–71): 225–75; Robert A. Guelich, "The Matthean Beatitudes: 'Entrance Requirements' or Eschatological Blessings?" *JBL* 95 (1976): 415–34.

39. On Matt. 7:7–12, see Walter Grundmann, *Das Evangelium nach Matthäus*, ThHK 1.

40. Burchard, "Versuch," 418.

41. See Barth, "Understanding," 123–24.

satisfied until the eschaton. Such a thirst, of course, is not just a Platonic ideal. Those whom it seizes it dominates here and now, making them cry out for divine justice but also to strive for it. In any case, righteousness is a gift of grace, not just a requirement to be fulfilled.[42]

In 5:20 and 6:1, the genitive "your" specifies the righteousness as being that of the disciples; 6:33 ("But seek first his kingdom and his righteousnes") makes it clear, however, that this righteousness is conceived of not merely in human terms but as God's righteousness, since "his" refers to the heavenly Father mentioned in v. 32. It is important to analyze this association of righteousness with the kingdom. Strecker himself asks[43] whether the parallelism between righteousness and the kingdom is not significant for understanding the notion of righteousness, since for Matthew the kingdom of God is a present entity, not something yet to come. He nevertheless follows the analogy of James 1:20, arguing that for Matthew, too, righteousness is a human attribute brought about by human means. The kingdom, he claims, belongs to the future and righteousness to the present; their relationship is that of cause (righteousness) and effect (kingdom). Even the word order of 6:33 suggests the contrary: seeking righteousness is the result of seeking the kingdom of God. But it is not really clear that the parallelism should be interpreted as representing cause and effect.

In my opinion, 5:6 also casts doubt on this interpretation. We must agree with Bornkamm[44] that the blessed of the beatitude are those who cannot live without the righteousness God alone can vouchsafe and establish in the world. Since for Matthew, however, righteousness undoubtedly means also the conduct of the disciples in accordance with God's will, it is better to say with Eichholz[45] that the beatitude refers to those who hunger and thirst for the realization of God's righteousness and justice throughout all the earth, that is, those who look for God to set this world aright and draw appropriate conclusions from their own expectation.

C. THE CHRISTIAN LIFE IN LUKE

1.1 According to the programmatic statement of Luke's prologue (Luke 1:1–4), his purpose is to record a relatively complete and systematic account intended as a reliable basis for instruction and tradition within the church. His increasing distance from the original events that laid the groundwork for

42. See Martin J. Fiedler, "'Gerechtigkeit' im Matthäus-Evangelium," *Theologische Versuche* 8 (1977): 63–75; in the Old Testament, Fiedler points out, righteousness means both "salvation" or "deliverance" and "right conduct." Cf. also Peter Stuhlmacher, *Gerechtigkeit Gottes bei Paulus*, FRLANT 87 (Göttingen: Vandenhoeck & Ruprecht, 1965), 189ff.

43. *Weg*, 154.

44. Bornkamm, *Jesus of Nazareth*, 76; cf. Fiedler, "Gerechtigkeit," 66; Kretzer, *Herrschaft*, 269–70.

45. George Eichholz, *Auslegung der Bergpredigt*, 2d ed., BSt 46 (Neukirchen: Neukirchener Verlag, 1970), 44. See also Ernst Käsemann, "The Beginnings of Christian Theology," in *NT Questions of Today* (London: SCM Press, 1969), 82–107, esp. 104–5.

Christianity makes him seek to give assurance by harkening back to the basic Jesus tradition. He exhibits an unmistakable tendency to provide historical warrant, guaranteed by a chain of tradition, for the Christian faith and Christian life. Luke constructs a schema of sacred history in which God's action is manifest in secular history. He does this to show that his entire narrative took place within the framework of the real world, but above all to describe the divine plan of salvation and establish a comprehensive framework of sacred history. It remains unclear whether he intended to describe the time of Jesus as an age of salvation already past, or even to depict the early days of the church as an era that has come to an end.

According to Conzelmann,[46] Luke deliberately distinguishes his picture of the early church from his own age. This distancing has ethical consequences: the summaries in Acts, for example, do not present ideals for the present. On the other hand, Conzelmann himself retreats from this position when he states that Luke distinguishes teachings of the Lord meant only for the immediate situation (e.g., the missionary discourse) from teachings meant to be permanent, such as the Sermon on the Plain[47] or the "timeless" exhortation in Luke 3:10–14.[48] Such distinctions, required by the passage of time, have already been noted in Mark (cf. Mark 2:19–20) and are certainly also present in Luke (for example, the evolution of the mission to the Jews into a mission to the Gentiles, or the contrast between observance of the law in the infancy narrative and partial freedom from the law in Acts 15). On the whole, however, they are the exception. The theory of Schottroff and Stegemann[49] that Luke 6:20b–26 is addressed to the disciples while vv. 27ff. are addressed to "those that hear" can hardly be maintained. According to Luke, the Sermon on the Plain is addressed to "a great crowd of disciples" (6:17; cf. v. 20), distinct from the Twelve: in other words, all Christians. The new beginning in v. 27 does not envision a different audience, but is due to the intervening woes addressed to the rich. In chapter 12, too, Luke exhibits no interest in distinguishing various groups addressed.

Even the life of Jesus is a prototype for the way of the church. Luke's concern for continuity with the time of Jesus is illustrated, for example, by the proclamation of the kingdom not only by Jesus (Luke 4:43; 8:1; 9:11; 16:16) but also by the disciples both before (Luke 9:2, 60) and after Easter (Acts 8:12; 20:25; 28:23, 31). For Luke, too, this kingdom of God is a central element of ethics (cf. Luke 18:29 in contrast to Mark 10:29), even if his understanding of the kingdom differs from Jesus'. Above all, "repentance," one of Luke's favorite themes, is identical both before (Luke 5:32; 15:7) and

---

46. *Theology*, 14–16; similarly Sanders, "Ethics," 25.
47. *Theology*, 13.
48. Ibid., 102.
49. L. Schottroff and W. Stegemann, *Jesus von Nazareth—Hoffnung der Armen*, 92–93.

after Easter (Luke 24:27; Acts 2:38; 3:19; 11:18; 17:30), as well as the consequent "fruits" (Luke 3:8) or "works" (Acts 26:20).

1.2 Despite all Luke's sense of the past, his awareness of the passage of time and distance from the beginnings, the crucial element is his sense of continuity—in other words, his awareness of the need to make these beginnings real in the present moment, because God's work continues in the present of the church. Just as Jesus was led by the Spirit (Luke 4:1ff.), so is the church (Acts 8:29, 39; 10:19; 11:12, 28; etc.). In the era of the church, the proclamation of the kingdom both before and after Easter is intended not to shift the kingdom to a far-off time but to bring it near in the present (cf. Luke 10:9). Although it is not robbed of its future aspect (cf. Luke 19:11), it is identified primarily with "the Lord Jesus Christ" (Acts 28:31). In the preaching of the kingdom, the kingdom is present, and therefore also Jesus himself (Luke 10:16).

In sum, the course of sacred history prefigured in the ministry of the earthly Jesus repeats itself in the experience of the church, and the church is the church only when it makes way for Jesus and the kingdom, as well as for the ethics of Jesus. Luke's exemplary christology and ethics (cf. Luke 22:27 or the Passion, described as the paradigm of a Christian art of dying [*ars moriendi*]) are based on the existence of an analogy between the time of Jesus and the time of the church. Both are a time of salvation and a history of promises fulfilled (cf. the proemium or Luke 4:21). In Jesus' good news for sinners and the poor, Luke gives full weight to "by grace alone" (*sola gratia*).[50] Despite a substantial tendency to moralize, he has preserved many examples of how God's mercy calls people to lifelong service in holiness and righteousness (Luke 1:72, 74) and to show mercy in turn (Luke 6:36), although this transformation of life is itself a prerequisite or an element of salvation (cf. Luke 19:8 with 19:9 or Luke 7:47a; Acts 3:26).

2.1 Especially urgent for Luke is the problem of ethics in the light of the delayed Parousia. Many exegetes even maintain that this delay led him to eliminate the eschatological perspective. It is undoubtedly true that Luke no longer shares the original form of expectation that the end was at hand (cf. Luke 19:11; 21:18). An interim has come between present and future (cf. 19:12). This does not mean, however, that he has given up waiting for the Parousia, not to mention the future, but he has shifted his emphasis to patience (cf. 8:15) and readiness (cf. 12:35ff.; 21:36). It is wrong to ask about the day (Acts 1:7) and the hour of the Lord's coming; they are uncertain (Luke 12:35). But the sudden return of the Son of man (17:20–21) bringing final judgment makes Luke, too, warn against losing oneself in worldly affairs (cf. 17:24ff.). In addition, for Luke expectation of the resurrection and

50. See, for example, Walter Klaiber, "Eine lukanische Fassung des sola gratia," in *Rechtfertigung* (Festschrift Ernst Käsemann), ed. J. Friedrich, W. Pöhlmann, and P. Stuhlmacher (Tübingen: Mohr, 1976), 211–28, esp. 226.

judgment are eschatological motives for Christian conduct. The resurrection, for example, will bring reward to those who have invited the poor, the maimed, the lame, and the blind (14:14), and according to Acts 24:15–16, hope for the resurrection is the reason why the Lukan Paul "takes pains to have a clear conscience before God and before men." The judgment to come rules out judging others. Acts 24:25 associates it with "justice and self-control."

2.2 Far more than by eschatology, however, Luke's theology is dominated by the idea of the Spirit, sent by the exalted Lord himself (Luke 24:49; Acts 2:33).[51] Besides the traditional association of the Spirit with prophecy (Acts 2:18), Luke makes the Spirit directly responsible for instructing the church and its members. He does not, however, introduce the Spirit into ethics as the driving force behind the new life. The guiding intervention of the Spirit is intended primarily to realize the divine plan of salvation, although this purpose does of course have ethical implications.

In Acts 10:19 and 11:12, for example, intervention of the Spirit is responsible for overcoming the distinction between clean and unclean food and for including Gentiles in the Christian community. In 13:2, the Spirit sets Barnabas and Saul apart and in 16:6, the Spirit forbids preaching in Asia, and so forth. For Luke this intervention of the Spirit does not rule out human mediation but rather implies it (cf. Acts 15:28, which mentions the Spirit and apostolic authority in the same breath). Nor does it render responsible human choice superfluous (cf. Acts 5:3; 21:4).[52] The way of the church as a whole is determined by Scripture (cf. Luke 24:44) and divine providence (cf. Acts 2:23; 4:28; etc.). Primarily, however, this holds for its overall framework and general outline. It hardly applies to ethical decisions. We do not find a special basis for ethics apart from tradition.

3.1 It is undoubtedly true that parenesis had special significance for Luke. Matthew's Sermon on the Mount is more parenetic than Luke's Sermon on the Plain, which has a more eschatological and soteriological perspective, but this is of little importance for Luke's ethics, since his hand is scarcely visible here.[53] It is nevertheless striking how he preserves the eschatological element and how little interest he evinces in the Old Testament law and legalism. The Sermon on the Plain does show clearly, however, that the law—which for Luke belongs to the era of the old covenant (cf. Luke 16:16)—does not play any special role in Luke's ethics, at least for gentile Christians (cf. Acts 15:10; 21:24–25). Of course this does not mean that the law was simply abrogated as an ethical norm (Luke 16:17), especially since the apostolic decree lists a minimal catalogue of requirements that are still binding even on gentile Chris-

51. Eduard Schweizer, "pneuma," *TDNT* 6:404–5.
52. Ibid., 407 n. 481.
53. See Hans W. Bartsch, "Feldrede und Bergpredigt," *ThZ* 16 (1960): 5–18; reprinted in *Entmythologisierende Auslegung*, ThF 26 (Hamburg: Reich, 1962), 116–24.

tians (cf. Acts 15:20 and 10:35).[54] On the whole, however, there is not much emphasis on the law, and passages like Luke 18:9 show that the law alone is not enough (with respect to v. 8, cf. Lev. 6:1ff.[55]).

Despite Luke's tendency to moralize, we should also hesitate to speak of legalism. One cannot cite as evidence his consistent use of the plural "sins" (e.g., Luke 3:3; 7:37, 39), his use of the plurals "fruits" (Luke 3:8 in contrast to Matt. 3:8; elsewhere [3:9; 6:43; etc.] he uses the singular) and "works" (Acts 9:36; 26:20), or his emphasis on changing one's way of life (e.g., Luke 3:10ff.). Luke's substitution of "iniquity" for Matthew's "unlawfulness" (Luke 13:27; cf. also Luke 16:8–9; Acts 1:18) show that he is concerned not merely to define such notions as "sin" in theological terms but also to depict them concretely in the sense of ethical misconduct (cf. also "sin" in Luke 15:18, 21 and "sinner" in 7:39; cf. v. 47; 19:7–8). The great importance of parenesis is underlined by the frequent repetition of the characteristic question "What shall we do?" (Luke 3:10; 10:25; 16:3, 18:18; Acts 2:37; 16:30).

3.2 It is noteworthy that all the so-called exemplary narratives of the Synoptic tradition appear in the Gospel of Luke: the good Samaritan, the rich landowner, the rich man and poor Lazarus, the Pharisee and the tax collector (10:29ff.; 12:16ff.; 16:19ff.; 18:9ff.). These stories have no figurative aspect, but describe models of proper conduct. It has been suggested recently that the exemplary narratives originally did contain figurative elements and that only moralistic misunderstanding of Jesus' metaphorical discourse turned them into concrete illustrations of behavior.[56] We may leave this question open, because in any case Luke himself was not responsible for such alteration. He alone included them, however, thus showing how important such exemplary rules are for Christians with the passage of time.

Luke probably is responsible for the parenetic reshaping of such parables as that of the great banquet. In 14:21, he describes in detail those who are invited: the poor, the maimed, the blind, the lame. This corresponds precisely to 14:13 in the banquet discourse: "When you give a feast, invite the poor, the maimed, the lame, the blind." This latter passage is meant to make even the details of hospitality at breakfast or supper a concrete manifestation of love. Luke clearly interpreted the invitation he introduced into the parable in the same way.

3.3 We find additional manifestations of Luke's concern in his encouragement of humility and warning against lust for power (cf. Luke 1:51–52; 18:9ff.; 22:24ff.), as well as in his emphasis on commitment (cf. Luke 14:26; Acts 15:25) and renunciation of security (Luke 17:33). He also stresses the

---

54. See Georg Sellin, "Lukas als Gleichniserzähler," *ZNW* 66 (1975): 19–60, esp. 52ff.
55. O'Hanlon, "Story," 16.
56. See, for example, John Dominic Crossan, "Parable and Example in the Teaching of Jesus," *NTS* 18 (1972): 285ff.; for a contrary view, see Werner G. Kümmel, "Jesusforschung seit 1965, IV," *ThR* 43 (1978): 134–35, 136.

need for Christians to suffer. To the saying about taking up one's cross he adds the word "daily" (9:23), and Acts 14:22 states: "Through many tribulations we must enter the kingdom of God."

4.1 Luke is quite concerned to prove that the Christian religion does not represent any danger to the state: there are no grounds for accusing Christians of subversion or disrespect for the authority of the Roman Empire. We find clear traces of political apologetics throughout both parts of Luke's work, culminating in the famous last word of Acts: "unhindered" (28:31). Luke has a burning interest in seeing that Rome continues to concede this unhindered preaching. The first example is the advice given to various classes in the preaching of John the Baptist (Luke: 3:10–14), which Bultmann thinks resembles a catechism.[57] Those who have two loaves are exhorted in radical terms approaching the bare necessities of life to give one away and meet the needs of the hungry. At the same time, tax collectors and soldiers are told to remain within commonly accepted limits: tax collectors should not enrich themselves by collecting more than is due, and soldiers are told: "Rob no one by violence or by false accusation, and be content with your wages" (v. 14). The fruits of repentance (v. 8) are to be manifest in the social and political world in such a way as not to jeopardize its basic structures. The admonition not to rob or extort and to be content suggests that there is no conflict in principle between faith and military service, and indeed implies a fundamental loyalty. The statement in Luke 4:5–6 that Satan has power over all the kingdoms of the world must not be misunderstood as suggesting that the state is satanic.[58] This power has only been "delivered" to him.

Luke repeatedly stresses directly and indirectly that Jesus himself is politically innocuous. Herod wishes to see Jesus (Luke 9:7ff). The Roman centurion calls Jesus not Son of God but an innocent man (23:47). Luke 20:20 states explicitly that there were attempts to trap Jesus in subversive statements reflecting political messianism "so as to deliver him up to the authority and jurisdiction of the governor." Jesus, however, is anything but a Zealot or an agitator. Above all, the Roman procurator personally affirms Jesus' innocence three times and refuses categorically to condemn him (23:4, 14, 22). These declarations of Jesus' innocence from the mouth of Pilate are all the more important because Luke has the Jews accuse Jesus explicitly of agitation and refusal to pay tribute (23:2, 5). Luke maintains that these are false accusations, emphasizing again that the Jesus movement is politically innocuous.

4.2 The same point is made in Acts, above all through the example of Paul

57. Rudolf Bultmann, *History of the Synoptic Tradition*, rev. ed. (New York: Harper & Row, 1976), 145. See also Traugott Holtz, "Die Standespredigt Johannes des Täufers," in *Ruf und Antwort* (Festschrift Emil Fuchs) (Leipzig: Koehler & Amelang, 1964), 461–74.

58. On Luke 4:5–6, see Heinz Schürmann, *Das Lukasevangelium*, HThK 3/1; also Thériault, "Les dimensions," 214-15; for a different view, see Aland, "Verhältnis" (B5), 169.

and his correct conduct toward the Roman authorities. Here, too, the accusation—which Luke considers totally baseless—reads: "They are all acting against the decrees of Caesar, saying that there is another king, Jesus" (Acts 17:7). Many other passages also seek to show the accusation of endangering the state was false (e.g., Acts 18:12ff.; 25:18ff.; 26:31).

In reality—Luke wishes to show—the apostle and his message do not represent any threat to *pax romana*. Unprejudiced officials can only certify that—as Claudius Lysias writes to the governor Felix—the accusations brought by the Jews involve nothing more than internal disputes (Acts 23:29; cf. 24:5, 14; 25:19). Thus it is only logical for the authorities to intervene on behalf of the Christians to protect them from the excesses of the Jews (e.g., 18:12ff.; 22:23ff.). Christians are not involved in anything punishable by death or imprisonment (23:29; 25:25; 26:31); they do not incite to riot (24:12) or offend against Caesar (25:8). The representatives and authorities of the empire therefore treat Paul fairly or favorably; they respect his Roman citizenship (16:37ff.; 22:25ff.), apologize to him (16:39), save him from the religious violence of the Jews (23:10, 17), refuse to condemn him (23:29; 24:22; 25:24), and lighten the terms of his custody (24:23).

4.3 This is not to suggest, of course, that Luke is looking for an easy compromise or a solution that will avoid conflict at all costs. He includes critical sayings (e.g., Luke 3:19; 13:32–33), knows that circumstances may demand confession before kings and governors (Luke 12:11), and has Peter say that one must obey God rather than human authority (Acts 5:29; cf. 4:19). Indeed he emphasizes the necessity of following Jesus at the cost of one's own life (cf. Luke 14:26 with Matt. 10:37). But his dominant purpose is clearly to show that Christianity does not represent a political danger and to sue for the rights accorded by Rome, as illustrated by Paul's appeal to his Roman citizenship and to Caesar. But Luke must not be made out to be simply a conformist who trims his sails to the wind and agrees with everything. The contrary is illustrated by his interest in the importance of women in the church, which ran counter to certain tendencies of his own era.

5. It has been noted frequently that Luke displays a particular openness and sympathy toward women. In fact they play a remarkably central role in his work, and are equal before God to men in honor, ability, and responsibility.[59] This motif begins in the infancy narratives with Elizabeth, Mary, and Anna. It continues with the widows in Zarephath and Nain, the notorious sinner, the women who follow Jesus, Mary and Martha, and so forth. All these episodes appear only in Luke, and it is noteworthy that he introduces narratives concerning women in parallel with narratives concerning men. Acts emphasizes similarly that the Holy Spirit is poured out upon both men

---

59. See Helmut Flender, *Heil und Geschichte in der Theologie des Lukas*, BEvTh 41 (Münich: Kaiser, 1965), 15–16; Eugene H. Maly, "Women and the Gospel of Luke," *BTB* 10 (1980): 99–104; Schottroff, "Frauen" (B2), 121ff.

and women (2:17) and stresses the importance of women for the missionary work of the church (e.g., 18:26; 21:9). Here, too, we do not find any program for social reform, but in the special Lukan material Jesus' conduct transcends the typical androcentric barriers of the ancient world (cf. the unusual role of Martha and the words of the Magnificat in the mouth of a woman). In Luke, Jesus defends women "against forces that would reduce them to the role of housewife and mother."[60]

On the other hand, it is Luke who insists that in cases of conflict it may be necessary for a man to leave his wife (cf. Luke 14:20; 18:29), although this should not be understood to suggest that celibacy is an ideal or a duty. It can hardly be correct to interpret Luke 20:34–36 as meaning that marriage is what characterizes the "sons of this age." It is more likely that the phrase encompasses all people and that celibacy, as in Mark 12:25, is reserved for the age to come.[61]

6. Luke is greatly concerned with the problem of possessions and their renunciation, the proper place and use of worldly goods. This concern is illustrated by the exemplary narratives, which describe vividly how riches and possessions can stand in the way of salvation. Luke clearly included everything recorded by tradition concerning these questions. No one can serve both God and mammon (Luke 16:13): it is difficult for the rich to enter into the kingdom, more difficult than for a camel to go through the eye of a needle (18:24–25)—these and other sayings go back to Jesus himself, and above all the beatitude that calls the poor blessed (6:20). The woe pronounced against the rich (6:24) is also pre-Lukan. Luke himself sets the fulfillment of the promises of salvation for the poor in a context that transcends economics (4:18), but he does not thereby restrict poverty to the metaphorical signifi-cance of a "religious" category. Both social and religious alienation are overcome. Luke clearly resisted the temptation to mitigate the harshness of Jesus' sayings about riches.

Like Jesus, Luke does not simply espouse a fundamental ideal of poverty or universal renunciation of possessions. He is not concerned to discredit worldly goods but to warn against their danger and encourage their proper use. He condemns the egoistic view that what people have is their "own" (Luke 18:28; cf. "everything" in Mark and Matthew; also Acts 4:32) or is theirs to do with as they wish. Interestingly, Levi is said to have "left everything" and at the same time to have given a great feast (Luke 5:28–29). Naturally Luke also cautions against covetousness and greed (12:15; cf. also 3:11–13; 16:14), because life does not consist in abundance of possessions.

The social aspect, however, is more important than the individual aspect. Luke therefore inculcates above all the obligation to show charity and un-

60. Schottroff, "Frauen," 123, citing Luke 11:27–28 and 10:38ff.
61. Pace Schottroff and Stegemann, *Jesus*, 110; cf., however, Schrage and Gerstenberger, *Frau* (B2), 144.

limited readiness to make sacrifices on behalf of the poor and dispossessed. It is at this point that we find several redactional alterations. Luke 18:22 ("Sell all that you have and distribute to the poor"), except for the Lukan "all" (cf. Luke 5:11, 28; 14:33), is taken directly from Mark 10:21 (but cf. Luke 18:28 with Mark 10:28). Luke himself, however, clearly added 12:33: "Sell your possessions and give alms." Degenhardt is wrong to limit this injunction to the leadership (cf. v. 32).[62] The "disciples" are not officials but all the faithful (cf. Acts 11:26). Nor are such verses as Luke 14:26–27, 33 addressed to a "special group" or an "inner circle" of Jesus' followers.[63] Luke's focus on the Twelve and the apostles is irrelevant here. In the dispute with the Pharisees, who cleanse the outside of the cup and of the dish but are inwardly full of extortion and wickedness, Luke adds: "But give for alms those things which are within; and behold, everything is clean to you" (11:41). Such charity renders questions of what is clean and unclean superfluous and puts cultic ceremonies in their proper perspective. The conduct of Zaccheus, who gives half his goods to the poor (19:8), is exemplary. Luke may also have in mind "economic equalization between wealthy and needy Christians within the community,"[64] like that described in Acts 11:28, where relief is sent to the poor according to the ability of each. In addition the application at the end of the story of the rich landowner (Luke 12:21) may be Lukan. Here it is laying up treasures "for oneself" that is castigated, that is, self-centeredness and unwillingness to put one's possessions at the disposal of others.

The application concluding the parable of the unjust steward is probably pre-Lukan, but quite in the spirit of the evangelist: "Make friends for yourselves by means of unrighteous mammon" (Luke 16:9). Its interpretation is disputed, but the most likely explanation, in my opinion, agrees with Luke that worldly goods should be used in the service of love. What matters is to have the right attitude and to show charity. Wealth and possessions are unjust when they are "served" and not shared. This gives rise to injustice, especially when more is accumulated than one needs[65] (see also Luke 8:3; 10:38ff.; Acts 9:36; 10:2; 20:35).

There is no hint that all these sayings are responses to an "extreme situation" and a reaction to persecution of the community, as suggested by Schmithals.[66]

Of course the motivating force has nothing to do with the dream of the simple life common among the rich.[67] The disciples' total and voluntary renunciation of possessions illustrates, I think, a kind of tendency to cast

62. *Lukas*, 87.
63. Cf. Mealand, *Poverty and Expectation in the Gospels*, 58.
64. Schottroff and Stegemann, *Jesus*, 138.
65. Cf. Nickelsburg, "Riches," 336–37, 341, according to whom Luke's sympathy for the poor parallels his sympathy for the outcasts.
66. "Lukas," 164–65.
67. Cf. Schottroff and Stegemann, *Jesus*, 106–7.

them in a heroic mold (notice the omission of such verses as Mark 14:50). It is meant to encourage members of the community not to become attached to goods and possessions, and possibly also[68] to criticize the luxury of the rich.

The example of responsibility for the poor basically shows that love, to Luke, is always concrete and practical. In particular he interprets the injunction to love enemies as doing good and lending money without expectation of return (Luke 6:27, 35). He also emphasizes that love knows no social, political, or racial boundaries and dares to ignore prejudice and convention (cf. once again the exhortation to invite the poor to dinner [14:12ff.] and the story of the Good Samaritan [10:25ff.]). Of course Luke is equally concerned for charity within the community itself, as we see in the account of how relief was provided (Acts 11:29–30) as well as in the accounts describing community of goods (Acts 2:44–45; 4:32). Luke interprets community of goods in the community as exemplary, an implicit call to surrender worldly possessions to those in need, not as a demonstration of Christian unity.[69] The sayings quoted force us to this conclusion. The unity of the church cannot be established solely on the spiritual and religious plane. Even if Luke no longer considers the community of goods a realistic possibility for his own church, it has parenetic implications. Paul's programmatic farewell discourse at Miletus, which resembles a testament, confirms Luke's concern always to stand up for the weak and remember the Lord's saying that it is more blessed to give than to receive (Acts 20:35). This certainly implies a social dimension.

Of course it would be mistaken simply to apply the words of Luke's Gospel to social problems. But to declare that the category "social" is anachronistic and alien to Luke[70] is at least as misguided as to call him the "socialistic evangelist."[71] Luke knows nothing of a conflict between charity, which operates between individuals, and social welfare, which allegedly springs from the head, not from the heart, and is governed by natural law. For Luke, "poverty" is far from being an exclusively religious category. In his commentary on Luke 4:18, Ernst rightly maintains that "deliverance" is understood here as "liberation from social and economic pressures."[72] According to Luke, this is where the reversal of fortunes for the poor and needy can and must begin.

---

68. Ibid., 108–9.
69. As suggested by Conzelmann, *Nie Mitte der Zeit*, 218.
70. Josef Ernst, "Das Evangelium nach Lukas—kein soziales Evangelium," *ThG* 67 (1977): 415-21.
71. J. Schmid.
72. Josef Ernst, *Das Evangelium nach Lukas*, RNT, 171.

IV

THE CHRISTOLOGICAL
ETHICS OF PAUL

BIBLIOGRAPHY

General

Bornkamm, Günther. *Paulus.* 4th ed. UTB 119D. Stuttgart: Kohlhammer, 1979. Eng. trans. of 1st ed.: *Paul.* New York: Harper & Row, 1971.

Campenhausen, Hans von. *Die Begründung kirchlicher Entscheidungen beim Apostel Paulus.* 2d ed. Sitzungsberichte der Heidelberger Akademie der Wissenschaften, 1957/2. Heidelberg: Winter, 1965.

Dodd, C. H. "The Ethics of the Pauline Epistles." In *The Evolution of Ethics,* ed. E. H. Sneath, 293–326. New Haven: Yale Univ. Press, 1927.

Eichholz, Georg. *Die Theologie des Paulus im Umriss.* Neukirchen: Neukirchener Verlag, 1972.

Enslin, Morton Scott. *The Ethics of Paul.* Nashville: Abingdon Press, 1957 [1930].

Furnish, Victor Paul. *Theology and Ethics in Paul.* Nashville: Abingdon Press, 1968.

Hasenstab, Rudolf. *Modelle paulinischer Ethik.* Mainz: Matthias-Grünewald, 1972.

Juncker, Alfred. *Die Ethik des Apostels Paulus.* 2 vols. Halle: Niemeyer, 1904–19.

Käsemann, Ernst. *An die Römer.* 4th ed. HNT 8a. Tübingen: Mohr, 1980. Eng. trans. of 3d ed.: *Commentary on Romans.* Grand Rapids: Eerdmans, 1980.

————. *Paulinische Perspektiven.* 2d ed. Tübingen: Mohr, 1972. Eng. trans. of 1st ed.: *Perspectives on Paul.* Philadelphia: Fortress Press, 1971.

Luz, Ulrich. "Eschatologie und Frieden." In *Eschatologie und Frieden* (IA), 2:225–81.

Merk, Otto. *Handeln aus Glauben.* MThSt 5. Marburg: Elwert, 1968.

Preisker, Herbert. *Ethos* (B). Pp. 168–95.

Sanders, Jack T. *Ethics* (B). Pp. 47–66.

Schnackenburg, Rudolf. *Botschaft* (B). Pp. 209–46.

Schrage, Wolfgang. *Die konkreten Einzelgebote in der paulinischen Paränese.* Gütersloh: Mohn, 1961.

Stalder, Kurt. *Das Werk des Geistes in der Heiligung bei Paulus.* Zurich: EVZ, 1962.

Strecker, Georg. *Glaube* (B). Pp. 17–35.

Theissen, Gerd. *The Social Setting of Pauline Christianity: Essays on Corinth.* Ed. and trans. with an introduction by John H. Schütz. Philadelphia: Fortress Press; Edinburgh: T. & T. Clark, 1982.

Wendland, Heinz-Dieter. *Ethik* (B). Pp. 49–88.

A. The Basis of Pauline Ethics (pp. 167–86)

Bornkamm, Günther. "Taufe und neues Leben (Röm 6)." In *Das Ende des Gesetzes,* 34–50. BEvTh 16. Munich: Kaiser, 1952. English: "Baptism and New Life in Paul." In *Early Christian Experience.* New York: Harper & Row; London: SCM Press, 1969. Pp. 71–86.

Bottorff, J. F. "The Relation of Justification and Ethics in the Pauline Epistles." *SJTh* 26 (1973): 421–30.

Bultmann, Rudolf. "Das Problem der Ethik bei Paulus." *ZNW* 23 (1924): 123–40. Reprinted in *Exegetica,* 36–54. Tübingen: Mohr, 1967.

Gäumann, Niklaus. *Taufe und Ethik.* BEvTh 47. Munich: Kaiser, 1967.

Grabner-Haider, Anton. *Paraklese und Eschatologie bei Paulus.* NTA 12. Münster: Aschendorff, 1968.

Grech, Prosper. "Christological Motives in Pauline Ethics." In *Paul de Tarse,* ed. Lorenzo De Lorenzi, 541–58. Série monographique de Benedictina, section Paulinienne, 1. Rome: Abbaye de S. Paul, 1979.

Halter, Hans. *Taufe und Ethos.* FThSt 106. Freiburg: Herder, 1977.

Käsemann, Ernst. "Gottesdienst im Alltag der Welt (Zu Röm. 12)." In *Exegetische Versuche und Besinnungen* 2:198–204. 2 vols. Göttingen: Vandenhoeck & Ruprecht, 1960–64. English: "Worship in Everyday Life: A Note on Romans 12." In *Questions of Today,* 188–95. Philadelphia: Fortress, 1969.

———. "Gottesgerechtigkeit bei Paulus." In *Exegetische Versuche* 2:181–93. English: "'The Righteousness of God' in Paul." In *NT Questions,* 168–82.

Keck, Leander E. "Justification of Ungodly and Ethics." In *Rechtfertigung* (Festschrift Ernst Käsemann), ed. J. Friedrich, W. Pöhlman, and P. Stuhlmacher, 199–209. Tübingen: Mohr, 1976.

Körtner, Ulrich H. J. "Rechtfertigung und Ethik bei Paulus." *WuD* 16 (1981): 93–109.

Laub, Franz. *Eschatologische Verkündigung und Lebensgestaltung nach Paulus.* BU 10. Regensburg: Pustet, 1973.

Romaniuk, Kazimierz. "Les motifs parénétiques dans les écrits pauliniennes." *NK* 10 (1968): 191–207.

Schlier, Heinrich. "Vom Wesen der apostolischen Ermahnung nach Röm. 12,1–2." In *Die Zeit der Kirche.* Vol. 1 of *Exegetische Aufsätze und Vorträge,* 74–89. 2d ed. Freiburg: Herder, 1958.

Soden, Hans von. "Sakrament und Ethik bei Paulus." In *Urchristentum und Geschichte,* 239–75. Tübingen: Mohr, 1951.

Steensgaard, P. "Erwägungen zum Problem Evangelium und Paränese bei Paulus." *ASTI* 10 (1975–76): 110–28.

Wendland, Heinz-Dieter. "Ethik und Eschatologie in der Theologie des Paulus." *NKS* 41 (1930): 757–83, 793–811.

———. "Das Wirken des heiligen Geistes in den Gläubigen nach Paulus." *ThLZ* 77 (1952): 457–70.

B. The Nature and Structure of the New Life (pp. 186–98)

Bornkamm, Günther. "Glaube und Vernunft bei Paulus." In *Studien zu Antike und Urchristentum,* 119–37. 3d ed. BEvTh 28. Munich: Kaiser, 1970. English: "Faith and Reason in Paul." In *Early Christian Experience* (IVC), 29–46.

Niederwimmer, Kurt. *Der Begriff der Freiheit im NT.* Berlin: Töpelmann, 1966. Pp. 168–220.

Richardson, Peter. *Paul's Ethic of Freedom.* Philadelphia: Westminster Press, 1979. Pp. 79–98.

Ridderbos, Herman. *Paulus.* Wuppertal: Brockhaus, 1970. Pp. 184–204. English: *Paul.* Grand Rapids: Eerdmans, 1975. Pp. 105–52.

Schrage, Wolfgang. *Einzelgebote* (IV). Pp. 49ff.

Schürmann, Heinz. "Die Gemeinde des Neuen Bundes als Quellort des sittlichen Erkennens nach Paulus." *Cath* 26 (1972): 15–37. Also appeared in *Orientierungen am NT,* 64–88. Düsseldorf: Patmos, 1968.

———. "Haben die paulinischen Wertungen und Weisungen Modellcharakter?" In *Orientierungen,* 89–116.

Schweizer, Eduard. "Ethischer Pluralismus im NT." *EvTh* 35 (1975): 397–401. (See also my comments ibid., 402–7.)

Sessolo, Pietro. "Bleibende Bedeutung der paulinischen Gebote." *ED* 32 (1979): 191–210.

C. Material Criteria (pp. 198–217)

Austgen, Robert J. *Natural Motivation in the Pauline Epistles.* 2d ed. Notre Dame, Ind.: Univ. Notre Dame Press, 1969.

Drane, John W. "Tradition, Law and Ethics in Pauline Theology." *NT* 16 (1974): 167–78.

Dungan, David L. *The Sayings of Jesus in the Churches of Paul.* Philadelphia: Fortress Press, 1971.

Gibbs, John G. *Creation and Redemption.* NT.S 26. Leiden: Brill, 1971.

Fjärstedt, Biörn. *Synoptic Tradition in 1 Corinthians.* Uppsala: Teologiska Institutionen, 1974.

Halter, Hans. *Taufe* (IVA). Pp. 457–92.

Hasenstab, Rudolf. *Modelle* (IV). Pp. 31–66.

Herr, Theodor. *Naturrecht aus der kritischen Sicht des NT.* Munich: Kösel, 1976.

Holtz, Traugott. "Zur Frage der inhaltlichen Weisungen bei Paulus." *ThLZ* 106 (1981): 385–400.

Hübner, Hans. *Das Gesetz bei Paulus.* 3d ed. Göttingen: Vandenhoeck & Ruprecht, 1982. English: *Law in Paul's Thought.* Edinburgh: T. & T. Clark, 1984.

Joest, Wilfried. *Gesetz und Freiheit.* 4th ed. Göttingen: Vandenhoeck & Ruprecht, 1968.

Lillie, William. *Studies* (B). Pp. 12–23.

Luz, Ulricht. *Gesetz* (IB). Pp. 89–112.

Pedersen, Sigfred. "Agape—der eschatologische Hauptbegriff bei Paulus." In *Die paulinische Literatur und Theologie / The Pauline Literature and Theology,* 159–86. Göttingen: Vandenhoeck & Ruprecht, 1980.

Schrage, Wolfgang. *Einzelgebote* (IV). Pp. 187-271.

Schürmann, Heinz. "'Das Gesetz des Christus' (Gal. 6, 2)." In *NT und Kirche* (Festschrift Rudolf Schnackenburg), 282–300. Freiburg: Herder, 1974.

D. Concrete Ethics (pp. 217–39)

Coleman-Norton, Paul Robinson. "The Apostle Paul and the Roman Law of Slavery." In *Studies in Roman Economic and Social History in Honor of Allan Chester Johnson,* 155–77. Freeport, N.Y.: Books for Libraries Press, 1969 [1951].

Delling, Gerhard. *Paulus' Stellung zu Frau und Ehe.* Stuttgart: Kohlhammer, 1931.

———. *Röm. 13,1–7 innerhalb der Briefe des NT.* Berlin: Evangelische Verlagsanstalt, 1962.

Gayer, Roland. *Die Stellung der Sklaven in den paulinischen Gemeinden und bei Paulus.* EHS.T 78. Bern: Lang, 1976.

Kähler, Else. *Die Frau in den paulinischen Briefen.* Zurich: Gotthelf, 1960.

Käsemann, Ernst. "Röm. 13:1–7 in unserer Generation." *ZThK* 65 (1959): 316–76.

———. "Grundsätzliches zur Interpretation von Röm. 13." In *Exegetische Versuche* (IVA), 2:204–22. English: "Principles of the Interpretation of Romans 13:1–7." In *NT Questions* (IVA), 196–216.

Preiss, Théo. "Vie en Christ et éthique sociale dans l'épître à Philémon." In *La vie en Christ,* 65–73. Neuchatel: Delachaux & Niestlé, 1951.

Strobel, August. "Zum Verständnis von Röm. 13." *ZNW* 47 (1956): 69–93.

Suhl, Alfred. "Der Philemonbrief als Beispiel paulinischer Paränese." *Kairos* 15 (1973): 167–79.

Wilckens, Ulrich. "Röm. 13,1–7." In *Rechtfertigung als Freiheit,* 203–45. Neukirchen: Neukirchener Verlag, 1974.

Zsifkovits, Ventin. *Der Staatsgedanke nach Paulus.* WBTh 8. Vienna: Herder, 1964.

Paul so integrated his ethics into his theology that any presentation of the basis of Pauline ethics must perforce sketch an outline of Pauline theology. This will be done here without differentiating among the "authentic" Pauline epistles (Romans, 1 and 2 Corinthians, Galatians, Philippians, 1 Thessalonians, and Philemon). Suggestions of fundamental change—from passionate asceticism at the outset to a purely conventional position[1] or from apocalyptic eschatology to a sense of responsibility within this world (cf. below, 184)— rest on untenable hypotheses. We must remember, of course, that in Paul's disputes with legalistic Judaizers and enthusiasts of both ascetical and libertine persuasion he sometimes shifts the emphasis of his argument. Important as this observation is for understanding Paul's ethics, the situational context can no more account satisfactorily for Paul's christological ethics (cf. below, 190–91) than can the early Christian tradition, in which Paul already stands, ethics included.

A. THE BASIS OF PAULINE ETHICS

1. "Indicative and Imperative"

It has become a commonplace to treat the relationship between soteriology and ethics under the catchwords "indicative" and "imperative." The schema is not without its problems, but is justifiable so long as it is not taken as suggesting interchangeable motivations and purely formal ethical statements, but as a shorthand way of referring to substantial assurances of salvation and substantiated injunctions for action.

1.1 We take as our point of departure the well-known fact that several of the Pauline epistles clearly comprise two sections (Romans, Galatians, Thessalonians; later also Colossians and Ephesians). The first section of these letters, generally speaking, deals with the kerygma or "dogmatics": christology, eschatology, and so forth. The second section deals with "ethics." Thus ethics follows "dogmatics." This sequence is not simply the result of chance or a purely formal reflection of early Christian missionary preaching. We already find here a suggestion of the highly significant fact that God's eschatological act of salvation in Jesus Christ is the absolute basis, foundation, and prerequisite for all Christian conduct.

More striking and more problematic than this simple sequence is the fact that both sections contain statements in the indicative and injunctions in the imperative (or optative); between them there is some tension. On the one hand, we find assurance in an indicative: "You have been set free from sin" (Rom. 6:22); on the other, Paul can exhort his readers, "Let not sin therefore reign" (Rom. 6:12). On the one hand, we read: "You have put on Christ" (Gal. 3:27); on the other: "Put on the Lord Jesus Christ" (Rom. 13:14). We

---

1. Houlden, *Ethics* (B), 28, following J. C. Hurd, *The Origin of 1 Corinthians* (London: SPCK, 1965).

could cite similar instances referring to sanctification and righteousness, for example.

What is the relationship between the indicative of assurance and the imperative of ethical admonition? At first glance they appear mutually exclusive, an unintentional self-contradiction. The problem is exacerbated by the fact that statements with the same content are sometimes formulated in the indicative, sometimes in the imperative. Our immediate conclusion is that the imperative is not to be understood as a kind of supplement, as though its sole purpose were to exhort us to be rid of the last remnants of our old godless nature and life. The imperatives address the whole. But how can exactly the same statements appear in both indicative and imperative? When Paul uses the indicative, has he forgotten the imperative? When he uses the imperative, is he ignoring the indicative?

This is far from the case. Paul is not being inconsistent when he uses now the imperative, now the indicative, to formulate the same statement. This may be seen from the fact that both forms can occur side by side: "Cleanse out the old leaven, as you really are unleavened" (1 Cor. 5:7) or "If we live by the Spirit, let us also walk by the Spirit" (Gal. 5:25).

1.2 How have exegetes accounted for this remarkable phenomenon? Those who have not simply complained about the allegedly contradictory nature of Paul have usually emphasized one side at the expense of the other, turning the indicative into an abbreviated imperative or the imperative into a disguised indicative.

At one time it was the fashion to reduce the bipolarity of these statements to a compromise between ideal and reality or theory and practice, or to speak of enthusiastic religiosity on the one hand and realistic empiricism on the other. The indicative then represents Paul's ideal and the imperative serves as a corrective to his idealism or optimism. This corrective is allegedly forced upon the apostle by harsh reality and bitter experience or occasioned by pedagogical concerns. In this case, the indicative is nothing more than an idea, a principle, or at best a valid anticipation at certain moments or even in certain moods. But for Paul the way of Christian life is not marked by theories, ideas, and doctrines, however much vision and hope can effect transformation.

There are other exegetes for whom it is not the indicative but the imperative that is inconsistent. For them the indicative stands for the only adequate expression of the Pauline gospel. The imperative is a retreat into Jewish legalism. Ethical conduct would seem to be a matter of course. It is guaranteed to evolve naturally from anyone who is justified—or at least so the argument runs. We are assured in any case that only in an emergency does Paul descend to the level of the imperative, a level that in fact has been transcended. Such exigencies and compromises are forced on him by the actual condition of the newly established missionary communities and become unnecessary with the passage of time. The imperatives are, as it were, a kind of starter to get the motor of ethical conscience running, a necessary medicine until the communities outgrow their religious and ethical childhood diseases.

Such judgments are not just symptomatic of a past era of scholarship. The spirit of the so-called practical Paul, forced more or less clearly to retreat from his allegedly idealistic theories, lives on in books and sermons. The common element in all these theories is their understanding of the relationship between indicative and imperative as a contradiction to be resolved, historically or psychologically, regardless of whether the indicative or the imperative is found inconsistent.[2]

1.3 It was Rudolf Bultmann's epochal study[3] that first defined the relationship between indicative and imperative as a necessary antinomy and paradox, as the relationship between two statements formally contradictory but mutually complementary in substance, a phenomenon found elsewhere in Paul (e.g., Phil. 2:12-13). In positive terms, Bultmann declares that the imperative is grounded in the fact of justification and derives from the indicative.

Although Bultmann's initial position may be criticized in detail, it must be recognized as a substantial step forward. Of course Bultmann views the problem only from the perspective of an anthropology defined by existential dialectics. Furthermore, by treating righteousness and sin as realities of faith inaccessible to the senses, he separates them from the total life and ethical conduct of those who are justified. The priority (extra nos) of God's acquittal with respect to the plane of empirical conduct is maintained, but human participation in establishing God's righteousness in real life receives short shrift and must take a back seat.[4] According to Bultmann, the meaning of the Pauline paradox of indicative and imperative is expressed by the ancient words of Pindar: "Become what you are." It is dubious, however, whether this sufficiently explains the relationship between indicative and imperative in Paul. Serious questions arise above all with respect to eschatology and christology, even though Bultmann has continued to find supporters even for his notion that the problem arises from human existence as such, because the self can be truly realized only in the imperative.

Without explicitly parting company with Bultmann, Bornkamm and others go beyond his position. Bornkamm, for example, finds that the need for admonition has its origin in the hiddenness of the new life vouchsafed in baptism. But this hiddenness of each individual's life is now viewed in a

2. See the material cited by Werner G. Kümmel, *Römer 7 und die Bekehrung des Paulus*, TB 53 (Munich: Kaiser, 1974 [1929]), 98ff.; Alfons Kirchgässer, *Erlösung und Sünde im NT* (Freiburg: Herder, 1950), 3ff.; Schrage, *Einzelgebote*, 26ff.; Körtner, "Rechtfertigung," 97ff.

3. Bultmann, "Problem."

4. Kümmel, "Römer 7," 110; idem, "Sittlichkeit" (B), 75; Luz, "Eschatologie," 251-52.

broader context than anthropology: Christ has brought the old eon to an end, but the new world has not yet dawned universally and openly. In this view, the basis of the indicative/imperative antinomy rests ultimately in eschatological dialectics, which comprises christology and pneumatology as well as anthropology: for Christ is both the present Lord and the Lord to come, the Spirit is both an eschatological gift and a "down payment," Christians are a new creation and still live in hope. A similar position is taken by Merk: "The interplay of indicative and imperative is the interweaving of the two aeons that pervades the Christian life."[5]

Because the present wicked aeon exists simultaneously with the dawning of the new creation, Christians are situated "between the ages," standing in the midst of this eschatological event, since the old era is passing away and the day of salvation is dawning. In the new era, parenesis is superfluous. Now, however, ethics is *ethica viatorum*, ethics for those still tempted who have not yet reached the goal. Those who are tempted repeatedly need repeatedly to be reminded and exhorted. Encouragement and admonition are not unique events; they must be heard again and again. If Christians are not immune to temptation but are constantly threatened by it, exhortation is all the more necessary. Therefore Pauline parenesis is not addressed to sinners, backsliders, stragglers, and laggards, as is commonly thought, but to the saints, the justified, the baptized—those who are still pilgrims in the new life that is theirs.

1.4 Käsemann has found Bultmann's answer inadequate and anthropologically limited from another perspective. He cautions that the indicative can be misunderstood onesidedly as a gift easily dissociated from the giver, and expresses concern that Bultmann has not totally escaped the influence of idealism. He suggests that "Become what you are" can be understood to mean that it is up to each individual Christian to actualize what has been given in principle, whereas God's demand is a constitutive element of the gift itself. Indeed, the imperative is not a mere afterthought; it is implicit in the indicative. To take the indicative merely as justifying the imperative can in fact suggest that the imperative calls on the individual Christian to realize or actualize only a possibility vouchsafed by God. In truth, however, the imperative is "an integral part of the indicative."[6]

Bultmann himself, it should be noted, explicitly rejects the idealistic interpretation and states that the formula is not meant to suggest that "the ideal of perfect humanity is increasingly realized in infinite progress." Instead, freedom from the power of sin is "already realized" in the righteous-

5. *Handeln*, 37. Cf. also Preisker, *Ethos*, 64ff.; Kümmel, "Sittlichkeit," 74; Robert C. Tannehill, *Dying and Rising with Christ*, BZNW 32 (Berlin: Töpelmann, 1967), 78; Sanders, *Ethics*, 54ff.; Schnackenburg, *Moral Teaching*, 278ff.

6. Käsemann, *Romans*, 175; cf. idem, "Righteousness," 168ff., esp. 175–76. Similar comments are made by Furnish, *Theology*, 225; Tannehill, *Dying*, 82; Bottorff, "Relation," 426, 429–30. For criticism of this approach, see Sanders, *Ethics*, 48 n. 6.

ness of God. Its "divine dimension" is "God's judgment" and it finds expression in the obedience of faith.[7]

What is more important, Käsemann holds that God's universal eschatological righteousness—which for him represents the indicative, as justification does for Bultmann—cannot be understood exclusively as a gift but must also be understood as potential; it is inseparable from the giver. The absolute and unconditional promise of righteousness and salvation is not thereby restricted. Instead, Christians are so incorporated into the eschatological establishment of God's righteousness through Christ (Rom. 6:12ff.) that the very texture of their lives is determined by this salvific power, which permeates the world, so that they can now bring forth "fruits of righteousness" (Phil. 1:11; cf. also Rom. 8:10). This shows at the same time that the dialectic of indicative and imperative is not merely formal. It can be understood correctly only from the perspective of christology. According to Käsemann, the sense of the parenetic imperative that follows from and ratifies the indicative is better expressed by the formula: "Stay with the Lord who has been given you and in his kingdom."[8] Christ as Lord both gives and demands. When the imperative is not heard, the indicative has no power. Stählin[9] and Schlier have also studied the Greek verb *parakalein*, which can mean both "exhort" and "encourage" or "comfort," showing that the demand implies a promise and the promise a demand, so that ethics is not limited to the domain of the law.[10]

1.5 The priority of the indicative assurance of salvation lets us treat it as fundamental: in other words, the indicative, whatever its substance, implies and justifies the imperative. Alternatively, the imperative harkens back to the indicative, on which it is based. This observation is confirmed by the beginning of the specifically parenetic sections of the Pauline epistles, and above all by the logical connective "therefore" (Rom. 12:1; 1 Thess. 4:1; Gal. 5:1). This causative particle introducing parenesis allows us to conclude that Paul considers his ethics a consequence of the kerygma he has expounded in the prior sections of his epistles. Nauck argues therefore that Paul's ethics is neither autonomous nor telic but sequential.[11] It is necessary to insist, however, that this consequence is neither random nor optional, as though Romans 12—13, for example, might be a kind of supplement or appendix. When Nauck speaks of an "ethics of gratitude," he must not be misunderstood to mean that ethics is a purely human affair. It would be totally wrong to think that Romans 1—11, for example, the "dogmatic" chapters, speak of God's action, whereas chapters 12—15 speak of human response. For Paul, ethics is not a human reaction that brings God's action to fruition;

7. *Theology* (B), 332–33.
8. "Righteousness," 176.
9. Gustav Stählin, "parakaleō," *TDNT* 5:779–80.
10. Schlier, "Wesen," 75ff.; on Bjerkelund's denial of the term's complexity, cf. Hasenstab, *Modelle*, 69ff.
11. Wolfgang Nauck, "Das ουν-paräneticum," *ZNW* 49 (1958): 134–35.

the actions of Christians are grounded in the actions of God. Nor is synergism involved, as though God did something and then humans joined in or both worked hand in hand. Any attempt to quantify the relationship can only misrepresent the dialectics of indicative and imperative.

Our discussion has demonstrated the fundamental formal significance of the indicatives. The following sections will deal with the content of these statements and attempt to fill in the details. It is important not to absolutize particular elements motivating the parenesis and claim that the entire Pauline ethics is "telic," "pneumatic," "sacramental," or the like. Paul's ethics cannot be categorized so easily. The innumerable various motifs[12] are interdependent, as is shown by the simple observation that the individual texts bring together a variety of motivations. If some attempt must be made to summarize their content, we would have to say that God's saving eschatological act in Jesus Christ is the basis and root of Pauline ethics.

2. Christological Basis

2.1 The starting point and basis for Paul's ethics is the saving eschatological event of Jesus' death and resurrection, in which God acted, eschatologically and finally, to save the world. The doctrine of justification in particular is an explication of the Christ event. In the death of Jesus, God demonstrates his righteousness, which also benefits and claims every human being. This saving act is the basis for justification and reconciliation. At the same time, it shapes the concrete reality of the lives of those justified and reconciled (cf. 2 Cor. 4:10–11). Indeed, they are so incorporated into this eschatological event that Christ now lives and reigns "in them" (Gal. 2:20); they are "in Christ" and live for him. According to 2 Cor. 5:14, Christ died for all, that those for whom he died might live no longer for themselves but for him who died and rose again for them. Power is here ascribed to Jesus' act of love. The death of Christ establishes the new life and the obedience of Christians, not just as an ethical duty but as reality. According to Rom. 14:9, too, Jesus Christ died and rose again that he might be Lord both of the dead and of the living. Jesus' liberating lordship is the beginning and the end of Christian life and Christian ethics. The sovereignty of Jesus Christ is nothing else than the sovereignty of God's saving righteousness, manifested in Jesus Christ "so that in him we might become the righteousness of God" (2 Cor. 5:21; cf. 1 Cor. 1:30; Rom. 3:21ff.). The sovereignty of grace that comes through righteousness (Rom. 5:21) leads to the sovereignty of righteousness even in the "mortal body" (Rom. 6:12ff.). Even the injunction to avoid intercourse with prostitutes, seemingly so obvious, is based on the fact that Christians belong totally to their Lord (1 Cor. 6:12ff.).

It is therefore not by accident that Paul can use "in Christ" interchangeably with "in the Lord" (see his frequent use of "in the Lord" in parenetic

12. Cf. Merk, *Handeln;* Romaniuk, "Les motifs."

contexts such as 1 Cor. 7:39; 11:11; Phil. 4:4; 1 Thess. 4:1). Those who are "in Christ" are *eo ipso* subject to the Lord in obedience: "If we live, we live to the Lord" (Rom. 14:8). The term *kyrios*, "Lord," has great significance for Pauline ethics. Jesus Christ is called "Lord" not just because he is so acclaimed in worship or because he will return on the "day of the Lord"; these two elements were already present in pre-Pauline tradition (see above, 119). As Lord he is both source and power, but he is also the authority before which the concrete lives of Christians unfold in total dependence on their Lord (1 Cor. 7:22, 32; Rom. 16:18; 14:4).[13] Of course Paul can use the term "Christ" as well as "Lord" to express this same idea; "Christ" also appears in parenetic passages (Rom. 8:9–10; 1 Cor. 3:23). Christians, who have been freed by the Lord, are also slaves of Christ (1 Cor. 7:22). They remain obedient, for example, in the state in which they were called (1 Cor. 7:17ff.). Because "Christ, our paschal lamb, has been sacrificed," because through his death he has inaugurated the new age, breaking the power of sin and of the world, everything belonging to the passing eon can and must be put away. The anachronistic practices of the old world can and must be given up (1 Cor. 5:7–8).[14]

2.2 The close association Paul finds between basis and standard can be seen from the fact that the love manifested in Christ is also the criterion of Christian conduct. Paul can even find a substantial correspondence between the conduct of Christ and the conduct of those who belong to him. We may recall such passages as Rom. 15:2–3: "let each of us please his neighbor. . . , For Christ did not please himself." Note also v. 7: "Welcome one another, therefore, as Christ has welcomed you." Here the saving way of Christ is not only the christological *basis* of ethics but also its guiding principle. But even here, to use Luther's terminology, Christ is not primarily *exemplum* but *sacramentum*. Christ did not please himself; Christ welcomed us—this is not conduct to be emulated by Christians in their lives but the point of departure for a life of love. Of course there is to be a correspondence (cf. v. 3), however, even if it can never be more than partial.

The christological hymn in Philippians 2 also serves primarily as motivation, despite Luther's translation: "Let everyone be minded as Jesus Christ was minded." In his analysis of this well-known hymn, Käsemann convincingly rejects the interpretation of Phil. 2:5ff. as an ethical ideal, which would see the humility and self-denial of the earthly Jesus as an example of the proper Christian attitude.[15] Of course the self-abasement of Christ implies obedience and self-denial on the part of Christians, but this self-abasement

13. See Werner Kramer, *Christ, Lord, Son of God*, SBT 50 (London: SCM Press, 1966), 151ff.
14. For further discussion of the christological basis of Paul's ethics, see Merk, *Handeln*, 237ff.; Eichholz, *Theologie*, 265ff.; Wendland, *Ethik* (B), 51–52.
15. Ernst Käsemann, "Kritische Analyse von Phil. 2,5–11," in *Exegetische Versuche und Besinnungen*, 2 vols. (Göttingen: Vandenhoeck & Ruprecht, 1960–64), 1:51–95. See also Ralph P. Martin, *Carmen Christi*, 2d ed (Grand Rapids: Eerdmans, 1983), 84ff.

appears not in the life of Jesus but in the relinquishing of divinity by the preexistent Christ. This rules out any possible imitation (cf. also 2 Cor. 8:9). If the thought focuses on Christ's incarnation and Passion primarily as the basis for parenesis, humility is also required of Christians as reflecting the self-abasement of Jesus Christ (Phil. 2:3). For this reason we shall return to the question of what Paul means by "imitation" or "mimesis" in other passages (cf. below, IV.C.3).

2.3 That there can be no doubt of the fundamental significance of the christological motivation is confirmed by statements of principle introducing parenetic passages, such as 2 Cor. 10:1: "I entreat you by the meekness and gentleness of Christ" (cf. also Rom. 15:30). Here, too, the point is the principle and motivating force behind the apostolic parenesis and the Christian way of life. More is involved, however, than simple recollection or a reference to the binding motivations for the new life, nor are such appeals mere entreaty. Paul is instead attempting both to declare effectually the basis of the new life and to actualize it.

This is illustrated by the first clause in the statement of principle introducing the ethical section of Romans (12:1–2), which Paul inserts before his parenetic chapters: "I appeal to you therefore by the mercies of God." We must note at once that "mercy" here does not refer in general terms to God's merciful favor and protection: "mercies" refer rather to the mercy of God made manifest in Christ, in other words, to what Paul has described in chapters 1—11. Furthermore Paul does not merely speak of God's mercy here, but lets this mercy speak for itself, so that it may intervene through the apostolic parenesis.[16] "By" is not a Latinism,[17] but has its usual instrumental sense. It is Paul's purpose to offer, declare, and communicate anew God's mercy and love as the basis of ethics and Christian living. Since, however, Paul is writing to converted Christians, this means that Christ not only stands at the beginning of the Christian way, initiating and making possible the new way of life, but also must constantly intervene through continued exhortation on the way. Christ is the measure and source of all things. In his word, including the word of parenesis, he wishes the voice of his mercy to be heard.

3. Sacramental Basis

3.1 This section does not really introduce a new theme. It is in fact a subdivision of the christological basis of Pauline ethics. For Paul, a sacrament is nothing other than the present reality of the Christ event. The sacramental basis of ethics as such was part of the tradition Paul inherited, because the early Christians thought baptism implies sanctification (cf. 1 Cor. 6:11), but the christological emphasis is specifically Pauline. We may recall the paral-

---

16. Schlier, "Wesen," 78–79; Wilfred Joest, *Gesetz und Freiheit*, 4th ed. (Göttingen: Vandenhoeck & Ruprecht, 1968), 152.
17. Pace Albrecht Oepke, "dia," *TDNT* 2:67–68.

lelism between Rom. 6:5–7 and 6:8–10, according to which the baptismal event and the Christ event coincide in such a way that the Christ event is present in the baptismal event. Baptism is an event that takes place "with Christ"—dying with Christ, crucifixion with Christ, burial with Christ—or a "putting on of Christ" establishing that the Christian belongs to Christ (Gal. 3:27, 29).

The ethical significance of this idea appears in the opening verses discussing baptism in Romans 6, where it is quite clear why Paul speaks of baptism.

Romans 5 emphasizes that, because sin increased, grace abounded all the more (5:20). Precisely because sin was powerful and strong, the superior power and strength of grace could take effect. This suggests an apparently logical conclusion, which Paul has already alluded to in Romans 3, only to reject it immediately and emphatically: if the grace of God has really abounded beyond measure because of the increase of sin, does it not follow that God be given new opportunities to document his grace more and more abundantly? If abundant sin yields abundant grace, is it not true that the more sin there is, the better, because it means more grace? Should we not abide in sin so that grace may still have the chance to abound?

As is well known, this perverse logic is not limited to early Christianity. Bornkamm has cited the much abused formula *pecca fortiter* ("sin bravely"), and has also addressed the widespread misconception that, while rejecting perfectionism and moralism, claims Pauline authority in support of actualizing a continual dialectic between sin and grace. Paul passionately rejects such blasphemous logic. Bornkamm puts it perfectly: "What this dialectical pseudotheology refuses to accept and turns on its head is the simple fact that the victory of grace over sin, far from inaugurating a state of dialectical uncertainty, establishes a reality from which we cannot turn back."[18] For Paul, this reality is established by incorporation into Christ in baptism, which releases those baptized from the bonds of sin once and for all. To abide in sin is not to evoke the Lord's grace but to ignore it, through refusal to take seriously incorporation into the dominion of Christ's saving rule.

Through baptism Christians are so included in the Christ event that they belong irrevocably to Christ. The fate of Christ and the fate of Christians are here brought together once and for all: their correspondence is established (cf. the "as Christ . . . so we too" of v. 4). Paul deliberately shifts the analogy in the case of the resurrection, but this reveals the ethical elements of the analogy more clearly: as Christ was raised from the dead, we too should walk in newness of life. This means that Christians have not yet been raised like Christ, but the existence of those who are baptized is already characterized by a radical newness, a newness that manifests itself in their way of life. Paul not only links ethics with baptism but also links baptism with ethics.[19]

18. Bornkamm, "Baptism," 73.
19. Gäumann, *Taufe*, 126.

3.2 That the Christ who works in baptism becomes the Lord of those who are baptized, liberating them and claiming them for himself, is shown by the fact that they are no longer slaves to sin. In baptism they have been set free by a more powerful Lord, in whose service they now stand. Thus baptism is both a gift of freedom and a change of servitude. It effects release from sin and obedience to righteousness or to Christ (Rom. 6:18).

This confirms the point that one does not first receive a gift and then decide—or refuse—to serve Christ. Both must go together to be real. Those who are free are those who are obedient, and those who are obedient are those who are free (cf. also 1 Cor. 9:19: "*Because* I am free from all, I have made myself a slave to all"). The freedom Christians receive in baptism imposes servitude; it is the paradoxical mode of this servitude. More precisely, it coincides with this servitude in such a way that the one cannot exist without the other. This statement, too, is not just anthropological; it derives its meaning from christology. "All things are yours" only because "you are Christ's" (1 Cor. 3:21, 23). No one can be free without having Jesus Christ as Lord and standing in his service; freedom does not come through subscription to an individualistic or liberalistic ideology of freedom. Radical freedom does not consist in libertinism, but takes the form of service. Those who are free remain so only when they are also free of their freedom; their freedom evaporates when it is not also freedom for Christ and for others. Servitude and obedience of one sort or another are inescapable; no one is truly independent and autonomous, not even those who think they are. Those who claim to be free, as people are wont to do, are themselves slaves to a lord, even if this lord is their own passions.

The servitude of those who are truly free is due to him who becomes their Lord in baptism. It is therefore logical that the first imperatives appear in the chapter dealing with baptism and are based on what has taken place in baptism (esp. Rom. 6:12ff.). These exhortations, as Luther puts it, appeal for a return to baptism *(reditus ad baptismum)*. This guarantees that Pauline ethics will not exhort Christians to procure, advance, or augment salvation; nothing is required that has not been given already. The imperative does not appeal to Christians' good will or ability, but recalls what they have already received in baptism: freedom and a new lord. Bornkamm describes the situation succinctly: "Baptism is the appropriation of new life, and this new life is the assimilation of baptism."[20]

3.3 The same situation is also illustrated by another example of baptismal terminology. In 1 Cor. 6:11, for instance, Paul points out to the Corinthians, in what is probably a reference to baptism, that they have been washed, sanctified, and justified. It is not through their own abilities and efforts but in baptism that people are sanctified, that is, consecrated to God and declared to

---

20. Bornkamm, "Baptism," 84; emphasized in the original.

be his property. It is therefore not by accident that Paul in his baptismal parenesis calls for the "sanctification" of those who have been sanctified (Rom. 6:19). This appeal is addressed to those already "sanctified," those who are "saints," as they are called in the opening verses of the epistles—not to those who have merely been justified and now must achieve their own sanctification. It is wrong to associate justification with the indicative and sanctification with the imperative. Sanctification, too, is God's work in us. God himself sanctifies and effects sanctification. But it is equally true that sanctification is also God's will and is associated with the imperative. Being sanctified obligates us to active sanctification (cf. 1 Thess. 4:3).[21]

3.4 The ethical relevance of the sacrament finds expression not only in references to baptism but also in the reference to the Lord's Supper in 1 Corinthians 11, albeit less as a permanent foundation for ethics than as a continually renewed motivation and obligation in the realization of ethics. The fact that the Lord communicates himself in the Lord's Supper, in which he himself is present, has significant ethical consequences. The Lord's Supper incorporates Christians into the church as the historical body of Christ, in which each member is totally responsible for the others; it is therefore no longer possible to have one's "own meal" (1 Cor. 11:21). Those who think of the sacrament as analogous to the rites of the mystery religions and denigrate the common meal associated with the Lord's Supper in order to emphasize the sacramental act are reminded that in the Lord's Supper we share in the death of Jesus and are incorporated into the body of Christ (cf. 1 Cor. 10:16–17). Therefore to celebrate the Lord's Supper while disregarding social obligations perverts the celebration of the sacrament. Here, too, the sacrament has an ethical dimension encompassing everyday reality.[22]

4. Pneumatologic-Charismatic Basis

4.1 Under this heading, too, we are still within the realm of christology, because in Paul's view the Spirit, as the eschatological power of God, is associated with Christ. Since Paul develops his pneumatology out of his christology, the Spirit being *eo ipso* the Spirit of Christ (Rom. 8:9) or the Spirit of the Lord (2 Cor. 3:17), the centrality of the dynamic and renewing power of the Spirit in the new life can be considered a christological motif. "In the Spirit, the exalted Lord proclaims his presence and dominion upon earth."[23] The traditional understanding of the Spirit Paul inherited he corrected by interpreting the Spirit as the vital presence of Christ himself (2 Cor.

21. See also Stalder, *Werk*, 210ff.
22. Cf. Hans von Soden, "Sakrament und Ethik bei Paulus," and Günther Bornkamm, "Lord's Supper and Church in Paul," in *Early Christian Experience* (London: SCM Press, 1969), 123–60. On the social background of the conflict at Corinth, see Gerd Theissen, "Soziale Integration und sakramentales Handeln," *NT* 24 (1974): 179–206. (= *Social Setting of Pauline Christianity*, 145–74).
23. Käsemann, *Romans*, 213.

3:17). He rejects the enthusiastic view that the Spirit is manifest primarily in the spectacular and miraculous, in the extraordinary and supernatural. The Spirit is rather the very essence of the new life, in all its apparently insignificant and mundane details. The entire life of Christians, from beginning to end, is the work of the Spirit: it is "spiritual worship" (Rom. 12:1) and thus a sign of the new world that is dawning. The Spirit does not work just now and then, in particular phenomena and isolated manifestations, in exceptional situations and specially gifted people. The Spirit totally pervades the life of every Christian and of every Christian community: "All these are inspired by one and the same Spirit" (1 Cor. 12:11). This wonderful dominance of Christians by the Spirit extends to the realm of ethical conduct.

That Paul sees the Spirit at work in the ethical renewal of people's lives was already noted by Gunkel.[24] Although he exaggerated Paul's distance from the popular view and was in danger of wrongly spiritualizing and ethicizing Paul, his basic position has not been refuted: for Paul the Spirit is essentially the fundamental force and principle of the new life and the new way of living.[25] Those in whom the Spirit dwells are not given over to mystical experiences, ecstatic visions, and the like, but to service and obedience. The Spirit does not bestow powerful emotions and feelings, but rules Christians in their very core.

4.2 Above all, according to Romans 8 and Galatians 5, to walk in "newness of life" (Rom. 6:4) through baptism is to walk in the "newness of the Spirit" (Rom. 7:6). Both in the inauguration and appropriation of the new life in baptism and in the assimilation of baptism in the new life, Christians are not left to their own devices but are enabled and equipped for walking in newness of life through the miraculous power of the Spirit. The fact that Christian life is walking in the Spirit means not only a new motivation but a new orientation. The Spirit is first and foremost the power, the basis, and the context of Christian existence. But when Christians actually walk in the Spirit, then the Spirit is also their guiding principle ("according to the Spirit": Rom. 8:4–5).

The work of the Spirit is not limited to particular moments. This does not mean, however, that Christians as it were have the Spirit safely in possession. Even pneumatics are subject to temptation. Even charismatics do not have "indelible character." They, too, still stand within the promise of the Spirit and are still threatened by the "flesh." The continual struggle within the Christian between flesh and Spirit (Gal. 5:17) shows that Christian and *pneuma* are not identical; the Spirit remains a power external to the Christian. The miracle of the Spirit is not subject to human manipulation or control. Christians are seized by the Spirit; they are the object, not the subject. They are, as Paul can say, "driven" (Rom. 8:14; Gal. 5:18).

24. Hermann Gunkel, *The Influence of the Holy Spirit* (Philadelphia: Fortress Press, 1979).
25. See Bultmann, *Theology*, 331; Wendland, "Wirken," 457ff.; Eduard Schweizer, "pneuma," *TDNT* 6:415ff.

It is the Spirit who takes possession of the Christian, not the Christian who takes possession of the Spirit ("the other side of justification of sinners"[26]). Here, too, however, the reverse is immediately added dialectically: Christians are debtors (Rom. 8:12). Just as baptism does not effect a magical transformation, so the Spirit is not an irresistible force sweeping all before it. This distinguishes Christian existence from the passive drift that 1 Cor. 12:2 says is characteristic of the heathen.[27]

The same situation is expressed by the terminology Gal. 5:22 uses to describe life in the Spirit. Here the concrete Christian way of life, exemplified in a catalogue of virtues, is called the "fruit of the Spirit," a fruit produced by the Spirit. In Rom. 6:22, however, where Paul is clearly more concerned with what Christians themselves actually do, he can speak with equal ease of "your fruit." This twofold qualification of "fruit" once again vividly illustrates the paradox. The "fruit of the Spirit" is not to be understood after the analogy of an automatic natural process. If the Spirit bears fruit, the Spirit also demands that Christians bear fruit. Therefore love, the first of the fruits of the Spirit, is not only a gift and fruit but also a demand of the Spirit (Rom. 13:8ff.). The obedience of the pneumatic is an act of the *pneuma*, and yet the Christian is to be caught up and involved in this action. But we must always keep in mind the irreversible trend of these statements, which implies the primacy of the Spirit.

4.3 The situation appears quite similar in the case of charismata or spiritual gifts, a notion closely related to that of the Spirit. In 1 Corinthians 12, for example, Paul can speak interchangeably of "gifts of the Spirit" and "gifts of grace." He introduces his catalogue of charismata by saying that they are given through the Spirit (v. 8; cf. v. 11; and Rom. 1:11). Following the terminology of Rom. 12:3, we might say that a charisma is the measure of the grace bestowed (cf. also Eph. 4:7: "the measure of faith"), the specific effect of the gift of the Spirit (cf. 1 Cor. 12:7, 11). As 1 Cor. 7:7 puts it: "Each has his own charisma from God."

This phrase "from God" insists above all that a charisma is not a human potential. It cannot be realized by one's own efforts, nor can it be commanded. Even here, though, Paul can exhort his readers to strive for a charisma such as prophecy (1 Cor. 14:1). The question, then, is what distinguishes charisma as the work of the Spirit from the "fruit of the Spirit" (Gal. 5:22–23), especially since both derive so clearly from the *pneuma* and thus have the same origin.

Gunkel thought that the difference lay in the context and nature of the resulting activity: the setting of charismata is public life and worship, whereas fruits of the Spirit involve one's private spiritual life. But the charismata cited

---

26. Käsemann, *Romans*, 226.
27. See Gottlob Schrenk, "Geist und Enthusiasmus," in *Studien zu Paulus*, AThANT 26 (Zurich: Zwingli, 1954), 107–27, esp. 115–16.

in Rom. 12:6ff. are by no means limited to the realm of worship. An especially striking feature of this passage is its interweaving of ethical phenomena with themes connected with worship and the life of the community. Nor are charismata—as others have suggested—"natural powers," in contrast to fruits of the Spirit, which are "ethical powers." This distinction also will not chime with Rom. 12:6ff., for Paul does not consider prophecy, teaching, etc. to be natural phenomena. Celibacy and marriage as such are not charismata. They become charismata only as an opportunity for Christian conduct, for building up or "edifying" (oikodomē) the community, as diakonia (1 Cor. 12:5). Of course grace can also involve the natural realm, the created order; for Paul the example par excellence is the body. It is therefore pointless to create an unnecessary gulf between a natural talent on the one hand and a miraculous gift of the Spirit on the other. Yet another attempt to distinguish charismata from fruits of the Spirit associates charismata with the indicative and fruits of the Spirit with the imperative. This, too, will not hold water. It is not merely the fruits of the Spirit that Christians are told to strive after (Rom. 12:13; 14:19; 1 Thess. 5:15), but also charismata (1 Cor. 12:31; 14:1, 12, 39). Both are gifts that carry obligations with them. It is therefore not by accident that the catalogue of charismata in Romans 12 stands in the context of parenesis.

Paul clearly has a different reason for not exhorting his readers to prophesy, teach, and so forth, but only to seek the fruits of the Spirit. This reason also constitutes the crucial distinction between charismata and fruits of the Spirit. The real difference lies in the individual nature of charismata: according to 1 Cor. 7:7, each has his own special charisma, and 1 Cor. 12:11 states that the Spirit apportions to each his own specific unmistakable gift. Therefore Rom. 12:6 declares that we have different gifts according to the grace given to us. Of course even this distinction is only relative; Romans 12 also refers to liberality and aid as charismata. Galatians 5, too, derives in large measure from tradition. It is nevertheless roughly correct to say that, although every Christian is both a pneumatic and a charismatic, only the fruits of the Spirit develop in the same way in all Christians. The fruits of the Spirit listed in Galatians 5 are therefore equally binding on all: love, joy, peace, patience, kindness, etc. While it is also true that every Christian is also a charismatic and the community as a whole will never lack in any charisma (1 Cor. 1:7), individual Christians are not equally endowed with charismata. One has one charisma, another another (1 Cor. 12:8ff., 29ff.). Individual charismata are even mutually exclusive (cf. 1 Cor. 7:7).

It is likely that Paul would not use the term "charisma" for the totality of Christian life, but only for the specific features and elements that promote service to the community. Otherwise there is a general structural similarity between the pneumatological and charismatic foundations of the new life.[28] It

28. For the most recent discussion, see Siegfried Schulz, "Die Charismenlehre des Paulus," in Rechtfertigung, (Festschrift Ernst Käsemann), ed. J. Friedrich, W. Pöhlmann, and P. Stuhlmacher (Tübingen: Mohr, 1976), 443–60, esp. 456–57, following Käsemann.

would be wrong to draw too sharp a distinction, because Paul in practice extended the concept of charisma to the realm of ethics, although not relating it to all aspects of Christian conduct.[29]

5. Eschatological Basis

5.1 It is clear from all we have said that christology is for Paul the fundamental ethical principle. Pauline eschatology does nothing to alter this conclusion. To say that eschatology is primary and central for Paul, so that his ethics, too, is exclusively eschatological, is true only if we do not over-emphasize expectation of the Parousia and interpret the resultant ethics as pure passivity or alienation with respect to the present world.[30]

Pauline eschatology, too, belongs primarily within the context of christology, which furnishes its basis and focus.[31] This clearly holds true for the present, realized dimension of his eschatology. Jesus' cross and resurrection are understood as epochal eschatological events making salvation a present reality. But the future aspects of Pauline eschatology are also developed along lines that are primarily if not exclusively christological. Paul's hopes and expectations focus on the Parousia of Jesus Christ, above all on being "with the Lord" or "with Christ." Paul does not develop the content of the Christian hope systematically. It must be reconstructed on the basis of scattered fragmentary statements. In nearly all of them, however, Christ is both the ground and the goal of hope. This would seem to conflict with 1 Corinthians 15, which states that the ultimate goal of hope is God's absolute and undiminished sovereignty. Nevertheless, the eschatological motifs of *ethics*, including the notion of judgment—according to Paul, both God and Christ act as judge—are shaped by christology. The foundation of ethics is both "the future of the *kyrios*" and "the present Christ event."[32] We have already noted that salvation is simultaneously present and future; it follows that Christians are themselves caught up in this eschatological tension, because, although delivered from the power of the old eon, they still suffer and sigh, wait and hope. This does not imply a neat dichotomy but a dynamic relationship; we repeatedly find attempts to frame the ethical conduct of the community according to God's future and to anticipate this future in the present (cf. Rom. 14:17).[33] Of course the dimension of futurity cannot be ignored. Futuristic eschatology has a double significance for ethics: on the one hand, it makes us take seriously the time remaining and the unredeemed reality of this world, which is a crucial motive for Paul's adoption of an

---

29. See Ulrich Brockhaus, *Charisma und Amt* (Wuppertal: Brockhaus, 1972), 220ff.

30. For a discussion of the similarities and differences between Paul and apocalypticism with respect to the relationship between eschatology and ethics, see Christoph Münchow, *Ethik und Eschatologie* (Göttingen: Vandenhoeck & Ruprecht, 1981), 150ff.

31. See Luz, "Eschatologie," 227ff.

32. Grabner-Haider, *Paraklese*, 110.

33. Luz, "Eschatologie," 262–63; Münchow, *Ethik*, 165–66.

eschatological tradition that is futuristic or apocalyptic (cf. Rom. 8:18ff.). On the other hand, however, it prevents the temporary and provisional reality of the world from claiming absolute importance.

5.2 In 1 Cor. 7:29–31, for example, while discussing questions having to do with marriage, Paul speaks in fundamental terms of the Christian attitude toward the world as shaped by a futuristic eschatology. The *kairos*, the "appointed time," remaining until the Parousia, has grown very short; indeed the very nature of this world is already passing away. Paul draws the appropriate conclusions: those who have wives should live as though they had none; those who mourn or rejoice should live as though they no longer mourned or rejoiced; those who buy should act as though they did not own what they bought; and those who deal with the world should do so as though they had no dealings with it.

The call to be inwardly free and aloof from the world is here based on eschatology. For Paul this eschatological foundation is not simply one option among several, an irrelevant conceptuality that could equally well be replaced by the world view of the Stoics and Cynics. Such a substitution would be impossible if only because Pauline eschatology does not reduce to anthropology. It is not, as Braun claims, merely a useful fiction for inculcating the urgency of the present or the irrecoverable uniqueness of each moment. Were eschatology, with its christological and theocentric focus, to vanish, there would be negative consequences for ethics. If the dead are not raised— and resurrection is implicit in christology—"let us eat and drink, for tomorrow we die" (1 Cor. 15:32). But if the dead are raised, the body that God will raise up already belongs to the Lord (1 Cor. 6:14).

The christological focus of eschatology in 1 Corinthians 7 does not become clear until v. 32. Up to that point, Paul has more to say about the shortness of the time and the passing away of the world. This, I think, is due to his incorporation of an apocalyptic *topos* in vv. 29–31.[34]

It would be wrong, however, to treat christology and eschatology as opposites. The fact that Christ is already present as ruler and deliverer (cf. v. 22) puts the things of this world in their proper perspective every bit as much as does the prospect of their final passing away, which itself coincides with the coming of Christ. In any case, the perspective of the ultimate makes all else penultimate at best. The nearness of the Lord allays anxiety (Phil. 4:5): his coming judgment makes it impossible to pass judgment upon other Christians (Rom. 14:10; 1 Cor. 4:5); the abundance of blessings to come evokes generosity in the collection (2 Cor. 9:6; cf. Gal. 6:9–10); the eschatological

---

34. See Herbert Braun, "Die Indifferenz gegenüber der Welt bei Paulus und bei Epiktet," in *Gesammelte Studien zum Neuen Testament und seiner Umwelt* (Tübingen: Mohr, 1962), 159–67; Wolfgang Schrage, "Die Stellung zur Welt bei Paulus, Epiktet und in der Apokalyptik," *ZThK* 16 (1964): 125–54; Gottfried Hierzenberger, *Weltbewertung bei Paulus nach 1. Kor. 7,29–31* (Düsseldorf: Patmos, 1967).

promise teaches the proper attitude toward the concerns of everyday life (1 Cor. 6:2). This perspective does not stand or fall with the expectation of an imminent end, which Paul uses here to reinforce his parenesis (as also in Rom. 13:11ff.; Gal. 6:10; cf. also 1 Thess. 5:1ff., with more stress on the uncertainty of the time). It does stand or fall, however, with the specific expectation of the ultimate victory of God and of his Christ. This very fact suggests that what is penultimate cannot be ignored: eschatology must not be confused with the kind of the religious enthusiasm that would escape from the world.

5.3 This is confirmed by Rom. 13:11-14, a passage in which Paul concludes the two parenetic chapters 12 and 13 with an eschatological motivation. The verses are especially illuminating because they appear in the same letter as 13:1-7, which deals with the proper attitude toward civil authorities. They therefore answer the question whether we can look for an ethics only after expectation of the Parousia has lost its urgency.

Paul begins by exhorting his readers to do everything discussed in the two parenetic chapters 12 and 13 in the knowledge that the hour is "already" at hand to awake from sleep. The use of "already" is striking. Elsewhere in Paul, it is either a catchword of "realized eschatology," a favorite expression of the fanatics (1 Cor. 4:8; cf. 2 Tim. 2:18), or else Paul himself expressly negates the perfectionistic "already": "Not that I have already obtained this or am already perfect" (Phil. 3:12). Only here, in Rom. 13:11, does Paul use "already" in a positive sense: to motivate the proper conduct of Christians.

This use of "already" is highly significant. The eschaton, casting its beams ahead, is manifested in the "already" of ethics; this means conforming to the cross of the risen Lord. Ultimate salvation is still to come, even though it is "nearer" than at the time of conversion. This comparative, "nearer," is also noteworthy, for it signals not only the dialectical position of Christians, who in the present time of transition belong in a way to both ages, but also "the continued advance of the eschatological clock."[35] "The night is far gone, the day is at hand" (v. 12).

Paul is not thinking of the time of night, just before the dawn, when darkness is deepest, as though alluding to the apocalyptic idea that the world is growing increasingly evil and depraved.[36] Nor, of course, is the opposite true—that the approach of dawn is to be understood in terms of human progress, evolution, or teleology. Such allegorical readings are illegitimate. It is true, however, that the day is increasingly near and that its being "nearer" motivates Paul's exhortations (cf. also the causative particle in v. 12). But this means that ethics is here a consequence of eschatology, more specifically of futuristic eschatology (cf. also Gal. 6:9-10; Phil. 2:16; 3:14; 1 Thess. 2:12).[37]

35. Gustav Stählin, "nun," *TDNT* 4:1120.
36. Pace Gustav Stählin, "prokope," *TDNT* 6:716.
37. On Rom. 13:11-14, see esp. Anton Vögtle, "Paraklese und Eschatologie nach Röm 13,11-14," in *Dimensions de la vie chrétienne*, Série monographique de Benedictina, section biblico-oecuménique, 4 (Rome: Abbaye de S. Paul, 1979), 179-94.

5.4 Now if future expectation is an undeniable basis for ethics in Rom. 13:11ff., this has special significance in light of the injunction in 13:1–7 to be subject to the civil authorities. It has often been asserted that an early Christian ethics was not possible until the expectation of an imminent Parousia waned and the overheated energy of the initial period came to an end.

Weidinger, for example, claimed that only the inexorable demands of everyday life made it clear to the Christians that they still lived on this earth, a fact they had forgotten in the earlier period dominated by eschatology.[38] Dibelius, too, asserts that Paul's incorporation of secular ethics was occasioned by the delay of the Parousia.[39] And according to Dodd, belief in an imminent eschatological climax and "an exaggerated mood of expectation" had to recede in order to open the way for ethical injunctions. He seeks to trace in Paul and Paul's letters a shift from eschatological enthusiasm in the first letters to a growing surrender of this belief in the later letters. Only this revision of eschatology, which Dodd credits to the robust common sense of the apostle, made possible a new appraisal of how Christians should relate to the world.[40]

This alleged revision of eschatology is a fiction. In particular such texts as Romans 13—which, be it noted, is among the apostle's later letters!—show that for Paul ethics does not replace eschatology but follows from it. Not even at the outset was Paul a fanatic, fired with eschatological hope and refusing to take seriously the oppressive problems of this world. His urgent insistence on ethics is not an emergency measure forced upon him by the so-called realities of continuing history. It is neither a compromise nor an accommodation to the world, but a consequence and an expression of the fact that in Christ a new world has begun and that everything is moving toward Christ's universal victory and the absolute sovereignty of God. In any case, eschatology does not evoke in Paul an apocalyptic quietism or a burning desire to flee this world. Instead of impeding action, it works as a sustained goad to action.

5.5 This is confirmed by yet another text, which also introduces another frequent motif: judgment based on works (2 Cor. 5:9–10).

In 2 Cor. 5:1ff., Paul calls the attention of his community to the future, having first contrasted the magnitude of the glory that awaits to the brief and therefore bearable suffering of this transitory world (4:17–18). He gives voice to his confidence that, when earthly life is over, Christians can look forward to a heavenly dwelling. Without denigrating the body, he contrasts the state of exile in the earthly body to being at home with the Lord, which he pictures as nearness and communication (vv. 6–8).

But, he argues in v. 9, those whose aim is eschatological communion with the Lord must also aim to please him here and now. The passage reads literally: "Therefore whether we are at home [i.e., with the Lord] or en route

---

38. *Haustafeln* (37), 6–7, 8; cf. also above, 128.
39. Martin Dibelius, *Urchristentum und Kultur* (Heidelberg: Winter, 1928), 18, and elsewhere.
40. *Gospel* (B), 35.

[i.e., in the earthly body] let us seek eagerly to please him. For we all must be revealed before the judgment seat of Christ, so that each one may receive according to what he has done while alive in the body [or: through the body], whether good or evil."

In the first place, this says that the eschatological hope spoken of in vv. 1ff. is the basis of responsibility and steadfastness here and now. Yearning for communion with the heavenly Lord leads Christians to take their earthly obligations seriously. It is therefore absolutely wrong to say that yearning for the Lord makes life here and now irrelevant. Quite the contrary, as Phil. 1:21ff. also confirms. Eschatological hope gives a clearer vision and evokes responsibility for earthly existence between the ages. Here, too, the juxtaposition of eschatology and ethics in Paul is not a forcible linkage of two incommensurate quantities. Indeed, the call to remain steadfast in the world and in the body is incomprehensible without the eschatological dimension. Steadfastness is a consequence of expectation, not a substitute for it. Hopelessness cripples, but hope mobilizes.

Verse 10 then uses the idea of judgment to emphasize that people are responsible for their earthly way of life. Here Paul is of course borrowing from Judaism, which associates judgment with the end of the present eon or the end of the world. In the Jewish view, each individual will then stand alone before God and be called to account for each individual deed (cf. such passages as Ethiopic Enoch 95:5).[41]

We cannot deny that Paul borrows the Jewish notion of judgment based on works. This does not mean that Paul has made an insufficiently radical break with Jewish heritage and is not speaking forthrightly. It would be wrong to interpret passages like 2 Cor. 5:10 innocuously as pedagogical threats or reduce them to hypothetical statements. Paul's words about judgment based on works are meant quite straightforwardly and seriously. God is and always will be the judge. This is a fundamental principle of *sola gratia* ("by grace alone"): only because God holds us not just apparently responsible but truly responsible can he show grace to those under threat of judgment. The judge alone can let grace take precedence over justice, acquitting and justifying the sinner for the sake of Christ. Judgment preserves the principle that we have no righteousness of our own.

But Paul does not present a God of grace and mercy who has ceased to function as judge in the case of justified Christians, closing his eyes to whatever takes place. Christians above all are confronted with the message of judgment. It is not by accident that most of these judgment passages occur in parenetic contexts. Even in the case of Christians, God has the last word. Not

41. On the idea of judgment, see Herbert Braun, *Gerichtsgedanke und Rechtfertigungslehre bei Paulus*, UNT 19 (Leipzig: Hinrichs, 1931); Lieselotte Mattern, *Das Verständnis des Gerichtes bei Paulus*, AThANT 47 (Zurich: Zwingli, 1966); Ernst Synofzik, *Die Gerichts– und Vergeltungsaussagen bei Paulus*, GTA 8 (Göttingen: Vandenhoeck & Ruprecht, 1977).

that Christians are now to seek their own salvation independently, by their own power and according to their own lights! They are asked whether they have given full weight to the *sola* of *sola gratia*; they are asked what they have done with what God has given them, whether they have really lived in the light of the eschaton and in the power of the Spirit and have not strayed from the way of salvation in Christ. Works are far from irrelevant. It would only be a slight exaggeration to say that they are intended to proclaim the work of God or the work of the Lord in us (1 Cor. 15:58), thus manifesting that we have let God work within us. As in the case of Jesus, however, this shows clearly that the Lord claims radical obedience and that we are totally responsible to him, whether we stand or fall. Justification has a future dimension (cf. Rom. 5:9; 9:28ff.), but the concept of the last judgment, which stands in radical tension to this future justification, is meant to keep us from abusing the righteousness of God out of a false sense of security and failing to do God's will (cf. 1 Cor. 10:1ff.). Judgment based on works imposes ethical responsibility on Christians.[42]

It is significant that Paul speaks of bodily resurrection in v. 10, following his discussion of hope. This sequence shows that hope, not fear, is the fundamental attitude with which Christians approach the end. God, who has begun the work, will bring it to completion (Phil. 1:6; 1 Cor. 1:6). Elsewhere, too, Paul gives pride of place to joy and confidence rather than fear and uncertainty (cf. 1 Thess. 1:10; 2:19; 5:23–24). Therefore the concept of reward also plays an important role alongside the concept of judgment, especially in figurative usage (cf. 1 Cor. 4:5; 9:24; Phil. 3:14). It appears also in parenetic words of encouragement and exhortation (Gal. 6:9–10; 1 Cor. 15:58).[43] Paul is not of the opinion that bodily resurrection must be earned by works of merit. His point of departure is his great hope and assurance, the expectation of the returning Lord, who will draw Christians into his fellowship. And he comes to pronounce the message of judgment. This path cannot be reversed. In 1 Corinthians 15, too, the hope of resurrection, not judgment, is the basis of parenesis (vv. 34, 58). Phil. 4:4–6 finds grounds for joy in the nearness of the Lord; it dispels anxiety and looks for mercy and kindness to be shown to all.

B. THE NATURE AND STRUCTURE OF
THE NEW LIFE

1. The Integrity of the Christian Life

1.1 According to Paul, the liberation and new being that comes through Christ is an all-encompassing event, a fundamental transformation, a "metamorphosis" (Rom. 12:2; 2 Cor. 3:18). The human contradiction (Rom.

---

42. Luz, "Eschatologie," 278–79.
43. Herbert Preisker, "misthos," *TDNT* 4:705, 726ff.

7:14ff.), the dichotomy and division within the self, is a thing of the past. The radical nature of this new being implies an undivided integrity of God's claim upon us. Radically renewed Christians to whom all has been given can put themselves at God's service totally and be obedient totally, not merely now and then or to some degree. Therefore Pauline parenesis does not tally particular deeds or acts of obedience, but addresses the whole person. Of course Paul can speak in particular of renewing the mind (Rom. 12:2) or exhort his readers to have a new self-understanding (Rom. 6:11) or to sacrifice their bodies (Rom. 12:1). But the anthropological terms are used by synecdoche. That the totality of the gift implies a corresponding totality of demand and obedience is expressed vividly in the frequent use of "all" or "every": God works for good in everything with those who love him (Rom. 8:28), he gives us all things with Christ (Rom. 8:32), he has enriched Christians in every way (1 Cor. 1:5; 2 Cor. 9:11) so that now "all things are yours" (1 Cor. 3:21). Therefore, Christians are now to do all to the glory of God (1 Cor. 10:31), to be obedient in everything (2 Cor. 2:9), and to let all be done in love (1 Cor. 16:19).

As in the case of Jesus, there is no room here for mere outward obedience or observance of the letter, nor is there any room, however, for a spiritualization that would make Paul the proponent of an ethics of pure subjectivity. Overemphasis on intention, such as marks the ethics of intention (cf. above, I.B. 1.3), at the expense of obedience in the real world and shaping the Christian life in its corporeal dimension would be for Paul a wrong-headed spiritualization. God claims our bodies for his service (cf. below, IV. D. 1) and is to be glorified in our eating and drinking (1 Cor. 10:31). The best support for the argument that good intentions are more important than actions is 2 Cor. 8:10–11. But even if it is good that the Corinthians have begun "not only to do but to desire," the following verses make it clear that there is a corresponding action that follows unconditionally from the desire, namely, material aid for the "poor" in Jerusalem. This action, it is true, does not clearly show forth obedience as obedience, but at least it keeps obedience from vanishing into total invisibility. Newness of life may be grounded in the judgment and actions of God and can only be the object of faith, but the new life is not lived invisibly: it is corporeally manifest on earth (Gal. 5:19ff.). The spiritual dimension is not the realm of vague subjectivity; the power and reality of the Spirit are manifest in the corporeal particulars of our life and work (see above, IV.A.4).

1.2 Hand in hand with the integrity required of the Christian life goes the unity of Pauline parenesis. The obedience God demands cannot be subdivided or put together out of individual acts. Like Jesus, Paul has his eye on an integral approach to life, not a conglomerate of isolated acts of obedience to the law. It is noteworthy, for example, that for Christian conduct Paul almost always uses the singular, for example "work" (1 Cor. 3:13ff.; Gal. 6:4;

Phil 1:6) or "fruit" (Rom. 6:22; Gal. 5:22; Phil. 1:11; 4:17). This is probably not entirely accidental, for Paul can use the plural for what people do before becoming Christians, speaking of "works of darkness" (Rom. 13:12) and "works of the flesh" (Gal. 5:19).

The change of number is especially striking in Galatians 5: Paul categorizes the vices listed in his catalogue under the heading "works of the flesh," while using the heading "fruit of the Spirit" for his catalogue of virtues. The singular is all the more striking because several fruits, not just one, are listed. The differentiation of the fruits is clearly secondary to their single origin and single focus. The disintegration of the person and the splintered multiplicity of the person's acts are overcome. According to Paul, God does not require this, that, and the other, an endless list of details. God claims the whole self, with all that one has and all that one is.

1.3 Notwithstanding this integral basis of the apostle's ethics and the Christian way of life that issues from it, Paul's numerous particular admonitions and injunctions illustrate the concreteness of this ethics in a variety of instructions (1 Thess. 4:2) and commandments (1 Cor. 7:19), of ways (1 Cor. 4:17) and traditions (1 Cor. 11:2). Paul was not content to call unflinchingly for total and undivided obedience. He could also speak without hesitation of specific individual demands. In such demands the totality of the new obedience is manifest.

In 2 Cor. 8:7, Paul can assure a community that it is rich in everything. What matters to him, however, is that the love and zeal of the Corinthians should now find expression and demonstrate its genuineness in a very specific single act, the collection for Jerusalem. In such a concrete offering, the total offering of their lives can take the form of a concrete event, for which Paul commends the Macedonian communities in v. 5. In the particular act of love they gave themselves totally. In his parenetic chapters, too, Paul repeatedly exhorts and demands in quite concrete terms. An example is 1 Thess. 4:1ff.: according to v. 6, the Lord requires that specific commandments be observed and will take vengeance if they are not (cf. v. 8).

Pauline ethics does not allow individual acts and thoughts, individual words and deeds, to vanish in a strict but abstract demand for total integrity (cf. also 2 Cor. 10:5ff.; 1 Thess. 5:22; Phil. 1:9). An instructive example of how specific Paul's admonitions can be is provided by 1 Corinthians 7, where he does not hesitate to confront the community with his admonitions and instructions even in questions of sexual ethics.

The Pauline "catalogues" of virtues and vices, especially Galatians 5, also confirm that integrity and concretenenss go hand in hand and must relate to each other. Each individual virtue or vice is an instance, a symptom, and a consequence of a life that is good or evil as a whole. Of course both "flesh" and "Spirit" refer to a sphere and dimension that is all-encompassing, but the concrete details are not simply the realm of the devil. In them the new being as a whole is at stake. While Paul sees the individual items in his catalogue of virtues as growing out of the single fruit of the Spirit, he does mention the particular manifestations by name and refuses to leave the concrete development of the Christian life simply to the free will and spontaneity of each person possessed by the Spirit. Even abstract concepts lead to concrete acts.[44]

The same is true of the catalogues of vices. Human sin, although usually spoken of in the singular as a power, does not consist solely in general or even theoretical wickedness. Total wickedness is manifest in empirical conduct and specific transgressions. Paul's admonitions to Christians accordingly not only warn against sin in general but also refer to specific actions and decisions as sin, because the individual act once again establishes the dominion of sin (1 Cor. 8:12; 6:18; Gal. 6:1).

Paul was therefore not content to proclaim universal ethical principles, either positive or negative. He did not hesitate to develop the new obedience in detail. The concrete variety of the apostle's instructions must not be rejected as a moralistic disintegration of the integrity of Christian ethics, especially since Paul clearly does not attach the same importance to each specific case. Anyone who applies the term "moralism" to specific instructions that go beyond the law of love will obviously find moralism in Paul, but is also open to the charge of thinking along the lines of the mystery religions. In the mysteries, it is in fact true that what is reborn is not actually the concrete historical person but rather a something within that person.[45] Of course Paul does not wish to drown the life of Christians in a sea of casuistic trivia. Nor does he wish to provide laws applicable to every conceivable situation. But he does wish for concrete application to real life.

The difference between Paul's approach and casuistry lies not in a lack of concreteness but in the absence of any elaborate system embodying every possible injunction and reducing them all to a lowest common denominator of triviality. Comparison of Paul's approach to the question of food in 1 Corinthians 8—10 or Romans 14—15 with the myriad Jewish regulations concerning clean and unclean makes the difference clear. Another example is his advice to married couples to refrain from sexual intercourse only for a season and by agreement, without going into detail about the length of time (1 Cor. 7:5). The rabbis, of course, often give precise directions about the frequency or avoidance of sexual intercourse.[46]

1.4 The real question at issue, however, is not whether Paul thinks Christians should act correctly, but whether an outside person, particularly the apostle, can impose on them concrete requirements of what they must and must not do. Many scholars treat Paul's specific injunctions, although indisputably present, as an emergency or interim solution applicable only to the

---

44. Wibbing, *Lasterkataloge* (B7), 58–59, 108, 123; cf. Vögtle, *Lasterkataloge* (B7), 158–59.
45. Rudolf Bultmann, "Das Problem der Ethik bei Paulus," *ZNW* 23 (1924): 133.
46. Strack-Billerbeck, *Kommentar* 3:368ff.

missionary congregations, which were not yet firmly established. Individual self-determination with its concomitant rejection of all concrete instruction is, to them, the authentic Pauline ideal. As time passes, it will prevail in practice and render all individual commandments superfluous.[47]

If this were true, we would expect to find passages urging such ethical autonomy, suggesting the historical relativity of the admonitions, or deploring their continued necessity. In fact there is no trace of such desire or complaint. Paul's remonstrances refer to specific grievances, not the need for admonition. Essential to parenesis is not only the constant need to be timely but also the constant need to confront people with concrete injunctions. In 1 Corinthians 10, for example, Paul is not content with a general warning against overconfidence ("let anyone who thinks that he stands take heed lest he fall"). He gives it concrete application, warning, for example, against sexual immorality (v. 8). Note above all the appearance of many injunctions that, although concrete and specific, coincide in substance with the fundamental commandments and would really seem to be self-evident, as is especially true in this particular case. Paul does not, however, go beyond the obvious basics of ethics to propose an agenda or instruct those who are ethically advanced. Indeed, he has nothing to say on such matters. This very observation argues against the theory that the concrete injunctions are gradually to become superfluous.

A few examples may reinforce this position. In 1 Thess. 4:1–2 and 4:11, Paul refers expressly to his previous instructions, familiar to the community from his missionary parenesis. His letters, therefore, do much more than provide previously unfamiliar ethical instructions with new content; they repeat what has long been familiar. The community not only *knows* this familiar material, but also *does* it (1 Thess. 4:1, 10; 5:11; cf. also 1 Cor. 4:17); this is especially damaging to the theory that increasing maturity renders injunctions superfluous. What Paul criticizes is sin, not temptation, and certainly not the need for parenesis.

2. The Situational Pluralism of the Apostolic Commandment

2.1 The opposite of the notion that the concreteness of parenesis is actually unnecessary and superfluous is the theory that Pauline ethics is exclusively concrete and situational and for this very reason limited to unique historical cases. According to this theory, Paul does nothing more than give specific instructions for specific cases.[48] Now it is of course undeniable that many of Paul's injunctions were occasioned by highly topical problems and dangers

47. See Wolfgang Schrage, "Zur formalethischen Deutung der paulinischen Paränese," *ZEE* 4 (1960): 207–33.

48. Oscar Cullmann, *Christ and Time*, 2d ed. (Philadelphia: Westminster Press; London: SCM Press, 1964), 229.

and address specific situations (above all 1 Corinthians, where Paul refers explicitly to questions asked by the community, even quoting some of them, as in 7:1). Paul's ethics accordingly cannot be understood as timely moral truth, independent of all historical conditions. Its individual injunctions are not meant without exception for all people in all situations; in part they are unique and unrepeatable (cf. Philemon), in part quite pragmatic and practical (cf. 1 Cor. 16:2).

On the other hand, however, we repeatedly find sections of Paul's letters couched in quite general terms, which do not refer to specific situations. This is especially true of parenesis. Alongside specific situational injunctions we find others that do not have a unique situation and occasion. The specifically parenetic chapters (Romans 12—13; Galatians 5—6; 1 Thessalonians 4) with their distinctive style, comprising loosely articulated sayings or groups of sayings without apparent organization, in many cases exhibit hardly any direct relationship to the situation of the letter. These admonitions are "not formulated for specific congregations and specific cases, but for the common needs of the earliest Christians. Their significance is not topical but generic."[49] It can also be shown that Paul often uses topical admonitions to introduce others not related to the problem at hand or treats the particular problem from a more general perspective (cf. Romans 14—15; and 1 Corinthians 8—10; 13).

2.2 Emphasis on the situational nature of the apostle's parenesis must also be distinguished from an interpretation that sees Christian conduct in general as being determined primarily by the situation. There is a certain justification in treating Pauline parenesis from the perspective of situation ethics, because it is able to encompass freedom of choice and spontaneous love. Often, however, a false antithesis is established between contextual ethics and substantive commandments, an antithesis that cannot be justified on pneumatological grounds.

When life is lived in the Spirit, there is no place for laws and commandments. Those who walk in the Spirit do on their own what God's law would command, because the Spirit shows them the way. God no longer comes to pneumatics "from without." This is Lietzmann's classic formulation of the position.[50] Weiss speaks of the free creative power of religious subjectivity, which derives its own law from within.[51] Christ himself guides the life of Christians from above through direct communications of the Spirit.[52]

Exegetes who support this interpretation appeal, for example, to expressions like "the Spirit in us" or "Christ in us" (Rom. 8:1ff.). But the true point of these expressions is quite different, namely, to express the radical

---

49. Martin Dibelius, *From Tradition to Gospel* (Cambridge: Clarke, 1971), 238.
50. Hans Lietzmann, *An die Römer*, 4th ed., HNT 8, 71.
51. Johannes Weiss, *Earliest Christianity* (Gloucester: Peter Smith, 1970 [1954]), 556–57.
52. See Enslin, *Ethics*, 101, 130; for additional bibliography, see Schrage, *Einzelgebote*, 75.

nature of belonging to Christ, which involes the very core of the human person. There is no hint in any context where such expression occurs that the Spirit dwelling within Christians frees them from commandments that come from without or that, filled with the Spirit, they know God's will without outward aid. Romans 8:4 states that the Spirit makes it possible to fulfill the just requirements of the law, already familiar. Nowhere does the language reveal any predilection for autonomy or hostility toward the "external word." The Corinthian libertines, too, appealed to the Spirit, and yet as transgressors of the law forfeited inheritance of the kingdom (1 Cor. 6:9).

Even expressions that emphasize the personal element in the relationship between Christians and their Lord, such as "serving" or "obeying" Christ, never stand in opposition to the commandments of Christ or of his apostle. Personal obedience to the Lord manifests itself in obedience to his commandments. In Rom. 14:18, for example, "serving Christ" is related specifically to concrete admonitions (cf. also Rom. 16:18). Never, though, does Paul confuse or confound the judgment and will of Christians with the commandment of God, of Christ, or of the Spirit. The fact that 1 Thess. 4:9 says that knowledge of love of the brethren has been taught by God, even though the apostle exhorts his readers to love one another, is not a contradiction, even if instruction on the part of the apostle or others is only secondarily necessary— as long as the present eon endures.[53] Normally, of course, Christians do not encounter God's commandment apart from and independent of the apostle's exhortations, but in them. His exhortations are obligatory and binding because Christ himself exhorts and commands through them (2 Cor. 13:3; Rom. 15:18).

The obligation imposed by the apostolic instructions is connected with the role of the apostle, who speaks as representative and messenger of his Lord Jesus Christ, both binding and loosing. The apostle does not exhort and encourage, command and admonish, in his own name but in the name of Jesus Christ; those who disregard his commands transgress against Christ and against God (1 Thess. 4:6, 8). Of course Paul never merely imposes a formal authority. He calls on his readers to judge what he writes (1 Cor. 10:15). Dialectically, it is proper to speak at once of a mature and responsible community, which is not reduced to obeying blindly apostolic decrees. Nor, however, are Paul's admonitions a more-or-less optional contribution to the dialogue or an unauthoritative personal opinion. They establish the will of God with authority and demand to be followed (2 Cor. 2:9; 7:15; Phil. 2:12; Philem. 8–11). This is also the basis on which the apostle calls on his readers to imitate his conduct (1 Cor. 4:16–17; 11:1; Phil. 4:9; 3:17).

2.3 Although some passages even exhibit a claim to a certain universality (1 Cor. 4:17; 7:17; 11:16), not everything the apostle says is of the same

---

53. Schürmann, *Orientierungen*, 69.

weight and authority. Paul is aware of differences and limits, and is quite capable of making distinctions in what he demands of particular individuals or groups. He has no choice but to leave most specific decisions about everyday matters to the resourcefulness and responsibility of love. In many instances he naturally counts on the judgment of those concerned: for example, with respect to the amount of the collection (cf. 1 Cor. 16:2; 2 Cor. 8:7–8). He leaves many questions deliberately open: for example, what types of conduct require charismatic qualification. If a charisma is not a human possibility, for instance, Paul cannot preach celibacy as a commandment for all Christians. In some passages he even seems to reckon with a variety of decisions when both the question and the situation are the same.[54]

Of interest for this question of decisions is 1 Cor. 6:1ff., where Paul clearly considers the possibility of two different forms of Christian conduct. What he rules out as irreconcilable with the eschatological call of Christians is for Christians to become litigious against each other and take their disputes before pagan courts. On the positive side, Paul first suggests the possibility of appointing Christians as mediators to decide disputes before authorities within the Christian community (vv. 1–6). In vv. 7–8, however, he goes further, calling the very existence of lawsuits or the demand for personal vindication a "defeat." Christians should simply suffer wrong.[55]

The juxtaposition of the two passages makes it clear that Paul is not demanding renunciation of all rights as a general rule, but is presenting a choice between two possible courses of Christian action: assertion of rights or mediation on the one hand and renunciation of rights on the other—a renunciation that does not mean passivity, but, like nonresistance, is intended to overcome evil through good (cf. Rom. 12:17, 21). The two courses are not simply put forward as equivalent options: Paul clearly prefers renunciation of rights to legal proceedings or mediation within the community. But he does indicate that there can be different courses of action within the framework of the community.

The situation is quite analogous in the case of marriage and celibacy; here, too, Paul considers celibacy to be what the times demand (1 Cor. 7:38, 40), but it is better to marry than to burn (v. 9). Further evidence for variation in ethical judgment and conduct is the existence of strong and weak side by side in a single community (Rom. 14—15; 1 Cor. 8—10). Here Paul states clearly his opinion of how Christians with different styles of life should relate to each other.

At Corinth the majority of the community clearly have no reservations about eating sacrificial flesh, while a few who are weak refuse to do so out of ingrained scrupulosity. But the strong have no right to insist on their deci-

54. See the discussion by Schweizer and Schrage in *EvTh* 35.
55. Erich Dinkler, "Zum Problem der Ethik bei Paulus," *ZThK* 49 (1952): 167–200 (*Signum Crucis* [Tübingen: Mohr, 1967], 207–40).

sion, however correct it may be, as the only right one. At Rome each group clearly contests the propriety of the other's decision. To them Paul must therefore speak more forcibly about the conditions and consequences of variety in the Christian way of life. The "weak," who practice vegetarianism and abstain from wine, certainly do not seem to think of themselves as weak; they consider themselves more serious and conscientious Christians, suspecting and condemning the freer and more natural life style of the others. The latter clearly do the same in reverse (Rom. 14:3–4, 10, 13).[56]

Paul clearly ranges himself on the side of the "strong," for it is certainly true that nothing is unclean in itself (Rom. 14:14, 20). But although the strong are correct in principle, he demands mutual tolerance and community solidarity. Each group should accept the others, not in order to convert them to their own life style or denigrate their decisions, but unreservedly and with total respect. Thus Paul recognizes that a variety of decisions are possible in the context of a very concrete mandate (mandatum concretissimum).

2.4 This does not mean that Paul considered ethical variety a praiseworthy abundance on a par with the variety of spiritual gifts. He would prefer that God would guide the community to unity even in disputed questions (Rom. 15:5). Above all, ethical pluralism is not boundless. It is possible only within a specific circle, whose extent cannot be delimited precisely. There is certainly no neutral ground where Christians are exempt from responsibility before God, not even in questions of eating or not eating, observing or not observing days (1 Cor. 10:31; Rom. 14:6–7). But there are some areas of life where a variety in practice is possible, but only—as we must add if we are not to modernize Paul—when fundamental ethical principles are not involved. In principle the freedom of the Christian life cannot be limited, but love and responsibility toward others in the community set clear limits: "Not all things are helpful; not all things build up" (1 Cor. 6:12; 10:23). Another limit is set by personal danger. A typical statement is 1 Cor. 6:12, where Paul first limits freedom out of regard for others (v. 12a), but then also warns against letting oneself be dominated by anything, so that freedom is turned once more into slavery (v. 12b).

The limit imposed on all conduct acceptable within the community appears clearly when Paul enforces "ecclesiastical discipline" for reasons of "orthopraxy." Such limits are set only in extreme cases. This does not mean, however, that all limits are automatically open to discussion and revision.

According to 1 Cor. 5:1ff., for a Christian to live in irregular marriage with his stepmother is unacceptable within the community. Paul therefore definitively finalizes the break with the community already made by the offending Christian through his concubinage. Of course the ultimate purpose of this

---

56. See Von Soden, "Sakrament und Ethik bei Paulus"; Gerd Theissen, "Die Starken und Schwachen in Korinth," *EvTh* 35 (1975): 155–72 (= *The Social Setting of Pauline Christianity*, 121–44).

"excommunication" is meant to be deliverance, not damnation (v. 5). It is nevertheless striking how little Paul is ready to concede in the situation. This chapter, however, is a unique case and clearly a last resort.[57]

This borderline case shows that the holiness and responsibility of the community make it impossible simply to accept obvious sin in silence. For Paul, freedom and mutual respect do not imply simple affirmation of whatever takes place within a universal Christendom.

3. Free and Conscientious Obedience

3.1 There is no denying that conscientious decision is of great moment in Pauline ethics. Not as though isolated decisions of the individual play the deciding role in the question of what God requires, but the judgment of conscience cannot be left subject to an outside party if the sense of responsibility is to be preserved.

In using the term "conscience," Paul employs a concept of great importance for his contemporary world. Seneca in particular describes what is meant in his *De ira* 3.36: self-examination. In our consciences we confront ourselves critically; our self reflects on its own thoughts and actions. The conscience is the tribunal before which self-recognition *(recognitio sui)* takes place, in the form of subsequent self-examination and reflection on the basis of a norm. Paul himself probably borrowed the concept from Hellenistic Judaism, where we find (especially in Philo) ideas similar to those of Seneca.[58]

For Paul, too, conscience is where individual Christians confront themselves critically and judge their conduct. It is not as though they simply encounter themselves here: conscience is a voice remarkably independent of individuals and their desires, their subjective ideas, and their personal worlds. It bears independent witness, bears witness with us, as Rom. 2:15 would have us say. On the other hand, conscience is by no means itself the voice of God. The verdict of conscience may be determined by the Holy Spirit (Rom. 9:1), it may be identical with faith, but it is not therefore autonomous, absolute, or definitive (1 Cor. 4:4). Furthermore, Paul sees the function of conscience as more evaluative than directive and normative, even though it may precede an act. In any event, conscience is not so much a guiding authority, establishing in its own right the substance of what is required, as a critical authority, using certain criteria to judge what people do or fail to do. What is to be done is prescribed not by conscience but by the commandments, or else the community is to determine it.[59]

57. See Ernst Käsemann, "Sentences of Holy Law in the New Testament," in *Questions*, 66–81, esp. 70ff.; Siegfried Meurer, *Das Recht im Dienst der Versöhnung* (Zurich: Theologischer Verlag, 1972), 117ff.; Göran Forkman, *The Limits of the Religious Community*, CB.NT 5 (Lund: Gleerup, 1972), 139ff.

58. See Christian Maurer, "Synoida," *TDNT* 7:898ff.; Bultmann, *Theology* (B), 211ff.; P. Hilsberg, "Das Gewissen im NT," *Theologische Versuche* 9 (1977), 145–60.

59. Hilsberg, "Gewissen," 155; see also below, 197.

The criterion by which the concience of a Christian judges is not the logos of the universe or a philosophical ideal (e.g., what is immutably in harmony with nature and reason) but God's demand, which is also imposed at the last judgment (note the similarity of some passages dealing with conscience to eschatological statements). In Rom. 2:15, for example, the conscience refers to the requirements of the law, which are written on the heart. In Rom. 13:5, it is connected with the need to be subject to God's will and commandment. Of course Christian duty is no exception. Thus the judgment of conscience is not limited to the realm of universally acknowledged good and evil. Only in this sense is conscientious Christian decision the criterion of Christian conduct.

In this sense it is true to say that one must obey one's conscience. All Christians should be certain of their own convictions, fully convinced in faith and conscience that their judgment is correct (Rom. 14:5). The very self is at stake in the verdict of conscience; therefore those who have a "weak conscience" (1 Cor. 8:7, 12) are themselves "weak" (1 Cor. 8:9–11).

This does not mean that a conscientious decision continues to hold "even when it goes astray."[60] We must recall that the divergences described in 1 Corinthians 8—10 and Romans 14—15 did not involve fundamental questions of conduct; Paul would hardly have tolerated a decision of conscience that transgressed God's law, for example. Only on this condition does he approve the approach of the "weak," who cannot free themselves from their past and draw the appropriate conclusions from the confession of one God and one Lord, and therefore still cannot think of meat offered to idols as food like any other.

Above all, Paul sees conscience or its dictates as being limited by love. The question of whether it is right or wrong to eat flesh offered to idols is decided ultimately by reference to others, not to God. Paul states explicitly that love can even lead one to forgo what one's conscience has determined to be necessary and proper. Anyone who wounds the conscience of the "weak" (1 Cor. 8:12) sins against other Christians and against Christ. This means that an individual's conscientious decision cannot be made absolute. It also means that the opposite decision on the part of the "weak" cannot be imposed absolutely. Both groups must heed the dictates of conscience.[61]

3.2 Conscience in particular does not dispense Christians from the authority of the apostle's command, from accepting it freely and obediently. In 2 Cor. 2:9, Paul says that his reason for writing was to test whether the Corinthians were obedient in everything. Since this is not to be understood as authoritarianism or spiritual dictatorship, as Paul himself says a few verses previously (2 Cor. 1:14), such obedience is clearly to be free and unconstrained, informed and not blind. The ultimate object of this obedience is not

60. Bultmann, *Theology*, 220.
61. Hilsberg, "Gewissen," 148.

the apostle but the Lord who works through him; the apostle himself must be judged on the basis of his message (cf. Gal. 1:8). It would therefore be wrong to picture the relationship between the apostle and the community simply as that between leader and followers, with the community assigned the role of a docile and dependent inferior. Paul can only exhort "for love's sake" (Philem. 9) to do what love requires; he cannot press or coerce.

He is therefore unwilling to force Philemon to release the runaway slave Onesimus, whom he could make good use of in his captivity, by simply presenting him with a fait accompli. The "goodness" Paul expects from Philemon is not to be "by compulsion" but of free will (Philem. 14). Paul is neither willing nor able simply to issue commands; he counts on the free obedience and agreement of the one who obeys. To be under an obligation and yet do what is required freely and willingly is not a contradiction (cf. Rom. 15:27; 2 Cor. 9:7). But if true obedience is "from the heart" (Rom. 6:17), obedience shaped by one's inmost self, it is the antithesis of mere formal correctness and outward observance.

Proper obedience includes not only free assent but understanding. Respect for civil authority, for example, is to be a matter of conscience (Rom. 13:5). The recognition owed (cf. v. 1) must spring from inward conviction. The apostle therefore wishes his admonitions to be heard and heeded not as arbitrary law but as perspicacious and perspicuous instruction. There is no place, therefore, for mere outward acquiescence or uncritical servility toward the state. The undoubted will of God is not the whim of a despot who demands only subservience, but the will of a father toward his children, to whom he has made known his will (cf. Rom. 8:14ff.; Gal. 4:6) in order that it may be understood and acknowledged (Phil. 1:9; Rom. 12:2).

3.3 For Paul, however, all knowledge of God's will is only partial (1 Cor. 13:9). Life's complexities constantly confront us with new tasks, so that we are under a continual obligation, drawing on the apostolic commandments and traditions (cf. 1 Thess. 4:2–3; Phil. 4:9), to determine God's will in the present moment (cf. Rom. 12:2). It is therefore all the more necessary to renew our powers of knowledge and judgment (Rom. 12:2): they are "untrustworthy" for non-Christians (Rom. 1:28), but, like every other human faculty, are caught up in the new creation effected by Christ. Certainly reason does not have the last word in questions of Christian conduct; it cannot set aside the commandments of God. Nevertheless, reason and insight, wisdom and knowledge, play an important role in Pauline ethics. For Paul, love finds expression in knowledge, judgment, and discrimination (Phil. 1:9–10), a point that must constantly be remembered whenever we face calls for decision and action. For Paul, the "primary ethical stance" is a very specific way of thinking, for which there can be no substitute in the form of action, belief, or prayer.[62] Of course this way of thinking is not an end in itself; it is meant to

62. Karl Barth, *The Epistle to the Romans*, 436.

be followed up by action (cf. Phil. 4:9). But Christian obedience implies not only respect for what tradition commands but also the creative search for new pathways. The goal and direction of these pathways is determined, but the substance of Christian ethics (cf. Rom. 14:14; 1 Cor. 6:9, 15–16; 1 Thess. 4:2) is not a fixed body of knowledge that has no need for further judgment and decision. Knowledge informed by faith (Philem. 6) and love (Phil. 1:9) is not meant to rest content with what has gone before but to ask what God's will is in each new situation. What is tested is what is "excellent" (Phil. 1:10), that is, what is best at any given moment.[63] This inquiry into what is required here and now must by its very nature always be done afresh. What is "excellent" in any particular case naturally depends to a large extent on the changing situation and circumstances. The abundance of love spoken of by Phil. 1:9 in the context of ethical discrimination can increase and grow ("more and more"), but it can never reach a final limit. The Christian community can only advance one step at a time in the decisions it faces here and now.

It is important that these decisions are not simply the private affair of isolated individuals but are the concern of the community. This is why Paul emphasizes the common search for the right way. The locus of this search is not one's private chamber but worship,[64] where the community comes together to hear and to discriminate, but above all where prophets raise their voices in words of encouragement, warning, and direction (1 Corinthians 14). If the teachers of the community guarantee continuity and tradition in ethics, the prophets guarantee topicality. In the ongoing search for God's concrete will by the individual communities, the situational nature of prophetic discourse was probably very important for instruction in specific cases. Of course the imperfection (1 Cor. 13:9) and variety (1 Cor. 14:29–30) of prophecy makes it necessary to weigh what is said (1 Cor. 14:29). Like individuals, the community needs not only courage and inventiveness, but also criteria by which to judge. Paul repeatedly presents such criteria, both implicitly and explicitly.

In view of the importance of this discrimination, guided by the Spirit, which tests everything and holds fast to what is good (1 Thess. 5:19–20), it is better not to speak of "norms," even in the case of Paul. Norms easily evoke the legalistic misconception of a "deontological" ethics, which ignores the consequences of actions and "teleological" arguments.

C. MATERIAL CRITERIA

1. Relationship to Non-Christian Criteria

1.1 It is widely held that we should not look for the new and unique features of Pauline ethics in specific directives and criteria, but in the way

---

63. See Walter Grundmann, "dokimos," *TDNT* 2:260.
64. See Klaus Wengst, "Das Zusammenkommen der Gemeinde und ihr 'Gottesdienst' nach Paulus," *EvTh* 33 (1973): 547–59; Schürmann, *Orientierungen*, 64ff.

Paul fulfills and realizes universal ethical norms, infusing them with a new motivation. In this view, we do not find the authentically Christian element in substantial reformulation of ethical criteria, but in the acceptance of long familiar criteria in new ways or with deeper insight: all conduct now stands under the sign of God's grace in Christ. This view undoubtedly reflects a fundamental aspect of Paul's thought, even though we must note at once that motivations normally tend to influence the nature of conduct and to imply specific meanings.[65] One may remain celibate out of convenience or a sense of resignation rather than by accepting charismatic celibacy for the sake of the Lord and the special opportunity it provides for service, or one may practice hospitality based on hedonism rather than love; these motivations affect the action itself. Furthermore, the traditional virtues not only find a new context through being associated with the Lord, but also acquire a new meaning. The new and characteristic central feature of Pauline ethics is undoubtedly its christological motivation, the new being bestowed through grace alone that is prior to all human action. But this observation by no means settles the question whether there are not concrete ethical demands that are specifically Christian, or, more precisely, demands that are commensurate with Christianity.

1.2 Of course there are many who roundly deny that there is any new substance: they maintain that the content of Pauline ethics does not exhibit any new features from the Christ event.[66] According to Bultmann, the ethical demands imposed on Christians have "no new content" and do not as such require anything "that the judgment of non-Christians would not also acknowledge as good."[67] But is Pauline ethics really subsumed in a universal ethos? Has Paul merely changed motives and reasons? Is christology relevant only in the context of motivation and not also in the substantial shaping of the Christian life?

If we look at the evidence of Paul's own writings, the first thing we notice is the injunction not to live in conformity to this eon (Rom. 12:2) and to stay away from the activities of those who stand "outside" (1 Cor. 5:12–13). This rejection of everything worldly by the "saints" does not mean refusal to associate with those of this world—"for then we would have to go out of the world" (1 Cor. 5:10)—but it does mean unmistakable rejection of specific customs and practives and an irrevocable break with certain concrete ways of life common in the world (cf. 1 Thess. 4:5; Phil. 2:15). Without the contrast between the life style of the world and the will of God, passages like Rom. 12:2 would lose their meaning (cf. also the "formerly–now" schema). These passages alone make it hard for the schizophrenic theory—that Christians

65. Halter, *Taufe*, 475.
66. Dinkler, "Problem," 199.
67. Bultmann, "Problem," 138; cf. also Conzelmann, *Outline* (B), 282–83; Georg Strecker, "Ziele und Ergebnisse einer neutestamentlichen Ethik," *NTS* 25 (1978): 11–12. See the criticism in Luz, "Eschatologie," 226 n. 5.

live by the power of the new world but by the criteria of the old—to have Paul's support. It would also be wrong to take Romans 1—2 in isolation and interpret them as laying the foundation of Christian ethics. For Paul they play an auxiliary role, showing that human beings are without excuse (Rom. 1:20). In any case, "natural" ethics is never a fixed framework for Paul, especially since the context significantly limits the actual resources of reason and it is not Paul's purpose "to lay down a viable moral code."[68] This does not gainsay the fact that what is right can also be known and done outside the Christian community, even though Paul immediately establishes certain limits ("here and there, now and then" [Rom. 2:4]).[69]

On the other hand, Romans 1—2 makes it quite clear that, despite all sinfulness, Paul assumes the existence of moral norms and requirements among non-Christians. This law, "written on their hearts," is not the demand of some natural law; it is the divine law itself. This would lead us to expect that the nature and criteria of moral conduct are basically identical for Christians and non-Christians. Pauline parenesis itself confirms this partial ethical consensus. We may recall passages urging conduct that will engender respect in the eyes of "outsiders" (1 Thess. 4:12; cf. 1 Cor. 10:32; Rom. 13:13). This concern for the opinion of non-Christians certainly presupposes a common moral standard. Only if there is such a commonly accepted criterion does it make sense to take seriously what non-Christians think about the Christian way of life. The very fact that Paul borrows from the Hellenistic world the term *euschēmonōs* to describe morally irreproachable conduct suggests that there is general agreement as to what is correct in any given instance.[70]

1.3 We must also call attention to Paul's extensive borrowing of both formal and substantial elements of ethics from his contemporary world. This, too, reveals implicitly Paul's awareness of a universal ethics, known and accepted by all, to whose demands all are subject. Of course this process of borrowing cannot be discussed exhaustively here. It must suffice to cite examples that illustrate the complex relationship between open acceptance on the one hand and selective qualification on the other.

Philippians 4:8, a conventional catalogue of virtues made up of terms from popular moral philosophy, provides an instructive example of how Paul borrows common ethical forms and substance. Even here, however, we must note that, although it is impossible to ignore or scorn "natural" ethics, this ethics is not autonomous: the context of the passage proclaims that the Lord is at hand (v. 5), inculcates the law of love (v. 5), and promises the peace of

---

68. Schnackenburg, "Ethik" (B1), 196–97.

69. Cf. Schrage, *Einzelgebote*, 192 n. 15; Otto Kuss, "Die Heiden und die Werke des Gesetzes," *MThZ* 5 (1954): 77–98 (= *Auslegung und Verkündigung*, 2 vols. [Regensburg: Pustet, 1963–76], 1:213–45).

70. Heinrich Greeven, "euschēmōn," *TDNT* 2:770–71.

God (v. 7). "What appears at first glance to be a foreign body within Paul's 'ethics' proves to be a critical incorporation of what the world knows to be good, purified by walking in the Spirit under the norm of eschatological agape. Within the community, the ethos of the world ceases to be worldly, and the community of Christ, as the eschatological reality it is, must make a beginning in the revelation of Christ's lordship in the domain of ethics under the law."[71] Elsewhere, too, as we shall see in the next section, the strong influence of Jewish and Stoic ethics is clear, along with the popular morality of daily life, but everywhere we find specific accents and material differences that are unmistakably Pauline.

In any case, it is out of the question to claim the complete identity of Christian and non-Christian ethics. If we are not simply to reduce everything to a lowest common denominator, we must not forget that, with all Paul's incorporation of contemporary ethics, there is a concurrent process of selection and sifting applied to the diverse ethical material. Everything must be tested, but only what is good is to be retained (1 Thess. 5:21). This suggests a priori that the process of inclusion is also a process of selection.[72] All acceptance was therefore selective and critical, not absolute. Not only were the terms and concepts borrowed from the ancient world selected carefully, they were in part given specifically Christian meaning and reorientation. As will be shown, we often find their content reshaped.

The unmistakable congruity of Christian and non-Christian conduct does not exclude the possibility of certain differences between them. Again the crucial influence is christology. The term "humility" (*tapeinophrosyne*), for example, is used only pejoratively in secular Hellenistic Greek, because fundamental renunciation of self-assertion is alien to the Hellenistic Roman world; the Stoics in fact consider it a vice. Josephus, too, considers humility a typical characteristic of slaves, avoided by anyone with self-respect.[73] In Phil. 2:3 (cf. also 2 Cor. 1:7; Rom. 12:16), however, it takes on positive meaning, probably because we are told that Christ "humbled himself" (Phil. 2:8). Grundmann finds in the correspondence between human conduct and the Christ event "a possibility not seen by the Greeks and also transcending the statements of the Old Testament and Judaism."[74]

2. The Meaning of the Old Testament

2.1 Paul's borrowing of ancient ethics undoubtedly presupposes belief in divine creation. And yet we must note at the very outset that for Paul the theology of creation is, to coin a phrase, primarily a christology of creation (H. F. Weiss, *Schöpfung in Christus*, 24–32) analogous to Jesus' incorporation

71. Heinz-Dieter Wendland, "Zur kritischen Bedeutung der neutestamentlichen Lehre von den beiden Reichen," *ThLZ* 79 (1964): 321–26; quotation from 326.
72. Furnish, *Theology*, 81.
73. *Jewish War* 4.494.
74. Walter Grundmann, "tapeinos," *TDNT* 8:22.

of wisdom elements into his eschatology. Paul speaks of creation primarily in the context of new creation in Christ. In other words, he deliberately uses the theological language of creation when expounding his doctrine of justification (cf. Rom. 4:17; 9:19ff.; 2 Cor. 4:6). This means that creation can hardly be considered the general background of Pauline theology;[75] it is rather "a way of interpreting soteriology, and is therefore associated with and subordinate to the message of salvation."[76] But if there is no separate and autonomous doctrine of creation—and even in the Old Testament, belief in creation derives from the experience of salvation, that is, from God's liberating and redeeming acts—then there is also no such thing as a separate ethics of creation. There are no autonomous norms based on creation, not to speak of subsuming ethics within a universal natural law.

On the other hand, God's saving act in Jesus Christ reveals the world once more as God's creation. Therefore the "one God, who created all things" appears alongside the "one Lord, Jesus Christ," who is the mediator of creation (1 Cor. 8:6). This is why Paul, in contrast to the Gnostics, could never interpret and disparage the world as the work of a demiurge. For him the world is and always will be God's creation (Rom. 1:20) and God is the Creator (Rom. 1:25). All things come from God and belong to God (1 Cor. 8:6; 10:26). The eschatological age ushered in by Christ does not bring destruction. Instead, the Creator's will from the beginning is fulfilled and surpassed. Belief in creation is for Paul an important defense against extremes of asceticism and fear of the world on the part of Christians. Statements like "the earth is the Lord's and everything in it" (1 Cor. 10:25, citing Ps. 24:1) or "everything is clean" (Rom. 14:20) have substantial importance for Pauline ethics. If all things come from God's hand, this fact has ethical consequences, as illustrated, say, by Paul's resolution of the problem of food offered to idols, where he maintains this faith in creation: Christians may eat any meat sold in the marketplace (1 Cor. 10:23ff.).

If we contrast the passages that speak of remaining aloof from the world that is passing away, describing celibacy, for instance, as a sign revealing the limits of created reality (1 Cor. 7:29ff.), we see that a Christian's relationship to the world is neither purely positive nor purely negative, but dialectical. According to Paul, Christians neither condemn nor idolize the world; they neither flee it nor embrace it. The aim of Paul's exhorting Christians to let their conduct be shaped by creation is neither radical rejection—the world is indeed God's creation and has reached its goal in Christ—nor uncritical acceptance—the world is indeed passing away—but the critical mean between worldliness and unworldliness. Just as there is a "no" to the fallen world, there is a "yes" to the created world, seen now once again as God's creation. Eschatology, however, relativizes even the good of creation, because

75. Hasenstab, *Modelle,* 144, citing Käsemann and Stuhlmacher.
76. Ibid., 154.

Paul does not reduce eschatology to restoration and does not conceive the new creation solely within the framework and against the background of creation.[77]

2.2 With these reservations, Paul does not hesitate to appeal to criteria derived from belief in creation, such as "nature" *(physis)*. For Paul, nature and the natural order are not independent entities; they do not define an ultimate, absolute criterion. He can nevertheless appeal to them now and again. When nature becomes unnatural (Rom. 1:26; here such "unnatural" conduct clearly refers to homosexuality), it is a symptom of apostasy. The reverse is also suggested, namely, that "natural relations" are consonant with God's will and the divine order.

In Rom. 1:26, *physis* designates what is consonant with the order of creation. In 1 Cor. 11:14, the concept has even less to do with a static entity; it refers to an order that manifests itself historically in tradition and custom. Even here, however, it is only one argument among many; it does not have the force of absolute authority. This observation does not vitiate the provisional value of an appeal to *physis*, but it cautions against exaggeration. Weiss, for example, states in his commentary on this passage: "In nature we perceive the revelation of God even more directly than in Scripture." But this describes the position of the Stoics, not that of Paul. The very rarity with which Paul uses the concept of nature is in striking contrast to its frequency in Hellenistic usage and confirms that "there is substantially no room for 'natural theology' in the thought of the New Testament."[78]

In this context we must also recall the exhortations to respect convention already noted (Rom. 13:13; 1 Cor. 7:35; 13:5; 14:40). Inappropriate or improper behavior would be, for Paul, the wrong conclusion to draw from the message that the end of the world is near (cf. 1 Cor. 13:5). The opinion of non-Christians is not only important because of "outsiders" (1 Thess. 4:12); it is also an authority to be respected within the community. This is not to suggest false compromises or uncritical accommodation. For Paul, the authority of non-Christians and respect for their opinions have distinct limits. If absolutely necessary, he can easily ignore the judgment of others. There are causes of offense, however, that are intrinsically necessary and others that are neither necessary nor authentic. Paul cautions against letting improper and dishonorable conduct provoke justifiable and avoidable criticism on the part of non-Christians. He himself is not a nonconformist on principle, nor, certainly, is he a conformist on principle.

2.3 Paul's attitude toward work, marriage, and the state also shows that we must not be too hasty in ignoring the structures and circumstances of the life we have received from the Creator. Eschatological fanatics who put aside their obligation to work at their calling Paul calls "people without order" (1 Thess.

77. Schrage, "Stellung," 129; Duchrow, *Christenheit* (B), 129, 133.
78. Helmut Koester, "physis," *TDNT* 9:271; cf. also 272.

5:14; cf. later 2 Thess. 3:6–7, 11). And in the confused conflict between asceticism and libertinism typical of Corinth, Paul also maintains his faith in creation. For him marriage is consonant with the created order; it is an effective barrier against the demonic power of unchastity and the triumph of evil—which does not mean, be it noted, that this exhausts the meaning and purpose of marriage (1 Cor. 7:11ff.; cf. also below, IV. D. 2.5).

In Romans 13, too, we find Paul clearly acknowledging the perspective of a theology of order. The point of his admonitions, however, is not to develop a doctrine of the state but to exhort Christians to behave properly toward the civil authorities (cf. below, IV. D. 4). On the other hand, we must recognize clearly that Paul bases his argument on the divine institution of the state and authorization of what it does. Paul's statements about marriage and the state are shaped by a variety of factors and motifs, and these ordinances belong to a world that is passing away. Nevertheless, his faith in creation assures him that God does not simply give the world over to chaos until the final transformation of all earthly reality. This is not because of any fundamental dignity inherent in the world itself but because it is so ordained by the Creator God, who does not give up his creation.

Despite 2 Cor. 4:4, "this world" is not simply in the hands of Satan. It is still God's creation, just as human beings are still God's creatures even though sinners (*simul peccator et creatus*). The Corinthians obviously fear the infectious power of the "flesh," advocating separation from the world and its children. According to 1 Cor. 7:14, however, God's power does not retreat from the world into locked dungeons and inner recesses; it penetrates the secular world as sanctifying power. Christians live, as it were, in a field of force that also affects non-Christians. Even sexual relations with non-Christians are neither dangerous nor harmful; they do not interfere with the relationship between Christians and God (cf. also 1 Cor. 8:4; 10:25ff.).

Christians are therefore not called upon to retreat into pious ghettos or form monastic orders like those of the Neopythagoreans or Essenes; they can be confident that even the institutions of this world are touched by the power of the Spirit. The holiness of God is more powerful than the unholiness of the world (cf. Test. of Benjamin 8:2–3; for the opposite view, cf. Syriac Baruch 98:4–5). Even in their present provisional character, the forms and structures of the world are willed by God; they are to be respected, not fanatically rejected. Paul is well aware that the world as a whole is not too happy with the ultimate sovereignty of God, and Christians can live peaceably only so far as it depends upon them (Rom. 12:18). But this by no means vitiates the call to bear the reality of Christ into the domain of the world.

2.4 The significance of the Old Testament for Pauline ethics is not limited to belief in creation. The Old Testament law and its commandments also have a place here, especially since for Jews the Torah is associated with the order of creation.[79] Paul's battle against legalism is not against observance of the law but against the perverse interpretation of such observance as a condition for salvation. God "justifies without works of the law," and the law has ceased to be a way of salvation, a "yoke of slavery" (Gal. 5:1) and a curse (Gal. 3:10, 13); but this does not mean that Christians are dispensed from obeying the commandments (1 Cor. 7:19). Therefore the Old Testament and its law are presupposed and enforced as the criterion of Christian conduct. There are instances where Paul as it were instinctively and without further justification presupposes certain conclusions deriving from Jewish thought based on the Torah.[80] These are not as significant, however, as the passage where Paul, debating with gentile Christians, appeals explicitly *(expressis vebis)* and deliberately to the Old Testament and its Torah.

Not so immediately striking is the more or less faithful citation and application of several Old Testament quotations, above all from the proverbial parenesis of wisdom literature and the legal books (Rom. 12:16, 17, 19, 20). Even here, however, several passages are introduced by introductory formulas (Rom. 12:19; 1 Cor. 6:16; 2 Cor. 8:15; 9:9). This shows that Paul is not simply quoting by rote and without reflection. Romans 12:19, with its motivating clause "for it is written," shows also that the words of the Old Testament remained authoritative. The situation is similar in 1 Cor. 5:13; 2 Cor. 8:15; 9:9, where the Old Testament quotations conclude the argument; they are not just decorative, but confirm and summarize authoritatively what has been said. Even the quotations without introductory formulas clearly reveal a sense of continuity in the ethical commandments. Note also the substantiating "for" in Rom. 13:8.

Nevertheless, the words of the Old Testament as quoted have lost their absolute and binding authority. They obviously cannot be the final court of appeal for Christians. The argument of 1 Corinthians 9 is instructive; we may think of it as a cumulative demonstration of the apostle's right to support from the community. In v. 7, Paul begins with three examples from the world of soldiers, winegrowers, and shepherds. Verses 8–9 reinforce this argument by reference to the Old Testament (Deut. 25:4). Verse 13 cites a further scriptural proof, and v. 14 a Word of the Lord. Since the argument clearly leads up to a climax, it follows that for Christians the Old Testament has "greater authority than the customs of everyday economic life" and a natural sense of what is just and proper.[81] On the other hand, the Old Testament no longer has autonomous significance for Christians; it is transcended and downgraded by the authority of the Word of the Lord. We must note, however, that Paul does not play one authority off against the other but cites

---

79. Cf. Holtz, "Weisungen," 395.
80. Ibid., 387ff., discussing 1 Cor. 1ff., 12ff.; etc.
81. See Heinz-Dieter Wendland, *Die Briefe an die Korinther,* NTD, on 1 Corinthians 9.

them in mutual support (cf. also Rom. 15:3, where the passage quoted from the Psalter confirms and illustrates the exemplary conduct of Christ).

We may cite 1 Corinthians 10 as a further example. Here, in a midrash on several passages from the Pentateuch, Paul employs his typological understanding of the Old Testament for parenesis. The events of the Old Testament are types: what befell Israel serves to instruct the Christian community, upon whom the end of the ages has come (v. 11). It is this end that gives the Old Testament its directive authority for the eschatological people of God.

2.5 The Old Testament, however, is hardly ever (except in Rom. 12:19) cited as the sole or decisive argument. The fact that Rom. 8:4 can speak of "fulfilling the just requirements of the law on the part of those who walk according to the Spirit" does not mean wholesale acceptance or restoration of what the commandments of law require. In brief: the law of the Old Testament must first become the "law of Christ" and be interpreted with respect to its true intention (Gal. 6:2); only then can it be the measure of Christian life. The fact that the Old Testament is binding on Christians only a posteriori means that there is an objective criterion, usually unstated, as well as a process of sifting and selection as described in Phil. 4:8 and 1 Thess. 5:23. The ethics of the Old Testament is accepted selectively and therefore critically. When people lose their fear of the curse and the damning verdict of the law, they obviously also lose exaggerated concern for the letter of the law. Non-observance of the Torah is already implicit in rejection of the ritual law (cf. the distinction between circumcision and the commandments of God in 1 Cor. 7:19). The statement that nothing is unclean (Rom. 14:14) contradicts the view of the Old Testament and Judaism. But there are also many ethical judgments of the Old Testament that Paul can no longer accept as types. Such revision of Old Testament ethics probably took place in part silently and without drama.

It is nevertheless noteworthy, for example, that Gen. 2:18 says that it is "not good" for the man to be alone, while Paul says in 1 Cor. 7:26 that it is "good" to avoid marriage and remarriage—certainly not because being alone is good or marriage is evil *per se*, but only because and if this being alone means undivided service to the Lord. The difference is nonetheless striking. Another departure from Old Testament ethics is the prohibition of divorce (1 Cor. 7:10), although Paul, unlike Mark 10 and Matthew 5, does not discuss the Old Testament background at all.

As in the case of the doctrine of creation, then, we find in Paul a dialectical attitude toward the authority of the Old Testament. On the one hand, it is authoritative. On the other hand, it derives its authority only from Christ and the law of love, even though Rom. 13:8–10 maintains that the law of love, in which all the other commandments are summed up (cf. below, IV. C. 4), is itself found in the Old Testament.

"Summed up" does not mean either "brought to perfection" or "reduced to one"; it means rather that the various individual commandments are interpreted from one particular point of reference.[82] In addition, "law" in Paul does not always refer to the Torah.[83]

In any case, the whole of the law is fulfilled by love (Gal. 5:14). "Fulfilled" does not mean "replaced." If love is the summing up of the law and bond uniting the individual commandments, this certainly does not mean that these commandments are replaced or absorbed, but that they are summarized and recapitulated. Paul did not preach freedom from the law because he wanted to simplify the requirements of morality and reduce them to the law of love, or substitute qualitative for quantitative fulfillment of the law. Nevertheless, the "law of Christ" also imposes restrictions on the content of the commandments.

The "law of Christ" is the command to bear the burdens of others in love (Gal. 6:2). It is hard to decide whether this formulation is based on a messianic *Torah*, since the concept appears only once in rabbinic literature.[84] There are no grounds for interpreting it as meaning the "imitation of Christ" or basing one's ethics on the exemplary conduct and words of Jesus, as suggested by Schürmann.[85] Probably Paul is saying that in the "law of Christ" the Torah is fulfilled according to its true intention.[86] Even Schürmann, who claims that the expression has a double meaning, rightly points out a concentration of the Torah in the law of love in addition to the interpretation just mentioned.[87] It is certainly undeniable that fulfillment of the "law of Christ" is possible only through Christ, whose life exemplifies it.

3. Conformity to Jesus Christ and His Word

3.1 In the light of the central importance of Jesus Christ for Paul's theology, it is only natural that the concentration on soteriology and the foundations of ethics should result in a christological orientation of the new life. The saving work of Jesus Christ and his commands are absolutely authoritative for the conduct of Christians. But how is this authority to be described in detail?

It is frequently claimed that Paul shapes his ethics around the person of Jesus. Feine even espoused the daring theory that Paul saw the proper conduct of the community "reflected in the earthly conduct of Jesus" and

82. See Heinrich Schlier, "anakephalaioomai," *TDNT* 3:681; Raymond F. Collins, "The Ten Commandments and the Christian Response," *Louvain Studies* 3 (1971): 308–22, esp. 319.

83. The metaphorical use of "law" in Rom. 3:27 and 8:2 is discussed by Heikki Räisänen, "Das 'Gesetz des Glaubens' (Röm. 3,27) und das 'Gesetz des Geistes' (Röm. 8:2)," *NTS* 26 (1980): 101–17.

84. Strack-Billerbeck, *Kommentar* 3:557.

85. Heinz Schürmann, "Das Gesetz des Christus (Gal. 6,2)," in *NT und Kirche* (Festschrift Rudolf Schnackenburg), ed. J. Gnilka (Freiburg: Herder, 1974), 282–300.

86. Walter Gutbrod, "nomos," *TDNT* 4:1076; see also Edward M. Young, "'Fulfill the Law of Christ': An Examination of Gal. 6:2," *SBT* 7 (1977): 31–42.

87. "Gesetz," 290.

possessed a vivid picture of Jesus' life in all its details.[88] But the passages cited to support such theories, which claim to demonstrate the significance of the earthly Jesus for Pauline ethics, cannot bear the burden required. They probably do not refer at all to the earthly Jesus but to the obedience of the preexistent Christ.

This is true, for example, of the christological hymn in Phil. 2:5ff.: it says nothing of the exemplary conduct of the earthly Jesus and depicts the humility of Christ *becoming*, not *become*, incarnate (cf. above, IV. A. 2–3). Of course these are not mutually exclusive for Paul, but the emphasis is on the obedience of the preexistent Christ, who renounces his divine status and dignity. And 2 Cor. 8:9, which says that Christ "became poor for our sake," refers to the obedience of the preexistent Christ, not the impoverished life of Jesus as something to be imitated, even though (we must note at once) the notion of an example is not totally absent in either case.

3.2 Nor is the situation any different when Paul speaks expressly of imitating Christ (*mimesis:* 1 Cor. 11:1). In the first place, it is noteworthy that he speaks not of imitating Jesus but of imitating Christ (cf. also 1 Thess. 1:6, where the Thessalonians are called "imitators of Paul and of the Lord"). The statement in 1 Cor. 11:1 agrees totally with what we have already observed: an exemplary element is indeed present, but the example is not the earthly Jesus. What is to be "imitated" is concern for the good of others rather than self, as exemplified by Christ, who humbled himself "for us" (cf. 10:33). The "law of Christ," too, the commandment to bear one another's burdens, was also lived by Christ through his loving act of self-sacrifice (Gal. 2:20).

This brings us very close to Rom. 15:1ff. In fact vv. 3 and 7 are the clearest examples of what Dahl calls the "conformity schema,"[89] in which Paul inculcates correspondence to the conduct of Jesus Christ. The phrase "as Christ" includes not only a causal but a comparative element, the substantial content of which must not be downplayed: welcome one another *because* and *as* Christ has welcomed you. The content of both ideas, mimesis and conformity, is either the *theologia crucis* (Christ's suffering and death) or agape, probably both.[90]

Paul therefore could hardly have cited the historical life and ministry of Jesus as providing specific guidelines for Christian living. Certainly any attempt to copy or imitate the life of Jesus that views Jesus as a model is not Pauline. But the examples cited are nevertheless significant. They demonstrate that Christ's humbling himself in the incarnation or his self-sacrifice on

88. Paul Feine, *Die Apostel Paulus* (Gütersloh: Bertelsmann, 1927), 327ff.; cf. the similar position of W. D. Davies, *Paul and Rabbinic Judaism*, 4th ed. (Philadelphia: Fortress Press, 1980 repr.) 147ff.

89. Nils Alstrup Dahl, "Formgeschichtliche Beobachtungen zur Christusverkündigung in der Gemeindepredigt," in *Neutestamentliche Studien für Rudolf Bultmann*, ed. W. Eltester, BZNW 21 (Berlin: Töpelmann, 1954), 3–9, esp. 6–7.

90. Furnish, *Theology*, 223.

the cross not only establishes a formal purpose and intention but defines a fundamental orientation of Christian living. The righteousness of God at work in Christ implies ethical conformity (cf. Rom. 6:12ff.; 8:10).

3.3 What we have said about the life of Jesus does not apply in the same way to his message. The significance of Jesus' words is not subject to the same negative verdict as his significance as an earthly person or an ethical model, even though Paul is undeniably much more interested in Jesus' saving work than in his words. The words of the Lord are not in the forefront of Paul's parenesis. But it is hardly true to say that Jesus plays an even smaller role as proclaimer of God's will than as a human figure. Although there are few direct references to words of the Lord, we must not overlook *how* Paul refers to Jesus' words and the importance he ascribes to them.

In 1 Cor. 9:14, for example, the Word of the Lord is an authority superior to other authorities, including nature and the Old Testament. In 1 Cor. 7:10, Paul distinguishes his own command explicitly from the commandment of the Lord. It is not the apostle but the Lord himself who commands married couples not to separate. In v. 12, which follows, there is a clear contrast to this Word of the Lord: "To the rest say I, not the Lord. . . ." Both the beginning and end of the Lord's word are thus clearly delimited.

Paul therefore seems not only to be well aware of the extent of the subject matter covered by the quotation, but also to ascribe to the Word of the Lord an authority superior to his own: "Not I, but the Lord." Even for him, the apostle, the Lord's Word represents a higher authority. It is noteworthy, however, that comparison of the form of this logion in the Synoptic tradition with 1 Cor. 7:10 suggests that Paul is giving an interpretation rather than a literal quotation. The extension of the law concerning divorce to both sexes corresponds (as in Mark 10:12) to Hellenistic legal practice, but in Paul the law dealing with the wife comes first. In any case, it is clear that Paul, despite his consciousness of speaking in the Lord's name and with the Lord's authority, does not simply appeal to inspiration and revelation from the exalted Christ but cites words of the Lord as such and ascribes supreme authority to them.

There is nothing to indicate that Paul cites the Jesus tradition because Christ, who overcomes the law of Moses, "reinstates the original design of the Creator."[91] Of course Paul is also concerned to manifest the original will of the Creator. Here, however, it is not the ordinance of the Creator but the claim of Jesus Christ to obedience that ultimately binds the apostle.

The importance of this fact is hardly lessened by the small number of times words of the Lord are cited. It is therefore also difficult to think of Paul as deliberately suppressing traditional words of the Lord. Nor is Paul's conflict with his opponents a likely reason why he cites words of the Lord only in

91. Hasenstab, *Modelle*, 235.

1 Corinthians. There is also no reason to claim that Paul found it particularly necessary to appeal to a word of the Lord when dealing with questions of community order. Most likely the rarity of quotation is due to the peculiar literary genre of the epistle, which is not especially suited to inclusion of traditions concerning Jesus. Above all, however, we must remember that the stock of extant words of the Lord that could appropriately be addressed to Christian communities in a cultural and socioeconomic milieu so different from Palestine was rather limited and could not be expanded at will. In 1 Cor. 7:25, Paul regrets explicitly that there is no commandment of the Lord applying to the unmarried.

3.4 Besides the literal quotations, we find many echoes, references, and similarities that clearly suggest some knowledge of the gospel tradition but are no longer associated with the figure of Jesus. Compare Rom. 12:14 with Luke 6:28, Rom. 12:17 with Matt. 5:38ff., Rom. 13:8ff. with Mark 12:31, and Rom. 14:14 with Mark 7:15. In some cases it is reasonable to ask whether Paul is not referring deliberately to words of the Lord with which he was familiar. There is no need to assume literary dependence or to postulate a common source for Paul and the Synoptics, but somehow Paul and the Synoptics presuppose a common tradition.[92] It is probably not enough to say (with Bultmann) that all these instances involve no more than possibilities. Dibelius, while rejecting any dependence on the Synoptics on the grounds that there is no quotation formula, nevertheless correctly points out that it would be wrong to infer that these words were not recognized as words of the Lord.[93]

The many points of agreement with sayings of Jesus could point in the same direction as the fact, already mentioned, that Paul does not quote the actual words of the Lord verbatim but allows himself the liberty of modifying them: what matters is not the words themselves but what they say. The parenthetical statement in 1 Cor. 7:11a, where Paul appears to concede divorce in spite of the Word of the Lord, might also confirm that Paul does not think of Jesus' words as authoritative in an external and legalistic sense that is content with observing the letter of the law. In any case, it is certainly true that for Paul the authority of the earthly Lord is not simply made irrelevant by Easter.

3.5 Of course Paul did not understand Jesus' words apart from the person who spoke them, who is identical with the crucified and risen Lord. But Jesus Christ also speaks in the present through the remembered words of the Lord (cf. the present tense in 1 Cor. 7:10). The suggestion that Paul looked on these words as the words not of the earthly Jesus but of the exalted Lord[94] assumes an un-Pauline dichotomy. In 1 Cor. 11:23, it is even stated expressly

92. Cf. Fjärstedt, Tradition, 29ff.
93. Dibelius, Tradition, 241.
94. Rudolf Bultmann, "Paulus," RGG² 4:1028.

that Jesus spoke the words quoted "in the night when he was betrayed" (cf. also the aorist in 1 Cor. 9:14). The evidence of 1 Cor. 11:23ff. indicates that Paul was not content with the merely formal statement that Jesus lived an earthly life; he held fast to a concrete history of Jesus, including narrative elements and above all Jesus' own words.

It is noteworthy that except for 1 Cor. 11:23ff. all the words of the Lord cited by Paul have to do with the Christian life. If we examine the content of indirect allusions to words of the Lord, we note that Paul shows a distinct tendency to turn to the words of Jesus in questions related to the law of love, obviously "because he interprets Jesus' words from the perspective of the self-abasing love of the Son of God."[95] In this sense, Paul sees a large area of overlap between the exemplary character of Jesus and of his words.

4. Love, the Greatest Commandment

4.1 The extent to which love confirms the centrality of Christ for Paul's thought can be seen from Paul's use of the same terms to describe love that are predicates of Christ (cf. 1 Cor. 13:5 with Phil. 2:4 or Rom. 15:3). "To live in accord with love" (Rom. 14:15) means the same as "in accord with Christ Jesus" (Rom. 15:5). Christians are "controlled" (2 Cor. 5:14) and moved by the love defined through Christ (cf. Gal. 2:20); they can also be exhorted to have such love (1 Cor. 14:1; 16:14). This inevitable ethical aspect of love cannot be set aside as secondary.

It has often been emphasized that love cannot be subsumed in ethics; it refers in the first instance to what we are, not what we do. But it is surely of equal importance for Paul that love finds expression in specific types of conduct and ways of life (cf. the variety of verbs in 1 Cor. 13:4ff.). Love must not be confused with a vague feeling of good will or a conformist pragmatism. It is therefore easily recognizable and its genuineness can be tested (2 Cor. 2:4; 8:8, 24). Love is sometimes described as hidden and ambiguous; according to Bultmann, for example, an act of love cannot be proved to be loving either to outsiders or within its own context.[96] But this is true only if it does not conceal the fact that Paul is well aware of signs that distinguish those who love from those who do not love even in the concrete details of daily life.

Of course love cannot be proved, because it is not simply identical with any particular act. It can be absent even in the context of extreme charismata, in the surrender of possessions, in martyrdom or self-enslavement; none of the actions in 1 Cor. 13:1–3 can be equated directly with love. On the other hand, however, love seeks to be realized in these forms of conduct, not in addition to them or in contrast to them. When the signs of love cease to shine forth in concrete, visible life, the genuineness of love is in doubt. Individual specific

---

95. Schürmann, "Gesetz," 286.

96. Rudolf Bultmann, "Das christliche Gebot der Nächstenliebe," in *Glauben und Verstehen*, 6th ed., 4 vols. (Tübingen: Mohr, 1965–75), 1:229–44, esp. 239–40.

acts are not love, but love is known and embodied in such acts; love makes use of these forms of expression and does not remain invisible. It represents "the incursion of the divine realm into the human realm in this present aeon,"[97] but not just in the context of worship.[98]

Human love, like God's, is not an attitude or an emotion but an act (cf. "labor of love" in 1 Thess. 1:3), freedom from self and openness to others. According to 1 Cor. 13:5, such love that focuses on one's neighbor does not insist on its own way but supports the interests of others (cf. 1 Cor. 10:24, 33). Paul can therefore use such terms as "service," "self-sacrifice," and "edification" (meant ecclesiologically, not individualistically!) in parallel with "love." Love is self-denial, not self-realization; it is not an act in which a neighbor becomes an object through which to reach perfection. Romans 9:3 shows how far such total self-denial can go. Not that love has no set purpose to achieve! It certainly does not desire simply to endorse its recipients or promote their comfort and egoism, but to "benefit" them (cf. the citations below in IV.C.4.3), for example by overcoming evil with good (Rom. 12:21) or gently restoring those who have gone astray (Gal. 6:1).

This does not mean that love can only take the form of personal involvement and cannot be embodied in institutions. For Paul, love is not allergic or hostile to institutions. It urges effective institutional actions and functions.[99] Of course offerings (cf. 2 Cor. 8—9) or "aid" and "service" (1 Cor. 12:28; Rom. 12:7) operate within the Christian community and do nothing to establish economically or politically relevant social structures, but they are not limited to spontaneous I-Thou relationships. In such acts of love outside the personal sphere the domain of *agapē* is determined for the most part by the so-called primary social structures (marriage, family, household). The notion that love can also set its stamp on group behavior in the social and political realm is at best peripheral (cf. the discussion of Romans 13 below, IV.D.4). According to Paul, love is primarily (cf. 1 Thess. 4:9; Rom. 12:10; Philem. 5), although not exclusively (cf. 1 Thess. 3:12; 5:15), love for other Christians. Although not even enemies are excluded (Rom. 12:17ff.), the notion of solidarity within the Christian community (cf. Phil. 4:14–15) stands in the foreground in these instances of what are more or less isolated acts of help; social problems as such are hardly noticed. In principle, the statement that love bears the burdens of others (Gal. 6:2) knows no limits, but in the time remaining to do good before the Parousia, this obligation toward "all" is felt especially toward "those who are of the household of faith" (Gal. 6:10).

4.2 This self-sacrificing love for others is not only the heart and core but also the fundamental criterion of Pauline ethics. There can be no doubt that

---

97. Pedersen, "Agape," 177.
98. Pace ibid., 181.
99. Heinz Schürmann, "Das eschatologische Heil Gottes und die Weltverantwortung des Menschen," *Geist und Leben* 50 (1977): 28–29.

the law of love takes precedence over all other commandments, even though not all the individual injunctions can be derived from it. Here, too, Paul continues the tradition of Jesus (cf. above, I.C.2). In Gal. 5:22, *agapē* appears as one fruit of the Spirit among many (although standing at the head of the list). Much more typical, however, is 1 Cor. 12:31, where Paul calls the way of love the way of all ways, the way that transcends all other ways, the supreme way.[100] He can therefore say that all things are to be done in love (1 Cor. 16:14). According to Rom. 13:8–10, the law of love is the quintessence of all the commandments, the bond that unites them: in it they have their hidden unity and meaning, but also their true criterion (cf. above, IV.C.2.5). In other words, Paul does not interpret love on the basis of the law, but interprets the law on the basis of love.[101]

4.3 Paul states as a fundamental principle that love is the greatest good in the Christian life. This central position of love can also be observed in his specific injunctions. Paul frequently introduces love into his parenesis as a normative entity, making it the decisive criterion of Christian conduct. In Rom. 12:9, it is not clear whether *agapē* stands programmatically at the beginning of the series of admonitions in vv. 9–21. In practice, however, it is the dominant theme, reaching its climax in the love of enemies. Even 1 Corinthians 13 is neither a systematic excursus on the primacy of love nor a secondary poetic addition; despite its stylistic elegance, it is a necessary element in the logical argument of the letter (1 Corinthians 12—14). It alone prevents Christians from losing sight of others even when exercising spiritual gifts such as glossolalia in worship.

Even more clearly than in Paul's opposition to the importance of extraordinary pneumatic phenomena to the Corinthians, the critical power of love comes to the fore in his discussion of the relationship between the strong and the weak at Rome and Corinth. In both places, walking in love (Rom. 14:15) is to be the sole criterion by which other measures are evaluated and limited.

In these chapters, Paul returns repeatedly to this theme, which he expresses in many ways: "seeking the advantage of others" (1 Cor. 10:33), "building up" (1 Cor. 8:1; 10:23; Rom. 14:19), and similar expressions, all of which ultimately make the same point, both negatively in polemic against pneumatic individualism and subjectivism, and positively as an expression of love.

In 1 Corinthians 8—10, it is primarily knowledge and freedom that are subjected to the critical test of love. Those who have faith also have knowledge, but their knowledge threatens to turn into complacent arrogance if it is not directed and controlled by concern for others and their well-being. Those who have faith also have freedom, which permits everything, but this free-

---

100. Günther Bornkamm, "The More Excellent Way (I Corinthians 13)," in *Early Christian Experience*, 180–93; Oda Wischemeyer, *Der höchste Weg*, StNT 13 (Gütersloh: Mohn, 1981).
101. Schrage, *Einzelgebote*, 255.

dom finds its limit in others and shows itself paradoxically in renouncing freedom out of concern for others (1 Cor. 8:7ff.; 10:23ff.). Even the doctrine of creation, which knows there is only one God and that idols have no real existence (1 Cor. 8:4), cannot limit the law of love. Instead, love functions as a corrective even to creation. Christian freedom depends not only on the Lord (cf. above, IV.A.3.2) but also on love. Those who are free are not those "who live for themselves, not for others,"[102] but those who love. Freedom manifests itself in love for others.[103]

4.4 If love is the driving and controlling force of all Christian life, its critical and creative potential must also find expression where Paul does not speak of it explicitly, but resolves conflicts and renders specific decisions. We may note 1 Cor. 7:36–38, which discusses the question of betrothal, or 1 Cor. 7:4, where the statement that married people do not rule over their own bodies can be taken as a special instance of the fact that Christians no longer rule over themselves and no longer seek their own benefit.

Paul also viewed the relationship between master and slave in the light of the law of love, thus giving it added depth while at the same time transcending and relativizing it. In Stoic ethics, with its ideal of the self-sufficient individual, there is more emphasis on avoiding unwarranted anger than on the person of the slave. For Paul, however, the principle of love is determinative, a principle that involves the human relationship between master and slave in a momentous transformation. The very fact that Paul calls a slave, usually considered an impersonal possession, a "beloved brother" (Philem. 16) is significant enough. The slave Onesimus is now much more than a slave (Philem. 16). But love and brotherhood must be manifested not only in relationships within the Christian community but also in relationships in the world, outside the community, as Paul explicitly and deliberately adds ("both in the flesh and in the Lord").

Christian love involves more than the personal relationship or feelings between master and slave. It also has practical consequences in the realities of daily life, for example, in the administration of justice. In Paul's time, a runaway slave was pursued as a criminal. As a "thief of his own person" (*fur sui*), such a slave faced harsh legal penalties: severe corporal punishment, often branding, sometimes even death in the arena or on the cross.[104] Paul's asking pardon for the runaway (Philem. 12, 17) shows that love does not leave sociological and legal customs untouched; it penetrates and shapes the structures of society. Love not only changes hearts but also, by changing hearts, changes actions—not just "in the Lord," as in the case of common meals, the

102. Aristotle *Metaphysics* 1.2.982b.
103. See also Gerhard Friedrich, "Freiheit und Liebe im 1. Kor.," in *Auf das Wort kommt es an* (Göttingen: Vandenhoeck & Ruprecht, 1978), 171–88.
104. Heinz Bellen, "Studien zur Sklavenflucht im römischen Kaiserreich," *Forschungen zur antiken Sklaverei* 4 (1971): 17ff.

kiss of peace, and so forth, but also "in the flesh," that is, in the outward circumstances of earthly life.

4.5 Even respect for institutions can be construed as an expression of love. In any case, it is not enough to interpret and fulfill the ordinances on the basis of the law. The relationship of Christians to civil rights (*iustitia civilis*) and convention, for example, involves the law of love (1 Cor. 13:5), as does daily work. The obligation to work for a living (1 Thess. 4:11) is placed under the heading of love (v. 9). Here work is not meaningful in itself, nor is it performed for the sake of financial independence and moral improvement, but for "love of the brethren." Possibly even the relationship of Christians to the state cannot simply be kept separate from the law of love. It is true that Paul asks his readers to show respect and obedience, not love, toward rulers. It remains an open question, however, whether this excludes any relationship to *agapē* and its insistence of what is "good" (Rom. 12:21).

It has often been pointed out[105] that Rom. 13:1–7 is set in the context of exhortations seeking to define the relationship between Christians and non-Christians on the basis of love (Rom. 12:14ff.; 13:8ff.). Despite the absence of any systematic arrangement among the parenetic texts, it is therefore reasonable to suggest—but no more—that this framework is not entirely accidental but is meant to establish a relationship between the two. Ultimately, love for others (not for the state) came to dominate the Christian attitude toward the state.[106] Dahl, however, is certainly wrong when he sees in the allegedly independent juxtaposition "the seeds of a doctrine of 'two realms.' "[107] But except in general statements such as Rom. 12:14ff.; 1 Thess. 3:12; 5:15, it must be admitted that the discussion of love rarely moves outside the boundaries of the Christian community.

4.6 Love is intended not only to shape and permeate the relationship of Christians to the orders and structures of the world, but also on occasion to limit them and break through them. This is illustrated by the example of celibacy, which Paul sees as a charisma presenting a chance to serve others and edify the community. An equally illuminating example of how secular institutions can be restricted is found in 1 Cor. 6:1ff. The reason Paul finds it preferable to relinquish one's rights rather than submit to mediation is undoubtedly the eschatologically motivated renunciation of one's legal rights over others, which excludes the demand for personal vindication. Disputes and lawsuits prove that Christians are not yet seized by the eschatological reality of agape; they do not yet take seriously the fact that the "law of Christ" is the supreme commandment and that those who love do not demand

105. See, e.g., Cullmann, *State* (B5), 56–57.

106. See Schrage, *Einzelgebote*, 236–64; idem, *Staat* (B5), 53; Duchrow, *Christenheit* (B), 144; Wilckens, "Röm. 13,1–7" (IV.D), 209–10, 238.

107. Nils Alstrup Dahl, "Neutestamentliche Ansätze zur Lehre von den zwei Regimenten," *LR* 15 (1965): 441–63, quotation from 453.

216   THE CHRISTOLOGICAL ETHICS OF PAUL

vindication (cf. Rom. 12:17ff.; 1 Cor. 13:7). This chapter (1 Corinthians 6) is an unmistakable attempt "within the Christian community to apply the radical demand to the circumstances of secular life."[108] Love cares for others (1 Cor. 12:25); it does not go to court. This does not imply that the legal system should be abolished, certainly not for the secular world. It is not legal justice that love rules out, but the self-centered demand for justice as well as injustice.

Paul does not call for the abolition of legal and social structures; nor, however, does he approve them as fixed institutions. He tests them critically in the light of agape, putting them to use or rejecting them. When they cannot serve the realization of love, he renounces them. Once again love proves superior even to the criterion of creation. Love is indeed the ultimate criterion of Christian conduct.

4.7 It is clear from the above that love, despite all situational variation and relativity, has its own individual characteristics and signatures, which are constant and unchanging. Love is not stereotyped and immutable in its forms of expression, but neither is it chaotic and at the mercy of spontaneous improvisation.

The claim that the demands of love never encompass specific actions and that the law of love is by nature hostile to concrete positive requirements[109] can hardly appeal to Paul for support. Wilckens quite rightly calls it a serious misconception when Bultmann "says that in principle, because of love's eschatological nature, it cannot be burdened with concrete specifics."[110] Such a position cuts love off from the world.[111] The reduction of ethics to Augustine's *ama et fac quod vis*, "love and do what you will," is "too exposed to the danger of unproductive sentimentality."[112]

The individual commandments are subordinate to and on occasion limited by the law of love, but this subordination neither degrades them nor leaves them up to each person's judgment, as we see in 1 Corinthians 13 with the individual acts and expressions of love. Precisely because it is the supreme criterion, love presupposes other criteria. It would be a gross misinterpretation of Rom. 13:9 to understand the summary of the commandments in the law of love as annulling or trivializing the listed commandments of the Decalogue, especially since Paul states expressly in v. 10 that love does no wrong to a neighbor. I cannot love my neighbor and at the same time deceive him in the person of his spouse, rob him of his possessions or his reputation,

108. Martin Dibelius, "Das soziale Motiv im NT," in *Botschaft und Geschichte,* 2 vols. (Tübingen: Mohr, 1953–56), 1:178–203, quotation from 196; see also Luz, "Eschatologie," 262–63, discussing Rom. 14:17.
109. Bultmann, "Gebot," 235; idem, *Theology,* 231.
110. Wilckens, "Kommunismus" (II), 140.
111. Cf. Duchrow, *Christenheit* (B), 172.
112. Dodd, *Gospel* (B), 72. See also Wendland, *Ethik,* 63; Schrage, *Einzelgebote,* 268ff.; Osborn, *Patterns* (B), 179ff.; Holtz, "Frage," 393.

or seek to take his life. Whoever loves takes the other fundamental commandments and criteria seriously. If love sums up the commandments, the commandments expound and support the law of love. Clearly specific commandments cannot compensate for the absence of love. On the other hand, the
absence of concrete requirements can turn love into a vague benevolence or
impulsive improvisation based on romanticism.

If the commandments stand in the service of love, love will not reject the
good offices of the commandments, which help it take concrete form amid
the variety of everyday life. Christians will always find themselves in new
situations, confronting new conditions within which they must live and act,
conditions that càn be mastered only through reason guided by love (see
above, 197–98), but their lives need not do without any clear direction or
orientation. Though love transcends the individual commandments, it does
not ignore them. Paul did not merely point to the single way of love; he also
pointed to specific ways (1 Cor. 4:17), even if they all start from and return to
this way above all other ways (1 Cor. 12:31). To say "love" is to say what is
most important, but not everything. Love is the supreme criterion but not
the only criterion, the final but not the only commandment for the conduct of
Christians.

D. CONCRETE ETHICS

1. Individual Morality

1.1 In this section we shall discuss briefly a few points that are not directly
concerned with social ethics but show how statements concerning individual
morality can be illuminated and restricted by the love that takes one's
neighbor as its reference point. It is in fact impossible to make a sharp
distinction between individual and social ethics, because the two realms
overlap to a large extent. Decisions in the one always have consequences in
the other.

Paul exhibits no trace of anything corresponding to the Greek *kalokagathia*
("nobility of character," "excellence"), the famous ideal of physical, intellectual, and spiritual formation for Hellenism. Although the Old Testament and
Judaism took individual responsibility very seriously, their emphasis on
corporate social solidarity—the "thou" addressed in the Decalogue, for
example, is sometimes the people as a whole, sometimes the individual—
prevented the development of an ethics focused primarily on the individual in
isolation from the community.

It is most revealing that Paul uses the word *aretē* ("excellence, virtue") only
once (Phil. 4:8), and then in a very unusual way: the other terms in the list are
not subordinated to *aretē* in normal Greek fashion, but are set in parallel with
it. Bultmann rightly says that the central idea of Pauline ethics is not that of
an ideal or of excellence, but the notion that what is good is what God

commands.[113] Bauernfeind[114] and Schelkle[115] theorize that the term *arete* is almost totally absent from the New Testament because the word was felt to be "too anthropocentric, too concerned with human merit." Probably, however, the reason involves distrust not only of the pride and fame that go hand in hand with excellence, but also of its strongly individualistic cast. How peripheral Paul considers an individual's relationship to his own person is shown by the term *sōma*, "body," which is extraordinarily important for Pauline anthropology and ethics.

1.2 Bultmann sees in the Pauline concept of "body" the most inclusive characterization of what it is to be human: the existential and historical human self. Bauer, Käsemann, and others have asked whether Bultmann, contrary to his intention, has not remained trapped in an idealistic anthropology that separates the thinking subject, in its sovereign freedom and spontaneity, from all worldly ties and relationships, ignoring the fact that the body is also part of the subject. More important, Käsemann not only criticizes Bultmann's neglect of the ontic foundation, namely corporeality and involvement with the world, but in positive terms makes it clear that *sōma* refers to human beings in their relationship to the world and their ability to communicate, and that "body" maintains this solidarity with the world and with unredeemed creation.[116]

Examination of the Pauline texts shows that *sōma* refers in the first instance to the human body as a whole; this is why "body" and "limbs" can be used in parallel (Rom. 6:12–13). The body is therefore the locus where we experience life and death, sickness and sexuality—in short, our creatureliness and our position in the realm of nature. The body is the living, breathing person. The term can also alternate with the personal pronoun (1 Cor. 6:13–15; 12:27): this shows that "body" can simply stand for the self or person. Much more important is the reverse observation: this self cannot be separated from the body; it is body, from which it cannot be abstracted. Therefore the person before faith is not only a sinner but also a sinful body (Rom. 6:6). And therefore Christians do not look forward to redemption *from* the body, but redemption *of* the body (Rom. 8:23; cf. Phil. 3:21).

For ethics, special importance attaches to what takes place in the interim, between the "body of sin" that belongs to the past on the one hand and the "spiritual body" of the future on the other. There appear to be two important points. First, Christians are exhorted to present their bodies in sacrifice (Rom. 12:1): the Lord requires not only minds and souls but also bodies, just as for Paul the church does not consist of souls but of bodies (1 Cor. 6:15).

---

113. *Theology*, 121.
114. Otto Bauernfeind, "aretē," *TDNT* 1:460.
115. *Theologie* (B), 213.
116. "On Paul's Anthropology," in *Perspectives*, 17ff. See also Karl-Adolf Bauer, *Leiblichkeit— das Ende aller Werke Gottes*, StNT 4 (Gütersloh: Mohn, 1971).

Second, however, "body" is in fact a correlative concept, expressing a relationship (1 Cor. 6:12ff.)—less a relationship to oneself than the ability to communicate and a correlation to the Lord. The statement that the body belongs to the Lord (cf. 1 Cor. 6:13c) jibes with the undivided totality and concrete reality of obedience; it stands in the way of any idealistic spiritualization. More surprising is the reverse statement in 1 Cor. 6:13d ("The Lord belongs to the body"), which associates the Lord specifically with the body. Because the body is the primary place where Christ exercises dominion in the reality of the present world, it is here or nowhere that Christians encounter their Lord. This is where Christ asserts his sovereignty and lordship: in the bodies of Christians he now claims the world as his own.[117]

This is also the decisive argument against unchastity. Here we find a limitation on freedom that goes beyond the law of love, even for individual Christians. The body does not belong to the person embodied but to the Lord.

1.3 The problem of suffering and how to deal with it already plays an important role in the Old Testament and in Judaism. Various answers ventured over the course of time are repeated, more or less modified, in the New Testament: suffering is a healthy test and discipline (cf. Prov. 3:11–12; Job 5:17); people should stand in silent awe before the wonderful and incomprehensible majesty of God (Job 42:3); the good fortune of the wicked does not endure (Psalm 37); suffering can be vicarious (Isaiah 53); fellowship with God outweighs any suffering ("There is nothing I desire besides thee . . ."; Ps. 73:15ff.). Apocalyptic literature in particular looks forward to the age after the messianic woes, when suffering reaches its climax. This is the new eon that brings an end to all suffering; its glory is out of all proportion to the suffering of the present.[118]

Paul, too, borrows motifs from this tradition, especially the apocalyptic view that "the sufferings of this present time are not worth comparing with the coming glory" (Rom. 8:18; 2 Cor. 4:17). But the true interpretation of suffering on the part of Christians derives from the suffering and death of Jesus. Because Jesus' suffering and death have an eschatological significance transcending time and space, Christians are incorporated into the suffering of Christ, so that the Christian life can now be referred to as "suffering with Christ" (cf. Rom. 8:17). Such shared suffering is the precondition for shared glorification, but it is also the paradoxical locus, here and now, of God's power and the life of Jesus Christ. Both are illustrated vividly in the various catalogues of afflictions in the Pauline Epistles (1 Cor. 4:11ff.; 2 Cor. 4:8ff.; 6:4ff.; 11:23ff.).[119]

117. Käsemann, "Anthropology."
118. For further discussion, see Erhard Gerstenberger and Wolfgang Schrage, *Suffering* (Nashville: Abingdon Press, 1980).
119. See Wolfgang Schrage, "Leid, Kreuz und Eschaton," *EvTh* 34 (1974): 141–75.

For Paul, these sufferings are not a welcome chance to demonstrate indifference to the world and *ataraxia*, as they would be for the Stoics, but dangerous temptations. Paul does not owe his survival to his own struggles and will to resist, but to God's miraculous intervention, an external reality. Of course—and this is also important for Pauline ethics—the hour of God's miracle is also the hour of trial, so that Paul can say in 1 Cor. 4:12: "When persecuted, we endure." The support of God's presence does not dispense us from the necessity of personal endurance. This presence does not accompany endurance but comes within it. In addition suffering does not dispense us from loving our neighbor: "When reviled, we bless." Misfortune and suffering are not overcome, as among the Stoics, by retreating into oneself so as to achieve inward self-sufficiency. Paul sees the Christian as a single entity, beset by doubts and afflictions: "fighting without and fear within" (2 Cor. 7:5). Comfort and joy in the midst of suffering do not come, according to Paul, through knowledge of God's eternal plan, but from knowledge of being incorporated into Christ's own fate, in which God's eschatological love was revealed, from which nothing can separate us (Rom. 8:35ff.).

Because Christ both died and rose again, the living power of Jesus is also experienced in the death of Christians (2 Cor. 4:10). Weakness is the paradoxical mode in which the power of Christ is manifest (2 Cor. 12:9). But this epiphany of life and power in hidden and paradoxical form is not the end. Paul also looks forward to God's raising of the dead, which puts an end to this paradox and hiddenness. For Paul, suffering is both the locus where life is paradoxically revealed and a sign that the world is still unredeemed (Rom. 8:18). Of course the point is not so much that the new comes after and beyond the old as that it also exists within and despite the old ("as dying, and behold we live"; 2 Cor. 6:9). But it is also true that the future helps us bear these afflictions: they are transitory, and the paradox is not forever. Suffering does not thereby become any easier, but it does take on a different appearance and importance in the light of what is to come. Those who have hope do not need to close their eyes to harsh reality.

1.4 If only because of his belief in creation, Paul could not preach a dualistic asceticism hostile to the body, a radical withdrawal from the sensual secular world, involving above all rejection of corporeality and sexuality. But he did set great store by self-discipline. Here this is relevant only insofar as the theme is not touched on in the context of social ethics, for example, in questions of marriage and sexual relationships, but affects the isolated individual.

Paul only uses the term *enkratia* ("self-control") to conclude the catalogue of virtues in Galatians 5. Twice he uses the corresponding verb. In 1 Cor. 7:9, he concedes that there are situations in which those who are unmarried and widows can no longer practice sexual abstinence. Under these circumstances, it is better to marry than to burn with the fire of sexual passion. In 1 Cor.

9:25, the term does not refer specifically to sexuality. In the metaphor of an athlete competing in the stadium for the victor's crown, it refers to self-discipline in all things. Christians live like athletes, avoiding pleasures and luxuries during training because every victory has its price.

Paul does not require sexual asceticism of married people in 1 Corinthians 7, but rather cautions against it. In addition, the list in Galatians 5 applies to all Christians. In Gal. 5:23, therefore, *enkratia* cannot refer specifically to sexual abstinence. It probably refers more generally to self-discipline and self-control.

This *enkratia* plays an important role in the ethics of the classical world. Socrates, for example, holds that it is the foundation of virtue and religion. According to the Stoics, it is a mark of human dignity and self-respect, as well as a sign that reason has dominion over the body. It usually refers to dominion over sensuality: control of natural desires, especially sexuality and enjoyment of food and wine. Chadwick, for example, interprets 1 Cor. 9:25 from this perspective: Paul's purpose in writing is to persuade the ascetics of Corinth of his own asceticism.[120]

This ascetic interpretation is unlikely, however, if only because of the plural "all things." Paul is not trying to commend himself to ascetics by citing his own ascetic accomplishments. It is even doubtful whether asceticism is under discussion here. More likely, the passage alludes to the basic meaning of *enkratēs:* someone who has power *(kratos)* and dominion over himself. In contrast to the values of Hellenism, Paul is not praising *enkratia* to support the ideal of the free, self-sufficient personality or from dualistic motives. For Paul, it expresses the truth that being a Christian involves a struggle against one's own self, but such self-control can be achieved only through the power of the Lord.

Therefore he says in Phil. 4:11ff.: "I have learned, in whatever state I am, to be content. I know how to be abased, and I know how to abound; in any and all circumstances I have learned the secret of facing plenty and hunger, abundance and want. I can do all things in him who strenghthens me." There are similarities here to Stoic affirmations,[121] but we must be careful not to confuse Pauline *autarkeia* ("self-sufficiency") with indifference or aloofness. Above all, Paul achieves this freedom and independence only in the school of his Lord, not through self-confidence or inward indifference to outward circumstances. Those who rely on themselves rather than the power of the Lord, retreating into an allegedly impregnable inner fortress instead of putting all their trust in the Lord, are dependent, not independent; they are dependent on themselves. Furthermore, the catalogues of afflictions show that, despite the "abundance" mentioned in Philippians 4, which could also be translated "a full life," Paul generally led a life of self-denial. But the

120. Henry Chadwick, "Enkrateia," *RAC* 5:350.
121. Cf. Marcus Antonius 1.16.

222 THE CHRISTOLOGICAL ETHICS OF PAUL

purpose of all this is not self-improvement, as though Christians grow increasingly self-controlled and self-contained. What matters is rather that they remain true to their calling, always and everywhere.

We may cite two further examples from 2 Cor. 6:5. "Watching" means simply being forced to go without sleep. The word most likely alludes to passages where Paul speaks of working at night in addition to his missionary preaching so as to earn his living (1 Thess. 2:9). The community meetings, too, which could be held only in the evening, probably often lasted well into the night (Acts 20:7, 9, 31). The point is not to sleep as little as possible, but to carry out one's task under time pressure. "Hunger," the next word, is to be understood in the same sense. Its primary sense is simply "going without food." Although even in the New Testament the word can have the specialized meaning "fasting," in 2 Cor. 6:5, as in 11:27, it probably refers to enforced hunger.[122] This jibes with what is said in 1 Cor. 4:11 (cf. also 2 Cor. 11:27). Even though we are dealing with forced abstinence, the notion of self-discipline is not ruled out.

Besides outward self-discipline, which can accept all the circumstances of life as the Lord's discipline, Paul is also familiar with an inward, psychic, moderation (cf. Rom. 12:3). In classical Greek, sōphrosynē meant "knowing one's limits," the opposite of hybris, but it also meant "prudence" in the sense of "moderation." According to Rom. 12:3, such prudence shows itself in sober judgment of the measure given by God and the limits appointed by God for each individual. "Thinking of oneself more highly than one ought to think," the antithesis mentioned in the same verse, is the mark of fanatics, who disregard the functional variety of the members constituting the one body.

Looking back over all three passages, we may say that only rarely does Paul speak of personal, individual ethics. Even the phenomena outlined in this section are related primarily to the group or community. Paul shows no particular interest in the moral conduct of Christians as single individuals, even though he knows that every Christian stands or falls before the Lord (Rom. 14:4) and that each contributes a specific gift to the community. But this does not reduce ethics to a private moral code.

2. Man and Wife/Marriage and Divorce

2.1 The inferiority of women in Judaism and the discrimination against them are discussed above (I.D.2). The variety of positions represented in the Hellenistic world is much harder to describe: there were regional differences, as well as differences between the rural and urban populations, the lower and upper classes, theory and practice, reaction and emancipation.

On the one hand, the Hellenistic period seems to have brought a certain emancipation of women. They have the legal right to inherit, for example, to

122. See Johannes Behm, "nēstis," TDNT 4:925.

make wills, to serve as guardians, to sue for divorce, and so forth. We also hear of good marriages and high marriage ideals, in which the wife enjoys great esteem. On the other hand, there is an unmistakable tendency to reject and downgrade women. The figure of the misogynist is a product of Hellenism. On the whole, the idea that women are inferior seems to have been maintained; there is certainly no question of real equality. Seneca holds that men are born to rule, women to obey.[123] Indeed, he maintains that women are morally inferior to men.[124] While Seneca sees women as generally inferior beings, the Stoic Musonius emphasizes a kind of equality from birth. He states, for example, that "both women and men have received the same logos from the gods."[125] More will be said later about the position of women in marriage.[126]

2.2 The basic statement of Paul's position, although borrowed from others, appears in Gal. 3:28: "There is neither Jew nor Greek, there is neither slave nor free, there is neither male nor female; for you are all one is Christ Jesus"[127] (cf. 1 Cor. 12:13 and Col. 3:11). Even though the words may well derive from fanatical circles, for Paul they do not constitute an illusory watchword that leaves the real situation unaltered. In the one body of Christ, all secular categories are transcended, even distinctions inherent in the created order. Christ and those who belong to him constitute a single whole in which the new creation has already dawned; all human differences that separate people are removed. The body of Christ has many members with a variety of functions. The point of Gal. 3:28 is not a uniformity that reduces everything to the lowest common denominator. But the categories and structures associated with the ancient world have ceased to carry authority, and this change has social implications and consequences. In the first place, it means that men and women have the same value and dignity in the eyes of God; the inferior and marginal status of women is overcome "in the Lord." This means that men and women share the same privileges and the same responsibilities. The result is to break through social roles and stereotypes. Paul, for example, speaks of women as fellow workers and companions (Rom. 16:3; Phil. 4:3), even acknowledging women who hold the office of apostle (Rom. 16:7). Above all, Paul refuses to forbid women to prophesy, as 1 Cor. 11:5 clearly shows. The charisma of prophecy is not reserved to the male sex;

123. *De constantia sapientis* 1.1.
124. Ibid. 14.1.
125. Ibid. 9.1–2.
126. See also Leipoldt, *Frau* (B2), 10ff.; Carl Schneider, *Kulturgeschichte des Hellenismus* (Munich: Beck, 1967), 1:78ff.; Klaus Thraede, "Frau," *RAC* 8:197ff.; Schrage and Gerstenberger, *Frau* (B2) 108–9; Schottroff, "Frauen" (B2), 91ff.
127. See Dieter Lührmann, "Wo man nicht mehr Sklave oder Freier ist," *WuD* 13 (1975): 53–83; Hartwig Thyen, "'. . . nicht mehr männlich und weiblich,' eine Studie zu Gal. 3,28," in Frank Crüsemann and Hartwig Thyen, *Als Mann und Frau geschaffen*, Kennzeichen 2 (Gelnhausen: Burckhardthaus, 1978), 107ff.; Luz, "Eschatologie," 248 n. 60; Schrage and Gerstenberger, *Frau* (B2), 122–23.

it is also exercised by women. This verse is especially important: it merely speaks in passing of women who prophesy as nothing unusual.[128]

This epistle admittedly retreats from this position in 14:34ff, stating that women should keep silent in churches, but this reactionary section must be considered a deutero-Pauline interpolation. Fitzer has given a comprehensive demonstration that these verses are un-Pauline (the un-Pauline formula "as even the law says," the conflict with their context, etc.), so that there can hardly be any doubt that they are not authentic.[129]

2.3 It is not so easy to deal with 1 Cor. 11:2ff. Here Paul appears to disavow everything he has said in Gal. 3:28, with the exception of the prophesying mentioned in v. 5, which was discussed above. The detailed exegesis of this passage, however, is highly controversial.

Above all, it remains quite obscure why Paul should admonish women not to pray or prophesy during worship with their heads unveiled or their hair down. It is possible that the argument addresses some kind of emancipation movement with fanatical overtones. More important, however, is the nature of the justification Paul gives for his ruling. He clearly injures his own case, not arguing on his usual high level. Verse 3, which is clearly inspired by a traditional interpretation of Genesis 2, insists that the man is the "head" (or "origin"; cf. v. 8) of the woman. What is more, v. 7 says that the man is the image and glory of God, whereas the woman is the image of the man. This is clearly a step backward even with respect to Gen. 1:27, which says that the "human person," not the "male," was made in the image of God. According to 1 Cor. 11:7, the image of God in women is only derivative.

Only in vv. 11–12 does Paul, possibly shocked at his own one-sided argument, return to what one would in fact expect him to say: "Nevertheless, in the Lord woman is not independent of man nor man of woman; for as woman was made from man, so man is now born of woman. And all things are from God." These words in fact contradict v. 8 and in effect retract what has already been said, even though Paul does not surrender his position (cf. vv. 13–16).[130]

Of course we must take into account the difficult situation in which Paul finds himself. The Corinthian women obviously were skilled in theological debate and appealed to Paul's own teaching, namely, to the idea cited in Gal. 3:28 that men and women are equal "in the Lord." Does it not follow that at least in worship this equality should be put into practice and conventional roles disregarded?

In response, apart from the considerations already mentioned, Paul appeals

128. See Schrage and Gerstenberger, *Frau* (B2), 132ff.

129. Gottfried Fitzer, *Das Weib schweige in der Gemeinde* (Munich: Kaiser, 1963).

130. See also William O. Walker, "1 Cor. 11:2–16 and Paul's Views Regarding Women," *JBL* 94 (1975): 94–110; Jerome Murphy-O'Connor, "The Non-Pauline Character of 1 Cor. 11:2–16?" *JBL* 95 (1976): 615–21; Lamar Cope, "1 Cor. 11:2–16," *JBL* 97 (1978): 435–36; John P. Meier, "On the Veiling of Hermeneutics (1 Cor. 11:2–16)," *CBQ* 40 (1978): 212–26.

to convention, nature, the practice of other Christian communities, and the mythological notion of awakening desire in the angels. The very multiplicity of Paul's arguments demonstrates his embarassment. It is clearly not all that easy to accept the consequences of "emancipation" if Gal. 3:28 is taken seriously.

In fact, Paul does not demonstrate convincingly that women should keep their heads covered or their hair up. In the first place, specific conventions do not follow *eo ipso* from the subordination of women at creation. Furthermore, except for v. 11, all the arguments Paul cites refer to the order of creation, which he himself does not consider the ultimate criterion "in the Lord."

Despite the weakness of Paul's individual arguments, there is this to be said for his anti-fanatic polemic: it rejects the confusion or identification of Christian freedom with social emancipation.

In my opinion, Käsemann is right in saying that the Corinthian watchword of freedom, considered in isolation and with reference to the case in question, appears more persuasive than Paul's reaction, but suffers from the fundamental defect of fanatical religiosity. "It sees only freedom from burdensome constraint. Here as always, however, the apostle is concerned with the freedom that recognizes a call to service; he sees this freedom threatened when fanaticism undermines order and proclaims its own supposed rights in the name of the Spirit."[131] This is true, but it does not make Paul's argument in detail more persuasive. We must probably admit that Paul, finding himself in a bind, could discover no other expedient than to rely on arguments he himself could no longer accept. He seems aware of this situation when he disavows his own argument in vv. 11–12.

Schottroff proposes a different explanation,[132] which sees Paul as being interested primarily in a "visible demonstration of women's subordinate social role"[133] and accordingly finds a "logical connection" between 1 Corinthians 11 and 1 Tim. 2:11ff.—an unlikely theory. Even if Paul is concerned for the opinions of non-Christians (cf. 10:32) and the community comes under public pressure, it remains to be asked how Christian praxis, which constitutes "an absolute alternative to the reality and ideology of secular society,"[134] can be restricted to the internal life of the community and whether Paul is really concerned primarily with the opinion of non-Christians. If so, he should logically have forbidden women to prophesy, as does 1 Timothy 2.

2.4 A brief glance at the Hellenistic world will also introduce our discussion of Paul's attitude toward marriage.

It seems that here, too, there was a certain ambivalence. On the one hand,

131. Käsemann, "Principles," 211.
132. "Frauen" (B2), 116ff.
133. Ibid., 118.
134. Ibid., 119.

for example, one hears of many good marriages or better protection for women through marriage contracts. The ideal of marriage described by the philosophers is in part exemplary. Earlier the primary reason for marriage was considered to be reproduction; now there is more emphasis on companionship. This is true especially for the Stoics and above all Musonius, according to whom husband and wife should be so close that "they live and work together in full partnership, considering that everything belongs to both and no longer to the individual, not even their own bodies."[135]

Alongside these high ideals there is also a dark side, especially in the realm of sexual morality: widespread infidelity and sexual relationships with hetaerae, prostitutes, and slaves. There were few objections to men, married or single, having intercourse with slaves, hetaerae, and hierodules. Typical is the much-quoted statement in the speech against Neaira of Pseudo-Demosthenes: "We have hetaerae for pleasure, concubines for daily cultivation of the body [a euphemism], wives for the begetting of legitimate children and to be faithful guardians of the household."[136] On the whole, in matters of sexuality there was a remarkable alternation between overemphasis and devaluation.[137] The influence of dualism and *enkratia*, with their ideal of sexual asceticism, also important for an understanding of Paul's attitude, will be treated in more detail below when we discuss deutero-Pauline ethics.

2.5 When discussing Paul's viewpoint, we must first avoid the misconception that 1 Corinthians 7 provides something like a complete Pauline teaching concerning marriage. The chapter clearly addresses questions raised by the Corinthians. Verse 1, which states that it is well for a man not to touch a woman, is probably even a quotation from the letter sent by the community (like 1 Cor. 6:13; 7:26; 8:1; and similar passages). In v. 2, Paul states his own opinion, which opposes this option of sexual abstinence and celibacy. This verse has been subject to considerable attack from Paul's commentators. It has been said, for example, that Paul views marriage "solely from the primitive perspective of sensuality" as a "necessary evil," a concession to pacify "un-Christian longings," a mere "safety-valve" against evil perversions, a "middle way" between *enkratia* and fornication.[138]

No one can deny that Paul exhibits a certain reserve with respect to marriage (cf. the discussion of celibacy below, IV.D.2.6–7). But this hesitation is not based on rejection of sexuality or the body; its roots are quite different. Nor does Paul say that avoidance of unchastity is the only purpose of marriage. In response to the Corinthians, who, like many rigorous fanat-

---

135. 67.7ff.; cf. also Plutarch *Praecepta coniugalia*, 34.
136. 59.122; cf. Albrecht Oepke, "grammateus," *TDNT* 1:740.
137. See also Preisker, *Christentum* (B2), 13ff.; Albrecht Oepke, "Ehe I," *RAC* 4:650ff.; Konrad Gaiser, *Für und wider die Ehe* (Munich: Heimeran, 1974); Schrage and Gerstenberger, *Frau* (B2), 149–50.
138. See Wolfgang Schrage, "Zur Fronstellung der paulinischen Ehebewertung in 1. Kor. 7,1–7," *ZNW* 67 (1976): 214–34.

ics, obviously find marriage very close to unchastity, he has to make it clear that it is in fact hostility toward the body and sexuality that can lead to unchastity. Marriage is the appropriate way to avoid this threatened danger. Despite his own high esteem for celibacy, Paul was sufficiently sober and levelheaded not to follow the ascetics in minimizing the risks of sexual asceticism. For Paul, asceticism without charisma is fanaticism; in the face of reality it comes to grief all too easily. If the problem is to avoid unchastity, Paul's answer is clear: "Each man should have his own wife and each woman her own husband" (v. 2). In other words, marriage is the way shown by the Creator to keep human sexuality within bounds and to protect men and women from sexual excess. It would be wrong to put too much weight on "each," but it is clear that Paul generally considers marriage the norm even within the Christian community. Marriage in the sense of full partnership can be the locus of "holiness" (1 Thess. 4:4) and "peace" (1 Cor. 7:15).[139]

What a marriage partnership involves is described in 1 Cor. 7:3–5: "The husband should give to his wife her conjugal rights, and likewise the wife to her husband. For the wife does not rule over her own body, but the husband does; likewise the husband does not rule over his own body, but the wife does." The marital relationship *eo ipso* involves the bodies of both. Where there is a marriage, there is also the obligation of sexual relationships. "Conjugal rights" is first and foremost a euphemism, but it is not impossible that Paul understands this obligation in the light of Rom. 13:8 and 15:1, that is, in the light of "owing" *agapē* and mutual responsibility. Marriage implies that one no longer rules over one's own body. This fact may also remind us that *agapē* renounces all claims to personal autonomy. The statement that married Christians no longer rule over their own bodies would then be a special case of the fact that Christians no longer rule over themselves, no longer seek their own advantage. Love thus has its place in such secular institutions and relationships as marriage.[140]

It is also noteworthy that Paul always addresses both husband and wife. And it is essential to recognize that the demands of the body are not viewed in isolation: the "body" is more than just flesh and blood. Paul's overriding purpose is probably to show that both husband and wife depend on each other and have mutual obligations. It is not by accident that Paul does not simply address one of the marital partners: he always speaks of both man and wife, so that his statements are interrelated.[141] With only minor exceptions, chapter 7 does not address husband and wife independently, saying something different to each, but speaks to them in similar terms throughout (cf. vv. 2, 3, 4, 5, 10–11, 12–13, 14, 15, 16, 28, 32).

How seriously Paul takes the principle of mutuality can be seen in v. 5,

139. See Schrage and Gerstenberger, *Frau* (B2), 153–54.
140. See Greeven, *Hauptproblem* (B), 136; Schrage, "Frontstellung," 229–30.
141. Cf. Kähler, *Frau*, 14ff.

where he speaks of the conditions under which sexual companionship may be denied. Such abstinence is to be restricted to a short period. Above all, it is not to be decided on by one partner alone, but mutually agreed to. Paul does not say how this agreement is to be reached, but it is probably safe to assume that love and consideration play a part. The bottom line is a warning against hyperascetical excesses. For this reason Paul does not favor unconsummated marriages without sexual relations, such as are found in the early church, although several exegetes maintain that such marriages are presupposed in 1 Cor. 7:36–38. Possibly the Corinthians did in fact prefer such platonic relationships, and Paul did not quite realize the situation. It is unthinkable, however, that he himself favored such sexless marriages.[142] Probably 1 Cor. 7:36–38 has in mind a normal betrothal.[143] If a man who is betrothed thinks he is behaving "improperly" toward his betrothed because he is experiencing sexual tension or finds himself in "sexual distress"[144] that presses for sexual union so that his desire threatens to lead him astray, he should marry his betrothed. But if he has control over his sexual urge, Paul recommends continued celibacy, probably on the same grounds as in 1 Cor. 7:25ff.

2.6 The problem of divorce does not need further discussion (see our interpretation of the Word of the Lord in 1 Cor. 7:10–12). We must remember, however, that this insistence on the indissolubility of marriage stands in clear contrast to the usual practice outside the Christian community.

Even in the non-Jewish world, divorce was the order of the day. According to Hellenistic law, the wife could also initiate proceedings. Delling reports divorce to have reached almost epidemic proportions in Rome.[145] In one funeral oration, for example, we read: "It is rare to find long marriages, ended by death rather than interrupted by divorce." According to Seneca, women keep track of the years not by names of the consuls but by the number of their husbands: "They divorce in order to marry and marry in order to divorce."[146]

Paul, however, emphasizes Jesus' prohibition of divorce (1 Cor. 7:10–12) and in 1 Cor. 7:27 says that a man who is bound to a wife should not seek to be free (cf. also Rom. 7:2). Christians in mixed marriages should not divorce if the unbelieving partner wishes to remain married (1 Cor. 7:12ff.). Paul even expects that the unbelieving partner will share in redemption through the Christian (vv. 14–15), although how this is to happen remains obscure.

Obviously for Paul marital fidelity goes hand in hand with the indissolubility of marriage; he condemns both divorce and adultery (cf. Rom.

142. See also Baltensweiler, *Ehe* (B), 175ff.; Crüsemann and Thyen, *Mann*, 178ff.
143. Cf. Werner G. Kümmel, "Verlobung und Heirat bei Paulus (1 Kor. 7,36–38)," in *Heilsgeschehen und Geschichte* (Marburg: Elwert, 1975), 310–27.
144. Cf. Gottlieb Schrenk, "thelema," *TDNT* 3:60–61.
145. Delling, *Paulus*, 15.
146. *De beneficiis* 3:16; see also Oepke, "gynē," *TNDT* 1:777ff.; Gerhard Delling, "Ehescheidung," *RAC* 4:709–10.

13:9; 1 Cor. 6:9). His conviction that marriage is inviolable also stands in sharp contrast to the common permissiveness or uncertainty of the surrounding world.[147]

2.7 For Paul, Christian celibacy is a charisma (1 Cor. 7:7). This has two implications. First, it is not required of all Christians, but is a free gift of God's grace. Second, however, as a charisma, it gives special opportunity for special service to others—a capacity for *diakonia*. There is nothing about ascetic celibacy for the sake of cultivating one's own spiritual personality, based on disdain for the body, or celibacy based on egoism, contempt for the opposite sex, or the like.

A further argument in favor of celibacy is heard in 1 Cor. 7:25ff., where Paul advises against entering into marriage because of the impending troubles of the eschatological age, which he would like to "spare" the community (v. 28b). In his preference for celibacy, then, Paul does not argue simply from dogmatic theologumena; his concern for married members of the community moves him to counsel celibacy. The pain and suffering, fear and terror of this dying eon can only be worse for those who are married (cf. also v. 37).

The fundamental reason Paul prefers celibacy, however, does not appear until vv. 32d–33: those who are single can devote themselves totally to the Lord, whereas those who are married are anxious about worldly affairs. As v. 34 puts it, they are "divided" between the Lord and the world. In celibacy, on the contrary, Paul sees the opportunity for undivided devotion to the Lord (cf. also v. 35), in which "service to Christ" (Rom. 14:18) is determined by love for others (Rom. 14:15). The crucial reason Paul recommends celibacy is therefore eschatological and christological, not the disaffection with marriage typical of late antiquity or the hostility to marriage of ascetic dualism. Since both Jews and Stoics considered marriage a way of life in accord with nature's plan and therefore obligatory,[148] Paul is also at odds with their normal expectations. The usual attitude toward the unmarried was pity or ridicule. The Christian community, however, offers an opportunity "to remain honorably and happily single."[149]

3. Work, Property, Slavery

3.1 The attitude of Paul's world to work depends in part on social class. In theory all work was respected in the Greco-Roman world. But the growth of a ruling aristocracy and above all the spread of slavery made physical labor in particular appear degrading. In certain circles, work came increasingly to be seen as an evil inflicted by Zeus, part of the dark side of life like sickness or disaster. Free people preferred to occupy themselves with athletics, social

147. Friedrich, *Sexualität* (B2), 108ff.; Gerhard Delling, "Ehebruch," *RAC* 4:666ff.
148. Greeven, *Hauptproblem* (B), 119–20.
149. Adolf Schlatter, *Paulus der Bote Jesu*, 4th ed. (Stuttgart: Calwer, 1969), 245; cf. also Friedrich, *Sexualität* (B2), 62ff.

life, philosophy, and politics. It is therefore not surprising that many philosophers, especially if they were rich, did not achieve a proper appreciation of work. Cicero, for example, lumps all workmen together as part of the "unsavory mob." "What nobility can there be in a workshop?"[150] The Stoics, who expressly contrasted work to disgraceful idleness and pursuit of pleasure, considered it a means of self-improvement. Seneca can liken human labor to the purposeless scurrying of ants up and down a tree trunk, but he nonetheless states that anyone who is virtuous desires to work.[151] The papyri, which originate in working-class circles, exhibit a large measure of love, self-satisfaction, and care with respect to work.[152]

Paul's positive evaluation of work appears to derive primarily from his Jewish background. Judaism sees work as a task assigned by God. Human labor is known, of course, to stand under the curse (Gen. 3:17), but it is also known that even before the Fall God assigned Adam work in the garden of Eden (Gen. 2:15). The growth of the scribal class produced critical voices, arguing that it was difficult to reconcile intellectual labor with physical labor. In general, however, the rabbis in particular engaged in both. According to Aboth 2.2, for example, Rabbi Gamaliel III said: "It is good to study the Torah in combination with secular work [such as a trade or business], for the effort demanded by both makes one forget [to engage in] sin. But all study of the Torah that is not associated with gainful employment finally comes to an end and brings sin after it."[153]

3.2 Paul himself learned a trade. According to Acts 18:3, he was a tent maker. We learn from his letters that he earned his living by his own hands. The appearance of this statement in the catalogue of afflictions in 1 Cor. 4:12 warns us not to idealize this laborious work or interpret it as a means of moral self-improvement. Paul worked day and night so as not to be a burden to anyone (1 Thess. 2:9) and to make it clear to the community that he was seeking them, not what was theirs (2 Cor. 12:14).

Paul often had to defend himself against association with the enterprising behavior of popular Christian or even syncretistic missionaries and propagandists (cf. 1 Thess. 2:5; 2 Cor. 7:2; 12:14–18). Wandering preachers out for profit appear to have been no rarity in the ancient world. When Paul emphasizes that he is not enriching himself at the expense of the Christian community, he is not denying that as an apostle he would have every right to be supported by the community (1 Cor. 9). But he relinquishes his claim to this right—not everywhere, but where necessary for the sake of the gospel.

In 1 Thess. 4:9ff., he categorizes his own work under the heading of love for the brethren and exhorts the members of the community to work with

150. *De officiis* 1.151.
151. *De providentia* 2.
152. Cf. Friedrich Hauck, "Arbeit," *RAC* 1:585ff.
153. Cf. Strack-Billerbeck, *Kommentar* 2:745, with other similar citations.

their own hands so as not to need support from others. Later, in Ephesians, love is cited even more clearly as a motivation for work: one should work so as to be able to give to those in need (Eph. 4:28). Here, too, work is not done for natural or "bourgeois" motives. It is noteworthy that, according to 1 Thess. 4:11, Paul stressed this obligation to work even during his three-week stay with the Thessalonians to establish their community. Probably there was good reason to insist from the outset that eschatological hope must not lead people to give up their work and profession. Nowhere, however, does Paul appear to find it necessary to attack what might be called an aristocratic contempt for manual labor.

3.3 Paul has much less to say about property and possessions than did Jesus (cf. above, I.D.3). Of fundamental importance is 1 Cor. 7:30: "Let those who buy do so as though they had no goods." Eschatology does not call buying as such into question, but ownership and possession. Those who buy are to refrain not from buying but from thinking that they have future disposition over what they have bought. Paul insists that ownership must remain conditional, not because buying and consumption are inventions of the devil or because the economic and commercial practices of daily life should simply be given up, but because the provisional must not become absolute. Philippians 4:11ff., too, says nothing of a fundamental renunciation of possessions above and beyond inward detachment and outward self-reliance.

These statements (plus the warnings against covetousness in Rom. 1:9; 1 Cor. 5:10; 6:10) focus primarily on individual morality—as does 1 Thess. 4:6 with its warning against defrauding one's neighbor in business, going outside the private realm. More important, however, are the passages in which Paul, addressing the local community or the church as a whole, calls for mutual sharing in all things, including worldly goods. Galatians 6:6, for example, exhorts those being instructed in the Word to share all good things with their instructors; undoubtedly this includes material support (cf. also Rom. 12:13; Phil. 4:14–15).

We must remember above all the collection for Jerusalem, which Paul mentions frequently in his letters (cf. 2 Cor. 8:9; Rom. 15:26; Gal. 2:10). Certainly this offering is not simply a demonstration of personal charity (not to mention a tax imposed by the Jerusalem authorities). It is also an act of social welfare in an economic emergency. Paul urges that those with much should have nothing left over and those with little should not lack (2 Cor. 8:15).[154] In economic matters Paul also demands equalization, indeed "equality" (1 Cor. 8:13–14; cf. Cicero, for whom such *aequatio* is a terrible evil).[155] Here, too, love has the last word. Although 1 Cor. 13:3 points out that love can be absent even when one gives away everything, so that renunciation of possessions is not in itself identical with love, there can be no doubt that love

154. See Gustav Stählin, "isos," *TDNT* 3:348.
155. *De officiis* 2.73.

takes concrete form in renunciation of one's own financial and material resources. Of course alleviation of social problems is not the real purpose, but the communion of the body of Christ has an ethical and social dimension. The social aspects of the Lord's Supper have already been mentioned in our discussion of the sacramental basis of ethics (cf. above, IV.A.3.3–4). Here we need only recall that depreciation of common meals in favor of the sacramental celebration would hurt the poor and destroy the solidarity of the community (1 Cor. 11:17ff.). Paul obviously did not espouse or undertake social action for the benefit of unbelievers on the basis of the fundamentally unrestricted law of love.

3.4 The apostolic age was characterized by a host of slaves. The ancient world considered slavery both natural and obvious. Slaves were property and are therefore often listed in summaries of net worth alongside money, household goods, or real property. As chattels, they could be sold, pledged, inherited, and rented. A slave is a living possession,[156] an object (res). By virtue of dominical power (dominica potestas), masters have extensive power over their slaves, not just the right to their labor. Stoicism, however, by calling to mind the common humanity of all, contributed to the amelioration of the system. And it must be remembered that the lot of slaves in particular cases depended in large measure on the individual master. The slaves who worked as secretaries, musicians, or teachers obviously had an easier life than those who worked in the mines or were chained to the mills. When all is said and done, however, slavery was often a wretched existence, crying out to heaven. It was generally thought that, besides food and work, slaves needed punishment and beatings; the lash was among the milder forms of punishment. According to C. Cassius, "that rabble can be kept in check only through fear." Therefore when the prefect Pedanius Secundus was murdered by one of his slaves, Cassius persuaded the Senate to have four hundred of them executed.[157]

It is obvious that Christian slaves were as dependent on their masters as their unbelieving companions. It had become increasingly common to allow slaves free exercise of their religion, but in practice this held true only when this religion was not in conflict with the religion of the house and its practice was not at odds with the sentiments of the master. It is easy to see that there would be frequent conflicts. We know from Ignatius's *Epistle to Polycarp* 4:3 and other early Christian documents that Christian slaves often wished to have the community buy their freedom, and it is not impossible that this situation already obtained in the apostolic age.

3.5 If we look at what Paul has to say against this background, he ob-

---

156. Aristotle *Politics* 1.2.4.

157. Tacitus *Annals* 14.43–44. Cf. also William L. Westermann, *The Slave Systems of Greek and Roman Antiquity*, 3d ed. (Philadelphia: American Philosophical Society, 1964); Gayer, *Stellung*, 19ff.

viously disappoints such hopes for social reform. In 1 Cor. 7:20ff., we read: "Everyone should remain in the state in which he was called. Were you a slave when called? Never mind. But even if you can gain your freedom, make use of it. For he who was called in the Lord as a slave is a freedman of the Lord. Likewise he who was free when called is a slave of Christ." Paul does not glorify slavery as an institution ordained by God. Nor, however, does he espouse a progressive program of social reform to free the slaves. This is not because such emancipation often brought starvation and insecurity, and certainly not because he wants to whitewash the terrible situation with fine-sounding words. His purpose in the short time remaining before the Parousia is rather to establish obedience wherever Christians find themselves: the state in which they were called is the state, assigned by God, in which they are to be tested and endure.

The question of whether a slave should remain a slave if given the opportunity to be free is disputed. The philological, contextual, and historical arguments surrounding the interpretation of 1 Cor. 7:21b lead in part to contrary conclusions. It is clear that Paul is not simply sanctioning the status quo; what matters is how one "walks" within the given institutions. Most exegetes supply "slavery" as the object of the Greek verb translated "make use of it" above. This agrees with the basic tenor of the passage, unless Paul is specifically seeking to avoid the misunderstanding, suggested by the context, that one should even reject the chance for freedom. Against this interpretation of the clause as urging rejection of emancipation is the fact that slaves as a rule do not seem to have had any say in whether or not they would be freed (but cf. Exod. 21:5–6). This argument, however, also undercuts the opposite interpretation ("avail yourself of [the opportunity for freedom]"), based on the use of the aorist tense, which designates a single act. Possibly Paul's purpose is only to emphasize that, even if emancipated, Christians should live according to their call in Christ, which cannot be altered by any change in social status.[158]

It might appear that Paul, like the Stoics, is trying to downplay mere outward freedom when he says in v. 21a: "Never mind, don't worry about it." Many think all that matters is inward freedom, which cannot be impugned by outward circumstances. Paul's calling the slave a "freedman of the Lord" appears also to be similar to Epictetus's paradoxical concept of freedom, which holds that one can be free although outwardly a slave if one possesses true inner freedom. For Paul, however, subjective inwardness is not an impregnable fortress in which one may realize full autonomy. Freedom

158. This interpretation is supported above all by S. Scott Bartchy, *MALLON CHRHSAI: First Century Slavery and the Interpretation of 1 Corinthians 7:21,* SBLDS 11 (Missoula, Mont.: Scholars Press, 1973). Cf. Also Peter Trummer, "Die Chance der Freiheit," *Bibl* 56 (1975): 344–68; Peter Stuhlmacher, *Der Brief an Philemon,* 2d ed., EKKNT 17, 44–45. For other interpretations see, for example, Wendland, *Ethik* (B), 78–79; Heinrich Schlier, "eleutheros," *TDNT* 2:501; Gayer, *Stellung,* 206–7.

cannot be achieved through one's own efforts, nor is Christian freedom the same as Stoic *ataraxia* or *autopraxis*. A Christian is free only as a "freedman of the Lord" and a "slave of Christ" (v. 22). It is only the freedom given through Christ and the service owed Christ that break down the legal and social distinctions between slave and free. In freedom from the entanglements and enticements of this world, its cares and its claims, and in loving solidarity with Christ and other believers, even slaves are freed from the need to attach ultimate importance to the pain and humiliation of sociological reality.

3.6 The Epistle to Philemon shows that we must not interpret Paul as saying that everything remains as it was and nothing has changed. The slave Onesimus, we read in the letter, has run away from his Christian master Philemon, possibly not without having had his finger's in his master's till. He has been converted to Christianity by Paul. We may conclude first that the Christian master did not force his slave to accept Christianity, but gave him the freedom to continue to live as a non-Christian. More important, although Paul does not simply urge the termination of this master/slave relationship on ethical or theological grounds, he does see the relationship as being defined by the ethics and praxis of Christian solidarity. The old legal relationship continues in force, but the institution itself does not remain unchanged. The slave is no longer an object but a "beloved brother" (v. 16); the difference is important in both human and social terms (cf. above, IV.C.4.4), and it affects more than the master. The relationship of Philemon to his slave is far more than just a private matter, as we can see from the fact that the letter is addressed to the house church (v. 2), which is also affected.[159] If Onesimus is now "much more than a slave" (v. 16), and if the love Onesimus's master has toward all the saints (v. 5) includes his slave, this has real consequences not only within the community but also in the world, with all its institutions and relationships (v. 16). Any dualistic social ethics is ruled out.[160]

When Paul, for example, asks pardon for Onesimus (vv. 12, 17), he is not simply preaching an abstract freedom from all outward circumstances; we also note a love that influences the structures of property rights and society. This happens in two ways. First, Paul intercedes personally on behalf of the runaway slave, who was liable to severe punishment according to the law, reminding Onesimus's master that in this case, too, Christian solidarity suggests forgiveness.[161] This already touches on the second point: Onesimus's master should not do whatever might be legal or normal, but what love requires. In other words, he should respond to the theft of his "productive capital" with forgiveness rather than punishment.

Paul himself breaks through these structures on occasion. To show hospitality to a runaway slave was a criminal offense. The law required that a

159. Suhl, "Philemonbrief," 277–78.
160. Preiss, "Vie en Christ."
161. Contrast Plato *Laws* 777e.

fugitivus found on anyone's property be reported. The fact that Paul sends Onesimus back to his master and offers to take responsibility for any loss (vv. 18–19) appears to suggest that Paul is well aware of what the law requires him to do. Nevertheless he does not say that he is returning the fugitive Onesimus in accordance with the *lex Fabia de plagiariis*, in order to satisfy the law and straighten out the matter. Paul instead requests Onesimus's release, so that he may be of service to Paul or act as a "Christian ambassador" while Paul is in prison.[162] This confirms that, far from being concerned simply to see that property rights are kept inviolable, Paul maintains that such institutions must take second place to the demands of the gospel and love.

4. Christians and the State

4.1 The Pauline view of the Roman Empire is recorded primarily in Rom. 13:1–7, despite certain problems that have led some to go so far as to suggest non-Pauline authorship. Romans 13 has often been misused to support uncritical servility on the part of subjects and to lay a biblical foundation for a religiously tinged political metaphysics that gives the state a position of honor and dignity. It is easy to see why the passage has often been judged deutero-Pauline or "foreign." Such "foreignness," which is due primarily to the traditional nature of this section of Pauline parenesis, does not by itself make the passage a secondary interpolation, but it does emphasize the need to interpret Romans 13 from within its Pauline context.

4.2 In my opinion, one cannot evade the problem by assuming that Romans 13 responds to special dangers arising within the Christian community at Rome, such as revolutionary or anarchistic movements, or hostility to Rome influenced by Zealots or other Jewish partisans. The verses themselves make no reference to anti-Roman movements or hostility within the community. The absence of specifically Zealot interests is shown in v. 6 by the ease with which Paul can treat the payment of taxes (indicative!) as a given.

Nor is there any support for the claim that Romans 13 was inspired by the apostle's favorable experience with the Roman legal system during the first years of Nero's rule. This theory leaves out of account the stereotyped nature of the parenesis in which Romans 13 appears. In addition the very basis of the claim is mistaken. There is no denying that as a Roman citizen (*civis Romanus*) some of Paul's experiences with Roman authorities were favorable (cf. his appeal to the emperor). On the other hand, he clearly had negative experiences as well. Although he may not yet have heard anything bad about Nero, who later went on to murder his mother, brothers, and wife, even he could not have missed rumors about the imperial lunacy of a Caligula. And

---

162. Cf. Wolf-Henning Ollrog, *Paulus und seine Mitarbeiter*, WMANT 50 (Neukirchen: Neukirchener Verlag, 1979), 101ff.; see Gerhard Friedrich, *Die kleineren Briefe des Apostels Paulus*, 11th ed., NTD 8 on Philemon. It is often argued on the basis of Col. 4:7, 9 that Philemon did in fact release Onesimus for Paul's service; see Stuhlmacher, *Philemon*, 18–19, 57.

Paul had had long experience with physical abuse at the hands of the Roman administration. In 2 Cor. 11:25, for example, he speaks of being beaten with rods by order of the Roman authorities; this passage antedates Romans 13. The chapter, therefore, is not simply dictated by Paul's own experiences. This is not to deny that such experiences exercised a certain influence, nor a latent Christian fanaticism, which Paul might well fear, but reference to such influences is not sufficient to account for Romans 13.

4.3 Romans 13:1–7 is set between passages that have love as their theme (12:21 and 13:8–10; cf. above, IV.C.4.5). The contrast with the content of 13:1–7 is certainly not deliberate. Since Paul subordinates everything to love, however, and seeks to maintain this love even in the secular institutions of this world, the relationship of Christians to the official representatives of the state is also based on love.

Even if there are reservations on this point, it is beyond doubt that 13:1–7 is related to 12:1–2 and 13:11–14, which enclose and define the entire parenetic block. Romans 12:1–2, the introduction and theme of what follows, shows that obedience to the state authorities is part of the worship Christians owe in secular life.[163] Similarly, Rom. 13:11–14, the concluding coda to the preceding material, makes the eschatological proviso clear. The state, too, is provisional, belonging to the world that is passing away, not final and absolute but temporary and transitory.[164] Although political authority is provisional and obedience to it is limited in both time and extent, this does not mean that both are negligible quantities, totally unimportant. Precisely because of the eschatological orientation that makes Christians look forward to the "heavenly commonwealth" in which they have their citizenship even now (Phil. 3:20), Christians can and must respect the provisional order of God's created world and not be too hasty in ignoring or sabotaging their implicit obligations to the state.

4.4 Paul's parenetic purpose is above all to deal succinctly but responsibly with the secular obligations of daily life,[165] not to provide an exhaustive and fundamental doctrine of the state. Too much weight should not be placed on the traditional admonitions he cites and the reasons he gives for them; their significance is primarily functional. This holds true also for the notion of "order" (RSV: "authority"), which undoubtedly plays a special role (vv. 1, 2, 5); it must not be misused to overemphasize the importance of the powers that be or to elaborate some metaphysical or sacral order of authority. Of course it would be wrong to downplay the element of institutional order in favor of personal relations or God's actions in history,[166] but it does not carry independent weight (cf. above, IV.C.2.3).

163. Cf. Käsemann, "Principles," 199, 212ff.
164. Cf. Cullman, State (B5), 61–62; Schrage, Staat (B5), 54–55; Aland, "Verhältnis" (B5), 179ff.
165. Käsemann, "Principles," 200; idem, "Röm. 13," 325.
166. Cf. Duchrow, Christenheit (B), 156–57.

Evidence that Paul is not thinking of a fixed institution in Romans 13 may be found in the term "disposition" (*diatagē;* RSV: "authorities") a *nomen actionis* (v. 2). Paul does not speak of "the heavenly and earthly *ordo* but of the divine *ordinatio* or disposition, the ordering will of God."[167] There can be no doubt as to Paul's interest: the subordination of Christians must agree with the ordered disposition ordained by God. This subordination includes the hierarchy of office holders, authorities, officials, magistrates, and the like.

4.5 Now to the basis on which Paul urges obedience: without going into the legitimacy, nature, and limits of the existing political authorities, Paul unhesitatingly refers to the powers that be—not those that correspond to some particular ideal—as having their authority fundamentally "from God" (v. 1)—established and empowered by the Creator. The statement that the civil authorities are entrusted by God with the exercise of power does not imply any apotheosis of the state. Nor does the mandate of the authorities imply that the form of government and how it exercises its authority are irrelevant, even though Paul does not discuss these matters. Nor do all the individual laws promulgated by the state have to be considered ordained by God. Nevertheless, governments exercise their powers not simply by nature, history, or social contract; Paul has nothing to say of such things. They are empowered by God and stand in his service. It does not matter whether the authorities think of themselves as appointed by God; they are God's "servants" and "ministers" (vv. 4, 6).

This is why Paul enjoins Christians to obey the authorities. But if those who do good have no need to fear the power of the state (v. 3), the office and function of the state are defined indirectly. The state's task is not, in Cicero's words, "primarily to see that the private property of all citizens is protected,"[168] but first and foremost to defend and promote what is good. Besides upholding justice and promoting what is good, the organs of the state are charged with protecting its citizens against what is evil. The state, in other words, has the function of maintaining order and preventing chaos. Paul presupposes almost naively that as a matter of course the state not only can distinguish between good and evil but will in fact promote what is good and oppose what is evil. In exercising this function of opposing evil, the state "does not bear the sword in vain" (v. 4); it also has the power to punish. Only the wicked, on whom the civil authorities vent their "wrath," need fear this power. Those who do good receive not the "sword" but "approval" (v. 3).

In any case, those who do good benefit in this transient world from the proper function of the state. "For your good" (v. 4) means either securing an ordered society in which justice is protected or helping Christians put into practice the "good conduct" (vv. 3, 4b) required of them as citizens, which for them cannot be separated from works of love.[169]

167. Käsemann, "Principles," 201.
168. *De officiis* 2.73; cf. 2.78.
169. Wilckens, "Röm. 13,1–7," 209–10.

4.6 The proper attitude of Christians, like others, to the civil authorities is subservience. But such subservience does not mean uncritical servility or blind acquiescence. Barth spoke of "accepting the powers that be, without any fanfare or illusions."[170] This is certainly something less than what Paul has in mind, but Barth's coolness is closer to the mark than all the solemn exaltation of the "sovereign state" and obedience to it that was long read into Romans 13. What subservience means is "participation in an order established by God."[171]

Paul's failure to discuss cases of conflict, abuse of power, and the limits of obedience in Romans 13 does not mean that he was ignorant of such problems. This is shown by 2 Cor. 11:32–33, for example, where he mentions his threatened imprisonment by the ethnarch of King Aretas, which he evaded only by a daring escape over the city wall. It is also shown by 2 Cor. 6:5 and 11:22–25, where Paul speaks of his sufferings—beatings at the hands of the Romans, scourging at the hand of the Jews, and various imprisonments (cf. Acts 16:22–23). Finally, Paul's awareness that obedience has its limits and his unwillingness to confuse subservience with blind obedience is clear from his condemnation and execution at Rome. He would never have obeyed an order to cease preaching Christ (cf. Acts 16:19ff.), nor would he have allowed "Caesar is Lord" to pass his lips.[172] Such refusal of obedience is quite compatible with the notion that the civil authorities are ordained by God.

For this very reason, Christians do not respect civil authority for opportunistic reasons, merely to avoid the punishment threatened by the state or because under present conditions resistance is doomed to failure. Christians affirm civil authority out of responsible and conscientious obedience to God's will (v. 5). This is why (as Paul says in v. 6) Christians pay taxes: their fundamental sense of responsibility prohibits them from refusing such prosaic obligations as payment of taxes on the grounds that they are meaningless. And in v. 7 the apostle exhorts his readers once again to pay their taxes, both direct and indirect, to those to whom they are due.

In my opinion, it remains an open question to whom the "fear" (RSV: "respect") and "honor" mentioned in v. 7b are due—in other words, whether the civil authorities are included. There is certainly some evidence that v. 7b does not refer to the state. First, there is the contradiction with vv. 3–4, where fear is limited to those who do evil. Note also the injunction in 1 Pet. 2:17, which derives from a similar tradition, where fear is expressly reserved for God. If Romans 13 were influenced by Mark 12:17, even indirectly, the second part of the dominical saying would have a parallel here. We must also recall that "fear" is an element in Paul's concept of faith. But if fear is due God, not the civil authorities, the same is true of the "honor" that appears as

170. Karl Barth, *Romans*, 483.
171. Gerhard Delling, "hypotassō," *TDNT* 8:43.
172. *Martyrdom of Polycarp* 8:2.

the last of the four elements listed in v. 7, unless we prefer to interpret the obligation to honor as referring to all (cf. 1 Pet. 2:17a and Rom. 12:10). If "those to whom honor is due" refers to everyone (including the emperor, as suggested by 1 Pet. 2:17d), the transition to v. 8 would also be better. If this solution were correct, there would be a certain element of distance in the respect demanded, which would make it easier to reconcile the attitude of Romans 13 with that of 1 Corinthians 6.

There is nevertheless a certain undeniable tension between Romans 13 and 1 Corinthians 6, which is probably a sign that Paul is somewhat tentative in addressing these questions of "political ethics." At the same time, however, it reflects the dialectic of the Pauline world view and the supremacy of love.[173]

4.7 When Paul warns the Christians at Corinth in 1 Cor. 6:1ff. (see above, IV.B.2.3) not to make use of the secular legal system, it is not to deny the jurisdiction of the courts but to fulfill the demands of love, as we see from his recommendation to renounce one's rights rather than seek arbitration within the community. He does not deny in principle the power and right of the state to decide civil cases any more than he denies the state's general purpose of maintaining order and justice. He makes it abundantly clear, however, that the function of the state and its legal system do not in themselves necessarily serve the ends of the gospel and love, not even when the state is carrying out its legitimate mission.

173. See also Cullman, *State* (B5), 62–63; Aland, "Verhältnis" (B5), 197–98. Aland gives too much weight to 1 Corinthians 6 and Phil. 4:8 as over against Romans 13.

V

THE ETHICS OF RESPONSIBILITY IN THE DEUTERO-PAULINE EPISTLES

BIBLIOGRAPHY

A. The New Life in Colossians and Ephesians (pp. 244–57)

Crouch, James E. *The Origin and Intention of the Colossian Haustafel.* FRLANT 109. Göttingen: Vandenhoeck & Ruprecht, 1972. Pp. 120ff.

Culpepper, R. Alan. "Ethical Dualism and Church Discipline Eph. 4:25—5:20." *RExp* 76 (1979): 529–39.

Fischer, Karl Martin. *Tendenz und Absicht des Epheserbriefes.* FRLANT 111. Göttingen: Vandenhoeck & Ruprecht, 1973. Pp. 147–72.

Lohse, Eduard. "Christologie und Ethik im Kolosserbrief." In *Die Einheit des NT,* 249–61. Göttingen: Vandenhoeck & Ruprecht, 1973.

Sanders. *Ethics* (B). Pp. 68–81.

Schrage, Wolfgang. "Zur Ethik der neutestamentlichen Haustafeln." *NTS* 21 (1974–75): 1–22.

Stuhlmacher, Peter. "Christliche Verantwortung bei Paulus und seinen Schülern." *EvTh* 28 (1968): 165–86, esp. 174–81.

Völkl. *Christ* (B). Pp. 298–322.

Weiss, Hans-Friedrich. "Taufe und neues Leben im deuteropaulinischen Schrifttum." In *Taufe und neue Existenz,* ed. Erdmann Schott, 53–70. Berlin: Evangelische Verlagsanstalt, 1973.

Wendland. *Ethik* (B). Pp. 90–95.

B. Apostolic Precepts in the Pastorals (pp. 257–68)

Bartsch, Hans Werner. *Die Anfänge urchristlicher Rechtsbildungen.* ThF 34. Harmbert: Evangelischer Verlag, 1965.

Dibelius, Martin. *Die Pastoralbriefe.* 4th ed. Ed. Hans Conzelmann. HNT 13. Tübingen: Mohr, 1966. English: *The Pastoral Epistles.* Hermeneia. Philadelphia: Fortress Press, 1972.

Foerster, W. "Eusebeia in den Pastoralbriefen." *NTS* 5 (1958–59): 213–18.

Merk, Otto. "Glaube und Tat in den Pastoralbriefen." *ZNW* 66 (1975): 91–102.

Mott, Stephen Charles. "Greek Ethics and Christian Conversion." *NT* 20 (1978): 22–48.

Sanders. *Ethics* (B). Pp. 81–90.

Stuhlmacher. "Verantwortung" (VA). Pp. 181–84.

Trummer, Peter. *Die Paulustradition der Pastoralbriefe.* Frankfurt: Lang, 1978. Pp. 227–40.

Wendland. *Ethik* (B). Pp. 95–101.

C. Christian Life According to 1 Peter (pp. 268–78)

Delling, Gerhard. "Der Bezug der christlichen Existenz auf das Heilshandeln Gottes nach dem ersten Petrusbrief." In *NT und Christliche Existenz* (Festschrift Herbert Braun), ed. H. D. Betz und L. Schottroff, 95–113. Tübingen: Mohr, 1973.

Goppelt, Leonhard. "Prinzipien neutestamentlicher Sozialethik nach dem 1. Petrusbrief." In *NT und Geschichte* (Festschrift Oscar Cullmann), ed. H. Baltensweilen and B. Reicke, 285–96. Zürich: Theologischer Verlag, 1972.

————. *Theology* (B.I). 2:161–77.

Lohse, Eduard. "Paränese und Kerygma im 1. Petrusbrief." In *Einheit* (VA), 307–28.

Philipps, Karl. *Kirche in der Gesellschaft nach dem 1. Petrusbrief.* Gütersloh: Mohn, 1971.

Schnackenburg. *Botschaft* (B). Pp. 296–301.

Souček, I. B. "Das Gegenüber von Gemeinde und Welt nach dem 1. Petrusbrief." *CV* 3 (1960): 5–13.

Unnik, William Cornelis van. "The Teaching of Good Works in 1 Peter." *NTS* 1 (1954–55): 92–110.

Wendland. *Ethik* (B). Pp. 101–4.

Wolff, Christian. "Christ und Welt im 1. Petrusbrief." *ThLZ* 100 (1975): 333–42.

A. THE NEW LIFE IN COLOSSIANS
AND EPHESIANS

Both Colossians and Ephesians were written by disciples of Paul who considered themselves bound by the theological heritage of the apostle and tried to actualize this heritage in a new situation. Colossians is directed against a syncretizing heresy with significant judaizing and gnostic elements. The ethics of this heresy is characterized by asceticism and hostility toward the world (cf. Colossians 2). Ephesians seeks to mediate an ecclesiastical and theological crisis and deals primarily with the doctrine of the church. Both letters are not mere variations and extensions of Pauline teachings in every detail, but by no means are they a sellout of the Pauline heritage. Both in theology and in ethics, the two letters are fully on a level with the heights of genuinely Pauline thought.

1. In the fundamental basis and motivation of ethics we find no substantial departure from Paul, at least with respect to the structural relationship between indicative and imperative. Here, too, the imperative of moral admonition is based on the indicative of the message of salvation; the two are inseparable. This is clear already from the structure of the letters, which closely resembles that of Paul's (cf. the explicit reference to the indicative message of salvation at the beginning of the parenesis in Col. 3:1 and Eph. 4:1). The similarity extends to individual details. It is certainly wrong to speak of a contrived and artificial association of indicative and imperative.[1] Colossians 3:3, 5 is an illuminating example. Verse 3 reads: "You have died." Verse 5 draws the appropriate conclusion: "Put to death therefore what is earthly in you." If the old nature has died, its members must also be put to death, just as the "life hid with Christ in God" (Col. 3:3) implies an obligation to "put on the new nature" (Col. 3:10). In like manner the introductory verse (3:1) clearly unites indicative and imperative: "If then you have been raised with Christ, seek the things that are above."[2] Paradoxically it is on earth that concentration on what is "above" provides the only appropriate way to live the new life, because it focuses on Christ (cf. v. 1b). At the same time, we find a clear christological statement of the indicative, as in 2:6 "As therefore you received Christ Jesus the Lord, so live in him, rooted and built up in him . . ."; the reference to the tradition of the church's teaching, however, must be noted (cf. v. 7).

The same dialectic appears in Ephesians. If Christians are light only "in the Lord," it is only in the Lord that they live like "children of the light" and bring forth "fruit of light" (Eph. 5:8–9). The light that shines upon Christians from Christ causes the totality of Christian life to be lived and realized in

1. Contra Sanders, *Ethics* (B), 69.
2. Cf. Erich Grässer, "Kol. 3,1–4 als Beispiel einer Interpretation secundum homines recipientes," in *Text und Situation* (Gütersloh: Mohn, 1973), 123–51, esp. 131ff.

Christians (vv. 8b, 14a) as the reflex and medium of the true light. On the other hand, "awakening from sleep and rising from the dead" can be the basis for Christ's act (5:14). Normally, however, it is the saving act of Christ that provides the basis for the corresponding acts of Christians. For example, those who are already "rooted and grounded in love" (3:17) are called upon to love (4:2; 5:2). In other examples, the motivating relationship implies also a relationship of conformity: "Forgive one another, as God in Christ forgave you" (4:32); "Walk in love, as Christ loved us" (Eph. 5:2; cf. 5:25).

2. When we examine the substance of the indicative in detail, however, we find major departures from Paul, which are connected with the theology of the two letters. For example, the motif of eschatological expectation recedes into the background (despite the traditional motifs of judgment and reward in parenesis: Col. 3:6, 24–25; Eph. 5:6; 6:8–9, 13), as does that of God's righteousness (righteousness is now a purely ethical term; cf. Col. 4:1; Eph. 4:24; 5:9; 6:1, 14). Especially noteworthy is the increased emphasis on the exaltation and lordship of Christ, in whose triumph the Christian community shares (cf. Col. 2:11–12; 3:1; Eph. 1:21–25). The parenesis of both letters nevertheless cautions against associating them as a whole too closely with their hymnic tradition and "realized eschatology."

The emphasis on things heavenly rather than earthly (Col. 3:1–2) is not triumphalism but rather emphasis on the lordship of Jesus Christ, who "sits at the right hand of God" (v. lc) and is confessed as Lord by his community here on earth. The parenesis of Colossians and Ephesians is clearly intended to provide a corrective to the one-sided enthusiasm expressed by the hymns, according to which the powers have already lost their power. Colossians follows both its statements of Christ's lordship over the powers with parenesis (1:21ff.; 2:16ff.). The interpolation of "the blood of the cross" (1:20) and "the church" (1:18) in the traditional hymn[3] defines Jesus' lordship as that of the crucified Christ, concretely expressed in his lordship over the community; both notions are intended to prevent any flight from reality (cf. also 1:12– 14).[4] Above all, the parenesis insists on interpreting the lordship of Jesus Christ concretely and without any flights of fancy.

In Ephesians, too, the "new creation" of the human race through Christ is immediately interpreted as "creation for good works" (2:10). Light is no longer merely a predicate of heaven or of the redeemer, but of Christians upon the earth (Eph. 5:8). This light, however, must shine forth in their conduct (v. 8b). There is no longer a sharp boundary between heaven and earth, but when Eph. 2:6 says that Christians have been raised up to heaven, this is not to be taken in the sense of otherworldly ecstasy: the Christian life is still a

3. See the commentaries, and also Hans Jakob Gabathuler, *Jesus Christus—Haupt der Kirche—Haupt der Welt*, AThANT 45 (Zurich: Zwingli, 1965); Klaus Wengst, "Christologische Formeln und Lieder des Urchristentums," *StNT* 7 (1973): 170–80.

4. On Col. 1:12–14, see Eduard Schweizer, *Der Brief an die Kolosser*, EKKNT 12.

battleground (Eph. 6:12). Ephesians describes the resurrected life of the baptized in almost perfectionistic terms transcending the eschatological proviso. Even here, though, as Weiss rightly emphasizes,[5] there can be no doubt that christology is uppermost: this life is not inherent in Christians themselves, but is "in Christ."

Even in detail there are many similarities to Paul besides the use of the indicative to motivate the imperative. We may cite, for example, the fructifying power of the Word (Col. 1:6), Jesus Christ's lordship in the concrete historical existence of Christians (Col. 3:17ff.; Eph. 4:1ff.), the notion of charisma (Eph. 4:7), the motif of the "fruit" of the Spirit or of light (Eph. 5:9), the recollection of baptism (Col. 2:12; 3:1; Eph. 5:14, 26), and the putting off of the old nature in baptism and the putting on of the new nature (Col. 3:9–10; Eph. 4:22ff.).

Not even Eph. 2:10 would make Paul turn over in his grave:[6] despite the un-Pauline plural "works," the verse says not only that we were created in Christ Jesus for good works but that these works were "prepared beforehand" by God for us to walk in, almost as in a physical space. The extent of the parenesis shows clearly, however, that Ephesians places greater emphasis on the imperative. Fischer[7] suggests that because the author could not secure the unity of the church by institutional means, he aimed to inculcate a common Christian life style that would distinguish the Christian community from the surrounding world. This theory, he claims, best explains the disproportionate space Ephesians assigns to parenesis. Other explanations, however, are possible.

3. When we compare what these letters say about the nature and structure of the new life with what Paul says, again we notice both similarities and differences. The relationship between totality and specificity in obedience is similar to that found in Paul: both obviously go together. "Putting off the old nature" includes "its practices" (Col. 3:9), implying categorical rejection of its specific actions. Putting off particular vices is an expression and symptom of "putting off the old nature": practice of the virtues listed in the catalogue of virtues is an expression and consequence of the general injunction in Col. 3:1 to seek what is above. The single root brings forth a single "fruit," but it is described in concrete terms (Eph. 5:9).

In view of the increased importance attached to the apostle, as well as to the apostolic teaching and tradition, it is surprising that, like Paul, Colossians and Ephesians often enjoin the reader explicitly to test the divine will. Colossians 1:9–10 prays that the recipients of the letter may be filled with the knowledge of God's will "in all spiritual wisdom and understanding," that they may lead lives worthy of the Lord and bear fruit in every good work.

5. "Taufe," 56, 59.
6. Pace Sanders, *Ethics* (B), 78.
7. *Tendenz*, 146.

Here once again the argument moves in a single direction: from knowledge, through reason renewed by the Spirit (cf. also Eph. 4:23), to action. This does not mean that knowledge informed by the Spirit and according to Christ (cf. Col. 2:8) guarantees the doing of God's will, as some assume. That would be Socratic. But knowledge and understanding of the divine will are important to the author (cf. also Col. 4:12, which states that Christians should be fully assured in all that is the will of God). Ephesians speaks in similar terms. In 5:10, we read: "Try to learn what is pleasing to the Lord," and in 5:17: "Do not be foolish, but understand what the will of the Lord is." Such admonitions are all the more urgent in light of the danger that those addressed are "children tossed to and fro and carried about with every wind of doctrine" (Eph. 4:1; cf. also Col. 2:8, which warns against the Colossian heresy), or that they might revert to their traditional standard of conduct (Eph. 5:11). Scholars have often pointed out a kind of dualism in Ephesians that somewhat resembles that of the Dead Sea Scrolls; it is clearly intended to alert those addressed to the need for keeping separate from the world and its way of life.[8] But Eph. 5:3ff. also shows that, in contrast to the Qumran community, the conduct of the "children of light" does not consist in obedience to the Torah or in monastic seclusion, but aims at the conversion of darkness itself to light (5:13). Subjection to the lordship of Christ keeps Christians in the critical mean, neither cut off from nor caught up in the world.

4. If we look for the criteria on which the parenesis is grounded, we find that words of the Lord are never cited. The situation is similar with respect to Old Testament commandments, at least in Colossians. Ephesians, however, occasionally cites the Old Testament explicitly in ethical contexts. Two instances occur in the *Haustafel* (5:21–33).

The admonition to those who are married cites Gen. 2:24: "For this reason a man shall leave his father and mother and be joined to his wife, and the two shall become one" (5:31–32). This Old Testament quotation originally established the intimate union of man and wife in marriage. In it the author also sees a mysterious allusion to the intimate union between Christ and the Christian community, and therefore adds: "This is a great mystery, and I take it to mean Christ and the church." The great mystery, in other words, is not the institution of marriage, but the mysterious allegorical interpretation of the Old Testament passage or the relationship between Christ and the church.[9]

The second Old Testament quotation in the *Haustafel* appears in Eph. 6:1–3, which admonishes children to obey their parents and then reinforces the injunction by citing the Fifth Commandment from Exod. 20:12a (LXX): "Honor your father and mother." In line with Jewish custom, this commandment is referred to as the first commandment with a promise, expressed

8. Culpepper, "Dualism," 530, 532.
9. Cf. Günther Bornkamm, "mystērion," *TDNT* 4:822–23.

concretely in a modified version of Exod. 20:12b: "... that it may be well with you and that you may live long on the earth." The omission of the Old Testament reference to the Holy Land shows the problems involved in such borrowing. We may note also that originally the promise was addressed to the people as a whole.

Besides these two Old Testament passages, which underline the parenesis and are designated explicitly as scriptural quotations, there is also Eph. 6:14ff., which alludes to various Old Testament passages in describing the battle waged by Christians and their panoply. Ephesians 4:25–26 also cites Old Testament passages (Zech. 8:16 and Ps. 4:5), but without noting them explicitly as such. This is not due simply to the Jewish origin of this parenesis. The Jewish tradition of the Old Testament is rather already an integral part of the Christian tradition.

There is accordingly not much explicit citation of the Old Testament, even though the Pauline problem of the law—whether it can be a way to salvation—is no longer an issue. Surprisingly the Old Testament notion of creation is also almost ignored. This is actually what the ascetic dualism of the Colossian heretics might have led us to expect. Of course the author still believes in creation. Indeed, Col. 1:15ff. explicitly extols Jesus Christ as mediator of creation, denying the independent significance of all the cosmic powers, which are themselves part of creation: "Christ is the first-born of all creation; for in him all things were created, in heaven and on earth." The ethical significance of this doctrine is illustrated by Col. 3:10, where the new creature, remade after the model of Christ, who is the "image of God" (1:15), is recalled to the original order of creation. This renewal in the image of the Creator aims at knowledge of God's will and an ethical life (cf. also Eph. 4:22–23). But this exhausts the list of passages dealing with the theology of creation—here in fact the christology of creation. Of course rejection of the heretical injunctions "Do not handle, Do not taste, Do not touch" (Col. 2:21) is inconceivable apart from the doctrine of creation, but criticism of such taboos is based explicitly on the fact that the sway of the cosmic powers has been broken (Col. 2:15ff.). They have been disarmed by the one who is mediator of creation, namely Christ, who is the "head of all principalities and powers." The emphasis, however, is not on the doctrine of creation but on triumph over the principalities and powers. This is the real reason for rejecting the demands of the heretics.

5. The *Haustafeln* do not speak of God the Creator but only of the Lord Jesus Christ. This is quite astonishing and of far-reaching significance. Of course the *Haustafel* presupposes that the world is God's creation rather than a work of the devil, as in Gnosticism. Remarkably, however, it is not the Creator but the eschatological Lord who appears behind earthly authorities and social structures. It is he, not mortals, to whom obedience is actually

given (Col. 3:23). All that matters is "to serve the Lord Christ" (3:24), not to sanction the present state of the world as the order of creation.

The absence of any argument based on natural law or on reason is especially striking in comparison with the Stoics. Awareness of an "unwritten law" may well have played a part in developing lists of duties and obligations in the world of the New Testament. Paul's disciples may have known the reality of a universal divine law. It is nevertheless astonishing that the *Haustafel* itself is never described as being part of this law or as demanding obedience on these grounds.

In Eph. 5:31, marriage is established as being the Creator's will, but the urging of agape within marriage clearly reveals a christological orientation. Rengstorf is therefore less than persuasive in claiming that the *Haustafeln* are intended primarily "to guarantee the continuation of the *oikos* (house) and make it possible for members of the household to fulfill their obligations . . . in consonance with the will of God the Creator."[10] As in Romans 13, it is not the institution that is given christological justification, but the conduct of the Christian community within the institution.

Christology therefore plays an important role not only by laying a foundation but also by establishing guidelines, above all in Ephesians but also in Colossians. Colossians 3:13 is typical: "As the Lord has forgiven you, so you also must forgive." The attitude and conduct of Christians evolve from the love shown by Christ and must conform to this love. Colossians 1:10 already calls on Christians "to lead a life worthy of the Lord." This notion takes on special significance in the *Haustafeln*, where conduct within the social structures is to pattern itself after Christ. Specific social structures are not exalted and legitimized as reflections of God's eternal order; the existing order is instead reoriented. Instead of structures that reflect the cosmos or the order of creation, representing God or adumbrating an eternal law, we find conformity to Christ, which is to inform all human relations.[11] Marriage is not an ontological mystery representing the relationship between Christ and the church. Instead, rules governing the conduct of marriage partners are derived from this relationship. Even when Eph. 5:31–32 reverses the analogy and looks upon marriage as being able to represent the relationship between Christ and the church, v. 33 reestablishes the fundamental perspective. Marriage between Christians is to be lived as a reflection of and in conformity to that primary relationship between Christ and the church.

6. Both letters describe love as the decisive criterion and summary of all that the new person has to do. Therefore Col. 3:14 says that it is "above all these," surpassing and crowning them all and of supreme importance. This

10. *Mann* (B2), 29.
11. Schrage, "Ethik," 16ff.

does not mean that love is "added" to all the rest, but that it stands above them.

The verse continues somewhat obscurely, saying that love is "the bond of perfection." Scholars disagree as to whether the phrase refers to love as the bond that joins the individual virtues together in perfect harmony or whether it aims at the unity of the Christian community, which is perfected through love. Lohse[12] and Sanders,[13] among others, take the latter position, interpreting the genitive as final rather than qualitative: love leads to the perfect harmony that binds together the individual members of Christ's body. This interpretation is supported by 2:2, where love is likewise the unifying bond that holds the community together.

Love thus establishes and maintains the unity of the Christian community. That love is a mark of the church is also confirmed by Eph. 3:17 and 4:15–16, and especially by 5:2. A life that is "worthy of the calling" is revealed by "forbearance in love," displaying lowliness and patience (Eph. 4:1–2). In discussing the *Haustafeln*, we shall also go into greater detail concerning love in relationship to the structures of the secular world. Notwithstanding the supreme importance of love, the substance of the parenesis is highly traditional in its particulars.[14]

7. One specific feature, which might be called the ecclesiastical basis of ethics, is especially pronounced in Ephesians. But here, too, Colossians paves the way: the "body" in 1:18, which in the original hymn had cosmological significance, now refers to the Christian community, although the author does not simply translate the cosmic sovereignty of Christ into sovereignty over the community (cf. 2:9–10, 15) or the individual Christian (cf. 3:11). This is also the case in Eph. 1:20ff., with the addition of the statement that Christ is made head over all things "for the church." The fact that the church is the great theme of this epistle (in contrast to the Pauline Epistles) has ethical implication.

Not by accident does the author begin his parenesis in chapter 4 with an extended exhortation to unity within the church (a further instance of an imperative deriving from an indicative; cf. 2:14ff.). The church, comprising "God's holy chosen ones" (Col. 3:12), is the real ethical subject. In addition, the church is also the focus of ethical conduct (cf. already Col. 3:13, 15–16); it is itself the theme of the parenesis (cf. Eph. 5:22ff.). The variety of spiritual gifts (4:7ff.), which prevents the unity of the church from turning into sterile uniformity, has an ecclesiological end, even though v. 12 states that the gifts are bestowed "to equip the saints for the work of service," an expression that

12. On Col. 3:14, see Edward Lohse, *Colossians and Philemon*, Hermeneia (Philadelphia: Fortress Press, 1971).
13. *Ethics* (B), 68.
14. See, for example, Joachim Gnilka, "Paränetische Traditionen in Epheserbrief," in *Mélanges bibliques en hommage au R. P. Béda Rigaux*, ed. A. Descamps and A. de Hallek (Gembloux: Duculot, 1970), 397–410; Ernst Käsemann, "Epheserbrief," *RGG*[3] 2:518.

may look beyond the limits of the church. Since Christ's sovereignty and hegemony over the cosmos (cf. also Col. 2:19) are established indirectly and historically through the universal mission of the church (cf. Eph. 4:10 in context and Eph. 4:13ff.),[15] everything depends on the growth of the church, both intensive and extensive. The specific injunctions also deal primarily with the life of the community, "not the formation of the individual person."[16]

Solidarity between Jewish and gentile Christians is especially important to the author. He uses it, for example, to historicize the traditional cosmic language of the hymn to peace in Eph. 2:14ff. The pacification and reconciliation of the universe are documented on earth in the bringing together of Jews and Gentiles in the one church. Reconciliation of the divine realm with the earthly realm also means reconciliation in the human realm. Salvation does not simply establish privately and inwardly the right relationship between the individual and God; it brings peace to a broken world.

The two go together, even though they belong historically to different stages. To a world that felt terribly threatened by supernatural powers and cut off from the heavenly realm by the cosmic barrier of the firmament, the hymn to Christ incorporated by the author may well have been a liberating answer: it extols Christ's destruction of the cosmic barrier between heaven and earth and the incorporation of the cosmic powers into the universal body of Christ. Ephesians itself confronts a different danger: enthusiastic fanaticism, without any historical anchor, believes that it has transcended all historical restrictions. This belief has ethical implications. Those who do not take history seriously are set free to drift aimlessly in their arrogant fanaticism, losing sight of both God's salvific purpose and the solidarity of the Christian community.[17] Weiss[18] also points out that the "enthusiasm" of the hymn is immediately "brought down to earth" by vv. 8–10.[19]

8. That heavenly salvation goes hand in hand with earthly living is confirmed by the specifics of the parenesis. In particular, the heavily christianized *Haustafel* of Ephesians uses the Christ event to orient earthly life in the framework of secular institutions. The *Haustafel* (Col. 3:18ff.; Eph. 5:23ff.) is a feature common to both letters that distinguishes them from the letters of Paul. It is a parenetic passage with formal analogies. Its content,

15. See Ernst Käsemann, "Christus, das All und die Kirche," *ThLZ* 81 (1956): 585–90, esp. 587–88; Eduard Schweizer, "Die Kirche als Leib Christi in den paulinischen Antilegomena," in *Neotestamentica* (Zurich: Zwingli, 1963), 293–316, esp. 314–15.

16. Hans Conzelmann, *Die Briefe an die Galater, Epheser, Philipper, Kolosser, Thessalonicher und Philemon*, 14th ed., NTD 8, 75.

17. Ernst Käsemann, "Sonntage nach Trinitatis (Eph. 2:17–22)," *Göttinger Predigtmeditationen* 12 (Göttingen: Vandenhoeck & Ruprecht, 1958), 169.

18. "Taufe," 60.

19. On Eph. 2:8–10, see Joachim Gnilka, *Der Kolosserbrief*, HThK 10/1; Fischer, *Tendenz*, 131ff.; for a different view, see, e.g., Helmut Merklein, *Christus und die Kirche*, SBS 66 (Stuttgart: KBW, 1973); Peter Stuhlmacher, "'Er ist unser Friede' (Eph. 2,14)," in *Neues Testament und Kirche* (Festschrift Rudolf Schnackenburg), ed. J. Gnilka (Freiburg: Herder, 1974), 337–58.

too, is not simply formulated ad hoc with reference to a specific situation. Many scholars think the *Haustafel* is directed against a fanatical overemphasis on the nearness of the eschaton, which thinks it can ignore the institutional structures of this world. Others find polemic against gnostic fanatics with ascetic or emancipatory programs. The *Haustafel* of 1 Peter, however, cautions against any one-sided reference to such dangers.

In any case, the *Haustafel* focuses Christians' attention soberly and realistically on the world they live in amid the complex relationships and institutions of daily life. Notwithstanding any implicit antifanatic position, the *Haustafel* cannot be thought of solely as a defensive reaction. It also goes over to the offensive. It is not by chance that the first *Haustafel* appears in Colossians, whose author attacks the ascetic demands and taboos of the Colossian heretics by demythologizing the cosmos and proclaiming the victory of *kyrios* Jesus over the principalities and powers. This lordship of Jesus Christ is meant to be realized within the Christian household.

The cosmos is not identical with the body of Christ, but Christians, who live within the sphere of Jesus Christ's saving lordship, belong even in this world to the *kyrios* to whom they owe allegiance. The two kingdoms "intersect."[20] "The kingdom of God invades the kingdom of the world"[21] so that "the social structures and relationships of the human world are altered, but without being destroyed."[22] In the realm of relationships between the sexes and social groups the Lord remains the supreme authority. It is he who motivates the way Christians live their lives, as many expressions in the *Haustafeln* suggest: "in the Lord" (Col. 3:18, 20; Eph. 6:1); "as to the Lord" (Col. 3:23; Eph. 5:22; 6:7); "serving the Lord Christ" (Col. 3:24); "as to Christ" (Eph. 6:5). These formulas are not simply tacked on like labels to indicate that the *Haustafeln* are Christian. Instead, the admonitions—including those whose content conforms to the non-Christian conceptuality of the ancient world—are set in the framework of the lordship of Jesus Christ.

It is not by accident that the *Haustafel* is preceded immediately by the words: "Whatever you do, in word or deed, do everything in the name of the Lord Jesus" (Col. 3:17; cf. the similar statement in v. 23 in the midst of the *Haustafel*). The purpose of the *Haustafel* is therefore to subject the life of Christians to the lordship of Christ within the institutions of the secular world. Even at home Christians do not live by an autonomous law deriving from secular institutions but by the will of the Lord. The title *kyrios* appears as often in the *Haustafel* of Colossians as all the rest of the letter: of fourteen occurrences, seven are in the *Haustafel*; several of the rest are in parenetic passages like 3:17 and 1:10.

This Lord (*Kyrios*), who appears with such striking frequency in the

20. Wendland, "Sozialethik" (B1), 76.
21. Wendland, "Welthorschaft" (B1), 94.
22. Ibid., 93.

Haustafel, does not require obedience in a religious ghetto set apart from the reality of the world, into which Christians can retreat, in pure subjectivity, or solely in the domain of the church, but also in the social realm.

9. What this means is that social structures and institutions become the opportunity for and locus of *agapē.* There is some tension between this ideal and the occasional uncritical acceptance of the patriarchal and authoritarian structure of the ancient extended family, in which, for example, the father is responsible for the education of the children (only fathers are addressed in Col. 3:21). The notion of "subjection" as typifying, for example, the conduct of wives toward their husbands reflects the conventions of the day. Nevertheless, the classical models are drawn on selectively, with many modifications and shifts of emphasis in specific instances.

In the matter of "subjection," for example, it is no longer assumed that the husband determines the "religion" of his wife, so that it is a wife's duty "to know and to worship only those gods in which her husband also believes."[23] This is shown by the fact of mixed marriages, not all of which necessarily involved non-Christian wives with Christian husbands. Furthermore, this "subjection" means "subordination," not "subjugation": Eph. 5:24 compares the "subjection" of the wife to the subjection of the church to Christ (cf. also 1 Cor. 15:28).

What is more important is that the admonition that the wife be subject to her husband must not be interpreted in isolation; it must be seen in correlation with the admonition to the husband. The admonitions must be interpreted as a body, not from the perspective of the isolated individual. In particular, the substance of the admonition addressed to husbands prevents the household and its organization from becoming the setting for oppression, domination, and alienation. The husband is not charged to rule over his wife but to love her (Col. 3:19; Eph. 5:25). Therefore the *Haustafel* of Ephesians can interpret the admonitions of the *Haustafel* meaningfully as requiring mutual subjection (Eph. 5:21).

The admonition calling on husbands to love their wives, in the sense demanded by the context of the whole of Ephesians, is something new and unique in the ancient world.[24] The occasional appearance of *agapē* outside the New Testament, usually in a relatively neutral or emotional sense, and its more frequent occurrence in the LXX (Samson's love for Delilah [Judg. 16:4]; Rehoboam's love for Maacah [2 Chron. 11:21]; cf. Gen. 24:67; 29:18; 34:2) are unimportant, especially since the term never appears in admonitions like those of the *Haustafeln.* Judaism did occasionally extend the commandment to love one's neighbor to the love of a man for his wife (Tob. 6:19; Jub.

23. Plutarch *Praecepta coniugalia* 19.
24. See, for example, Greeven, "Aussagen" (B2), 122; idem, "Ehe (im NT)," *RGG* 2:319; Konrad Gaiser, *Für und wider die Ehe* (Munich: Haimeran, 1974), 99.

36:34).[25] In any case, the *Haustafel* does not use *agapē* in the sense of erotic love but in the sense of the selfless love of self-surrender: "as Christ loved the church and gave himself up for her" (Eph. 5:25; cf. also Col. 3:12–14). When Eph. 5:23 calls the husband the "head" of his wife, it implies not simply superiority but also a mutual relationship favorable to the wife (cf. Eph. 4:15–16, 25).[26] Here love is clearly defined in terms of Christ's self-sacrifice; everything else is a commonplace or mere emotionalism.

The common notion of what a man's attitude should be toward his wife was also different in this period. Reduced to a formula, it would not be "love your wives," as in the *Haustafel*, but something like the famous words from the *Praecepta Delphica*, which, like similar passages, see the function of the husband as exercise of authority and dominion: "Rule your wife." Even Plutarch, in the passage where he extols the subjection of the wife, speaks of the husband as "ruling," albeit with nobility and moderation ("not like a despot, but as the soul rules the body, with sympathy and affection").[27] But Seneca, for example, says quite bluntly: "The one was born to obey, the other to rule."[28] Josephus, too, states that God gave the husband dominion over his wife.[29]

It would be wrong to assume that this attitude was universal, but these passages are not untypical. Against this background, the admonition that husbands love their wives loses all traces of conventionality and appears in its true light. Men are not exhorted to exercise their privileges or acknowledge their rights but to practice love and kindness, especially within their own households. This has far-reaching consequences for social ethics.

Goppelt, on the contrary, maintains that love is never made the guiding principle for conduct involving various classes. Christians, he claims, did indeed act "out of obedience to the exalted Lord and to do his will, but on the basis of rules inherent in this world and permeated with sin."[30] But a doctrine of the two kingdoms or a sharp distinction between the religious and social spheres fails to deal adequately with the text. The christological argument does not legalize the existing social structures and their accustomed codes of conduct, but "radicalizes the existing order, while both limiting and criticizing severely the current system of authority."[31]

In any case, it seems to be a fundamental theme of the *Haustafel* that love should enter through Christians into the secular structures of society. For the

---

25. Strack-Billerbeck, *Kommentar* 3:610.
26. See Friedrich, *Sexualität* (B2), 88–89, 91–92; Schrage and Gerstenberger, *Frau* (B2), 160–61.
27. *Praecepta coniugalia* 33.
28. *De constantia sapientis* 1.1.
29. *Against Apion* 2.201.
30. Leonhard Goppelt, *Christologie und Ethik* (Göttingen: Vandenhoeck & Ruprecht, 1968), 130.
31. Friedrich, *Sexualität* (B2), 89.

period in question, this means nothing more or less than that the household becomes the locus of *agapē* for Christians. Married life is not to be spiritualized by *agapē* but made subject to the law of love, even in domestic routine. The duty to love is not limited to a religious sector of marriage: the life of Christians is not divided into a secular sphere of the home and a religious sphere of the church.

10. Probably this love that shapes legal and sociological relationships obtains elsewhere as well and is not limited to the relationship between husband and wife. Where but in the love that is not irritable or resentful (1 Col. 13:5) would the admonition not only to avoid harshness toward one's wife (Col. 3:19) but also not to provoke one's children (Col. 3:21), lest they become discouraged, find its meaning and its possibility?

Rengstroff,[32] for example, has rightly stressed that the guiding principle in the admonition to fathers is not their position as head of the family—nothing is said of rights and privileges—but their special duties and obligations. Schrenk[33] thinks that Col. 3:21 and Eph. 6:4 are directed against paternal power (*patria potestas*) that takes the form of arbitrariness and brutality. This idea is undeniably present, at least implicitly. One need only contrast Col. 3:21 and Eph. 6:4 with what even Hellenistic Jews like Philo and Josephus say about this *potestas*: "A father is *empowered* to upbraid or beat his children, to impose harsh punishments on them and keep them locked up. But in case the children nevertheless remain obdurate, ... the Law has even authorized parents to go so far as to impose the death penalty."[34] Just as in Hellenism (Menander, Plutarch) and among the rabbis (e.g., bGittin 7a), occasional voices were raised within Hellenistic Judaism against harsh use of force on the part of fathers: according to Pseudo-Phocylides 207–9, a father should refrain from disciplining a spoiled son and leave his reproof to others. Nevertheless, the idea of strict discipline, already characteristic of wisdom literature (Prov. 13:24; Sirach 30:1, 11), continued to prevail.

In any case, the *Haustafel* does not stress the notion of a father's discipline or unlimited authority, but rather his duties. Even if not quite so clearly as in the relationship of husband to wife, these duties are ultimately determined by agape. This confirms the observation that the relationships and institutions of this world are to give Christians a place and opportunity for conduct based on love.

It is true that masters are not told to love their slaves but rather to treat them justly and fairly. The *Haustafel* is concerned above all that the owners of slaves, probably not very heavily represented in the Christian community, should see that their slaves receive justice, respecting and protecting their

---

32. *Mann* (B2), 35.
33. Gottlob Schrenk, "patēr," *TDNT* 5:1005.
34. Philo *De specialibus legibus* 2.232; cf. also 243ff.; similar sentiments are expressed by Josephus *Antiquitius* 4.260ff.

rights—in other words, they should do what was expected in fairness of non-Christian masters also. Such conduct was undoubtedly practiced in part, but it was also enjoined by various writers.[35] In any case, it is not simply a foregone conclusion that the *Haustafel* should depart from the view of Aristotle, who maintained that the owner of a slave could never do the slave an injustice, since the slave is his property and no one treats his own property unjustly.[36] Slaves, too, have their rights. This does not mean that Christian masters are dispensed from loving their slaves (cf. Philem. 5, 16); it is a reminder that love does not dispense Christians from the requirements of justice and fairness. Earthly masters are reminded that the Lord is their heavenly master. Here, too, social structures are not simply sanctioned or left to individual option. Nor is there any appeal to the Lord as their guarantor. Instead he furnishes the point of reference and the guideline in all matters; this means that all of life is a proving ground for our relationship to the Lord, with love as the standard.

11. This still leaves us with a problem: how are the admonitions to subject and subordinate classes—the admonition to slaves to obey their masters in everything is the most sweeping—to be reconciled with this christological ethics? Here the author's primary purpose is obviously to prevent confusing Christian freedom with social freedom, even while paying some attention to the otherwise generally disregarded responsibilities of women, children, and slaves, as well as putting earthly lords and masters in their proper place, concentrating on the true Lord and the eschatological perspective. It is nevertheless easy to agree with the many critics of the *Haustafeln* in their disapproval of the admonitions defending subjection. Here "christianization" has been least successful, and the basic conservative attitude even lags behind the possibilities of contemporary practice. If the exhortation to "put on love" above all (Col.3:14) applies and to walk in love "as Christ loved us" (Eph. 5:1)—and it is nowhere suggested that these exhortations are irrelevant to conduct within the institutions of the secular world or are limited by a kind of "inner law"—then the specific admonitions addressed to the underprivileged in the *Haustafel* must be judged by this standard and not excluded from the general context. In this case, however, these specific applications are especially problematical today. The problem does not lie in social stratification and distinctions, nor in the later tendency to legitimize ancient institutions as being eternal and unchangeable. The problem is the lack of counterpoise when those in a position of superiority abuse the assumed conditions through oppression.

12. Finally, we turn our attention briefly to 2 Thessalonians, which is likewise not Pauline but has a different author than Colossians or Ephesians. Here, too, the notion of the apostolic tradition and its authority plays an

---

35. E.g., Seneca *Epistolae* 47.10; Pseudo-Phocylides 224.
36. *Nicomachean Ethics* 5.10.8.

important role (2:15), especially in parenesis (3:6, 10, 12). Of particular ethical significance is 3:6ff., where the idle are rebuked and the apostolic example of self-support is inculcated as an obligatory norm requiring Christians to work. The community is obviously upset by intense apocalyptic expectations, as though the day of the Lord had already come (2:2). Whether this apocalyptic excitement is responsible for the "disorderly" life of aimless idleness or the problem is a general disinclination to work is not entirely clear.[37]

B. APOSTOLIC PRECEPTS IN
THE PASTORALS

The Pastoral Epistles are less documents of a Pauline school following in the spirit of the apostle than are Colossians and Ephesians. Here everything is much more prosaic, pedestrian, bourgeois, moralistic. There is more emphasis on traditional formulas and more interest in ecclesiastical and institutional matters. The focus is on attacking heresy, on ecclesiastical tradition, and on the organization and governance of the Christian community. The goal is a regular and reliable ecclesiastical hierarchy with clear assignment of responsibilities. The local Christian community no longer exists as an independent entity operating on its own initiative. Parenesis, too, aims primarily to prevent disturbance of the peace and to support a solid ecclesiastical praxis. For the most part parenesis stands unrelated to the indicative. Its content is more traditional, set down didactically in fixed rules of conduct and morality.

To say all this is not simply to reduce these epistles to second-class status. The hypertrophy of the principle of legitimacy in ecclesiastical office is clearly open to criticism, but the epistles of this period also deserve credit for having brought down to earth a theology that threatened to degenerate into ascetic speculation and fanaticism. The parenesis illustrates this clearly. The sudden assault of Gnosticism was clearly so successful that proven doctrine and effective rules were needed. Whether it was necessary to accentuate pragmatism and traditionalism to the extent illustrated by these epistles is another question. Furthermore anyone with a sense of historical change, recognizing the need to apply Paul's principles to new situations or even go beyond Paul instead of seeking to recover the purity of historical Paulinism, must be painfully aware that the charismatic and eschatological corrective is absent. Even if the gnostic pneumatics appealed far too often to the Spirit, it is difficult to accept the conclusion that only hierarchical organization and bourgeois morality could keep gnostic fanaticism in check, as though internal and external threats had to be neutralized primarily through the stabilizing influence of institution and convention. Nevertheless, the praiseworthy at-

37. For further discussion of 2 Thess. 3:6ff., see Wolfgang Trilling, *Der Zweite Brief an die Thessaloniker*, EKKNT 14.

tempt to maintain and develop the Pauline heritage must not be overlooked or scorned.

1. Here, too, we must inquire first into the fundamental principles of ethics. We note that the Pastorals, too, base imperative on indicative, but the paradoxical aspect of this relationship, still present in Colossians and Ephesians, has vanished. Titus 2:11ff., for example, contains an admonition like those found in the *Haustafeln*, based on the statement that the grace of God "has appeared for the salvation of all men, training us to renounce irreligion and worldly practices, and to live sober, upright, and godly lives in this world." Although the Pastorals base their ethics on soteriology and interpret this ethics as a response to God's grace, they associate this soteriology more with the incarnation that do Paul's earlier disciples and give it a different accent. This is not to deny the presence of authentic Pauline elements, but the differences are more significant, especially in pneumatology and eschatology.

There is only the barest hint, for example, of baptism or the work of the Spirit. Titus 3:5–6 states that God saved us in virtue of his own mercy by the washing of regeneration and renewal in the Holy Spirit, which he poured out upon us richly through Jesus Christ. The purpose and result is that those who are baptized will come to good works through justification and as heirs. It is also possible to cite 2 Tim. 1:7 in this context and even interpret it in a Pauline sense: "God did not give us a spirit of timidity but a spirit of power and love and self-control." This recalls Paul's description of the Spirit as the power of the new life. But these are the only passages in all thirteen chapters of the three epistles to suggest that the life of Christians is based on the work of the Spirit.[38]

The Spirit is no longer understood as an eschatological gift; now the Spirit is closely associated with ecclesiastical office. Therefore the Pastorals say nothing of a variety of spiritual gifts, but speak only of the charisma of grace in connection with ordination. The Spirit given in ordination has become more important to this church than the Spirit given to every Christian in baptism as the power of new life. It is not by accident that this Spirit makes it possible to guard the entrusted truth of pure doctrine (2 Tim. 1:14). Future hope is mentioned, but it has lost its critical and motivating function, and can neither hold in abeyance the enduring structures of this world nor force the Christian community to advance. The author certainly continued to maintain the nature of the Christian life as an act of witness (above all for church officers, but also more generally: 1 Tim. 5:14; 6:1; Tit. 2:5, 8, 10) and likewise the centrality of the saving gospel (cf. 2 Tim. 1:10) and faith; this life, however, is anything but charismatic, and faith itself has become a Christian virtue, "decked out with the attributes of good conduct."[39] Never-

38. See also Eduard Schweizer, "pneuma," *TDNT* 6:445.
39. Merk, "Glaube," 93.

theless, despite all the substantial modifications of Paul's approach, we must conclude that on the whole ethics is based on the presence of salvation. But it must remain an open question whether, despite the Pastorals' onesidedness and dullness, we are dealing with a legitimate extension of Pauline thought, because "grace is understood as a power that shapes everyday life."[40]

2. If we turn our attention to the criteria and substance of ethics, we note, alongside the doctrine of creation, extensive agreement with the ideals of bourgeois Hellenistic morality. The Pastorals do not mention the schema of conformity to Christ or any words of the Lord. They do not draw on the proverbial or sapiential tradition of the Old Testament or on its legal parenesis (according to 1 Tim. 1:9, the law is reserved for the lawless and disobedient). Instead we find the tradition of catechetical parenesis, which serves as a trustworthy and authoritative basis for Christian praxis (cf. 1 Tim. 4:9; Tit. 3:8).

Although the Pastorals do not mention Old Testament law, they do draw on the motif of creation, which must have been especially helpful and important for the author in his battle with dualistic asceticism. Therefore 1 Tim. 4:3–4 explicitly uses creation to refute the heretical prohibition of marriage and eating certain foods: the heretics forbid what God has created to be received with thanksgiving, "for everything created by God is good, and nothing is to be rejected if it is received with thanksgiving; for then it is consecrated by the word of God and prayer."

Although it is not entirely certain that this passage alludes to the divine Word of creation, the doctrine of creation is here a fundamental corrective and criterion for guidance in Christian living. Titus 1:15–16 is similar: "To the pure all things are pure, but to the corrupt and unbelieving nothing is pure; their minds and consciences are corrupted. They profess to know God, but they deny him by their deeds." It would be wrong to understand this passage simply as an expression of enlightenment or as "a statement to which enlightened persons of all countries subscribe as against cultic asceticism regarding food."[41] But it is easy for the doctrine of creation to enter into a limited alliance with enlightenment, as in the case of Jesus and Paul. That the idea of creation does not suffice by itself to explain Tit. 1:15 with its Pauline echoes is shown by Judaism, which makes a sharp distinction between clean and unclean despite its doctrine of creation. That the doctrine of creation can also be used to support models of patriarchal authority is shown by 1 Tim. 2:13. With reference to 1 Timothy 2 and 6, as well as Titus 2, Stuhlmacher is

40. Bultmann, *Theology* (B), 536; this view is defended by Norbert Brox, *Die Pastoralbriefe*, RNT 7, 175, and is attacked by Ulrich Luz, "Rechtfertigung bei den Paulusschülern," in *Rechtfertigung* (Festschrift Ernst Käsemann), ed. J. Friedrich, W. Pöhlmann, and P. Stuhlmacher (Tübingen: Mohr, 1976), 365–83, esp. 379 n. 2.

41. On Titus 1:15–16, see Martin Dibelius and Hans Conzelmann, *The Pastoral Epistles*, Hermeneia (Philadelphia: Fortress Press, 1972), 137–38.

justified in speaking of a "static theology of creation."[42] Furthermore, the words of Tit. 1:15, unlike Romans 14, for example, are not restricted by the motive of love and concern for the weak.

Quite generally, in the Pastorals love does not play the important role it did for Paul or even for his disciples in Colossians and Ephesians. Only 1 Tim. 1:5 sounds Pauline, calling love the "aim of our charge," in contrast to the myths, speculations, and empty chatter of the heretics—a clear reference to active love. In all the other passages that mention agape, however, it has lost its dominant role, even when it stands alongside such other important concepts as faith and purity (1 Tim. 4:12), power and self-control (2 Tim. 1:7), righteousness and peace (2 Tim. 2:22), or patience and steadfastness (2 Tim. 3:10). But a passage like Tit. 2:2 shows clearly that it has been downgraded by the author in favor of other values and priorities: he admonishes the older men to live serious and sensible lives, sound in faith, in love, and in steadfastness (cf. also 1 Tim. 6:11). Here love is nothing more than one virtue among many.

3. It is easy to see from all three epistles what has taken over the preeminence of love. The central concept and fundamental attitude is now *eusebeia*—reverence, piety, conduct that is pleasing to God.

Foerster has shown that in *eusebeia* neither the religious nor the ethical element predominates; both go together. In Greek the term is used for "any kind of deferential behavior," whether toward one's parents, the dead, one's homeland, or the law. It is "respect for the structures . . . that support all of life: family relations, political relationships, even relationships between sovereign states."[43] Since, however, the gods serve as guarantors of these structures, *eusebeia* can also mean simply "religious devotion." In short, *eusebeia* is characteristic of those who "respect the structures that make social life possible and protect the gods."[44]

It is in this light that Foerster interprets the passages in the Pastorals where the term serves as an antonym to the fanatical Gnosticism of the heretics, who reject the structures of the natural order. It does not mean religious conduct in general, but respect for those structures that is rooted in reverence toward God.[45] This interpretation is supported above all by 1 Tim. 4:7–8: "Train yourself in *eusebeia*, for while bodily training [i.e., asceticism] is of little value, *eusebeia* is of value in every way, as it holds promise for the present life and also for the life to come." Similar usage appears in 1 Tim. 5:3, which speaks of *eusebeia* toward members of one's own family.

In other passages, however, despite what Foerster says, the term has more religious overtones and seems to refer to devotion in the sense of proper and

42. "Verantwortung," 184.
43. "Eusebeia," 215.
44. Ibid.
45. Ibid., 217.

well-ordered conduct (cf. 1 Tim. 3:16; Tit. 1:1). Commenting on Tit. 2:12, Foerster himself recalls the Greek distinction between conduct toward oneself, toward one's neighbor, and toward God, which corresponds to the triple admonition to lead a sober, upright, and godly life (cf. also 1 Tim. 6:3, 5–6; 2 Tim. 3:5).[46] On the other hand, this devotion finds concrete expression in an honorable way of life, in which respect for the opinion of the surrounding world plays a major role (cf. 1 Tim. 3:7; Tit. 2:3ff.).

4. All these words such as *eusebeia* or *semnotēs* ("propriety," "decency") likewise play an important role in Hellenistic ethics. The nature of the Christian life thus agrees in large measure with the Hellenistic ideal. Of the four classic cardinal virtues only "courage" or "manliness" is not mentioned, but Mott has shown that there are also parallels to the group of three including *eusebeia*—also, as in Titus, in the context of deliverance from vices in favor of virtues,[47] to which grace provides access.[48]

Dibelius speaks of the "ideal of Christian citizenship" in the Pastorals. In the light of the other possible way of being reconciled for the time being to living in this world (namely Gnosticism), he claims that this bourgeois Christian way of life may be understood "as a genuine expression of an existence in the world based on faith," even though "the dialectic of the eschatological existence is no longer understood in its original keenness."[49] If the "ethics" of Gnosticism and that of the Pastorals really did constitute an either/or, the greater theological acceptability would be on the side of the Pastorals. It remains an open question, however, whether the gnostic world view is really the only alternative to the orderly life of "bourgeois Christianity."

Paul was clearly able to incorporate elements of the classic ethics of order. Colossians and Ephesians did the same in a changed situation, as did 1 Peter. Only the Pastorals, however, arrived at such a static bourgeois ideal. Such a statement as 1 Tim. 2:2, calling on Christians to lead a quiet and peaceable life, godly and respectful in every way, is unique in the New Testament. Here, too, of course, the *status confessionis* constitutes an inviolable boundary beyond which the bourgeois devotion to order cannot go. According to Dibelius and Conzelmann, the description of readiness for death in 2 Timothy also transcends "the realm of ideas that describe the normal, virtuous life of the good citizen."[50] Brox adds that, despite the evident influence of "a pragmatic, 'opportunistic' mentality," there is a crucial difference: "the vitality and motivation that grow out of the preaching of Christ."[51] The question nevertheless remains whether this is not something like an ultimate barrier, while in

46. See also Brox, *Pastoralbriefe*, 174ff.
47. E.g., Philo *De virtutibus* 180.
48. Cf. Philo *De sacrificiis* 63; 4 Macc. 10:10.
49. Dibelius and Conzelmann, *Pastoral Epistles*, 39–41.
50. Ibid., 40.
51. Brox, *Pastoralbriefe*, 125.

general the ideal of bourgeois morality dominates and the boundary between Christian and secular ethics becomes ill-defined. Wendland, for example, commenting on the family ethics of the Pastorals, notes that there is no trace of Jesus' call to discipleship that can break even family ties. "To put it rather crudely, God becomes the sustainer and preserver of the family, taking the place of the pagan household gods."[52] The point is clearly well taken.

5. It would be wrong simply to identify bourgeois virtues with secularism or worldliness. This is clear in the attitude of the Pastorals toward worldly goods and especially their emphasis on moderation, which contrasts on the one hand with asceticism and hostility to the world and on the other with "worldly passions" (Tit. 2:12) and the pagan past associated with "various passions and pleasures" (Tit. 3:3).

First moderation (*sophrosynē*): "If we have food and clothing, with these we shall be content" (1 Tim. 6:8). This recalls similar sayings about moderation attributed to the Cynics.[53] What is espoused is not renunciation of worldly goods but a kind of middle way and compromise between poverty and wealth. Those who are rich can only fall victim to senseless and hurtful desires that plunge them into ruin and destruction (1 Tim. 6:9), indeed, 1 Tim. 6:10 states that the love of money is the root of all evil—a common ancient proverb. On the one hand, then, we find warnings against the dangers of wealth and lust of possessions; on the other, we find the natural expectation that Christians have some means at their disposal (cf. such passages as 1 Tim. 5:16). The rich are admonished "not to be haughty, nor to set their hopes on uncertain riches but on God who richly furnishes us with everything to enjoy" (1 Tim. 6:17). Above all, the rich are to be generous and thus show themselves to be rich in good deeds (v. 18). Quite similar in tone and typical of the author's attitude is his advice about wine. It would be wrong to be overly devoted to the enjoyment of wine (1 Tim. 3:2; Tit. 1:7) or be slaves to drink (Tit. 2:3). With respect to total abstinence, however, we read: "No longer drink only water, but use a little wine for the sake of your stomach and your frequent ailments" (1 Tim. 5:23). In other words, neither no wine nor much wine, but some wine. This middle road between total abstinence and drunkenness well characterizes the attitude of the Pastorals to worldly goods and pleasures.

6. Quite striking is the relationship between ecclesiastical discipline and ethics. The obligations of bishops, deacons, and presbyters amount to an obligation to live by the norms of bourgeois morality: "A bishop, as God's steward, must be blameless; he must not be arrogant or quick-tempered or a drunkard or violent or greedy for gain, but hospitable, a lover of goodness, master of himself, upright, holy, and self-contained" (Tit. 1:7; cf. also 1 Tim. 3:2). The precepts for deacons are similar: "Deacons likewise must be

52. *Ethik* (B), 98.
53. Cf. Diogenes Laertius 6.105.

serious, not double-tongued, not addicted to much wine, nor greedy for gain. . . . Let deacons be married only once, and let them manage their children and their households well" (1 Tim. 3:8ff.). Finally, much the same virtues are required of elders (Tit. 1:6).

Comparison of the requirements shows immediately that the lists are almost identical; there is hardly anything related to a specific office. They really apply to all Christians rather than specific offices, although a few additional requirements appear in the canon of duties for bishops and deacons. "The Christian ministry thus becomes another ordinary profession."[54] Much more striking than the absence in these catalogues of specific requirements for a particular office is the observation that the requirements are not even specifically Christian. They refer to universal human or moral qualities that are also demanded by the bourgeois ethics of the Hellenistic world. It is hard to account for this remarkable limitation to the expectations of any run-of-the-mill ethics. There are Hellenistic parallels to such admonitions to officials in the form of a schematic catalogue of virtues;[55] this is another striking example of the author's dependence on the ideals of contemporary moral philosophy.

A deeper reason for this dependence may be reflected in the statement that only someone who manages his own household well can fulfill the duties of office properly (1 Tim. 3:4). The church is referred to explicitly as the "household of God" in 1 Tim. 3:15, and Tit. 1:7 calls the bishop "God's steward." Therefore 1 Tim. 3:5 asks: "If a man does not know how to manage his own household, how can he care for God's church?" Church and household are closely related. But even the application of managing a household to fulfilling an office is not unique; it appears elsewhere in Greek parenesis.[56] In any case, the author sees an intimate connection between the institutional church and bourgeois morality. He also considers it obvious that the heretics have lax morals, although this contradicts their asceticism. What is contrary to the "sound doctrine" of the church can therefore be listed in a catalogue of vices (1 Tim. 1:9–10).

Undeniably the author has moralized the Christian message. Membership in the church now takes the form of a properly regulated ecclesiastical life and bourgeois rectitude, and sin has become primarily a moral lapse. This marks a momentous shift. Wendland maintains that the church of the Pastorals has not yet succumbed to the danger of becoming a "moral institution," because it still holds fast to the Lord Jesus Christ, the grace of God, and the substance of sound doctrine.[57] However that may be, it is perilously close to the line, and, in my opinion, has already crossed it at several points.

54. Hans von Campenhausen, *Ecclesiastical Authority and Spiritual Power in the Church of the First Three Centuries* (Stanford: Stanford Univ. Press, 1969), 106ff., quotation from 113.

55. On 1 Tim. 3:1ff., see Dibelius and Conzelmann, *Pastoral Epistles*.

56. Ibid., on 1 Tim. 3:4–5.

57. *Ethik* (B), 100.

This is certainly also connected with what Weber has called the "routinization of charisma," which is associated in turn with rationalization and banality. It is more significant, however, that eschatology has vanished as a critical and inspiring force; the provisional nature of the present world is no longer taken seriously. At the same time, despite 2 Tim. 2:11, the crucifixion had lost its centrality to theology and ethics, making accommodation to normal life all the easier.

7. Finally, a few concrete examples that are symptomatic. First we shall examine the relationship between men and women.

The author of the Pastorals was probably responsible for 1 Cor. 14:34 with its requirement that women keep silent in church, especially since similar words appear in 1 Tim. 2:11–12: "Let a woman learn in silence with all submissiveness. I permit no woman to teach or to have authority over men; she is to keep silent. For Adam was formed first, then Eve; and Adam was not deceived, but the woman was deceived and became a transgressor. Yet woman will be saved through bearing children, if they continue in faith and love and holiness, with modesty."

Whether this refers to the position of women in the created order or their conduct in worship is debated. Bartsch, making a virtue of necessity, states that the impossibility of drawing a clear line between rules governing worship and universal rules shows that the author is not interested in such a distinction.[58] If the Christian community takes the rules governing worship as applying to all of life, this demonstrates its awareness that all of life is lived in the presence of God.[59]

Traditio-historically, however, the situation is exactly the reverse: rules that were originally universal are applied to worship, as in the case of the code of conduct for bishops, where the requirements for episcopal office are stated in terms of universal qualities. In other words, the author does not make a fundamental distinction between worship and the secular world—not because worship extends to the everyday world, but because the world has invaded the realm of worship and the rules of bourgeois society now govern worship. If v. 12, which forbids woman to teach, refers to speaking in the Christian assembly, where women must not interfere in the teaching office reserved to males, moralism has permeated worship, and ecclesiastical structure and hierarchy have won the day against charisma. The Spirit of God, who, according to Paul, moves and speaks through women, must be silent, because convention forbids women to speak in public—a demand that, like 1 Cor. 14:34–35, contradicts 1 Cor. 11:5.

Even more problematic is the argument on which this prohibition is based, which requires submission to whatever is taught by males. The principle that what is older is better and male was created before female may still claim Old

<hr/>

58. *Anfänge*, 60.
59. Ibid., 70.

Testament sanction (cf. 1 Cor. 11:8–9). Much more problematic is the statement that Eve alone was responsible for the fall (v. 14). This contradicts both the Pauline view stated in Rom. 5:12 and the Old Testament account, which clearly expresses the shared guilt of Adam and Eve. It echoes instead such statements as Ecclus. 25:24: "From a woman comes the origin of sin, and on her account we will die." There may even be an allusion to the Jewish tradition of Eve's fornication with the serpent. This would explain v. 15, a problematic statement that bearing children is part of the way of salvation. Atonement and deliverance must, as it were, take place in the same sphere as the sin committed—an extraordinarily dangerous and suspect claim. Even if v. 15 may possibly be directed against a heretical ascetic denigration of marriage and sexuality (perhaps even against the heretical view that bearing children renders salvation impossible) and represents an attempt to include natural processes in the life of faith, the salvific role accorded them (albeit somewhat modified by v. 15b) is highly problematic.[60]

All the same, we must keep the contrary position in mind if we are to understand the author's overreaction. It is not entirely certain that Paul's opponents at Corinth maintained that it is good not to touch a woman. In my opinion, 1 Cor. 7:1 is a quotation from the letter sent by the community.[61] In the Pastorals, however, we clearly encounter people who forbid marriage (1 Tim. 4:3). This prohibition appears in the context of a dualistic hostility to the body, which leads as a rule to sexual asceticism and rejection of marriage, although occasionally the same fundamental denigration and demonization of the body could lead to libertinism (cf. 1 Cor. 6:12ff.). The later polemic of the church against heretics repeatedly speaks of Gnostics who claim that marriage and childbirth come from the devil,[62] that sexual intercourse is an obscenity,[63] and so forth. Gnostic texts themselves attack sexual procreation as a "filthy practice,"[64] claim that Jesus came "to destroy the works of the feminine,"[65] and so forth. Of course ascetic features are also found apart from Gnosticism, especially cultically imposed sexual abstinence, but this is limited almost entirely to priests and priestesses[66] and does not indicate fundamental rejection of marriage and sexual intercourse.

An even more revealing passage on the same topic is Tit. 2:2ff., which, unlike the *Haustafeln* of Colossians and Ephesians, says nothing about the love of a husband for his wife. Such love is not the counterpart to the wife's subordination to her husband: both are required of the wife. Also noteworthy is the use of *philia* rather than *agapē:* the love in question is the natural love of

60. Wendland, *Ethik* (B), 97; for a positive treatment, see Trummer, *Paulustradition*, 150.
61. See the citations in nn. 126, 127, 128, 137, and 138 of chap. IV.
62. Irenaeus *Haereses* 1.24.2.
63. Tertullian *Marcion* 1.29.
64. *Sophia Jesu Christi* 106.5.
65. *Gospel of the Egyptians*.
66. See Theodor Hopfner, "Abstinenz (sexuelle)," *RAC* 1:41ff.

a woman for her husband and children. It is not by accident that particular emphasis is put on the woman's familial role as mother (cf. also 1 Tim. 2:15; 5:14).

Just as a bishop or deacon is supposed to be "the husband of one wife" (1 Tim. 3:2, 12; Tit. 1:6), a woman is supposed to have been "the wife of one man" (1 Tim. 5:9). It has been suggested that the passages dealing with males refer to polygamy, but that is out of the question here. "Husband of one wife" has also been interpreted as referring to the prohibition of adultery[67] or to remarriage after divorce or the death of the first spouse. Marital fidelity, however, is usually described in different terms. Furthermore, young widows are counseled explicitly to remarry (1 Tim. 5:14). The most likely meaning, therefore, is that those who are divorced should not remarry.[68]

8. An admonition unique in early Christianity concerns widows (1 Tim. 5:3–16).[69] This extensive section deals with two matters: the support of widows and their office or status. With respect to the former, it is easy to see that the author is concerned to limit the number of widows to be supported by the community. The special duty of the community to care for widows and orphans is obvious from the Old Testament and Judaism (Isa. 1:17; Jer. 22:3; Zech. 7:10; Sirach 4:10). This duty is extended, however, by 1 Tim. 5: it is not only the spontaneous love on the part of individuals that is addressed, but the responsibility of the community to care for one of the classes that were socially, economically, and legally deprived. Not until Justinian did the law provide for widows to receive a quarter of their husbands' estate; otherwise the laws governing inheritance treated them very poorly.[70]

Now 1 Timothy 5 also shows that the community was not in a position to spend its resources openhandedly for charitable purposes, but had to calculate very carefully (v. 16b). The reader is therefore reminded repeatedly that material support of widows is primarily the concern of their own families. Those who do not provide for the widows of their own family deny the faith (v. 8). The contributions of the community are reserved solely for those who are "real widows," clearly those who do not live with a family and are left all alone (v. 5). Verse 6, however, speaks of another category in contrast to real widows: those who are self-indulgent and live for their own pleasure. In other words, there are moral as well as social criteria for those supported by the community (cf. also v. 10). The charitable work of the community is thus contingent upon both social and moral conditions.

The difference is clear if we ask whether the Good Samaritan could have interrogated the traveler who fell among thieves about the morality of his life

67. E.g., Trummer, *Paulustradition*, 151; idem, "Einehe nach den Pastoralen," *Bibl* 51 (1970): 471–84.
68. E.g., Albrecht Oepke, "gynē," *TDNT* 1:789.
69. See Johannes Müller-Bardoff, "Zur Exegese von 1. Tim. 5,3–16," in *Gott und die Götter* (Festschrift Erich Fascher) (Berlin: Evangelischer Verlagsanstalt, 1958), 113–33.
70. See Gustav Stählin, "chēra," *TNDT* 9:441ff.

before offering help. Even so, it is important to recognize the problem and not be too quick to pass judgment. It is hard to blame this church for refusing to spend its money on projects that make it appear self-indulgent. The difficulty is that moral criteria are now being used to judge people's behavior. On the positive side, we may note that the importance of the institutional element is recognized without being exaggerated and made absolute as in the case of the ecclesiastical hierarchy (v. 8).

It is also disputed whether the same criteria specified for the care of widows apply also to those officially enrolled as widows or whether v. 9 introduces a new theme unrelated to the question of support. The functions of official widows may have included pastoral or charitable visitation; in any case, they engaged in intensive prayer (v. 5; cf. Luke 2:26–38). It is probably true that the support of the community was contingent not only on social and moral expectations but also on sharing in the work of the community. This did not eliminate the possibility of helping others, but regular support was linked with some function within the community, however defined. In other words, those receiving assistance were expected to provide assistance.

Young widows, however, are forbidden explicitly to enroll as official widows (v. 11). We must remember that people in those days married at a very early age, and the number of young widows was probably not inconsiderable. The author clearly seeks to spare these young widows the conflict between the office of widow and remarriage. He prefers that they should remarry (v. 14) rather than the untrue to their vows after giving their lives entirely to Christ by refusing to remarry (vv. 11–12).

According to Müller-Bardoff, the author presupposes the ideal of a celibate "widow of God," which may also have been attractive for other than religious reasons. He is concerned "to prune certain excrescences and restrict the undesirable hypertrophy of an ascetic ideal."[71]

9. There are two admonitions addressed expressly to slaves: 1 Tim. 6:1–2 and Tit. 2:9–10. The Pastorals differ strikingly from the *Haustafeln* in Colossians and Ephesians in not including any corresponding admonition addressed to masters. Slaves' fulfillment of their temporal duties within the household adorns the Christian message (cf. also 1 Tim. 6:1).

Gülzow has pointed out the widespread view that foreign religions corrupted slaves. It may therefore be correct to assume that the Pastorals are intended to counter the charge that Christians were poor and worthless slaves and treated their masters with surliness and arrogance.[72]

10. In 1 Tim. 2:2 we find the injunction, obeyed to this day, to pray with intercession and thanksgiving for kings or emperors and all in authority. This duty is clearly linked with Jewish custom and may already reflect early

71. "Exegese," 133; but see Kähler, *Frau*, 163.
72. *Christentum* (B4), 75.

Christian practice.[73] As is well known, prayer was offered in the Jerusalem temple for the emperor and the empire, and sacrifice was also offered on their behalf. Besides Hananiah's injunction to pray "for the well-being of the government" (Aboth 3:2), there are passages in Philo and synagogue inscriptions showing that affirmations of loyalty to the authorities were known in the synagogues of Hellenistic Judaism outside Palestine.[74]

The call for intercession in the Pastorals does not suggest the danger of Erastianism; the injunction is independent of the situation. The representatives and organs of the state constitute, as it were, the framework within which the community can realize the ideal of a life pleasing in the eyes of God and of the world. Intercession continued in times of official hostility and persecution, but was not inconsistent with civil disobedience, as we know from the *Epistle of Polycarp*, which is roughly contemporary. In any case, the author considers it the function of the state to protect against chaos and make it possible for people to live together in an orderly society as well as to lead Christian lives according to God's will. But that is all. This last reservation, which the Pastorals share with the other New Testament witnesses, lays the foundation for intercession. "Intercession, however positive, is an absolute denial of worship. Anyone who stands in need of intercession—emperor, king, or governor—is human."[75]

C. CHRISTIAN LIFE ACCORDING TO
1 PETER

It may appear surprising to find 1 Peter included among the deutero-Pauline epistles. There are good reasons for this inclusion, however, even though the author appeals to Peter rather than to Paul. The anonymous author in large measure espouses Pauline and deutero-Pauline views and can have appeared only in the sphere of influence of Pauline preaching and theology; this is shown by his close relationship to the Pauline corpus. Certain similarities are due to common traditions (above all the christological statements and the parenetic passages); besides this, however, there is sufficient other material that can be called typically Pauline.

Apart from the traditions common to Paul and 1 Peter, the epistle contains numerous additional primitive Christian traditions. It has been possible to reconstruct early Christian hymns and confessional formulas and above all parenetic forms that bear the stamp of primitive Christianity as well as the

---

73. See Bartsch, *Anfänge*, 27ff.; idem, "Das Gebet für die Obrigkeit in 1. Tim. 2," in *Entmythologisierende Auslegung*, ThF 26 (Hamburg: Reich, 1962), 124–32. Bartsch (wrongly) sees here an "indifference to the current authorities" (125). See Aland, "Verhältnis" (B5), 207.

74. See Wolfgang Schrage, "synagōgē," *TDNT* 7:826–27.

75. Gerhard Kittel, "Das Urteil des Neuen Testaments über den Staat," *ZSTh* 14 (1937): 651–80, quotation from 665.

Old Testament and Judaism. Clearly the author was less concerned with originality than with transmitting and actualizing received traditions.

The epistle is addressed to a community besieged by suffering and under pressure from the surrounding world to conform. Christians are distrusted and vilified, and even prosecuted on the charge of being Christians. The author hopes to avoid unnecessary confrontations, but realizes that the alienation and discrimination resulting from Christian nonconformity, leading even to treatment of Christians as criminals, cannot always be avoided.

1. As in the case of Paul, the promise of present and future salvation provides the basis for parenesis, even when the imperative comes first, followed by a reference to the will or acts of God.[76] Characteristic is the causal "for" that introduces the motivation for ethical injunctions (cf. 1 Pet. 1:15–16; 3:17–18; 5:5). Examination of the content of the indicative that motivates the parenesis shows that the real and ultimate basis for ethical exhortation is christological and soteriological. At times, of course, even here this theme is sounded somewhat formulaicly, in order at least to suggest the new background against which ethics must be viewed. For example, 3:16 speaks simply of good behavior "in Christ," and in 2:13 the author uses the phrase "for the Lord's sake" to suggest a christological motivation. Much more typical, however, are extended motivations based on kerygmatic statements, confessions, and hymns that bear witness to the fundamental saving event of Jesus' crucifixion. According to 1 Pet. 1:17–19, for example, Christians are to lead responsible lives because they can know that they have been ransomed from their futile ways by the precious blood of Christ. In 3:17–18, we are told that it is better to suffer for doing right than to do wrong because Christ suffered for sins once for all, the righteous for the unrighteous. This is followed by a hymnic passage that draws on traditional formulas to describe the saving work of Christ, placing the fate of Jesus Christ before the eyes of the community as a source of encouragement in the hour of need. Similarly, the admonition to slaves in 1 Peter 2 cites christological tradition to support its *Haustafel* parenesis, applying this tradition to the situation of Christian slaves (2:21ff.). They are to realize that the vicarious atoning death of Jesus makes it possible for them to live in righteousness instead of straying in sin (2:24–25). In light of the suffering experienced by those to whom the epistle is addressed, it is not by chance that the suffering Christ appears repeatedly. Christians in their suffering and temptation are confronted with Christ in his suffering and temptation as a source of comfort and courage. It goes almost without saying that this crucified Jesus is also the risen (1:3) and living (3:18) Christ and the exalted Lord (3:22).

2. Unlike Colossians and Ephesians or the Pastorals, 1 Peter cites as one of

76. See Lohse, "Paränese," 325.

the primary driving forces of Christian life and ethics a "living" (1:3) eschatological hope based on the resurrection of Jesus. As hope (cf. 1:21), faith always looks forward to the "inexpressible" joy (4:13) that will accompany the return of Christ (cf. 1:8–9). In 4:7, we are told explicitly: "The end of all things is at hand; therefore keep sane and sober for your prayers. Above all hold unfailing your love for one another." Here we have a clear and unmistakable eschatological admonition to draw the proper conclusions from the imminent end of all things—a highly important point, because we are dealing with a document from the close of the first century in which eschatological hope nevertheless plays a dominant role. Here, too, ethics is not a substitute for but a consequence of eschatology (cf. 4:17, an eschatological statement motivating the admonition of v. 16). In 1:13, awareness of the eschatological hour issues in an admonition to be ready and sober: the transitory nature of this world makes true wisdom and understanding possible. Christians need not be enraptured by this passing age: the future revelation of Jesus Christ strips away their illusions and urges them to action. They place their hope entirely in the Lord and are thus "children of obedience" (1:14), free of any need for conformity to the world and ready to act with patient calm.

Especially important is the introduction to the great *Haustafel* in 1 Peter 2, which addresses Christians as "aliens" and "exiles" in this world (v. 11), the "eschatological diaspora community of the exodus."[77] All of Christian life and Christian conduct in the secular world falls within this category. Without this perspective, which reverses all values and establishes new criteria, the place of Christians in the midst of earthly institutions is beyond comprehension. Even as citizens of the state, even within family and society, and despite the responsibility with which they fulfill their political, social, and familiar responsibilities, these "aliens" and "exiles" have a homeland outside this world; despite their loving involvement, they look for their salvation and their future from another source (cf. also the eschatological motifs in 1:17; 3:7; 4:5, 17; 5:1, 4; 3:9–12).[78] But during their "time of exile" (1:17) they can rightly await the Lord who is to come and bear witness to him in their lives because the fulfillment of salvation is already guaranteed by Christ's ransom (1:18).[79]

3. In 1 Peter, therefore, baptism as well as eschatology is the basis of Christian life, endowing Christians with courage, strength, and comfort. Baptism, too, derives its power from the resurrection of Jesus (1:3; 3:21) and the Word (1:23). The new reality created by God in new birth is described in 1:22–23 as the motive for ready love. Baptism leads by nature to obedience.

77. Goppelt, "Prinzipien," 285.
78. See John Piper, "Hope as the Motivation of Love: 1 Peter 3:9–11," *NTS* 26 (1979–80): 212–31.
79. Delling, "Bezug," 101.

The imperative "love one another" is enclosed by two perfect participles that motivate it, both referring to baptism: "purified" and "born anew."

There is yet another basis of the Christian life, also strongly reminiscent of Paul: the Spirit and spiritual gifts, which are closely linked with baptism. The opening of the epistle speaks of "sanctification of the Spirit" (1:2). This is clearly a subjective genitive, as are the other genitives in the salutation. The agent of sanctification is therefore the Spirit. Christians do not live their lives in order to be sanctified but as people already sanctified, already claimed by God and the Spirit. That Christians need the power of the Spirit is clear also from 1:12 and 4:14, but above all from the charismatic basis of all Christian conduct stated in 4:10–11: "Whoever renders service, do so by the strength that God supplies" (v. 11). The community does not act and serve by virtue of its own strength but by the strength God supplies—not "has supplied" but continually supplies (present tense).

All this shows that ethics has the same foundation as in Paul: God's present and future act of salvation in Jesus Christ is the basis and impetus of Christian conduct. Here, too, ethics is not autonomous but linked indissolubly with God's action. Without new birth, there is no new obedience. Without hope, there is no basis for Christian life.

4. Unlike the Pastorals, 1 Peter draws to some extent on the Old Testament for the substance and criteria of its ethics. This is because its christology and ecclesiology are grounded in *Heilsgeschichte*. The historical perspective of the epistle leads it to incorporate at least in part the ethics of the Old Testament. In 1 Pet. 1:15–16 we find what is almost a programmatic statement: "As he who called you is holy, be holy yourselves in all your conduct, since it is written: 'You shall be holy, for I am holy.'"

Of course we must not draw the wrong conclusions from the citation of this Old Testament quotation, arguing, for example, that the whole of Old Testament Scripture can claim scriptural authority for Christians. The quotation was not chosen at random: it is a central theologoumenon of the Old Testament. It is not the whole Old Testament that is normative. Instead, its fundamental thrust is incorporated: as a "holy nation" (2:9), the community must accept God's absolute and exclusive claim upon it in everything it does. Wholesale observance of all the Old Testament commandments would therefore hardly be in line with the author's intentions, even though he himself does not specify any criterion by which to judge the Old Testament, appearing rather to accept the formal principle of "it is written." This appearance, however, is deceiving. Not only does the author pick and choose, he also reinterprets. In 1 Peter, "holy" has clearly taken on a meaning different from its meaning in the Pentateuch. The notion of levitical purity, for example, is no longer involved.

Two other passages, however, confirm the ethical authority of the Old Testament. The exhortation to women cites an Old Testament exemplar as its authority, calling Christian women "children of Sarah" (1 Pet. 3:6). Here we see the internal reason why the Old Testament can be used as a source of ethical models: Christians are heirs of the promise (cf. 1:10–12). Paul calls Christians children of Abraham, a relationship he finds signified solely in faith. Here the author, describing Christians as children of Sarah, explicitly cites good works, basing his ethics on the Old Testament. Of course he adds a Christian interpretation. We also find a Christian interpretation in 3:10–12, the longest Old Testament quotation in the epistle. It comes from Psalm 34 and follows quite closely the wording of the LXX. The first thing we note is that this long quotation is not even cited as such. The proverbial wisdom tradition of the Old Testament has already become so fixed an element of early Christian parenesis that people are no longer aware of its origin.

We find the same phenomenon in 1 Pet. 5:5, which cites the familiar maxim that God opposes the proud but gives grace to the humble. This well-known saying from Prov. 3:34 is also cited by James 4:6, Ign. Eph. 5:3, and 1 Clem. 30:2. These quotations not only illustrate its popularity in the early church but also show that certain Old Testament sayings no longer needed to be identified as such. Of course they were often reinterpreted, as 3:10–12 in particular shows. The psalmist undoubtedly looked for salvation in the present world. The good days he looks forward to are good days during his life on earth. The author of 1 Peter, however, interprets the passage eschatologically: "life" is eternal life, and "good days" are the eternal blessedness of the eschaton. A bit of worldly wisdom from the Old Testament here takes on an eschatological aspect.

The goal and presuppositions have been radically changed, but the concrete application to daily life is the same. Christians also must eschew evil; they too must do right and seek peace. The author may also have in mind an analogy to the conduct of Jesus: just as no guile was found on his lips (2:22), so Christians are to keep their lips from speaking guile (3:10).

5. Other substantive parallels to Jesus' conduct are also emphasized in 1 Peter. The injunction in 3:9, "Do not return evil for evil or reviling for reviling," is a direct allusion to 2:23, which says that when Jesus was reviled he did not revile in return. This conformity of the Christian life to the life of Christ finds programmatic expression in 2:21: "Christ also suffered for you, leaving you an example, that you should follow in his steps." Christians are to follow the way and the example of their Lord.

The passages collected by Schrenk[80] make it clear that the notion of a model or example originally had a pedagogical background, as when children are given a memory aid or a model to follow. The corresponding verb is used when a teacher draws lines with a stylus for children who have not yet learned to write, so that they can follow these lines when they make their first

80. Gottlieb Schrenk, "hypogrammos," *TDNT* 1:772–73.

attempts. Of course the author uses this image figuratively and supplements it at once with a different image, that of footprints, picturing Christ as a leader whose followers walk in his footsteps.

Both images point to the exemplary significance of Jesus and flesh it out in some detail. The way the servants are to follow their master is the way of suffering. Here the passion of Jesus Christ is clearly set in the context of an exemplary ethics (cf. Heb. 12:2). The dominant notion, however, is not that of a model but that of a path. A path cannot be imitated but only followed, and there is always a sense of the distance between the one who has gone ahead and those who follow.[81] Simple imitation in every detail would be out of the question; the notion of atonement and vicarious suffering does not admit imitation and in fact destroys the idea of a model. It is nevertheless indisputable that the author would have Christians follow in the footsteps of their Lord.

6. Another important point in the ethics of 1 Peter is the emphasis on missionary apologetics. The fundamental principle is stated in 2:12: "Maintain good conduct among the Gentiles, so that in case they speak against you as wrongdoers, they may see your good deeds and glorify God on the day of visitation" (cf. 3:16; 4:14–15). The theme of these injunctions remains constant: the charges of non-Christians must not be based on Christian failings. Christians must not withdraw into isolation, but must silence the accusations of the pagans through their good works.

The juxtaposition of these two motifs—the "alien" nature of the church (2:11) and the influence of the Christian community on the world (2:12)—has with good reason led Schelkle to state that the history of the church shows "that the more the church has sensed its alienation from the world, the more it has been able to influence the world."[82] The world is not impressed by attempts at familiarity or strenuous efforts to appear more worldly than the world. It must be asked, however, whether this is the real point of 2:12. What leads to conversion is not the alienation of Christians but their good works. At least this is the opinion stated in 1 Peter, even though the two can go hand in hand.

The primary importance of good works is restated in 1 Pet. 3:1–2, an exhortation to wives: "Be submissive to your husbands, so that some, though they do not obey the word, may be won without a word by the behavior of their wives, when they see your reverent and chaste behavior." Although the author characterizes Christian life as obedience to the Word, wordless conduct may have a chance when the Word itself does not succeed. This assumes, of course, that Christian life "without a word" is nonetheless determined by the Word and that the Word has already been spoken to the husband, since he

81. Albrecht Stumpf, "ignos," *TDNT* 3:404.
82. On 1 Peter 2:11–12, see Karl Hermann Schelkle, *Die Petrusbriefe; der Judasbrief,* 5th ed., HThK 13/2.

has in fact rejected it. It is nevertheless astonishing that Christian conduct in a mixed marriage is thought capable of achieving what the rejected Word could not, the "winning" of non-Christian husbands. The author therefore expects missionary success from Christian life, lived in the power of the Word and representing its reality—not with a zeal for conversion, but in the knowledge that one's life is a form of proclamation, which can affirm or deny the authenticity of the gospel.

Of course the author knows from experience that the Christian way of life can evoke negative as well as positive reactions from non-Christians. In particular, the inescapable rejection by Christians of their own previous conduct probably often caused painful separations and conflicts with the surrounding world. Those with whom Christians had shared the transgressions listed in 4:3 (including drinking partners, but others as well) felt alienated because their Christian friends had bid a final farewell to their previous way of life.

This meant a break not only with various forms of depravity but also with such everyday customs as participation in religious exercises. Christians most likely kept their distance from public celebrations (which almost always involved cultic observances), certain forms of social intercourse such as cultural events and theatrical productions, non-Christian marriage practices, and the like. The "then/now" schema applies not just to the catalogue of vices, whose individual items (except for idolatry) may in fact be called "somewhat vague, random, and trivial";[83] Christians renounced many other shared experiences, especially in the realm of cult and ethos.[84]

But such rejection of one's own previous life style engenders unpopularity, resentment, and suspicion. Those who break the common mold are vulnerable to insinuation and slander. We can see from 4:14 that Christians are defamed not just on account of their generally alien way of life but also simply for being Christians. In any case, alienation and difference constitute one side of Christian life. We must keep this side in mind, along with respect for the opinions of others and the apologetic stance described in 3:15, when we speak of a life style embodying missionary responsibility.

7. When we come to the place of love, it is impossible to speak of special emphasis on the law of love; at least there is no particular stress on love of one's neighbor or enemy. The author is certainly not concerned that Christians attain spiritual perfection, cultivating their own spirituality and interior life, but that they engage actively in love for others. In this sense we find here the same opposition to all kinds of individualistic devotion and mysticism that promote cultivation of one's own soul and isolation from the world. In 1 Peter, however, the emphasis is not on *agape*—love of one's neighbor—but on *philadelphia*, "love of the brethren," those in the Christian community

83. Norbert Brox, *Der erste Petrusbrief,* EKKNT 21, 193.
84. Ibid., 194.

(1:22; 2:17; 3:8). The community is seen as the family of God, in which love rules and all live in mutual solidarity. The repeated injunction to practice *philadelphia* suggests that the author sees it as something more than one virtue among many. And no wonder—in the midst of suffering and persecution, hardly anything is more important than the solidarity of the community. This finds explicit expression in 5:9: the family of Christians throughout the world, knowing the same experience of suffering, is now called upon to resist.

The obligation of mutual love is therefore singled out in 4:8 as being important "above all." Here, too, with the change just described, love is described as the highest duty of Christians. The primacy of the law of love is maintained in the form of "love for the brethren." This is admittedly something of an abstract principle: love is never mentioned as regulative in actual parenesis. It is easy to show, however, that this love has consequences and seeks to be manifest in concrete form.

This is seen, for example, in the fact that love has the power to cover sins, as 4:8b says (on the basis of Prov. 10:12). The hospitality mentioned in 4:9 should also probably be considered an expression of love.[85] This hospitality is clearly owed primarily to traveling brothers and sisters, whose journeys serve the Christian community (cf. Acts 18:2–3, 26; 3 John 5–8; Philem. 22). We must remember that in this period there were as yet no inns or hotels and that traveling was often very burdensome. The situation of persecution may also have lent an element of urgency to this exhortation: open doors are obviously vital to the oppressed and persecuted. "Ungrudgingly" reminds us that hospitality can also be burdensome, costing both time and money and requiring selfless love.

The call for sympathy in 1 Pet. 3:8–9 is ultimately also an appeal for concrete expression of love. One Christian should experience the joys and sufferings of another, sharing with understanding and sympathy the other's fate. It is uncertain whether the tenderness and humility enjoined in the same passage also refer to conduct within the community or, as a transition to v. 9, look beyond its limits. In any case, v. 9 ("Do not return evil for evil or reviling for reviling, but on the contrary . . .") is so reminiscent of the love of enemies enjoined in the Sermon on the Mount that at least in this passage love transcends the realm of community solidarity. The epistle is not interested in maintaining sharp distinctions. What is at issue is Christian humanity toward the persecuted in a hostile environment. The conduct of Christians is not to be simply a reaction to standards imposed by this environment, repaying evil with evil. Contrary to all common sense and logic, evil is to be answered with good, cursing with blessing.

8. Finally, a few concrete words about various aspects of life treated in 1 Peter. First, there is the passage addressed to wives and husbands (3:1–7).

85. See Denys Gorce, "Gastfreundschaft," *RAC* 8:1104.

With the exception of vv. 1b–2, which speak of the missionary opportunity in mixed marriage, and v. 6, which speaks again of "not being terrified," a theme that appears repeatedly, there is nothing specifically Christian in 3:1–6. In particular, vv. 3–5 present a tradition that cautions against outward luxury and display.

Exaggerated finery and luxury on the part of women have been a target of moral criticism in every age (cf. Isa. 3:18ff.; 1 Tim. 2:9). There are numerous examples from non-Christian literature—Plutarch, Epictetus, and Philo. Although we may realize that this attitude is historically conditioned and "puritanical," we must not lose sight of its true intention: freedom from dependence on outward show and luxury. The statement that a women's true adorning is hidden within the heart nevertheless comes perilously close to the position of Hellenistic dualism. Of course outward appearance is not identical with the person, but it is equally true that people are not abstractions, dissociated from their outward appearance. To say that the real person lies within leads easily to a false introversion, which forgets that God claims the whole person and that obedience must be embodied.

In comparison to the exhortation to wives, the exhortation to husbands in 3:7 is quite terse.[86] Most explanations of this brevity are unconvincing. Most likely the author here pays tribute to the limitations of his time. On the other hand, in contrast to the duties of wives, there is little to suggest that the substance of the verse is traditional. It may well go back to the author himself, who sensed what was not intrinsically obvious—that the duties of husbands must also be stated.

In 3:7, unlike 3:1–6, the author probably is thinking only of Christian marriages, not mixed marriages, since wives are called "joint heirs of the grace of life." The question is whether this refers only to an "equality of husbands and wives with respect to the gift of salvation and their eternal heritage," with husbands still "being required to play the primary role socially and liturgically."[87] It is more likely that "the unquestioned rights of the husband's privileged social position" are here rejected.[88]

The equality of grace motivates an injunction affecting the relationship between husband and wife here and now, in the everyday conduct of their marriage. The fact that there is no longer any difference with respect to salvation has implications for the relationship between husband and wife in their married life. No one who knows that God values everyone can be a domestic tyrant, refusing to honor another's value. Husbands must therefore exhibit kindness, understanding, and respect in their daily lives. Husbands also owe their wives such loving understanding because the latter are the

---

86. See Bo Reicke, "Die Gnosis der Männer nach 1 Petr. 3,7," in *Neutestamentliche Studien für Rudolf Bultmann*, ed. W. Eltester, BZNW 21 (Berlin: Töpelmann, 1954), 298–304.

87. Ibid., 303.

88. Brox, *Petrusbrief*, on 1 Peter 3:1–7.

"weaker sex"—in other words, the injunction is based also on the wife's weaker constitution. Only when husbands treat their wives with understanding are their prayers not hindered (3:7c). This does not refer to interruption of prayers by domestic strife or marital quarrels, but to fundamental spiritual incapacity for prayer. Absence of love and consideration for others distorts and destroys one's relationship with God.

9. When addressing slaves in 1 Pet. 2:18ff., the author does not go beyond the standards of the day, except for the christological motivation for enduring suffering. He espouses neither social revolution nor abject servility. Here, too, the central concept is submission (v. 18), not only—as the author expressly adds—to kind and gentle masters but also to those who are overbearing, who treat their slaves harshly and unfairly. That such harsh treatment was not exceptional (see above, IV.D.3.4) is shown by the whole exhortation, which is really addressed only to slaves who suffer. There is no question that such unfair treatment of slaves is "unjust," but in the opinion of the author those who suffer injustice, that is, harsh treatment in the form of physical or verbal abuse and similar wrongs, receive God's special approval. The author is not suggesting apathy and *ataraxia,* but he does urge slaves not to provoke such suffering by improper behavior. But he does admit the realistic possibility that they will be mistreated even when they do good and therefore points to the example of Jesus' innocent suffering. The life of a slave can exemplify conformity to the suffering of Christ.

The absence of any parallel admonition to masters constitutes a problem. We can only speculate on the reasons. Possibly the community addressed in 1 Peter was made up primarily of Christians in socially underprivileged positions. Possibly the author is also dependent here on the ethical standards of his age. Possibly he felt that parenesis based on the suffering of Christ was all too absurd when addressed to masters.

10. In the situation presumed by 1 Peter, with the civil authorities apparently no longer tolerant of the Christian community, the relation of Christians to the state perforce takes on special urgency. It raises the question whether disloyalty should be met with disloyalty. The author deals with such questions in 2:13–17. Like Paul (cf. above, IV.D.4.3–4), he does not respond with a doctrine of the state but enjoins conduct based on a tradition like that in Romans 13. Immediately before this exhortation, he addresses Christians as aliens and exiles traveling through this world, whose way of life is temporary; this perspective is as important as the reference to "freedom" within the exhortation itself. Christians must maintain their freedom also within the context of the state. As in the case of Paul, this means in the first instance "subjection"—more precisely, "subjection to every human creature" (2:13).

Whether "human creature" is the right translation of the Greek expression is a matter of dispute. Most exegetes take the word to mean "institution," in some cases more specifically the institution of the state together with its divine origin. This interpretation, obviously inspired by Romans 13, is far from convincing. Nowhere else does *ktisis* mean "institution," either in secular Greek or in the LXX. Since 2:13–14 and 17 use personal terminology to expand on it and since 2:18a (cf. also 3:1 and 5:5) also speaks of subjection in personal terms, the translation "creature" is much more likely.[89]

The obedience referred to is therefore owed concretely to individual human beings, who are still "creatures" even when acting as agents of civil authority. We may note in addition that there is no statement analogous to Rom. 13:1b–2, despite the fact that both passages draw on the same tradition. The shift of emphasis is therefore unmistakable. The emperor and the imperial governors are not *eo ipso* appointed by God or even possessed of divine dignity; their authority is the authority of creatures (cf. also the negative attitude toward Rome exhibited by the apocalyptic codeword "Babylon" in 1 Pet. 5:13).[90] Christians are to be subject to them not because their authority is from the Lord but "for the Lord's sake," that is, because it is the Lord's will. The function of the civil authorities is described in terms similar to those used in Romans 13, but even this relationship to the constitutional state does not derive directly from God (cf. Rom. 13:3–4: "God's servant"). It is not God but the emperor who appoints governors "to punish those who do wrong and to praise those who do right" (2:14).

The basis and mode of Christian obedience to civil authority, however, is freedom (1 Pet. 2:16). Such obedience is the obedience of those who are free: it rules out blind and docile subordination as well as Christian abuse of freedom. Christians are not slaves of the state but "slaves of God" (v. 16) and therefore free. Therefore they do not fear the emperor but God, as the saying from Prov. 24:21 quoted in 1 Pet. 2:17 declares, noting the difference. The author does not say that those in authority are "God's servants," and certainly does not enjoin fear of the emperor. Only God is properly to be feared. According to 2:17d, Christians owe the emperor what they owe to all (2:17a): honor. They are free with respect to the authorities, and normally this freedom manifests itself in respect and loyalty, submission and honor.

11. Finally, we shall take brief note of 2 Peter and Jude, which belong to the latest stratum of the New Testament. Here we find the ideals of Hellenistic ethics (cf. 2 Pet. 1:5–11). Primary emphasis is on vitriolic polemic against heretical libertinism (cf. 2 Peter 2). The major charges include worldly pleasure and lawlessness, debauchery and greed. The recommended remedies are escape from the world (2 Pet. 2:20), virtue, and morality, supported by recourse to the "holy commandment" delivered by the apostles (2 Pet. 2:21).

89. See Werner Foerster, "ktizō," *TDNT* 3:1034–35; Martin Dibelius, "Rom" (B5), 191 n. 28; Horst Teichert, "1 Petr. 2,13—eine crux interpretum?" *ThLZ* 74 (1949): 303–4.

90. See Claus H. Hunzinger, "Babylon als Deckname für Rom und die Datierung des 1 Petr.," in *Gottes Wort und Gottes Land* (Festschrift Hans-Wilhelm Hertzberg), ed. H. G. Reventlow (Göttingen: Vandenhoeck & Ruprecht, 1965), 66–70; Aland, "Verhältnis" (B5), 203.

VI

PARENESIS IN
THE EPISTLE OF JAMES

BIBLIOGRAPHY

Blondel, Jean-Luc. "Le fondement théologique de la parénèse dans lépître de Jacques." *RThPh* 29 (1979): 141–52.
Dibelius, Martin. *Der Brief des Jakobus*. 12th ed. Ed. Heinrich Greeven. KEK 15. Göttingen: Vandenhoeck & Ruprecht, 1984. Eng. trans. of 11th ed.: *James*. Ed. Heinrich Greeven. Hermeneia. Philadelphia: Fortress Press, 1976.
Eichholz, Georg. *Glaube und Werk bei Paulus und Jakobus*. Munich: Kaiser, 1961.
Goppelt. *Theology* (B1). 2:197–209.
Lohse, Eduard. "Glaube und Werke." In *Einheit* (VA), 286–306.
Maston, Thomas Bufford. "Ethical Dimensions of James." *SWJT* 12 (1969): 23–29.
Perdue, Leo G. "Paraenesis and the Epistle of James." *ZNW* 72 (1981): 241–56.
Sanders. *Ethics* (B). Pp. 115–28.
Schawe, Erwin. "Die Ethik des Jakobusbriefes." *WuA* 20 (1979): 132–38.
Schnackenburg. *Botschaft* (B). Pp. 281–95.
Via, Dan Otto. "The Right Strawy Epistle Reconsidered." *JR* 49 (1969): 253–67.
Wendland. *Ethik* (B). Pp. 104–9.

No other New Testament document is as dominated by ethical questions as the Epistle of James. This has not made the position of the epistle easy in the church. At first its rigorism led to difficulties. Later the problems that Reformation exegesis had with the epistle because of its theological opposition to Paul and his doctrine of justification often cast an unjustified shadow on the ethics of James. The epistle is parenetic through and through. It is a rigorous protest against a quietistic Christianity, merely verbal or cognitive in nature, that considers it possible to ignore the practice of Christianity in everyday Christian life. Such theoretical Christianity is pseudo-Christianity.

As Dibelius points out, the only form-critical genre found in the epistle is parenesis, a loose assemblage of individual injunctions, series of aphorisms, and brief discussions of various topics. From beginning to end, injunctions and admonitions follow without apparent organization or logical development. It is possible to distinguish sections comprising loose collections of individual sayings or groups of sayings and sections with a relatively homogeneous theme (e.g., James 2:1—3:19). These latter are clearly the passages where the author speaks most independently and expresses his own concerns most clearly. Elsewhere he draws on a broad stream of parenetic tradition fed by a variety of elements from ancient ethics. This eclecticism—called by some "internationalism and interconfessionalism"[1]—also accounts for the relative scarcity of specifically Christian features. The author's purpose is not to be original, but to collect in a kind of catechism what he considers the bare essentials of a Christian life.

A. WORKS IN RELATIONSHIP TO FAITH, HEARING, AND HOPE

The real purpose of the epistle is neither proclamation of the gospel nor instruction in theology. It is a clear call to the active realization and obedient preservation of a Christian way of life without any ifs or buts. Admittedly, even when we recognize the primarily ethical thrust of this didactic parenesis, the deficient foundation and motivation of its ethics remains questionable. Apart from James 2:1, there is no hint of a specifically Christian or christological foundation. This is not to suggest that the epistle is dominated by the notion of merit or that the author was unaware that Christians had been accepted by grace (cf. 1:17). But this realization is not utilized as a foundation for ethics and there is no trace of it in the central section of the epistle, 2:14ff. We cannot totally deny that the author is familiar with the message of salvation (cf. 1:18), bears witness that "the Lord is compassionate and merciful" (5:11), and espouses a "consequential ethics."[2] If we recognize that works alone evince true "wisdom" and that "wisdom" is oriented totally toward practical ethics, the statement that wisdom (described as peaceable,

---

1. Dibelius and Greeven, *James*, 21.
2. Blondel, "Le fondement," 150.

gentle, full of mercy and of good fruit) comes "from above" (3:17; cf. 1:5)[3] takes on the nature of an indicative motivation for realizing God's will (cf. also 1:5). But this perspective is not maintained. Nor can we ignore the statement that the "word of truth" brings forth the new reality of human life (1:18). Since this is identical with the "perfect law of liberty" (1:25), gospel and law are ultimately one and the same.[4] The problem is not so much that gospel and law are merely two sides of the same coin as that the text unfortunately does not say that the law of liberty requires and guarantees ethical engagement.[5] The imperative stands in relative isolation, without motivation. The mention of baptism in 2:7, for example, has nothing to do with the otherwise common indicative justification of the imperative. Therefore there is little emphasis on faith as acceptance of the message of salvation. Of course faith must prove steadfast (1:3): for example, it must not show partiality (2:1). But it cannot be considered the driving force or basis of Christian life and ethics.[6] James insists—with good reason—on works but not—with less good reason—on faith, which is not especially surprising in the light of his concept of faith.

1. This is illustrated by the example that the author places in the center of the epistle, the relationship between faith and works (2:14ff.). The thesis of this section is stated at the outset in 2:14: only faith and works together bring salvation. Without works, faith is empty and dead, a statement repeated no less than three times (vv. 17, 20, 26).

In James 2:18a, the author presents a fictitious opponent who proposes ascribing faith to one person and works to another. In 2:18b–20 he objects to this approach and in particular to any isolation of faith. "Show me your faith apart from your works"—in the opinion of the author, any such attempt is doomed from the start, even though v. 18a renders all proposed interpretations hypothetical and fraught with problems.[7]

Many interpreters read 2:18b as suggesting that faith and works are interdependent or even equivalent, but the text does not support this reading. It is not the equal status of faith and works that the author is emphasizing but the meaninglessness of any hypothetical faith apart from works. In the author's opinion, works are logically primary: the presence of faith may be argued on the evidence of works. The reverse argument is impossible.

On the basis of what has gone before, one might suppose that the author is criticizing a faith that has become so subjective as to be invisible. In the discussion that follows, he appears rather to be attacking a faith that is merely intellectual and theoretical. Even here, however, he is less concerned with a

3. See Rudolph Hoppe, *Der theologische Hintergrund des Jakobusbriefes*, FzB 28 (Würzburg: Echter, 1977), 44ff.
4. Goppelt, *Theology* 2:202–3.
5. Pace Blondel, "Le fondement," 149.
6. Pace ibid., 146–47; Goppelt, *Theology* 2:210.
7. See now Hoppe, *Hintergrund*, 101ff.; Christoph Burchard, "Zu Jak. 2,14–26," *ZNW* 71 (1980): 17–45, esp. 35ff.

different kind of faith than with the manifestation of faith in works.[8] Of course James has no objection to faith like that in v. 19, which believes that God is one. The second half of v. 19, however, reveals unmistakably the insufficiency, indeed the irony, of such faith: it does not distinguish human believers from demons.

The example of Abraham also serves to refute the possibility of faith without works, and is intended to support the theory of justification through works. Here the author follows a traditional Jewish interpretation: Judaism, too, sees in Abraham not only an individual of exemplary righteousness and obedience but also a great example of faith, but the "faith" of Gen. 15:6 is interpreted as referring either to Abraham's entire life of devotion (cf. also Heb. 11:8ff.) or to his outstanding work in his willingness to sacrifice Isaac (Gen. 22; cf. 1 Macc. 2:52). In short, Abraham's faith and Abraham's works are identical. For James, too, Abraham is justified by his willingness to sacrifice Isaac—in other words, by a good work (v. 21b). Genesis 15:6 is nothing more than a prediction realized by Genesis 22. The author concludes (v. 22): faith worked together with Abraham's works, it merely "cooperated" in the attainment of justification (cf. 1:20) or in the works (v. 22b).[9] There is no hint that Abraham's faith was the crucial or even primary source of his works, or even that it was equally important.

This position is explained in part by the purpose of the epistle. Verse 24 in particular, which states that faith does not save and justify, clearly reveals a polemic against the theory of justification by faith alone. The impression that this is a deliberate counter to Pauline statements is thoroughly correct. The problem of justification by faith alone does not appear before Paul. It could hardly have done so, since Judaism does not and cannot consider faith and works to be mutually exclusive. The question certainly remains whether the "Paulinists" the author has in mind, who may already have devalued and perverted the theological heritage of Paul, did not misunderstand the apostle quite as seriously as did James. It is doubtful, however, that James himself was familiar with the Pauline message and understood it correctly. The different historical context and theological background are clearly not sufficient to explain the discrepancy. In any case, almost nothing is said about the source of good works or the basis of ethics. Nowhere in the entire passage is there any mention of the Christ event, the Spirit, or baptism.

Of course the author is concerned that faith be genuine when put to the test (cf. 1:3). One might even conclude from the ability of works to demonstrate faith (2:18) that he is interested in the manifestation and embodiment of faith in works (cf. also 2:1). But this is canceled out by his ascription of equal status to both, or actually his subordination of faith to works. Faith is reduced to a mere theory or doctrine (v. 19). Even though the author may be working

8. See Via, "Epistle," 256.
9. See also Burchard, "Jak.," 42.

within a tradition, reflecting the degraded concept of faith of his own period or current among exaggerated pseudo-Paulinists, he exhibits no desire to set the matter straight. Of course such a degraded, intellectualized faith cannot save. On this point Paul and James agree. Unlike Paul, however, James considers works to be necessary for salvation. Not only does he defend the unity and interdependence of faith and works, he also places works before and above faith. Indeed, he ascribes to human acts the power to remove sin (5:20).

2. Of course criticism of the epistle's concept of justification cannot serve as an excuse to rule it out of court entirely or reject it as no more than moralism. The author is right to protest against a "faith" that has been reduced to a formula or degenerated into ethical laxness.[10] The very variety of his arguments should caution us not to interpret him solely on the basis of 2:22. He is not interested in a new doctrine of justification or intense theological debate over the nature of faith. His theme is the consistent realization in practice of an active Christianity, concretely embodied. His lack of concern for subtle theological precision is illustrated by the confused outlines of his concept of faith.

The author's central concern is reflected in 1:22ff., where he calls on the readers to be "doers of the word, and not hearers only," deceiving themselves. This word to be done is described in James 1:21 as the implanted word, which is able to save (cf. also 1:18). But 1:21a ("Put away all filthiness and rank growth of naughtiness") and 21b ("Receive the implanted word") are not related as cause and effect, as though power to fulfill the ethical demands came from acceptance of the word. The acceptance of the word enjoined in v. 21 effects eschatological salvation only when what has been heard is embodied in action. Any theological reservations about the value of works would only be a distraction. James maintains that Christians cannot deceive themselves with what they do, but only with what they fail to do. The simile of the mirror (1:23–25) undoubtedly suggests careful and patient "reflection" on the word. It is therefore reasonable to say that patient and reflective hearing is necessary for action. But the emphasis is not on the need to hear before doing, but on doing what has been heard.

3. Elsewhere, too, we sense the absence of any explicit basis for ethics. The eschatological perspective of the epistle is less a foundation than a motivation. The eschatology of James, primarily a hope for the future, is not so much a foundation as an incentive. Even though it would be wrong to exaggerate the difference, an eschatology of the present (cf. 1:18) is primarily a foundation— action depends on what has already been vouchsafed—whereas an eschatology of the future is primarily a motivation—action is motivated by what is yet to come.

10. Wendland, *Ethik* (b), 109.

In any case, the Epistle of James records primarily a motivation based on an eschatology of the future, possibly even expectation that the end of the world is imminent. James 5:7, borrowing the style of prophetic exhortation, calls for patience until the Lord appears with power and glory at the end of time: "You also be patient. Establish your hearts, for the coming of the Lord is at hand. Do not grumble, brethren, against one another, that you may not be judged; behold, the Judge is standing at the doors" (5:8–9). Farmers cannot hasten the growth and ripening of the fruit, but must wait with hope and patience; Christians must follow their example (vv. 7–8; cf. also 1:3). This seems to suggest some delay of the Parousia, but does not mean rejection of imminent eschatological hope or of patient expectation.

Elsewhere in the epistle, too, the judgment to come motivates proper conduct (cf. 2:12–13; 5:12). Although the notion of judgment predominates, the motif of promised salvation at the Parousia cannot be overlooked (cf. 1:18, 21; 4:10). The one who stands at the doors in 5:9 is not only judge but also the advocate who comes to the aid of the afflicted and oppressed (cf. vv. 4, 6; also 4:12, where the judge can both save and destroy). And according to 2:5, God has chosen the poor to be heirs of the kingdom.

There is also a different expectation, however, which raises a problem. We read in 1:9–11, for example, that the rich will pass away like the flower of the grass. It is not clear whether the author has the eschatological future in mind or the transitoriness of earthly life. As in Syriac Baruch 52:6ff. and 83:12 the text here borrowed from Isa. 40:6ff. clearly refers to the eschatological transformation of the world, so that James, too, might be thinking of the coming revaluation of all values. On the other hand, apocalypses also speak of the transitoriness of human life without reference to the coming end of all things. The future tenses in James 1 can hardly refer solely to the Parousia; they describe an eternally valid truth. Possibly the author saw in the transitoriness of life a hint or a kind of anticipation of the eschatological judgment. In any case, these verses are not simply examples of imminent eschatological expectation, but show that the author can also criticize the rich in other ways.

The situation is similar in 4:13ff., where the author inveighs against confident plans and transactions, pointing out that those engaged in commerce for profit are a mist that appears for a little time and then vanishes. This passage is aimed primarily at the arrogance and self-righteousness of the merchants who do not take God into account and think they can tell every detail of when and where and why and how long they will be gone. The author suggests instead that it is madness to count on the future, since mortals cannot even know what the next day will bring. Everything is contingent on the Lord's will—which does not mean God's law but God's sovereign governance. We are dealing here with a kind of belief in providence. James certainly does not conceive this God on whose sovereign will all depends as a kind of fate that gives rise to resignation or despair: God's salvific will engenders confidence (cf. 1:17–18; 4:6; 5:11). But eschatological expectation must not be taken as the single dominant basis of ethics. It stands as one element alongside a sense of human perishability and God's governance.

More serious is the fact that the author does so little with christology. Jesus Christ is mentioned only twice: once in the salutation (1:1) and again in 2:1, where we are told that "faith is our Lord Jesus Christ in his glory" is irreconcilable with partiality. But this verse is trivial as a foundation for ethics.

There are no other foundations or motivations for ethics to be found in the Epistle of James. The stock of ethical principles is therefore quite modest, even though this disappointing observation does not allow us to say that the conclusion is totally negative.

B. "THE LAW OF LIBERTY"

1. If we turn our attention to the criteria for ethics explicitly emphasized by the author, we must first deal with the understanding of the law found in the Epistle of James.[11] Even if the author does not actually cite it very frequently, he appears to ascribe to it a decisive role in the orientation of Christians.

Especially important is James 2:8–12:

> If you really fulfill the royal law, according to the scripture, 'You shall love your neighbor as yourself,' you do well. But if you show partiality, you commit sin, and are convicted by the law as transgressors. For whoever keeps the whole law but fails in one point has become guilty of all of it. For he who said, 'Do not commit adultery,' said also, 'Do not kill.' If you do not commit adultery but do kill, you have become a transgressor of the law. So speak and so act as those who are to be judged under the law of liberty.

This is a didactic discourse on the relationship between individual commandments and the law as a whole. Those who show partiality to the rich transgress the law contained in Scripture, which enjoins love of one's neighbor. This law is described and cited as "the royal law" (Lev. 19:18). Coming from Jesus and Paul, we might think that this expression singles out the law of love as the most important and greatest commandment. But such a conclusion would be at odds with the text. The law is called "royal" not to suggest the primacy of the law of love but because it comes from the king of the kingdom of God (cf. 1 Esd. 8:24; 2 Macc. 3:13). Having this authority it brooks no disobedience.

Otherwise we would expect v. 8 to speak of a commandment rather than of the law (cf. Mark 12:18, 31). Above all, vv. 10 and 11 make sense only if the law of love is taken as one commandment among many.[12] The author is not

11. Cf. Walter Gutbrod, "nomos," *TDNT* 4:1082.
12. Pace Hoppe, *Hintergrund*, 88–89, 92.

concerned with the relationship between the great commandment and a particular commandment but with the relationship between the law as a whole and a particular exemplary commandment—with the notion that the law as an indivisible whole constitutes a homogeneous entity and is binding upon all. The same God who gave the Seventh Commandment gave the Sixth.

The fact that the author cites these two commandments is not related to his previous citation of the law of love, as though refusal to love were a kind of spiritual murder or adultery. It is simply that the Fifth or Sixth Commandment was the traditional point where citations of the Decalogue began (cf. Mark 10:19; Rom. 13:9). In any case, the individual commandments are inseparable. As part of the Old Testament, they are part of the "perfect law of liberty," which is also binding on Christians.

James 2:10 states that anyone who keeps the whole law but fails in one point has become guilty of all of it. This suggests that the literal wording of the law is binding in all particulars. In fact, however, despite the programmatic statements in 2:8–12, the theme of the law and its interpretation do not play any outstanding role in the parenesis of the epistle. Furthermore, as we shall see, the author silently discards the cultic and ceremonial law. The example in v. 7, where the author paradigmatically cites two commandments of the Decalogue, already betrays his lack of interest in the ritual law. He is concerned primarily with the application of the law's fundamental ethical commandments. In contrast to Matthew, however (cf. above, III. B. 4), he does not particularly stress the double law of love or see it as a canon for interpreting the law.

James certainly does not think in perfectionistic terms: according to 3:2, "we all make many mistakes" (cf. also 5:16). He nevertheless maintains the full force of the ethical law. It remains the norm by which Christians are judged (2:12). Whoever transgresses one of the commandments transgresses the entire law. God's will cannot be divided to suit human preferences. Even those who, unlike James, are convinced that distinctions must be made according to some canon of judgment will heed the warning that they cannot adapt God's law at will or select from it only what comports with their own ethical notions. It is clear that James sees this danger primarily in partiality toward the rich. Such conduct cannot be justified by citing the law of love. Divisive partiality is an offense against the law, which is binding as a single whole.

2. The "perfect law of liberty" (1:25) is the whole law; the phrase does not mean the law's perfection but its totality. This law does not enslave; it sets free. It does so in being obeyed, not in remaining vague and vouchsafing "contextual freedom."[13] For James, freedom is not freedom from the law, but freedom through the law and in the law. That Christians must respect the law

---

13. Pace Via, "Epistle," 261–62; but cf. 266.

is stated also in 4:11–12: "He that speaks evil against a brother or judges his brother, speaks evil against the law and judges the law. But if you judge the law, you are not a doer of the law but a judge. There is one lawgiver and one judge, he who is able to save and to destroy."

Because Christians, too, are bound by the absolute authority of the law, their only appropriate role is that of doers, not that of judges and critics. God is the only judge; he gave the law and will one day judge all by it. This suggests that the only possibility is unlimited respect for and obedience to the law. The author clearly is unaware of his own indirect criticism expressed in nonobservance of the ceremonial law. Once again he is thinking only of the ethical requirements, more specifically those associated with the law of love (cf. the concluding phrase of v. 12, "judge your neighbor," and the similarity of Lev. 19:16 to 19:18 = James 2:8).

3. James's total lack of interest in ritual matters is shown above all by 1:27: "Worship that is pure and undefiled before God and the Father is this: to visit orphans and widows in their affliction, and to keep oneself unstained from the world" (cf. also v. 26). True worship consists in care for widows and orphans and separation from the world. It would be hard for the author to express more clearly his reservations about everything cultic. It is highly revealing that James can touch on the theme of pure and undefiled cultic behavior without mentioning a single word of the ritual law. This is clear evidence for the priority of the ethical and social dimension in his thought. Only those who take up the cause of orphans and widows, the poorest of the poor, worship God rightly.

The author does not even say that both must go together, as in the familiar words of Bonhoeffer during the Holocaust: "No one has the right to sing Gregorian chant unless he is crying out for the Jews." James does not even mention "Gregorian chant." Of course we must not press the argument from silence too far, and we certainly do not mean to imply here that the author knows of no other form of worship than that in 1:17. Worship is presupposed in 2:1ff., and other passages clearly have in mind a spiritual life that includes prayer (cf. 1:6; 5:15). The emphasis, however, is clearly on the obligation to care for widows and orphans.

These observations also make it clear that "keeping oneself unstained from the world" does not mean retreat from social activism and from support of the weak and oppressed. The final phrase confirms the ethical reinterpretation of cultic terminology, for "without spot" or "without stain"—originally a cultic concept—is understood in an ethical sense. A similar statement appears in 4:8: "Cleanse your hands, you sinners, and purify your hearts, you men of double mind." This, too, was originally a cultic exhortation; now it is a call to single-minded obedience. All this shows that the author considers the ethical law of the Old Testament, but not the cultic law, to be a guideline and criterion of Christian ethics.

4. Besides citing actual passages from the law, the epistle makes use of Old Testament examples, as already illustrated by the example of Abraham. Unlike Paul, the author does not see Abraham as the prototype of a justified sinner: Abraham is an exemplar of active obedience yielding justification. It is unlikely that Abraham is also meant implicitly to be an example of hospitality.[14] Rahab the harlot is mentioned along with Abraham in 1:25: she, too, is an example of justification by works, because she took in the spies sent by Joshua to Jericho and saved them from entrapment by the king of Jericho by secretly lowering them from her roof with a rope (Joshua 2). The author probably cites this example because Rahab is the prototype of the proselyte, so that there can be no doubt that even for a Gentile there is no possibility of justification except by works. Additional Old Testament examples appear in James 5. In 5:10, the author cites the prophets as "an example of suffering and patience," clearly intending them as models Christians should strive to imitate. Verse 11 speaks of the exemplary steadfastness of Job, and v. 17 of the exemplary fervent prayer of Elijah. With this examples, the epistle exhibits a similarity to the long series of Old Testament exempla in Hebrews 11 and to mimetic ethics in general.

Besides these passages, the Epistle of James also cites the Old Testament in 2:8, 11, 23 and 4:5–6. The first of the two sayings in 4:5–6 does not in fact appear in the Old Testament. This shows that for the author there is only a vague dividing line between "Scripture" (2:8) and the extensive traditional material he borrows from Hellenistic Jewish parenesis. Conversely he sometimes includes Old Testament passages without citing them explicitly (cf. 1:10–11 and 5:11, as well as the vague introduction of the quotation in 4:6 "Therefore it says"). The explicit statement in 2:8 that the "royal law" is scriptural, the absence of an interpretation of Old Testament law, and the identity of law and gospel all indicate that the author does not limit the concept of "law" to the Torah of the Old Testament.

5. This is confirmed by the observation that the Epistle of James also considers the traditional words of the Lord authoritative for proper conduct, since it often exhibits both formal and substantial points of contact with sayings of Jesus.[15]

In at least one passage, the epistle has preserved a version of one of Jesus' sayings earlier than that found in Matthew, as we may see by comparing James 5:12 with the prohibition of swearing in Matt. 5:37. It is clear that Jesus forbade all oaths (as may still be seen in Matt. 5:34); he insisted that "yes" should be "yes" and "no" be "no." This is exactly what James 5:12 says, whereas Matthew makes a concession, allowing a repeated asseveration formula (cf. above II. B. 2). But if James 5:12 goes back to Jesus himself, it is quite possible in principle that elsewhere, too, James has incorporated tradi-

14. Roy Bowen Ward, "The Works of Abraham, James 2:14–26," *HThR* 61 (1968): 283–90.
15. Greatly exaggerated by Schawe, "Ethik," 313–14.

tions going back to Jesus, even if they have no parallel in the Gospels. The stream of oral tradition continued on even after the Gospels were composed: note, for example, the Word of the Lord in Acts 20:35, which has no equivalent in the Gospels. But this theoretical possibility does not in fact turn into a tenable hypothesis anywhere in the epistle.

There is a further problem: passages that sound like words of the Lord, James does not cite or identify as such. This is not unique to James in early Christian literature, as we see in the Didache and also in Paul, who, while citing some sayings of Jesus explicitly (1 Cor. 7:10; 9:14), also introduces several allusions to dominical traditions without making them explicit (cf. above IV. C. 3. 4). Here, too, there is no convincing explanation why James does not identify sayings of Jesus explicitly, in partial contrast to injunctions from the Old Testament. All we can say is that the epistle also includes early Christian parenetic traditions, some of which may go back to Jesus himself. But there is no special emphasis on these words of the Lord.

C. SPECIFIC FOCAL POINTS

1. We must first emphasize that the author repeatedly insists on a radical either/or, together with wholehearted and undivided obedience. Already in James 1:4 the author exhorts his readers to be whole ("perfect") and complete; in 1:8 he warns against doubt and double-mindedness. For James, a doubter is not a radical skeptic but someone inwardly torn, like a wave of the sea tossed to and fro by the wind (1:6), possessed of two minds (1:8) and a divided heart. James, however, looks for unity and wholeness.[16]

In particular, a blunt either/or pervades 4:1–12; it is especially clear in v. 4: "Unfaithful creatures! Do you not know that friendship with the world is enmity with God?" Those who become involved with the world commit infidelity—an allusion to the Old Testament image of a marriage covenant between Yahweh and his people. The statement that one cannot love both God and the world recalls certain Johannine passages (cf. 1 John 2:15). It does not represent either philosophical dualism or a tendency to withdraw from the world, but ethical rigorism. Those who decide in favor of the world as an entity that imposes its own obligations apart from God decide against God, who demands for himself alone the Spirit that he created and implanted as his gift (v. 5).

In 3:13ff., the author states the either/or by contrasting heavenly and earthly wisdom. Wisdom "from above" is characterized by good works and a morally responsible way of life. Jealousy and selfish ambition, on the other hand, are the signs of false wisdom, which cannot be divine by nature and origin: it is earthly, unspiritual, and demonic. A concrete example of failure to respond to the either/or is use of the same tongue to bless God and curse

16. See Gottfried Schille, "Wider die Gespaltenheit des Glaubens," *Theologische Versuche* 9 (1977): 71–89.

others, blessings and curses proceeding from the same mouth (3:9ff.). According to James, this incomprehensible ambiguity and division is contrary to nature: in nature two things that are irreconcilable cannot proceed from the same source.

2. Elsewhere, too, traditional polemic against so-called "sins of the tongue"[17] plays an important role. The entire passage 3:1–12 treats the dangerous power of the tongue at length and describes its destructive effects.

The tongue is not a minor nuisance; like a spark in the forest, it has devastating consequences. It is the essence of unrighteousness, a very universe of unrighteousness. Its baleful fire is traced to the fires of hell itself (v. 6). The conquest of nature, which other ancient authors consider a glorious page in human history, here becomes an indictment: our control over the forces of nature shows all the more painfully how little control we have over the deadly poison of sins of the tongue (vv. 7–8). This sounds pessimistic, but is intended to unleash contrary forces. The metaphors of v. 12—a fig tree cannot yield olives, a grapevine figs, or a salt spring fresh water—show that the pessimistic view must not be taken as encouraging surrender to the so-called "realities." The entire section is intended rather to promote especially intense efforts to obviate the dangers. Other warnings have the same purpose as 3:1ff.: people should be quick to hear, slow to speak, and slow to anger (1:19); those who do not bridle their tongues worship in vain (1:26).

The same chord is struck by the admonition not to let words and actions go separate ways: they go together (2:12). If a brother or sister lacks clothing or daily food, it is useless to say, "Go in peace, be warmed and filled," if one does not give them the things needed for the body (2:15–16). Just as 1:19 deals with the unity of hearing and deed, so this passage deals with word and deed. Kind words are not enough. Those in need of the bare essentials of food and clothing cannot be fed with kind words and wishes, which must be mockery in the ears of the needy. This is not just polemic against unctuous platitudes and pious clichés. Friendly and well-meaning words, seriously intended, are not enough; they do not fill the hungry and warm the freezing. Those who are starving and suffering need material support more than verbal support.

3. Criticism of wealth plays a major role in the Epistle of James (cf. especially 2:1ff. and 5:1ff.).[18] It is clear from 2:1 that the assembly includes rich people. We are not told whether they come as members or as unbelievers. The latter is more likely, especially because assignment of seats (v. 3) points more in that direction. Nothing is said about the motives for preferred treatment—the rich are shown to comfortable seats while the poor are left standing—but it is likely that the community expected support and prestige

17. See Johannes Behm, "glōssa," *TDNT* 1:721–22.
18. See Bent Noack, "Jakobus wider die Reichen," *StTh* 18 (1964): 10–25.

from the rich and felt the poor to be a burden. The community is not simply admonished to be impartial: it is expected to show partiality, but toward the poor. This is what God has done (v. 5).

The reference to God's preference for the poor is followed by a reminder of the unfortunate experiences the community has had with the rich: "Is it not the rich who oppress you, is it not they who drag you into court? Is it not they who blaspheme that honorable name by which you are called?" (vv. 6–7). The first charge of oppression recalls the social accusations leveled by the prophets against the wealthy upper classes, who exploit and oppress the poor (cf. Amos 4:1; 8:4; Zech. 7:10; Mic. 2:2; Mal. 3:5; Ezek. 18:12; 22:7). James also resembles the prophets in accusing not just individuals but the entire class (the article is generic; the present tense indicates habitual action).

Besides oppressing the poor socially, the rich haul them into court. This hints at the impotence of the poor in legal proceedings, where the rich can rely on their economic power (cf. Isa. 1:23; 10:1ff.). It is not clear whether these forensic disputes involve charging the poor with being Christians. The Christian message clearly represented a threat to the commercial interests and profits of well-to-do citizens (Acts 16:16ff.; 19:23ff.). But the "blasphemy of the honorable name"—the name of Jesus Christ pronounced in baptism—mentioned in v. 7 probably represents a third, additional accusation against the rich and does not belong to the forensic context of v. 6.

Since blasphemy against the name of Christ is possible only on the part of non-Christians, the author seems again to assume that the rich are outside the community. On the other hand, the example in v. 2 involves the rich coming to worship. Indeed, the author appears to fear a certain influence on the part of the rich, engendering conflict within the community. It is reasonable to assume that the readership of the epistle comprised primarily members of the lower classes, but it is impossible to be certain whether the rich stood within, without, or on the fringes of the community. Perhaps the most realistic theory is that there had been only a few well-to-do Christians (but cf. 4:13ff.) and the author was fearful that their influence might increase.

A clear pauperistic and apocalyptic perspective appears in James 5:1–6, a section recalling the woes against the rich found in the Old Testament and Judaism. As in the judgment discourses of the Old Testament prophets, the author begins with a call to wail and howl. In both cases the call is based on the coming eschatological day of judgment (cf., e.g., Isa. 13:6). This threat of judgment and disaster, however, is not directed against the nations or the people of God, but the rich. The apocalyptic writers also inveighed against the rich with these woes (cf., e.g., Ethiopic Enoch 98:4–5; also above, I.D. 3.1).

James 5:2 ("Your riches have rotted and your garments are moth-eaten") should probably not be interpreted as an imitation of the prophetic perfect, anticipating what will come to pass. The author is not trying to transport himself and his readers to the time when the riches of the wealthy will be at an end. What we have in vv. 2 and 3 is instead the basis for the threat of eschatological judgment: v. 3 states that the rust will testify as evidence, obviously because it bears witness to an overabundance of riches accumulated without regard for social responsibility.

In short, James charges the rich with preferring to let rust and moths devour their wealth rather than using it to help the needy. The "rotting" of riches (probably thought of as stores of grain), the devouring of clothing by moths, and the rusting of silver and gold are meant to recall not so much the perishability of all earthly wealth (as in Matt. 6:19) as the inhumanity and antisocial conduct of the rich.

The rich are unrighteous as well as inhumane. "Behold, the wages of the laborers who mowed your fields, which you kept back by fraud, cry out; and the cries of the harvesters have reached the ears of the Lord of hosts" (v. 4). This shows that the wealth of the rich derives from their cruel exploitations and brutal oppression of the poor. The author is probably thinking of large landowners who keep back the wages earned by their agricultural laborers, conduct he views as an offense that cries out to heaven. The cries of the exploited are heard by God, and God himself will surely intervene on behalf of the powerless. At the same time, this is a social accusation against the rich, who are charged in v. 5 with living lives of luxury and pleasure, fattening their hearts in a day of slaughter.

Verse 6 makes the most serious accusation: the rich condemn and execute the righteous, whose nonresistance makes this bloody crime all the more heinous. The helplessness of the poor is set in sharp contrast to the brutal power of the rich. Whether we can interpret these final accusations in vv. 4–6 as showing indirectly the real duty of the rich, namely social responsibility and justice, is uncertain. It is an open question whether the author thinks such conduct is even possible. Wealth may be so hopelessly intertwined with injustice and lack of social responsibility that change is out of the question; it may be *ipso facto* a mark of guilt. Such passages as 1:27 and 2:15 nevertheless show clearly how much importance James attaches to social responsibility and humane conduct.

Finally, we observe briefly that the author also criticizes the inward motivation of greed. In 4:1–2, he writes: "What causes wars, and what causes fightings among you? Is it not your passions that are at war in your members? You desire and do not have." The passionate desire for wealth and pleasure causes outward strife; it is also ultimately profitless. Desire does not attain its end but sends the greedy back with empty hands. The only remedy is the wisdom that comes "from above," which aims at peace and is full of kindness and mercy (cf. 3:17). Mercy is a crucial mark of the Christian life (cf. 1:27; 2:13, 15–16; 3:17).

VII

THE COMMANDMENT OF BROTHERLY LOVE IN THE JOHANNINE WRITINGS

BIBLIOGRAPHY

Bultmann, Rudolf. *Evangelium des Johannes*. 19th ed. Göttingen: Vandenhoeck & Ruprecht, 1968. English: *The Gospel of John*. Philadelphia: Westminster Press, 1971.

Collins, Raymond F. "'A New Commandment I Give to You, that You Love One Another . . .' (Jn 13:34)." *LTP* 35 (1979): 235–61.

Käsemann, Ernst. *Jesu letzter Wille nach Joh. 17*. 3d ed. Tübingen: Mohr, 1971. Eng. trans. of 2d ed.: *The Testament of Jesus*. Philadelphia: Fortress Press, 1978.

Lattke, Michael. *Einheit im Wort*. StANT 4. Munich: Kösel, 1975.

Lazure, Noël. *Les valeurs morales de la théologie johannique*. Paris: Lecoffre, 1965.

Morris, Leon. "Love in the Fourth Gospel." In *Saved by Hope* (Festschrift Richard C. Oudersluys), 27–43. Grand Rapids: Eerdmans, 1978.

Prunet, Olivier. *La morale chrétienne d'après les écrits johanniques*. Paris: Presses universitaires de Frances, 1957.

Sanders. *Ethics* (B). Pp. 91–100.

Schnackenburg. *Botschaft* (B). Pp. 247–80.

Schottroff, Luise. *Der Glaubende und die feindliche Welt*. WMANT 37. Neukirchen: Neukirchener Verlag, 1970.

Thyen, H. "'. . . denn wir lieben die Brüder' (1. Joh. 3,14)." In *Rechtfertigung* (IVA), 527–42.

Völkl. *Christ* (B). Pp. 393–439.

Wachs, H. J. "Johanneische Ethik." Diss., Univ. Kiel, 1952.

Wendland. *Ethik* (B). Pp. 109–16.

Wittenberger, Werner. "Ort und Struktur der Ethik des Johannes-Evangelium und des ersten Johannesbriefes." Diss., Univ. Jena, 1971.

John writes his Gospel to awaken or increase faith in Jesus Christ as Son of God and thus bring life (John 20:30–31). Such a purpose need not ignore specific dangers to which the addressees are exposed (cf. the attacks on the followers of the Baptist or "the Jews" in the Gospel and on the gnostic heretics in 1 John) or problems within the community. But despite all their polemic and apologetic elements and their historical background, the Gospel and the Epistles of John cannot be interpreted primarily as arising from a particular historical situation. Furthermore both their historical and their religious background are vigorously debated, as are the question of sources, the problem addressed, etc. In any case—to cite just two thematic complexes that are important for ethics—it would be wrong to take dualism alone or the restriction of love to the community of believers as the key to understanding the disputes with nascent Jewish orthodoxy.[1]

Because of their similarity in style and intellectual content, the Johannine writings are treated here largely as a unit. Despite the differences that undoubtedly exist, even in the realm of ethics—it is important to note, for example, that there is more emphasis on parenesis in 1 John—it is neither necessary nor reasonable to differentiate between the Fourth Gospel and the Johannine Epistles. In my opinion, it is likely that the author of 1 John is closely related to the so-called ecclesiastical redaction of the Fourth Gospel, or is at least not identical with the author of the Gospel, but such a distinction between Johannine and deutero-Johannine or redactional passages in the Gospel would be much too complicated and hypothetical, not to mention reconstruction of the theological history of the Johannine community or school on the basis of various stages and strata. All we can do is note a few specific accents here and there.[2]

We may ask whether a chapter on the Johannine writings even belongs in a book on the ethics of the New Testament, whether it would not be better to limit ourselves to evaluating the place of John within the theology of the New Testament. Wendland is right to note the "impression of an enormous reduction of ethical questions and statements."[3] Especially when we set the writings of the Johannine school and their ethics alongside the New Testament documents already discussed, we note immediately an almost total absence of specific injunctions or detailed parenetic passages. Nothing is said about marriage or wealth, and discussion of the state is indirect at best. Nevertheless, even John knows nothing of "'dogmatics' without 'ethics.'"[4] The ethical dicta of the Johannine writings are integrated quite differently into their total theology than is the case with the other New Testament writings.[5] "Being"

1. Pace Wittenberger, "Ort," 29ff., and others.
2. See also Hartwig Thyen, "Aus der Literatur zum Johannesevangelium," *ThR* 43 (1978): 357; 44 (1979); 132, 134.
3. *Ethik* (B), 109.
4. Bultmann, *John*, 274.
5. Prunet, *La morale chrétienne*.

and "doing" are practically identified, and various theologoumena have ethical aspects and implications.[6] Here the two go hand in hand; because the structure of Johannine theology—which appears so simple but is in fact enormously obscure—is so difficult, this makes our task substantially harder.

A. CHRISTOLOGICAL BASIS

1. Here, too, we shall devote our first section to the basis and foundation of ethics. But this section cannot follow the guidelines of anthropology. It is really limited to a single theme: the eschatological sending of the preexistent Son of God to bring salvation and revelation into the world. Since christology is the dominant theme and clear focus of John, the ethics of the Johannine writings is exclusively christological in a way not encountered elsewhere. God's love for the world, fallen victim to darkness and death, is the basis for the sending of Jesus Christ; this sending brings the believer salvation from judgment and destruction (John 3:16; 1 John 4:9). The Son sent into the world through the Father's love is, as the many "I am" sayings show, the good shepherd, the way, the truth, the life, the bread of life, and the light of the world. Above all, the image of the door (John 10:9) illustrates the exclusivity and absoluteness of the revelation given and the salvation vouchsafed in Christ. Salvation, life, joy, light, fulness—all exist only in association with Jesus, and this association is eternal. For if Jesus is the way and the truth (14:6), it is not the case that he merely shows the way or teaches a truth that would be valid apart from him or could render him superfluous. He is the one in whom God is personally present. Because the Son and the Father are one (10:30), the Father bestows his blessing only in the Son. All things have been given (3:35; cf. 10:18) and shown (5:20; cf. 8:28) to the Son; those who believe in the Son believe in the Father, and those who see the Son see the Father (12:44–45). The Son is therefore honored equally with the Father (5:23), and Thomas even confesses the Son "my Lord and my God" (20:28). It chimes with this repeated emphasis on the Son's unity with the Father that elements of glory dominate the description of Jesus' earthly life.

It is true that the incarnation of the divine Logos remains a scandal, but Käsemann has emphasized with some reason that the focus is not on the paradox of the incarnation, in which the revealer appears as a pure human being (Bultmann). The crucial clause in the Gospel is 1:14b ("We have beheld his glory"), not 1:14a ("The Word became flesh"). In other words, v. 14a is ultimately only the prerequisite for v. 14b.

Käsemann does not totally deny the humble features of the earthly Jesus in the Fourth Gospel, but asks whether they are anything more than "the bare minimum of scenery necessary for someone . . . who dwells for a while among men and women, appearing to be one of them, but without being

6. Lazure, Les valeurs morales.

reduced to earthly dimensions."[7] There is an important point in this criticism of popular presentations of Johannine theology, which emphasize the truly human (*vere homo*): not the humanity of Jesus but the glory of Christ actually dominates the scene. Jesus' heavenly nature is recognizable even through the flesh. This holds true even of the cross, which is seen from the outset in the light of the resurrection. Jesus' crucifixion is thus robbed of its offense: the way of the cross is represented as the sovereign triumphal procession of the Christ returning to the Father, victorious over all temptation and horror (see, e.g., 12:27–28). Death is glorification. Käsemann states that the cross "is no longer the pillory of one who associated with criminals. It has become a demonstration of Jesus' self-sacrificing divine love and victorious return from an alien realm to the Father who sent him."[8]

This argument against John's alleged theology of lowliness is basically correct but in part exaggerated. It is hardly accurate to speak of "naive docetism," since Jesus is in fact truly human. But even in human form he is still the Logos "tabernacling" upon earth, upon whom the angels of God therefore ascend and descend (John 1:51). He reveals the heavenly glory of the Father, to which the Son returns after death. The incarnation makes possible the saving encounter with the heavenly glory or the knowledge of grace and truth, which Jesus brings from the Father (1:18). "Behold the man"—crowned with thorns: these are the words of Pilate, an unbeliever. The Passion is only the culmination and conclusion of Jesus' mission. It is part of the work of redemption (19:30 refers to the whole work of salvation), but the emphasis is on the fact that the man on the cross is the exalted Lord, not on the fact that the exalted Lord was crucified. There are certainly other features in the picture of Christ, as shown, for example, by his washing the disciples' feet, but also by the simple fact that Jesus is called the son of Joseph of Nazareth (1:45; cf. also 2:3; 7:10). It is especially significant for ethics that John does not simply espouse a theology of glory (*theologia gloriae);* he did not extend the christology of *doxa* ("glory") into anthropology. Those who meet Christ enter "the realm of triumph and share in it."[9] But this stands in contrast to John's picture of the temptations and sufferings believers encounter in the world: "In the world you have tribulation" (16:3).

2. Whatever disputes there may be about Johannine christology in detail, one thing is certain: it is of fundamental significance for the Christian community and its conduct. Jesus' discourse about the vine and the branches (John 15:1ff.) is particularly instructive as an example of the influence of christology on ethics. Here it is absolutely clear that the Christian cannot bear

7. *Wille*, 28–29.
8. Ibid., 29; see also Lattke, *Einheit*, 142ff.
9. Käsemann, *Wille*, 41.

fruit without abiding in Jesus, the one true vine. But abiding in him so as to bring forth fruit is itself based on Jesus' abiding in those who belong to him.

Heise rightly interprets the "and" in John 15:4a ("Abide in me, and I in you") as meaning: "Abide in me as and because I abide in you." The abiding of Jesus "makes it possible for those who belong to him to abide in him" and thus bear fruit.[10] John, too, considers it necessary for discipleship "that Jesus constantly comes to us—promising, reminding, teaching, warning, comforting," but "neither our experience nor our decision determines who Jesus is."[11]

Above all, it is important that those who belong to Jesus derive their growth and fruitfulness solely from their indissoluble association with him, apart from whom they would wither and die. Such intensive association is not to be interpreted as mystical communion: it is mediated by the Word, as we see from 15:3 and 7 as well as from the use of "hear" as a synonym of "abide." According to 15:16, it is Jesus himself who chooses his disciples and appoints them to bear fruit. All that a Christian is and does can be realized and understood only in connection with Jesus.

But John also stresses conversion, and not just as polemic against over-emphasis on the indicative of salvation.[12] Not only is there no fruit apart from the vine, but the reverse is also true: without fruit, the connection with the vine will be severed—indeed the absence of fruit in itself already indicates separation from Jesus (15:2 and 6). There is a deliberate tension between vv. 2 and 4–5: according to v. 2, a branch that does not bear fruit will be cut off; according to v. 4, it is necessary to abide in the vine in order to bear fruit. Bultmann finds here the dialectic of indicative and imperative,[13] with the indicative once again prior to the imperative. Nothing more is expected of Christians than what has accrued to them. Only those who have been loved can love. Elsewhere, too, John repeatedly grounds love in being loved. The Johannine ethics of love stands and falls solely on God's having demonstrated his love by sending and sacrificing his own Son; God's love attains its goal only in the love of those who belong to him. It is vouchsafed them and required of them. In 1 John, too, ethics—the law of love—is grounded in the demonstration of God's love in Christ (cf. 1 John 4:10–11).[14]

Because the footwashing scene is of great parenetic importance (cf. below, VII.B.3), we must stress here that there is no conflict between the soteriological and ethical interpretations of John 13:1–7. Jesus' crucial salvific act ("perfect love" or "love to the end" [v. 1]), symbolized by his act of loving

10. Jürgen Heize, *Bleiben: Menein in den johanneischen Schriften* (Tübingen: Mohr, 1961), 85; cf. 81ff.; see also Rainer Borig, *Der wahre Weinstock*, StANT 16 (Munich: Kösel, 1967).

11. Käsemann, *Wille*, 59–60.

12. See Günter Klein, "'Das wahre Licht scheint schon,'" *ZThK* 68 (1971): 261–326, esp. 264 n. 17.

13. *Theology* (B), 2:80.

14. See Georg Eichholz, "Glaube und Liebe im 1. Joh.," *EvTh* 4 (1937): 411–37.

service in washing his disciples' feet, is the prerequisite for the disciples' own acts of love. This makes two points clear. First, it is hardly accurate to call Johannine ethics "legalistic" or "moralistic."[15] This is all the more true because the divine commandment of love is "given" (15:10); such "giving" refers elsewhere to God's gift (cf. 3:34; 6:11; 10:18). Second, the love demanded finds not only its norm and measure but also its basis and possibility solely in Jesus' love. Only as they are loved can those who love continue to experience the love of Jesus and thus continue to love in their own right. This statement presupposes that their love cannot be separated from Jesus and made an ethical principle or program, to be practiced apart from him. It is not by accident that the context of the new commandment of love in 15:12 speaks of the vine and of bearing fruit.

3. People cannot set themselves in motion, activate themselves, and bring forth fruit on their own initiative; this truth finds expression in the Johannine doctrine of predestination. In 3:27, we are told that no one can receive anything "except what is given from heaven." All receiving depends on giving. How can anyone receive when nothing is given—or, in christological terms, how can anyone abide with Jesus or come to Jesus unless "drawn by the Father" (6:44; cf. v. 65)? Of course this deterministic statement is followed in v. 45 by a variant: "Everyone who has heard and learned from the Father comes to me." This obviously refers to the "drawing" of the Father in v. 44: this drawing takes place in hearing and learning. "The drawing of the Father does not take place prior to the decision of faith but in it."[16]

Bultmann puts too much emphasis on this decision. In his view, the decision is fundamental for a person's being and past.[17] In other words, it reveals what one truly is and always has been. "The decision for the future is also decisive for one's past. . . . That a person encountering the revealer must decide for or against him on the basis of his own past is only an audaciously paradoxical way of saying that this decision reveals what the person truly is."[18] This resolves the paradox too one-sidedly in favor of the decision.

For John, on the contrary, God's choosing and human responsibility are dialectically related and intimately interwoven, like the being drawn and hearing or willing spoken of in 7:17 or 8:44 and other passages. In 6:27, we find juxtaposed an admonition to labor for the food that endures and the recognition that such food can only be given. In 1 John, too, we read both that those who are born of God do not sin (3:9) and overcome the world (5:4), and also that those who do or love righteousness are born of God (2:29; cf. 4:7; etc.).

15. Pace Preisker, *Ethos* (B), 209.
16. Bultmann, *John*, ad loc.
17. Ibid., 317.
18. Ibid., 159.

Schenke[19] sees the tension in 1 John between sinlessness and sin as expressing the interrelationship of indicative and imperative, but associates it with
the supernatural and natural aspects of the Christian life.[20] It is true that
determination and ethics do not cancel each other out but rather belong
together. It is not clear, however, that the notion of obligation derives specifically from the natural or earthly aspect and thus exists prior to any "theory"
(as he terms the indicative).[21]

4. The same situation appears in the Johannine interpretation of sacrament
and Spirit. Here, too, it is presupposed that human beings are excluded by
nature from salvation and therefore from the new life: "what is born of the
flesh is flesh, and that which is born of the Spirit is spirit" (3:6). But birth
from the spirit, which is rebirth by water and the Spirit (3:5) and being "born
again," is not simply a corrective that makes those who are reborn better; it
can only mean establishment of a totally new human nature. This is a divine
miracle, not a human possibility. If we may cite 1 John 5:1 in this connection,
this rebirth also involves faith: only those who believe or have faith are "born
of God." It follows that there is no more reason to play off sacrament and faith
against each other than indicative and imperative.

The work of the Spirit may be understood in similar terms. The Spirit
blows where it will (John 3:8). It is the Spirit that gives life (6:63), and yet the
following verse (6:64) speaks of the faith that is intimately bound up with
love. If we remember that the Spirit continues the work of Christ, it is clear
that christology and pneumatology together determine how Christians live
and love. But the priority of christology is unmistakable, even in the passages
dealing with the sacraments and above all those that speak of the Spirit. It is
the Spirit in whom Jesus himself returns (cf. 14:16–17, 26) and who recalls
the words of Jesus (cf. 14:26), which is also important for love (cf. 14:18 with
14:23).

5. The greatest difference between John on the one hand and Jesus and
Paul on the other with respect to the indicative of salvation is certainly John's
radical realization of eschatology. Here we must make a distinction between
the Gospel and 1 John. The former espouses an eschatology that refers clearly
to the present (cf. 5:24, 3:36; 6:47; 8:51; 11:25–26). It cannot be denied, of
course, that the author has included remnants of a future hope, quite apart
from the question of whether the Gospel in its present form is original or
most of the references to the future are due to an ecclesiastical redaction.
Even Bultmann ascribes to the evangelist such passages as 14:2, which speaks
of many rooms in the Father's house, to which Christ will bring his followers
(cf. also 12:32; 17:24).

19. Hans-Martin Schenke, "Determination und Ethik im ersten Johannesbrief," *ZThK* 60
(1963): 203–15.
20. Ibid., 215.
21. Ibid., 214.

But Bultmann rightly stresses that John has totally realized and historicized the traditional Jewish-Christian futuristic eschatology. The decisive event has already taken place; all that remains of early Christian cosmic and apocalyptic eschatology is the hope of the individual for the heavenly perfection. Apocalyptic expectation of a coming new world is reduced to anthropological hope, in which—if such passages as 5:28–29 are not secondary interpolations—-the hope of resurrection is also implicit.[22] The crucial point in any event is that those who have faith already have life, the judgment has already taken place, and the future will not bring anything truly new. Here, too, the point of departure and coordinate system is christology: the presence of the one who is the resurrection and the life.[23]

Apart from the christological context, the Gospel scarcely develops directly the ethical consequences of this life in the present. The situation is different in 1 John, where, however, we again find traces of future eschatological expectation, including the Parousia and judgment, motivating Christians to "do righteousness" in conformity to Christ (cf. 1 John 2:28ff.). According to this passage, although hope is linked indissolubly with the salvation of being God's children in the present, "it does not yet appear what we shall be," and the hope that we shall be like him (3:2) leads to corresponding conduct. "Every one who thus hopes in him purifies himself as he is pure," that is, the future of those who hope affects the present, setting Christians free to be pure. And according to John 4:17, those in whom the love of God is perfected can have "confidence for the day of judgment." According to John 4:12 (cf. also 2:5), this includes mutual love within the Christian community.

B. CHRISTOLOGICAL IMPERATIVE

1. If christology is the dominant theme of the Johannine indicative, we should expect a priori that it would have its reflex in the substance of the imperative. And in fact John sees the life of Christians as related fundamentally to Christ. It finds expression in such largely synonymous terms as believe, love, hear, continue, know, come, receive, serve, and follow. The emphasis is not in the first instance on sharing Christ's fate ("Where I am, there shall my servant be" [12:26; cf. 13:36]) or conformity in one's way of life as on remaining with the Lord, who alone has "the words of eternal life" (6:68). As such he is the Son of God, distinct from others, who goes before them and calls them to service and discipleship (cf. 12:26). The Christian's relationship to Christ is dominated not by Jesus' equality but by his priority. Faith, for example, is hearing the voice of Jesus Christ (cf. 10:26–27; 10:4), not a personal and mystical relationship. The Gospel therefore repeatedly calls Christians to hear and obey Christ's word. Continuing in this word is the proof of true discipleship (8:31).

22. Käsemann, *Wille*, 36ff., 146ff.
23. Ibid., 42.

But what is the substance of this word? Bultmann claims that Jesus' words "never convey anything specific and concrete." The theme of his discourses is "always the single fact that the Father has sent him, that he has come as the light, the bread of life, a witness to the truth, etc."[24] More pointedly: "Jesus' words convey no palpable content except that they are words of life, words of God; in other words, it is not their content but the fact that they are his words, the words of him who speaks them, that makes them words of life, words of God."[25] Their crucial uniqueness thus consists in their actually being spoken.

There is truth to this claim insofar as Jesus does not in fact reveal any truths—cosmological, soteriological, or whatever—or any esoteric mysteries. It is also true that we find in the content of his words an unmistakable tendency to reduce everything to christology. Nevertheless, the word of Jesus has "a clearly definable content":[26] the witness of the fathers, the words and ministry of the earthly Jesus—in short, the tradition recorded by John. John is well aware that fanaticism and anarchy would result "if Jesus' word can be determined only through the prophetic spirit and the immediate situation."[27]

2. If we now ask in detail about the content of Jesus' word, the first element bearing on ethics is "keeping the commandments." These commandments, however, are no longer identical with those of the Old Testament. If we compare the ethical instructions of Jesus with those of the Gospel of John, we notice at once that the law no longer plays any role as a guide to conduct.[28] Of course the Johannine Jesus refers occasionally to the law—standing by synecdoche for the Old Testament as a whole—but only in the sense that the law already points to Christ.

This point is made by Philip's words to Nathanael: "We have found him of whom Moses in the law and also the prophets wrote, Jesus of Nazareth, the son of Joseph" (1:45). In Jesus the Old Testament hope for salvation is fulfilled. Of course Nathanael's skepticism ("Can anything good come out of Nazareth?" [v. 46]) shows that even here the witness to Christ does not take the form of an exegetical demonstration: there is much support for objections based on tradition. Is the Messiah not to be of Davidic lineage and to come from Bethlehem, the city of David?

We may conclude that Jesus not only fulfills the promises but shatters them; therefore Christ and Moses can be presented antithetically (1:17; cf. also 6:32; 9:28). This combination of destruction and fulfillment also appears in 5:39: "You search the scriptures, because you think that in them you have eternal life; and it is they that bear witness to me." Occupation with the

24. *Theology* (B), 2:62.
25. Ibid. 2:63.
26. Käsemann, *Wille*, 102.
27. Ibid., 102; cf. 82–83.
28. See Severino Pancaro, *The Law in the Fourth Gospel* (Leiden: Brill, 1975); Ulrich Luz and Rudolf Smend, *Gesetz* (Stuttgart: Kohlhammer, 1981), 119ff.

Scriptures does not guarantee eternal life, for "the scriptures as such are of no value . . ., they give life only insofar as they bear witness to the one who is the life."[29] Searching the Scriptures can in fact cause us to miss the voice of Jesus. On the other hand, it is already Christ who speaks in the Scriptures. If people really would listen to Moses, they would also believe in Christ (5:46). If they do not, Moses becomes their accuser (5:45). According to Luz,[30] John consciously distinguishes between the law ("almost a Jewish term") and the Scriptures ("the Old Testament in its true sense, namely as a witness to Christ").

There are a few other passages bearing more directly on the realm of conduct, above all those dealing with Jesus' failure to observe the Sabbath (cf. 5:9, 16–18; 7:22–23; 9:14–16). These transgressions, which call into question the Torah as well as the Sabbath, bring not only Jesus (5:16; 9:16) but also those he heals into conflict with the Sabbath commandment (5:10; 9:15, 18, 34); those who are healed ascribe this to Jesus' power and authority (5:11; 9:15, 30ff.). Of course Sabbath observance is no longer a real problem; the conflicts are meant primarily to emphasize the uniqueness of Jesus.[31] In 7:19ff., conversely, the evangelist describes the Jews as breaking the law while appealing in error to Moses: they circumcise on the Sabbath, but condemn Jesus for healing on the Sabbath.

The argument is not entirely clear in detail. Verse 19 accuses the Jews of transgressing the law of Moses, whereas v. 23 accuses them of breaking the Sabbath commandment by circumcising in obedience to the law of Moses. According to Bultmann, the only possible interpretation that makes sense of the whole passage is this: "The Jews break the law of Moses because, although they are trying to obey the law of circumcision, they do not ask what Moses' real intent was."[32]

We must therefore distinguish the apparent meaning of the law from its true meaning. When we read in 8:17, "In your law it is written that the testimony of two men is true," the context almost turns the words into mockery. The sense of alienation is already clear from the expression "in your law."[33] Overall we find a dominant conviction that the revelation of grace and salvation is superior to the revelation of the law (cf. 1:17). The Old Testament is not considered binding in the sense of its moral injunctions and examples. Indeed, the term "commandment" is reserved for the injunctions of Jesus. The law has no significance for ethics. We do not even find the law of love as the focus and summary of the law. Luz is therefore right in denying that John

---

29. On John 5:39, see Walter Bauer, *Das Johannesevangelium*, 3d ed., HNT 6; similar views are espoused by Bultmann, *John*, and Jürgen Becker, *Das Evangelium nach Johannes*, 2 vols. (Gütersloh: Echter, 1979–81).
30. Luz and Smend, *Gesetz*, 120.
31. Becker, *Evangelium*, 233.
32. *John*, 278; cf. Pancaro, *Law*, 136–37.
33. See Walter Gutbrod, "nomos," *TDNT* 4:1084.

sees any continuity, direct or indirect, between the law of the Old Testament and Christian ethics.[34]

Only in 1 John 3:12 do we find mention of Cain's fratricide as a negative example: he "murdered" his brother because he was challenged by the latter's righteous deeds. This is intended to show the community that there is good reason why it, too, should feel the world's hatred. Especially if the casual introduction of this example, which is not intended as a model for the community, presupposes some knowledge of the Old Testament, it is all the more striking that this is the only example.

3. For John, it is self-evident that Jesus' commandments are inseparable from his person. His words and actions, what he says and what he does, are seen together (cf. 8:28; 14:10). Both are binding upon the disciples and guide them. Christology is the crucial foundation even in the case of the imperative; this is confirmed above all by the observation that conformity to Jesus' conduct is a basic theme of Johannine ethics. God's saving act in Jesus Christ is not only a central motif, the only thing that makes Christian love possible, it is also the absolute criterion of this love. It is clearly stated with respect to motivation that the Son can do nothing without the Father (5:19) and the disciples can do nothing without the Son (15:5); this is also reflected in the nature of what they do. The frequent repetition of "as" is characteristic: on the one hand, it reflects the relationship of the Father to Jesus and of Jesus to the disciples; on the other, it confronts Jesus' followers with Jesus' own conduct as an exemplary realization of Christian life.[35] Jesus loves his disciples and sends them, just as the Father loved him (15:9; 17:23) and sent him into the world (17:18; 20:21). Furthermore, many clear examples establish a substantial parallelism between Jesus and his followers. The identity of terminology, which naturally must be partial if only on account of the difference between "master and servant" (cf. 13:16; 17:11), underlines the correspondence. The exemplary character of Jesus as a prototype for his disciples extends to all aspects of his earthly life, including his surrender to death. The most frequently cited facet is love: as Jesus loved his own, so his own are to love each other.

A particularly vivid and impressive example is the pericope that describes Jesus' washing of his disciples' feet. Here Jesus' action is explicitly called a model and example (13:15); in other words, it has exemplary significance. "For I have given you an example, that you also should do as I have done to you."

The traditio-historical problems connected with this pericope, which bear upon its ethical relevance, are highly controversial. According to Bultmann, vv. 4–11 constitute a first interpretation, deriving from the evangelist himself. In vv. 12–20, however, we have a second interpretation, supposedly pre-

---

34. Luz and Smend, *Gesetz*, 124.
35. See Olivier de Dinechin, "Kathos," *Recherches de science religieuse* 58 (1970): 195–236.

Johannine. Richter[36] considers vv. 6–11 with their soteriological interpretation of the footwashing, as well as 13:3—14:31, to be Johannine and considers vv. 12–20, as well as v. 1b, a redactional addition by the later editor, which
nevertheless draws on pre-Johannine tradition. Thyen proposes a different
analysis:[37] the second interpretation is not pre-Johannine but is a reinterpretation of the first by the author of chapter 21. Now Jesus' action is "no
longer an unworldly *sēmeion*," as in the more dualistic basic document, but
"*is also* an exemplary demonstration of humble service to the lowly."[38]
Weiser,[39] too, is at least right in maintaining that other soteriological and
christological passages in John also introduce a call to mimesis (see, e.g.,
12:25–26 following 12:24). Compare also 1 John 3:16: "By this we know love,
that he laid down his life for us; and we ought to lay down our lives for the
brethren." Here, too, soteriological and ethical interpretation go hand in
hand, so that it is unnecessary to call the relation in John 13 artificial.[40]
Wittenberger also considers the separation of christology and parenesis totally un-Johannine.[41] There is some conflict between service to and service of
the disciples, but the different accents are intended to be complementary.[42]

Whether or not the first, soteriological interpretation in vv. 6–11 is specifically Johannine, many parallel statements confirm that the second, ethical
interpretation comports well with John's thoughts. If we consider that washing someone's feet is a menial service assigned to slaves—a concrete, physical, dirty business, far removed from the liturgical action performed as a
solemn ceremony by bishops and abbots, popes and emperors—Jesus here
demeans himself to perform a degrading and humiliating act of love. And just
by doing so he sets an example. The fact that he is also something more, that
the "as" is constitutive as well as exemplary, does not alter this observation a
jot. In 13:34, too, where the "new commandment" is given—"that you love
one another even as I have loved you, that you also love one another"—the
love displayed by Jesus is not only the basis for love within the community, it
is also paradigmatic of its nature and manner (cf. also 15:12). Just as only
those who are loved can love, so those who love are bound by Jesus' example
of love. Bultmann's statement that Jesus' washing of the disciples' feet is to be
understood as a symbolic act representing the service of love in all its forms[43]

36. See Georg Richter, *Die Fusswaschung im Johannes-Evangelium* (Regensburg: Pustet, 1967).
37. Hartwig Thyen, "Joh. 13 und die 'kirchliche Redaktion' des vierten Evangeliums," in
Tradion und Glaube (Festschrift Karl Georg Kuhn), ed. G. Jeremias, H. W. Kuhn, and H.
Stegemann (Göttingen: Vandenhoeck & Ruprecht, 1971), 343–56.
38. Ibid., 350.
39. Alfons Weiser, "Joh. 13, 12–20: Zufügung eines späteren Herausgebers?" *BZ* 12 (1968):
252–57.
40. See also Collins, "Commandment," 353–54; Wittenberger, "Ort," 56ff.
41. Wittenberger, "Ort," 62–63.
42. On 1 John 3:16, see Siegfried Schulz, *Das Evangelium nach Johannes*, NTD 4.
43. On John 13:4–11, see Bultmann, *John*, 466–73.

must not be allowed to spiritualize the exemplary concreteness of this service of love.

In 1 John, Jesus' exemplary model is pictured in other terms besides the vocabulary of love. According to 1 John 3:7, those who do right (or "righteousness") are "righteous, just as he is righteous." Here Christ is exemplary in practicing righteousness, which is also binding upon his followers. Doing righteousness is the opposite of doing sin (v. 8), and v. 10 links it together with Christian love. In any case, the conduct of those who believe is meant to conform to the conduct of Jesus, just as 1 John 3:3 states that all should purify themselves "just as he is pure." Finally, 1 John 2:6 speaks of this conformity in quite fundamental and general terms, calling Jesus the prototype and model of the Christian life: "He who says he abides in him ought to walk in the same way in which he walked."

Schnackenburg is probably right to interpret this statement in the context of v. 4, which speaks of keeping the commandments. He writes: "Thus the general requirement to keep the commandments (which a devout Jew could also insist on) takes on a specifically Christian stamp. No general law code— not even the revered Decalogue—provides the immediate guideline for Christian conduct, but the personal instruction of Christ, and not only his word, but also the example of his life."[44] This anticipates the new commandment of love (1 John 2:7–8). Conformity to Christ and to his love determines the entire way Christians live. According to 1 John 3:16, this extends to actual sacrifice of one's life, the extreme case that exemplifies the normal case taken to its limit.

C. SEPARATION FROM THE WORLD AND FREEDOM FROM SIN

1. Critical separation from the world, a fundamental theme of Johannine ethics, is also connected with christology. Christ is alien to this world to an unexampled degree; he can be thought of properly only from outside the world, in which he merely "tabernacles" (John 1:14). Therefore his kingdom is not of this world (17:18), and Christians accordingly are not of this world (15:19; 17:14, 16), but are exposed to the same hatred shown by the world as he (15:18). The sharp contrast between the Christian community and the world (identified by several scholars only with the basic stratum of the Gospel) has significant ethical consequences. Even though Johannine dualism is not solely ethical, this dualism is documented ethically in the contrast between "doing evil" and "doing what is true" (3:20–21).

The Johannine writings are permeated by a dualism of light and darkness, truth and falsehood, above and below, spirit and flesh, and so forth. This dualism frequently recalls the radical dualism of Gnosticism, but John's belief in creation and incarnational soteriology preclude its association with a sharp

44. Rudolf Schnackenburg, *Die Johannesbriefe*, 2d ed., HThK 13, 105.

metaphysical antithesis between God and the world.[45] Since all things were created by the divine *logos* (1:3) and since the Word (*logos*) itself became flesh (1:4) and came into the world as "to its own home" (1:11), the physical universe and flesh cannot simply be identified with sin.

Nevertheless, no sharper dualism is found within the New Testament. It is characteristic that statements about creation appear only in the prologue and that John's picture of hope has no room for the world; expectation of a restored creation has been totally surrendered. Of course John speaks of God's love for the world (3:16), but the idea expressed in 3:16 is not taken up or developed elsewhere, and nowhere are ethical consequences derived from it.[46] Of course it is God's purpose to save the world (12:47), but when it is saved it is not renewed or restored as it was at creation, but rather "overcome" by faith (1 John 5:4). In fact it ceases to be the world.

The whole world is in the power of the evil one (1 John 5:19) and is called pejoratively "this world" (John 8:23; 9:39; 12:31; 16:11; 18:36). It is ruled by sin (16:8) or Satan (12:37); it is darkness (1:9; 8:12) and loves only its own (15:19). Of course the human world usually stands in the forefront, but the world is ipso facto a world that shuts out God, a negative quantity.

Christians are not called to shut themselves up in a ghetto. Nor are they taken out of the world, but are sent into it (17:18; 20:21)—not to engage in mysticism, contemplation, or cultic ceremonies, but in order "to enter into the labor" (4:38) and share in Jesus' work (14:12), which means primarily witness and love. But the world is expressly excluded from intercession, for example (17:9). Its social relationships are totally and rigorously disregarded. Christians should involve themselves as little as possible in the world. Ultimately it is of interest only as a setting and stage, but it remains dangerous as a source of infection and an agent of persecution.

2. It is therefore only logical that we should find the following parenetic exhortation in 1 John 2:15–17: "Do not love the world or the things in the world. If anyone loves the world, love for the Father is not in him. For all that is in the world, the lust of the flesh and the lust of the eyes and the pride of life, is not of the Father but is of the world. And the world passes away, and the lust of it; but he who does the will of God abides for ever."

This passage expresses Christian separation from the world and superiority to the world on unmistakable terms; "the believer and the hostile world" are in fact irreconcilable (L. Schottroff). This is more than a warning against the wiles of the world and more than a call to live by grace. All that is in the world is transitory and can only distract Christians from what makes their lives authentic: God's love. When one starts from the unreality of everything

---

45. See Karl-Wolfgang Tröger, "Ja oder Nein zur Welt," *Theologische Versuche* 7 (1976): 61–80; Günther Baumbach, "Gemeinde und Welt im Johannes-Evangelium," *Kairos* 14 (1972): 121–36.
46. Wittenberger, "Ort," 40.

worldly, it is hardly possible to achieve a perspective that is open to the world and affirms it. The author sees almost nothing but what is insignificant and indeed hostile to God—the lust of the flesh, the lust of the eyes, bragging over wealth. Only the last of these, an ostentatious style of life, appears to presuppose that the world and what is in it are not ipso facto negative but are made negative by egoistic glorification and antisocial exaggeration. The evil of the other two examples of worldly conduct obviously does not derive from their blinding Christians to God's love and thus making Christian love impossible: they are evil ipso facto and a priori.

This does not rule out the possibility that it is actually John's opponents who maintain their superiority to the world, disparaging social and material values because "they do not have to worry about material security" and have made a clear distinction between "their exalted spiritual consciousness and their worldly affairs."[47] Spiritualization of solidarity also founders on 3:17, which condemns refusal of the bare necessities to those in need. The author's concession to a Spartan or puritanical life style and his polemic against all desire for luxury nevertheless do not constitute a positive estimate of worldly goods.

It is therefore dubious whether victory over the world (1 John 5:4) means merely victory over "ungodly worldliness" and 1 John 2:15 is really "no more hostile or open to the world and no more 'dualistic' than Matt. 6:24."[48] But the author seems to mean more than an either/or in this latter sense. He appears to see something wrong in involvement in worldly affairs as such, an involvement that, like everything pertaining to the world, is neither true nor enduring. This observation is illustrated by two examples from the Gospel.

3. The first is the account of Jesus' trial, which documents the fact that no accommodation is possible between the Redeemer and the world together with its political representatives. The Johannine account of Jesus' trial makes it clear that the political authorities are quite unable to maintain objective neutrality toward Jesus. By nature and origin, Jesus' "kingdom" is not an earthly political kingdom (cf. John 12:36; 18:36; 6:15). The very fact that the "witness to the truth" (18:37) is put on trial by the representative of the state demonstrates abuse of political office. Despite his efforts to achieve justice, Pilate, who represents the kingdom of this world, cannot recognize the truth when confronted with its claims or the kingdom that is not of this world (18:38–39). It would not be accurate simply to say that Jesus' kingdom is not political: the unworldly nature of this kingdom "touches the political sphere at its roots and calls it into question."[49] But even though Jesus' kingdom is

47. Klaus Wengst, *Häresie und Orthodoxie im Spiegel des ersten Johannesbriefes* (Gütersloh: Mohn, 1976), 59.
48. Wachs, *Ethik*, 62ff.
49. Josef Blank, "Die Verhandlung vor Pilatus Joh. 18,28—19,16 im Lichte johanneischer Theologie," *BZ* 3 (1959): 60–81, quotation from 70. See also Aland, "Verhältnis" (B5), 170–71.

not limited to the realm of subjectivity,[50] it appears to be fundamentally at odds with the state; the "metaphysical" confrontation is inescapable. The evangelist is therefore unwilling to concede that Pilate's political office comes "from above," as 19:11 is often wrongly held to claim. Jesus says to Pilate, "You would have no power over me unless it [the situation, not the power] had been given you from above." These words are not meant to stress that the procurator was appointed by the emperor or that his official function and political authority were established by God. The emphasis is rather on the fact that Pilate is an instrument to realize God's plan (cf. 8:20; 11:50–51; 18:11).

The second example is John 4. Whether the narrative of Jesus' encounter with the Samaritan woman at Jacob's well in John 4 incorporates an ancient tradition in which Jesus overcomes the barriers of religious nationalism separating Jews from Samaritans is not certain. This analysis would jibe with what we know of Jesus' openness to the tax collectors, sinners, and prostitutes who were castigated as heretics.[51] But even if the tradition were much more extensive and this background irrelevant to the ideas of the evangelist, the message is clear.

According to John 4, the tension between Jews and Samaritans does not represent any problem at all. The choice of cultic centers is an outmoded internal problem, like the other differences between Jews and Samaritans. The Father is not worshiped rightly either on Gerizim or in Jerusalem, but in spirit and in truth. Jesus' purpose is not "to attack the barriers of worldly hatred; he has no interest in problems that for him are merely superficial and earthly."[52] In the evangelist's narrative, Jesus says nothing of earthly water (despite asking for water, he does not drink). He speaks of a totally different reality, which the woman does not understand. Nor is he hungry: his food consists of doing the will of God (4:31ff.), and even on the cross he thirsts only in order that the Scriptures may be fulfilled (19:28).

In a similar manner, the miraculous feeding is not associated, as in the Synoptic accounts, with Jesus' pity for the crowd that lacks a shepherd or suffers want (Mark 6:34; 8:2). Its sole purpose is to demonstrate Jesus' glory (John 2:11) and self-revelation (6:1ff.). The other miracles, too, are not so much concrete aid for those in need as symbols and illustrations of what is intended to be transparent in the earthly sphere. Jesus' healing of the blind shows that he is the light of the world. His raising of Lazarus shows that he is the resurrection and life. Even the most materialistic miracles merely point to the transcendent world. For John, there is no salvation within the reality of

50. See Bultmann, *John*, 657; and the comments of Dieter Lührmann, "Der Staat und die Verkündigung," in *Theologia Crucis, Signum Crucis* (Festschrift Erich Dinkler), ed. C. Andressen and G. Klein (Tübingen: Mohr, 1979), 359–75.
51. Luise Schottroff, "Joh. 4,5–15 und die Konsequenzen des johanneischen Dualismus," *ZNW* 60 (1969): 199–214.
52. Ibid., 206.

this world. All earthly goods are illusory and false; natural life is not authentic life.[53]

This is also the point of 6:63, which states that the spirit gives life, whereas the flesh is of no avail. John does not say that the flesh kills or is opposed to God. But it is transitory, worthless, irrelevant, inauthentic—it counts for nothing when weighed against heavenly reality, which is all that matters. Here, too, the doctrine of creation sets up a final barrier that is never crossed, although John comes perilously close to doing so. We cannot ignore the dangers of Johannine dualism. When all the concrete demands and basic necessities of life are dismissed as inauthentic and separation from the world is demanded, we have little in common with the earthly Jesus. Jesus, too, resists entanglement with the world, but he also resists separation from the world. Only when we remain between these two extremes are we close to Jesus and his kingdom.

4. The Johannine writings were unable to sustain this dualism totally; the antithesis of love and hate, life and death, for instance, clearly could not be made congruent with that of sinlessness and sin. In principle, of course, freedom from the world means freedom from sin, a freedom given by the Son (8:36). Here "sin" is not so much immorality and wickedness (5:14; 8:34) as unbelief (8:24; 16:9), which 1 John also identifies with absence of love and community solidarity (cf. 1 John 3:14ff.).

The situation grows more complex, however, when we examine other statements in 1 John. Here we find alongside the promised freedom from sin the realization that believers are quite capable of sinning. There are also fundamental distinctions in the concept of sin. On the one hand, we are told once again that "no one born of God commits sin" (1 John 3:9). On the other hand, 1:8 states that "if we say we have no sin, we deceive ourselves, and the truth is not in us." The same apparent contradiction is repeated immediately in a single verse: "I am writing this to you so that you may not sin; but if any one does sin, we have an advocate with the Father, Jesus Christ the righteous; and he is the expiation for our sins" (2:1).

Here we have an obvious paradox, which is cited with good reason as the scriptural basis for Luther's *simul iustus simul peccator:* Christians are both righteous and sinful, and therefore need to be forgiven every day.[54]

This dialectic of sinfulness and sinlessness is by no means to be understood as an expression of static resignation. We must note in the first place that the author is clearly attacking the claim of gnostic fanatics that those who are spiritual are no longer able to sin. The author does not attack this claim directly (cf. 3:9), but seeks to emphasize that Christians must always remain

---

53. Bultmann, *John*, 181.
54. See Ernst Käsemann, "Ketzer und Zeuge," in *Exegetische Versuche und Besinnungen,* 2 vols. (Göttingen: Vandenhoeck & Ruprecht, 1960–65), 1:168–87, esp. 182; Wittenberger, "Ort," 112–13; Klaus Wengst, *Der erste, zweite und dritte Brief des Johannes,* ÖTK 16, 55ff.

obedient to the Word. Therefore 1:10 reaffirms the point of 1:8: "If we say we have not sinned, we make him a liar, and his word is not in [or: among] us." But the evangelist also stresses that what makes clean is the Word (John 15:3). Christians are constantly dependent on this Word. The warning not to accept the alleged sinlessness of false perfectionists (1 John 1:8, 10) is further underscored by the admonition never to relent in the struggle against sin (2:1). The warning against claims of sinlessness is intended to assist the struggle against the power of sin and darkness, not to discount in advance all efforts to live in the light and in mutual fellowship (cf. 1:7). At the same time, those defeated in the struggle can find new courage and new strength. The paradox does not promote either defeatism or false confidence; its purpose is parenetic. It is intended to mobilize Christians for the battle against sin.

5. In this discussion of the problem posed by sin as a fact of life for Christians, the distinction in 1 John 5:16–17 between different types of sin is more problematic and theologically questionable. The plural in 2:1 is unobjectionable; it indicates that sinning can involve more than deficient faith or love. But 5:16–17 goes on to distinguish between "sin that is mortal" and "sin that is not mortal." The preceding two verses speak without qualification of praying and the assurance that God will hear our prayers. Verses 16–17, however, say that we should pray only for those whose sin is not "mortal." This assumes a significant difference among sins.

Scholars usually assume that this distinction reflects a distinction made by the Old Testament and Judaism, which could also call unpardonable sins "mortal." This expression refers to the difference between accidental sins and deliberate sin, which is punishable by death (cf. Lev. 4:2ff.; 5:1ff.; Jub. 21:22; 26:34). A similar distinction appears in Heb. 10:26. We cannot determine precisely what the author of 1 John had in mind by "mortal sin." Besides deliberate transgressions, various suggestions have been made: heresy (cf. the polemic against heretics and especially 5:21, the concluding verse), especially heinous sins like murder (cf. 3:15), or apostasy (cf. Heb. 6:4ff.; Hermas Similitudes 6.2.3).

The basic problem, however, remains this momentous distinction itself. It contradicts both 1 John 1:5—2:2 and 3:4–10, which maintain that we are always in need of forgiveness and that the blood of Jesus "cleanses us from all sin" (1:7). And could there be a more significant description of sin than the statement that those who sin show thereby that they are not born of God (3:4ff.)? It would be wrong, however, to jump to hasty conclusions. We must note explicitly that our criticism of 1 John 5:16–17, however justified, does not imply that individual actions and omissions do not matter, that, because we are all sinners at every moment, we need not always be too particular and that all distinctions are superfluous and meaningless. But the distinction between sins that can and cannot be forgiven and the restriction of intercession to those that can is quite another matter and goes far beyond such necessary distinctions. Here, as in the problem of apostate repentance (Heb. 6:4–6), criticism of the author's position is inescapable.

D. THE COMMANDMENT OF
BROTHERLY LOVE

1. When discussing Jesus as examplar and model, we repeatedly faced the question of what is actually required of Christians. According to John, Christian duty can be summed up in a single phrase: brotherly love. Although the initiative for love clearly lies with God and this commandment does not represent a statutory law, the author does not hesitate to speak explicitly of commandments, both singular and plural. Besides hearing the Word and abiding in the Word, nothing is more characteristic of the Christian life in John's eyes than "keeping the commandments." Those who love Jesus keep his commandments (John 14:15, 21; 15:10; 1 John 2:3–4), and the love of God consists in obeying God's commandments (1 John 5:2–3). The commandments of Jesus are identical with the commandments of God (cf. 1 John 3:22–24). When Christians keep the commandments, their obedience corresponds to Jesus' keeping of the Father's commandments: "If you keep my commandments, you will abide in my love, just as I have kept my Father's commandments" (John 15:10). But according to John 12:49–50, these commandments (plural) of the Father are a single commandment: "The Father who sent me has himself given me commandment what to say and what to speak." The situation with respect to the commandments given the disciples by Jesus is analogous. They, too, are not a jumble comprising every conceivable injunction; the plural merely expresses the various forms in which the one commandment is fulfilled.[55] In the last analysis, the commandments are but a single commandment, and this single commandment is the law of love. "This is my commandment, that you love one another as I have loved you" (15:12).

2. This commandment of love is termed a "new commandment" in 13:34. But what is new about it? Exegetes differ widely on this point, finding the novelty in the commandment's centrality, its restricted domain, the totality required in its fulfillment, its christological basis and character, its eschatological dimension, or the like.

According to Behm,[56] what is unique about the new commandment is that "the obligation of the disciples to love is based on the love of Jesus they have experienced." Schnackenburg,[57] citing John 13:34–35 and 1 John 2:8; 3:16, holds that the commandment "takes its 'newness' from Jesus' 'ultimate' love in sacrificing his life." Bauer[58] claims that the love commandment can be

55. See Gottlieb Schrenk, "entolē," *TDNT* 2:553–54; Wittenberger, "Ort," 138.
56. Johannes Behm, "kainos," *TDNT* 3:450.
57. Rudolf Schnackenburg, "Mitmenschlichkeit im Horizont des NT," in *Die Zeit Jesu* (Festschrift Heinrich Schlier), ed. G. Bornkamm (Freiburg: Herder, 1970), 70–92, esp. 78.
58. On John 15:12, see Walter Bauer, *Das Johannesevangelium*, 3d ed., HNT 6.

called new despite Lev. 19:18 "because in the preaching of Jesus and early Christian ethics it plays a totally different role than in the Old Testament." Lattke[59] suggests that the term "new" derives from the tradition of the Lord's Supper ("new covenant"). According to Bultmann,[60] the love commandment is new "not as a newly discovered principle or cultural ideal proclaimed by Jesus in the world"—in other words, neither with respect to the Old Testament nor to pagan antiquity—but as an ontological predicate. Wachs[61] follows Bultmann: "new" does not refer to historical uniqueness. The love commandment is new because it reflects the eschatological time of salvation.

All of these views have something to recommend them, although they disagree on many points. It is certainly true that the basis of the commandment is new: usually John does not call the love commandment "new," but refers to it as Jesus' own ("my") commandment (15:12; cf. 14:15, 21; 15:10). The christological element is therefore crucial, as the constitutive "as" in 15:12 suggests (cf. 13:15). It is also true that "new" is primarily an eschatological predicate. It appears in such contexts as "new covenant," "new song," "new creation," designating an eschatological quality. The law of love is "new" because "the true light is already shining" (1 John 2:8). Love is a sign of realized eschatology, an essential element implicit in the new reality of Christ.

This does not answer the question of whether a historical aspect is ruled out or implicit. Wachs continues the discussion as follows: "Even if 'new' designates a relationship that is qualitative rather than temporal, what is qualitatively new becomes 'new' in a temporal sense when it enters into history in the Christ event or in the conversion of an individual."[62] In support of this position he cites 1 John 2:7–8: "Beloved, I am writing you no new commandment, but an old commandment which you had from the beginning; the old commandment is the word which you have heard. Yet I am writing you a new commandment, which is true in him and in you."[63]

Here more than perhaps anywhere else we are forced to confront the difference between the Gospel of John and 1 John. For the author of 1 John, the law of love already possesses a Christian tradition, deriving from the authoritative beginnings to which the author calls the readers to return. In other words, he sees chronological significance in the temporal attributes. The commandment that is eschatologically "new" is also old, in that it can look back on a recorded history. According to Collins,[64] this view may be directed against gnostic opponents who offer experiences of spiritual novelty while ignoring love. There is an interesting difference between 1 John and 2

59. *Einheit*, 217.
60. Bultmann, *John*, 526.
61. *Ethik*, 51.
62. Ibid., 51–52.
63. See Klein, "Licht," 304ff.
64. "Commandment," 243.

John in this regard, in that the latter even says: "Not as though I were writing you a new commandment, but the one we have had from the beginning, that we love one another" (2 John 5). Here the historical and chronological perspective has taken over completely: the traditional nature of the commandment guarantees its authority and truth. Furthermore, doubts as to whether echoes of such a temporal element can already be heard in the Gospel do not prevent us from asking whether there is not a new element in the way love finds expression.

See above, pp. 73ff., for a discussion of the law of love in Judaism and especially the meaning of "neighbor." It is undoubtedly true that philanthropy and charity were also practiced in the Hellenistic world, even though the "neighbor" was seen more as a means of self-fulfillment and the *philia* of the Greeks denoted primarily eros, sympathy, and self-promotion. In this sense, a radically selfless love would be something historically new.

3. In John especially, "new" is a totally unsuitable description of love in this radical sense, because in John the radical inclusiveness of "neighbor" found in Jesus has vanished once more. As the object of *agapē* we find neither neighbor nor enemy but other Christians ("brother," "brethren"), as in 1 John, or "one another," as in the Gospel. Various attempts have been made to mitigate this observation, but they are not persuasive. It is not legitimate, for instance, to interpret "brother" as referring to one's neighbors in general rather than to fellow Christians. The close connection between discipleship and love (13:35) or brotherhood and being born from God (1 John 4:20ff.) rules out such an interpretation. One might still ask, of course, whether the analogy to God's love does not imply a universality of Christian love. John 3:16, for example, speaks of God's love for the world. But we must remember that 3:16 is unique (despite 1:29; 4:42; 6:33). Nowhere does the Gospel make God's universal love a standard for the life of the Christian community. Despite the notion of mission, there is no immediate parallel to God's sending of Jesus to save the world (3:17; 12:47). To abide in Jesus' love (15:9) means to keep his commandments (15:10), but these commandments speak only of loving one another (15:12). Of course a community living in solidarity can exercise an attraction and represent a challenge to the world despite its concentration on its internal life. But it is not clear that this is what John has in mind. Furthermore, the point would be more convincing if this solidarity did not draw a line at the boundaries of the community.

Those authors are probably correct who criticize John for narrowing the law of love from "neighbors" to "brethren" or for defining "unmistakable limits."[65] Wendland, too, rightly sees "a substantial reduction and onesidedness" in comparison with the Sermon on the Mount or the conduct of the Good Samaritan. Explanations of this tendency toward restrictiveness remain

---

65. Besides Käsemann, *Wille,* see also Collins, "Commandment," 235–36; Morris, "Love," 40 n. 1; Lattke, *Einheit,* 206ff.

hypothetical. Many authors speculate about concrete historical causes for the restriction or propose form-critical considerations.

Bultmann, for example, seeks to explain the commandment to love one another from the specific perspective of the farewell discourses: this is the bequest of the departing Lord to the eschatological community. It lives among the members in their mutual love through the gift of his love.[66] According to Collins, the farewell discourses typically comprise admonitions urging unity within the Christian community and mutual love.[67] The testamentary nature of these injunctions is undoubtedly significant and lends greater authority to the law of love. This observation does not suffice, however, since 1 John speaks of mutual love rather than love of neighbors without any reference to the farewell discourses.

Wachs finds a different explanation arising from an acute need. In his view, the situation among the readers of the Gospel should be thought of as resembling that addressed by Gal. 5:3–15: "Ardent love for enemies or neighbors is pointless if the Christian community is rent by mutual hostility or enmity."[68] The polemic against heretics in 1 John can easily suggest a concrete absence of love within the community, but it is hardly likely that such a problem is also acute in the Gospel.

The most likely background, as in the *philadelphia* of 1 Peter, would be persecution. In such a situation it is always reasonable for the persecuted community to close ranks. Persecution could also account for dualistic separatism. John 9:22; 12:42; and 16:2 show that an unbridgeable chasm has opened between the Christian community and the Jewish synagogue and that the Christians have been ejected from the synagogue because of their confession.[69]

Wengst[70] has focused on the inclusion of an anathema against heretics in the Jewish Eighteen Benedictions, pointing out its consequences in all areas of life, including economics (exclusion from commerce, occupational training, etc.). Such measures undoubtedly intensified the atmosphere of fear (cf. 3:1–2; 9:22; 19:38). Such a crisis indeed reinforces the solidarity of the community, a solidarity that is necessary if the community is to survive in the face of oppression and apostasy.[71]

It is therefore quite possible for a situation of outward crisis and persecution to induce the community to close ranks, but this does not in itself

66. Bultmann, *John*, 527–28.
67. "Commandment," 258.
68. *Ethik*, 61.
69. See Wolfgang Schrage, "aposynagōgos," *TNDT* 7:852.
70. Klaus Wengst, *Bedrängte Gemeinde und verherrlichter Christus*, 2d ed. (Neukirchen: Neukirchener Verlag, 1983), 48ff.
71. See also Wittenberger, "Ort," 31–32; Sanders, *Ethics*, 93; Morris, "Love," 37–38; also Thyen, "Brüder," 354 n. 32, according to whom the Christian communities had no other choice than to "form a cadre and concentrate on love within the community" if they were to survive at all.

legitimize a particularistic conventicle ethics—which is what "loving one another" actually comes down to.

This conclusion needs to be stated somewhat more precisely. In the first place, restriction of love to members of the community is indeed quite different from the sectarian hatred of outsiders found at Qumran; others are not explicitly excluded from love or "hated" (e.g., it is a commonplace to point out that Judas was among those whose feet Jesus washed). It is also true that the disciples are intended to carry the missionary message of God's love into the world, so that the mission of the disciples occurs within the setting of this divine love; in this sense, everyone is "potentially" included in "one another." It is also true that John sees love as proceeding from the Word and associated with the Word, so that it implies dialogue and communication.[72] The social nature of love within the community is analogous to the relationship of Christ to the Father. If the love with which God loved the Son is to abide in them (17:26), the communicative and reciprocal nature of love is understood (cf. the insistence on unity in 17:11–12), not a mere turning inward: for the Father loves not only the Son but also the world. But here we note once again that the statement in John 3:16 is not generally given full force; normally the love of God is "perfected" in mutual love (1 John 4:12). The problem of how far love extends remains a problem.

4. Our conclusions can be much more positive with respect to the meaning and substance of love in John. For him, too, love is clearly the highest demand, if not the sole demand, made of Christians. We do read occasionally of true love as the opposite of loving darkness (3:19), human praise (12:43), or one's own (15:19). The real dichotomy, however, is love and hate. Like light and darkness, life and death, love and hate belong to fundamentally different worlds. Therefore hate, which is the same as wanting to be oneself at the expense of others, can be identified with murder: "Anyone who hates his brother is a murderer" (1 John 3:15). Hate is therefore a sign that those who hate do not belong to the community, whereas love is a criterion for recognizing Jesus' disciples. This is true for both recognition within the community and recognition by others: John 13:15 says that "all" will recognize the disciples by their love. We find much the same idea in 1 John 3:14, which speaks of the assurance that comes through love: "We know that we have passed out of death into life, because we love the brethren." Love is the sign par excellence that one belongs to the sphere of life and salvation in which the disciples dwell.

The fact that love transcends the realm of ethics does not mean that there is no ethical dimension in what John says about love within the community. For John, too, love is not an emotion or an affect, not a theory or an idea, but simply living for others. The absence of a perspective on the world at large

72. See Käsemann, *Wille*, 127–28, 129.

must not cause us to overlook the fact that for John, too, love implies concrete behavior (cf. the washing of the disciples' feet, which is itself a demonstration of love). This love is so radical a demand that it can lead to sacrifice of one's own life: there is no greater love than to lay down one's life for one's friends (15:13), a statement that 1 John 3:16 applies to the disciples. "The extraordinary can teach us the commitment demanded in daily life."[73]

The ethics of 1 John, however, does not limit itself to ultimate sacrifice or deal solely with ethical high points; it also confronts the concrete demands of daily life with its needs and requirements, which put the solidarity of love to the test: "If any one has the world's goods and sees his brother in need, yet closes his heart against him, how does God's love abide in him?" (1 John 3:17). This shows clearly that for Johannine ethics, which often appears so abstract and theoretical, too ready to come to terms with dualism, love is not something poetic, not merely something radical: it is something very prosaic, concrete, material, earthly, and corporeal. Here, fortunately, we find an absolute limit standing in the way of any spiritualizing tendency to consider everything earthly as less than authentic. When suffering members of the community are not given palpable help in their everyday earthly need, love is not present. The author does not ask whether a feeling of unity or solidarity may not be present, or whether motives and intentions are pure. Those who refuse concrete, material aid have disrupted the community and closed their hearts. It is not the intention but the deed that counts. "Let us not love in word or speech but in deed and in truth" (1 John 3:18). Here, finally, Johannine ethics finds common ground with the ethics of James and the ethics of Jesus, from which it differs in so many respects.

73. Wittenberger, "Ort," 68.

EXHORTATIONS
ADDRESSED TO THE
PILGRIM PEOPLE IN THE
EPISTLE TO THE HEBREWS

BIBLIOGRAPHY

Glombitza, Otto. "Erwägungen zum kunstvollen Ansatz der Paränese im Brief an die Hebräer X 19–25." *NT* 9 (1967): 132–50.

Goppelt. *Theologie* (B1) 2:590–99.

Grässer, Erich. *Der Glaube im Hebräerbrief.* MThSt 2. Marburg: Elwert, 1965.

Käsemann, Ernst. *Das wandernde Gottesvolk.* 2d ed. FRLANT 55. Göttingen: Vandenhoeck & Ruprecht, 1957. English: *The Wandering People of God.* Minneapolis: Augsburg Pub. House, 1984.

Maxwell, Kenneth LeRoy. "Doctrine and Parenesis in the Epistle to the Hebrews with Special Reference to Pre-Christian Gnosticism." Diss., Yale Univ., 1953.

Nitschke, H. *Das Ethos des wandernden Gottesvolkes.* MThSt 46. Marburg: Elwert, 1957.

Sanders. *Ethics* (B). Pp. 106–12.

Schnackenburg. *Botschaft* (B). Pp. 302–7.

Völkl. *Christ.* (B). Pp. 343–60.

The Epistle to the Hebrews is not an epistle or a letter in the strict sense, but a "word of exhortation" (13:22). It is addressed to a community threatened by exhaustion, resignation, and indifference. The anonymous author cautions against cowardly retreat (10:39) and inculcates patience and constancy (cf. 10:36; etc.). The important thing is to run the race with perseverance (12:1), "lift your drooping hands and strengthen your weak knees" (12:12), and "hold our first confidence firm to the end" (3:14). Therefore the epistle is replete with exhortations. The theological statements appear to be subservient to parenesis, which appears repeatedly (2:1ff.; 3:1ff.; 4:14ff.; 5:11ff.; 10:19ff.; 12:14ff.)—not for its own sake, but undergirded by theological considerations.[1] The christological reflections and the scriptural exegeses, undertaken with the aid of Alexandrian hermeneutics, are intended to support the author's attempt to counter the frustration and stagnation of a second or third generation and undergird faith with assurance. Even christology is not an independent theme: the didactic christological sections of the epistle are interwoven with its parenetic sections. There is throughout a direct and indissoluble association between doctrine and parenesis.[2] According to Grässer,[3] Michel is the scholar primarily responsible for our insight into "the overall parenetic purpose of all the material" in the epistle.

1. For the Epistle to the Hebrews, the Christ event is central to the kerygma (cf. 1:2ff.; 2:5ff.; 4:14ff.; etc.). It is therefore not surprising that it is also cited as the motivating force in ethics. The focus is on confession of the exalted Lord as Son and High Priest, but we also see Christ dying "outside the gate" (13:12), subject to temptation and suffering, sharing our trials and our weaknesses (2:18; 5:7).[4] He is thus not only the "pioneer" or "source of eternal salvation" (2:10; 5:9–10) but also its model. The author nevertheless finds the true comfort and stimulus for Christians less in Christ's learning obedience through suffering and death as a human being of flesh and blood (5:7–8) than in Christ's sympathy for human weakness gained through his own experience of temptation (4:15). Effectual and convincing comfort and solidarity derive from the mercy of the Son of God and the sympathy of the eternal High Priest, which meet in him. We must therefore hold fast to him as the eschatological Savior (cf. 1:11ff.) and not reject his Word (12:25). Because we have become "Christ's partners" (3:14), we are warned against apostasy and called to mutual encouragement. Because we have become "brothers" of the Son (2:11–12), we have been delivered from fear and death (2:14–15).

Eschatological hope is just as important for the author as a basis of parenesis as is christology.[5] The two are in fact almost identical (cf. 6:11,

1. Schnackenburg, *Moral Teaching* (B), 373–74; Otto Michel, *Der Brief an die Hebräer*, KEK 13, 21ff.
2. Maxwell, "Doctrine," cf. Käsemann, *People*, 110ff.
3. Erich Grässer, "Der Hebräerbrief 1938–1963," *ThR* 30 (1964): 138–236, esp. 160.
4. See Erich Grässer, "Der historische Jesus im Hebräerbrief," *ZNW* 56 (1965): 63–91.
5. See Gerd Theissen, *Untersuchungen zum Hebräerbrief*, StNT 2 (Göttingen: Vandenhoeck & Ruprecht, 1969), 93ff.

18–19; 10:23). Those who belong to the "house" of Christ will "hold fast their confidence and pride in their hope, firm to the end" (3:6; cf. 3:14). Although the epistle does not date from the first generation and is dominated by a spatial dualism of this world and the heavenly world, it breathes eschatological hope. The "pilgrim people of God" are constantly reminded of the promises (4:1ff.; 10:19ff.), with special emphasis on the rest to be expected in the heavenly realm. Faith gives substance to what is hoped for, but must remain constant if hope is to be realized. Here on earth, Christians are strangers and exiles (cf. 11:13), living like Abraham or Moses in the exodus (11:8, 27; cf. 3:16); they have no permanent city but look for the city that is to come (13:14; cf. 11:16).[6] For this very reason they must be admonished to maintain their alien status.

In 10:25, for example, this admonition is motivated by a reference to the Day that is drawing near. Imminent eschatological expectation also appears elsewhere as a stimulus, especially in the context of parenesis (cf. 10:37; 6:9). Those who do not hear as long as it is still "today" (3:7ff.) will drift away from the goal (2:1) and will not enter into God's rest (3:11). The Word brings salvation, but it also exercises a critical function to which all are exposed (4:12–13). Although the notion of judgment cannot be missed (10:26ff.), in ethics as well as in eschatology (cf. 13:4), the dominant motif is promise. In particular, the notion of reward plays a major role; although the author is aware of prevenient grace (cf. 12:28), this emphasis on reward is open to the dangers of a religion of works.[7] Only here in the New Testament is "retribution" mentioned (2:2).[8] Confidence looks forward to a great reward (10:35), God will not forget work and love (6:10), and those who are hospitable may entertain angels unawares (13:2).

2. The author guides his readers primarily by the notions of model and imitation (cf. 4:11; 6:12; 13:7). The Old Testament generation of the desert, for example, serves as a warning against unbelief and apostasy (3:7ff.). Conversely in chapter 11 the long series of faithful suffering witnesses drawn from Israel's history serves as an example to the community, helping its members to know and preserve the faith and the conduct appropriate to it. It is not by chance that the example of Jesus culminates the series.[9] Elsewhere, too, Jesus himself is the great paradigm. The place of Christians is by his side, especially in his obedient suffering (5:8; 12:2). They also "go forth to him outside the camp" in order to bear his abuse (13:13). Despite Jesus' soteriological uniqueness, which makes him strictly beyond emulation, here

6. See William G. Johnson, "The Pilgrimage Motif in the Book of Hebrews," *JBL* 97 (1978): 239–51; according to Johnson, the parenetic sections are dominated by the notion of the pilgrim people (248). See also Gustav Stählin, "xenos," *TDNT* 5:31; Karl Ludwig and Martin Anton Schmidt, "paroikos," *TDNT* 5:851–52.

7. Völkl, *Christ* (B), 356.

8. See Herbert Preisker, "misthos," *TDNT* 4:726.

9. See Schulz, "Evangelium" (B), 294.

as in 1 Peter (cf. above, V. C. 5–6) we may speak of a paradigmatic ethics in which Christ serves as the true model.[10]

3. The parenesis of the epistle, like all its thought, is shaped by its view of the Old Testament, the "living and active word of God" (4:12), which must be heard as God's voice "today" (3:7, 15). The dominant theme is not prophecy and fulfillment but correlation, difference, and superiority, with the Christ event as the crucial reference point for interpretation.[11] It is noteworthy that the epistle does not distinguish between cultic law and moral law; many passages, however, can refer only to the cultic law (cf. 7:5, 12, 28; 8:4; 9:19, 22; 10:8). The law enshrining the sacrificial system of the cult represents the "Old Covenant" as a whole, which has been robbed of its meaning by the new order of salvation. In its "weakness and uselessness" (cf. 7:18–19; 8:13) it belongs to the realm of what is earthly and transitory, the sphere of shadow (10:1) and flesh (7:16; 9:10). Besides stressing the difference between the old covenant and the new (8:8, 13; 9:15), the author repeatedly emphasizes the superiority of the latter (7:22; 8:6; cf. 9:11, 23). The abolition of the Old Testament cult in favor of something better does not simply signify an attitude of enlightened superiority to the cult (cf. the heavenly cult in 12:22ff.); despite its inferiority, the law has indirect significance ("the shadow of good things to come": 10:1; cf. 8:5).

Citing Jer. 31:31ff., the author substantiates at length (the quotation is the longest in the entire New Testament) the promise of the new covenant and its implicit transformation of the law into a new law (8:8ff.; cf. 10:16–17), which means uninterrupted communion with God, immediate knowledge of God, and free obedience to the laws of God. Regulations concerning food and drink and ablutions are merely outward "regulations for the body." They cannot perfect the conscience, but achieve only a ritual purity, and must therefore yield to the better law (9:9–10). There is no way to forsake "dead works" and serve the "living God" except through the sacrifice of Christ (9:14–15).

4. If we examine the content of the admonitions, we note an obvious dualism reminiscent of Plato and Philo; this dualism devalues the physical world.[12] The visible world was indeed created through God's creative Word (cf. 1:2; 4:3; 11:3), but everything that has been created is earthly and must pass away, yielding to "what cannot be shaken" or a "kingdom that cannot be shaken" (12:27–28). "This [!] creation" (9:11) is not the only creation. We must therefore look to what is unseen (11:1) and trust solely in what will endure (cf. 10:34; 3:14). Even the Old Testament witnesses inculcate "rejection of the visible and expectation of the invisible that is to come,"[13] so that

10. See Grässer, "Hebräerbrief," 235.
11. Ibid., 207–8.
12. See Völkl, *Christ* (B), 343–44.
13. See Herbert Braun, "Die Gewinnung der Gewissheit in dem Hebräerbrief," *ThLZ* **96** (1971): 321–30, quotation from 329.

those who have faith, like Moses, do not place the invisible at risk to enjoy pleasures of the moment (11:25–27). Unlike Esau they will not sell their birthright for a single meal (12:16). Of course this lesson has its earthly and visible dimension—characteristically not in asceticism but in suffering, as exemplified above all in Christ.

We also cannot miss the influence of popular philosophical ethics looking to "regulate a middle-class Christian way of life,"[14] especially in 10:22–25. We find such traditional admonitions as "Let marriage be held in honor and let the marriage bed be undefiled" (13:4) and "Keep life free from love of money and be content with what you have" (13:5). The author nevertheless does not limit himself to normal and conventional ideals: the marital and sexual morality enjoined by 13:4 was not universally accepted. Furthermore, Christians are urged to stir up one another to love and good works (10:24).

The difference between love and good works is not made clear, however. Nor is it clear whether we may draw any conclusions from the fact that love is mentioned first, especially if "good works" is used in the Jewish sense to mean works of love and mercy. Strobel thinks that Hebrews follows the Jewish distinction between works of love and good works, disagreeing only in not subordinating the former to the latter. The epistle "loudly proclaims love of one's neighbor as its primary goal."[15] According to 6:10, service to the saints (probably some kind of financial support) evinces such work and such love. Many scholars see here an allusion to the great collection taken up by the early church (cf. Rom. 15:25, 31).

5. Another focus besides courage to live as a pilgrim is the exhortation to be patient and ready to suffer, vividly illustrated by the great examples of faith in the Old Testament. Moses, for example, "chose rather to share ill-treatment with the people of God than to enjoy the fleeting pleasures of sin. He considered abuse suffered for the Christ greater wealth than the treasures of Egypt, for he looked to the reward. By faith he left Egypt, not being afraid of the anger of the king; for he endured as seeing him who is invisible" (11:25–27). Within the series of examples of suffering, the author also speaks of witnesses who "conquered kingdoms and enforced justice" (11:33), but these "ethical" notes fade into the background beside the countless sufferings of Israel listed by the author in a long series.

The author's inability to rest content with middle-class ideals is illustrated by his refusal to allow apostates a second repentance (6:4–6; 10:26–27; 12:16–17). Whether the rigorous stance of a single conversion is motivated only by a sense that the end is at hand (cf. 10:25) or—more likely—by the christological recognition that Christ's sacrifice, single and unique (cf. 6:6), is rendered null and void by "deliberate" sins (10:26, 29), sin and repentance on

14. Grässer, *Glaube*, 117.
15. August Strobel, *Die Briefe an Timotheus und Titus; Der Brief an die Hebräer*, NTD 9, 198; cf. however on 6:10.

the part of Christians represented a difficult problem for the author. His uncompromising "impossible," however, is not intended as a dogmatic statement or absolute but as a parenetic warning.[16] The church rightly refused to support this rejection of a second repentance.[17]

6. The ethics of the epistle is above all an ethics of the people of God (on the basis of 10:21, one could call it an ethics of the household of God), always addressed as a group. Those who are on their way to the heavenly rest journey in company with the other members of the people of God. They must therefore "exhort one another" (3:13; 10:25), stir one another up to love and good works (10:24), so that those who are lame are healed rather than falling by the wayside (12:13). Those who know what "rest" means during their pilgrimage will naturally show hospitality (13:2). Community solidarity is the ideal. The author reminds the readers, for example, that they have become "partners" of those "publicly exposed to abuse and affliction" (10:32–33). They have "suffered with the prisoners [cf. also 13:3] and joyfully accepted the plundering of their property" (10:34), probably a reference to government confiscation. At the very end of the epistle, the reader is enjoined once more to do good and to share (13:16). But there is no mention of being sent into the world or of any relationship to the world other than passive suffering. Even the injunction to "strive for peace with all" (12:14) is probably limited to members of the Christian community (cf. the exhortation to love of the brethren in 13:1 and to exercise *diakonia* toward the "saints" in 6:10).

16. See Grässer, *Glaube*, 196; idem, "Hebräerbrief," 231–32.
17. See Luther's criticism in WA *Deutsche Bibel* 7:344.

ESCHATOLOGICAL EXHORTATION IN THE BOOK OF REVELATION

BIBLIOGRAPHY

Collins, Adela Yarbro. "The Political Perspective of the Revelation of John." *JBL* 96 (1977): 241–56.

Käsemann. *Ruf* (B). Pp. 225ff.

Lampe, Peter. "Die Apokalyptiker—ihre Situation und ihr Handeln." In *Eschatologie und Frieden* (IA), 61–125.

Sanders. *Ethics* (B). Pp. 112–15.

Schnackenburg. *Botschaft* (B). Pp. 307–13.

Schüssler Fiorenza, Elisabeth. "Religion und Politik in der Offenbarung des Johannes." In *Biblische Randbemerkungen* (Schüler-Festschrift Rudolf Schnackenburg), ed. H. Merklein and J. Lange, 261–72. Würzburg: Echter, 1974.

Schütz, Roland. *Die Offenbarung des Johannes und Kaiser Domitian*. FRLANT 50. Göttingen: Vandenhoeck & Ruprecht, 1933.

Völkl. *Christ* (B). Pp. 441–63.

Wendland. *Ethik* (B). Pp. 116–22.

A. ESCHATOLOGICAL FRAMEWORK

1. The Revelation of John has been a book sealed with seven seals since time immemorial. It has often had a shadowy existence within theology and the church. Certain chapters appear exempt from the general uneasiness about the book, namely the letters to the seven churches and the description of the Roman Empire—sections that are also the most important for ethics. Even these chapters, however, have often been shrugged off by ethics and theology. It is natural that an age when alliance between throne and altar was thought to embody the proper relationship between church and state should greet with incomprehension the notion that the Roman Empire was a satanic power, drunk on the blood of the saints, to be resisted to the death. But the book's harsh message of repentance and judgment could also explain why Revelation is often ignored in a middle-class church with a bourgeois theology. There is of course also the mythological imagery, the apocalyptic symbolism of colors and numerals in the visions, and the like. But resistance is probably due in large measure to the prediction of what lies in store for the church: it will not progress from glory to glory, enjoying increasing success and recognition until it achieves a universal happy end. It will instead be beset by worldwide persecution, during which the people of God will be decimated and take refuge in the desert. Power will be given to the beast to wage war against the saints and to vanquish them. Because the book is largely unfamiliar and alien, we must provide some general background before turning to the ethics of Revelation.

German theology is once again engaged in serious discussion of apocalypticism. That this is not considered a sign of theological perversity or an adherence to superstitious eschatological fantasies is largely due to Käsemann.[1] The relationship between history and eschatology is now viewed from a new perspective. It is acknowledged explicitly that there is no theological justification for giving up the Christian view of history, with its universal coordinates of salvation and damnation, in order simply to substitute the insight that all human existence is historical. There is no reason to replace the coherence of history with a sequence of more or less unrelated situations viewed from the perspective of the human psyche and to reduce God's future to a human tomorrow. The Book of Revelation in particular is concerned not merely with the independence of each individual from the present world but with the world itself, the question of whose it is and who has dominion over it. These questions bear on New Testament eschatology and the New Testament understanding of history, but they also have a clear ethical component, because there has never been an exodus of the true church "from its defensive position" without apocalyptic hopes and injunctions.[2] According to

1. Ernst Käsemann, "The Beginnings of Christian Theology," in *NT Questions of Today* (London: SCM Press, 1969), 82ff.; idem, "Primitive Christian Apocalyptic," in *NT Questions*, 105ff.
2. Käsemann, "Apocalyptic," 110.

Käsemann, the unsettling message of Revelation is especially relevant to a church that often slumbers in self-satisfaction, that comes to terms with the world and forgets that the sovereignty of Jesus begins here and now with the freedom of those who spurn the mark of the beast under the aegis of a *pax Romana* and bear witness that he who makes all things new is on the march.[3] These comments, of course, are not meant to trivialize the theological problems raised by the Book of Revelation, especially in comparison with other writings of the New Testament.[4]

2. With regard to its date, we can say that Revelation was probably composed in the last decade of the first century, during the reign of Domitian, when Christians were subject to increasing persecution. This appears to chime with the frequent claim that apocalyptic hopes—not just the hopes recorded in Revelation—compensate for unhappiness with the present world, as though the apocalyptic author were dreaming himself out of the cruel realities of this world into the elysian fields of the next. The inexplicable riddles and suffering of the present age can account at most for a certain pessimism or, more accurately, a realism based on the experience of those handed over to the authorities, but not the triumphant power of apocalyptic hopes. A hostile environment has often shattered worldly expectations, but has never by itself given rise to genuine hope. The extent of the suffering and disaster certainly precluded optimistic illusions, but we all know that suffering teaches us not only to pray but also to curse. During the period of nascent apocalypticism, others found different ways to deal with the tribulations of the hostile world—resignation, rebellion, or cynical skepticism. Historical oppression constitutes the background of apocalyptic, not its cause; apocalyptic masters its experience of the historical world by relying on the unfulfilled promise of God. This holds true also for Revelation, where eschatology is the primary motivating force for exhortations and warnings.

3. Here we can only touch on a few central statements, for ultimately the entire book is permeated by eschatology. According to 1:1, the seer's vision of the eschatological future derives finally from God himself, who alone can disclose the future and thus interpret the course of history. The content of the vision is "what must soon take place." This illustrates two points: first, the intensity of the expectation that dominates the entire book, which culminates deliberately in the promise of Christ's imminent coming (22:20); and second, its so-called apocalyptic determinism—although the necessary course of history comes not from a blind, impersonal fate but from the Lord of history. Despite these features of apocalyptic, which are a source of comfort rather than speculation for the seer, there is no attempt to calculate the end. The "when" is vague, though near (3:3). God is not slave to an apocalyptic calendar or a wound-up clock: he is the Almighty (1:8), who created all things

3. Käsemann, *Freedom* (B), 130ff.
4. See Ch. Münchow, "Das Buch mit sieben Siegeln," *ZdZ* 31 (1977): 376–83.

(4:11). It is not those who observe or calculate that the author calls blessed, but those who hear the words of early Christian prophecy, through which the exalted Lord speaks comfort and encouragement to his oppressed community (1:3; cf. the striking alternation between Christ and the Spirit as speaker in 2:1, 7; 2:8, 11; 2:12, 17).

More important is the actual substance of the author's eschatology, since the nearness and determinism of the eschaton we have noted are not peculiar to Revelation, as Jewish evidence amply attests. The unique feature of eschatology in Revelation is its expectation of Christ's presence—the Christ whom the community has already encountered and continues to encounter as Savior and Lord. Just as 1:4 speaks of God as the one who is and was and is to come, the Alpha and the Omega (1:8), so 1:7 speaks of Christ as coming, and 22:13 calls him the Alpha and the Omega, the first and the last, the beginning and the end. He is also the one who initiates the events of the eschaton (5:1ff.). The one who comes to this world in the person of Christ is also the one who has been alive and at work since the beginning, the Creator and Finisher (1:8), toward whose saving lordship the whole world moves.

4. Alongside this statement that the one who spoke the first word will soon also speak the last word, the book's soteriological christology effectively prevents restriction of hope to an apocalyptic future.[5] The grounds for confidence in the coming sovereignty of Jesus Christ and the source of strength to endure to the end through the struggles at hand are stated in the doxology of 1:5b–6: "To him who loves us and has freed us from our sins by his blood and made us a kingdom, priests to his God and Father, to him be glory and dominion . . ." The present tense ("who loves us") with its durative emphasis shows that the love of Christ is the constant that Christians have experienced and continue to experience, even in the midst of present oppression. The community is therefore not simply comforted with a vision of a better future but reminded of the enduring love of him who by suffering and death redeemed them from enslavement to sin and guilt (besides 1:5; cf. also 5:9), obtaining for the community royal and priestly prerogatives in the present (1:6; 5:10).[6] The community is already the locus of God's sovereignty, where this sovereignty is acknowledged and attested.

In other passages, too, the hope of the seer is grounded in what has already taken place and is taking place in Christ. The same "Lamb" whose blood redeems (5:9) is also victor over the "beast" (17:14). Hope is therefore not utopian or wishful thinking, but a consequence of the salvation accomplished by Christ's death and exaltation. Only those aware that Christ's love and power keep them safe from all terrors and tribulations can endure what is

---

5. See Traugott Holtz, *Die Christologie der Apokalypse des Johannes*, Tu 85 (Berlin: Akademie, 1962).

6. See Elisabeth Schüssler Fiorenza, *Priester für Gott*, NTA 7 (Münster: Aschendorff, 1972); idem, "Redemption as Liberation," *CBQ* 36 (1974): 220–32.

coming. The initial vision culminates in the words of Christ: "Fear not, I am the first and the last, and the living one; I died, and behold I am alive for evermore, and I have the keys of death and Hades" (1:17ff.). Indeed, according to 17:14 and 19:16, the Redeemer is already "Lord of lords and King of kings" (cf. "ruler of kings on earth" [1:5]).[7]

5. Because what will come to pass is grounded in what has already taken place, this experience of salvation can already influence the present; it is already possible to speak proleptically of Christ's victory and the fall of Babylon. The transitions between series of visions repeatedly culminate in hymnic passages that bear witness to this truth.

"The kingdom of the world has become the kingdom of our Lord and of his Christ, and he shall reign for ever and ever" (11:15). "Now the salvation and the power and the kingdom of our God and the authority of his Christ have come, for the accuser of our brethren has been thrown down, who accuses them day and night before our God. And they have conquered him by the blood of the Lamb and by the word of their testimony . . ." (12:10–11).

According to Jörns,[8] these hymns, heard in the context of the eschatological vision, serve to make clear the salvific message of the apocalyptic event in contrast to the disasters seen in the visions. Discussing the hymnic passages in chapters 4–7, for example, Jörns shows that even before the real battle with Satan and his followers begins and the satanic powers are brought low, the hymns extol the purpose and climax of the eschatological event, proclaiming the victory of God and the Lamb, so that the good news blots out the terrors of the judgment. According to 12:12, these hymns are sung by the heavens and those who dwell there (cf. also 4:11; 11:16; 15:3; 19:1); possibly, however, they may also echo the worship of the church on earth (cf. 5:8), elements of which frame the book as a whole (cf. 1:3 and 22:17, 20–21).

The book begins with a christological statement of what has already taken place, and the visions are interrupted repeatedly with hymns that proleptically glorify the victory of Jesus. The book concludes similarly with the great vision of the new heaven and the new earth and the new Jerusalem, where God dwells in the midst of his people. The vision of the future culminates not in judgment but in the new creation; we must remember this when we read of all the cosmic catastrophes and tribulations described in the visions. Not even the cry of woe over all who dwell on the earth (8:13) and the terrified question of 6:17 ("The great day of wrath has come, who can stand before it?") can drown out the heavenly rejoicing of the eschaton (19:6–7).

6. Chapter 20 shows that for Revelation eschatology does not mean abandoning the world. The millennial kingdom described there is the counterpart to the judgment of Babylon described in earthly terms in chapters 17–18.

7. Holtz, *Christologie*, 58–59, 154–55.
8. Klaus-Peter Jörns, *Das hymnische Evangelium*, StNT 5 (Gütersloh: Mohn, 1971).

Since "chiliasm" has played a certain role in the history of ethics, we shall discuss this subject briefly.

Expectation of a messianic interim is already found in Jewish apocalyptic where it is usually considered an attempt to reconcile two different kinds of hope. In 2 Esdras, for example, the two pictures of the future are related to each other sequentially: the messianic kingdom precedes the end of the world and the new eon. Thus the messianic kingdom becomes a kind of interim, while the following age of the new eon brings true and definitive salvation.[9]

The seer has virtually nothing to say about the millennium. This parsimony stands in marked contrast to the vivid descriptions found in Jewish apocalyptic, an observation that suggests a certain degree of caution. But theological literature is replete with all-too-easy victories over this conception of an earthly interim preceding final salvation, victories won in the name of an abstract and colorless hope for a world to come. We must remember that for Revelation the new eon that follows the millennial kingdom will bring a new heaven and a new earth. It is true that the appearance of Christ does not mark the beginning of a secular salvation that arrives by stages within this present world. But it would be wrong to ignore the legitimate element of this hope expressed in Revelation 20, even though its basis is largely traditional: the visible realization of Jesus Christ's lordship in this world, which cannot simply be adjudged satanic and left to the demons and the imperial lackeys of the beast. For the seer, the lordship of Jesus Christ must be manifested within this eon, and this is totally legitimate. Jesus Christ is "Lord of lords and King of kings" (17:14). This is true not only in the world to come but implicitly in all aspects of the present world, for all its lord and kings. How little this world is simply left to earthly lords and their claims is illustrated most vividly by the conflict with the Roman state (see below, IX.C).

Schüssler Fiorenza rightly stresses that victory over the powers hostile to God includes "destruction of all repressive human institutions, of suffering and death."[10] From the use of the same term "sovereignty" for both God and the Roman Empire, she even concludes that "these two kingdoms cannot coexist."[11] In another article,[12] despite the sixfold repetition of the number 1000, she disputes the interim nature of the messianic kingdom, seeing in the millennium one aspect of eschatological deliverance.

B. THE LETTERS TO THE CHURCHES

1. There can be no doubt that the seer's eschatological vision also determines his entire ethics, as we see above all in the juxtaposition of eschatology

9. For further discussion, see Hans Bietenhard, *Das Tausendjährige Reich* (Zurich: Zwingli, 1955); Walter Bauer, "Chiliasmus," *RAC* 2:1073–78; Eduard Lohse, "Chilias," *TDNT* 9:470–71.

10. "Religion," 266.

11. Ibid., 264.

12. Elisabeth Schüssler Fiorenza, "Die tausendjährige Herrschaft der Auferstandenen (Apk.20, 4–6)," *BiLe* 13 (1972): 107–24.

and ethics in the letters to the seven Christian communities of Asia Minor,[13] where promises and threats of judgment stand side by side. Here, too, however, the author's perspective is not limited to the future, pictured in words describing threats or triumphs to come. The communities are also reminded of what they have already been given: "Remember then what you have received and heard; keep that, and repent" (3:3). The community has not only a future but a past, something already received and heard. It is not a triumphalistic host secure in its salvation, nor is it a forlorn hope blindly groping toward the future with empty hands and hearts. In the very act of looking to the future, the community can be recalled to its beginnings (cf. also 2:25). The gift and word that have been received must become real. At the same time, the author cautions against self-deception and enthusiastic fanaticism: "For you say, I am rich, I have prospered, and I need nothing; not knowing that you are wretched, pitiable, poor, blind, and naked" (3:17). A Christian community that thinks itself rich is actually poor and does not enjoy God's promise. Riches and salvation come only through Christ, as 3:18 shows.

2. The number of motivations citing what has been given in Christ is of course far exceeded by those based on futuristic eschatology that the seer has worked into the letters. Christ's eyes are like flames of fire (1:14; 2:18; 19:12), which penetrate everywhere and from which nothing can be hid; a sharp two-edged sword issues from his mouth (1:16; 2:16). Such images point to Christ's role as judge over all, including his own community. The lampstand of a community can be removed (2:5). In other words, a community can be rejected, even without any change in outward appearances. "When stars go out, their light remains visible for a considerable period. The lampstand can be long gone, even while the church continues to go about its business."[14]

The letters threaten judgment against the church, whereas the visions threaten judgment against unbelievers. One probable purpose is to issue a final call to the heathen to forsake their evil ways: "Fear God and give him glory, for the hour of his judgment has come; and worship him who made heaven and earth, the sea and the fountains of water" (14:7). Earthly judgment is also intended to preach repentance, but people do not hear the message. After the fourth bowl of wrath is poured out, we are told: "Men were scorched by the fierce heat, and they [nevertheless] cursed the name of God who had power over these plagues, and they did not repent and give him glory" (16:9; similarly 16:11; 9:20–21). Other passages suggest that repentance is no longer possible and that the judgment against the heathen is irrevocable. God's own people, however, are called to go forth so as to escape

13. For a discussion of the letters, see Ferdinand Hahn, "Die Sendschreiben der Johannesapokalypse," in *Tradition und Glaube* (Festschrift Karl George Kuhn), ed. G. Jeremias, H.-W. Kuhn, and H. Stegeman (Göttingen: Vandenhoeck & Ruprecht, 1971), 357–94.

14. N. Hadorn, *Die Offenbarung des Johannes*, ThKNT 18, on Rev. 2:5.

the destruction: "Come out of her, my people, lest you take part in her sins, lest you share in her plagues; for her sins are heaped high as heaven, and God has remembered her iniquities" (18:4–5). The seer expects that the heathen who have laid waste the earth will fall victim to God's wrath while Christians receive their reward (11:18). According to 2:23, however, even Christians are judged (cf. above all 20:12; 22:12), but Christ will acknowledge them as his own.

3. The positive aspects of future hope, however, are much more important in providing ethical motivation. We see this once again especially in the seven letters, all of which end with a statement about "conquering,"[15] a word that has eschatological overtones in Revelation. It is the eschatological battle at the end of days in which the victor will conquer.

"Conquer" is a favorite word in Revelation, appearing no less than sixteen times. It suggests the struggle inherent in Christian life between the ages. As in Rom. 3:5 (Ps. 51:6), God's forensic controversy with the world is also in the background.[16] There is both an initial and a final victory: those conquered in the former may be victorious in the latter. Of course the seer is convinced that the Lion of Judah has already conquered (5:5): the host of those who belong to him are promised a victory like his ("as I myself conquered," 3:21) if they, like Christ, do not shun suffering. As "followers of the Lamb" (14:4) they know that they can conquer only through the blood of the Lamb (12:11).[17]

In any case, all the statements about conquering, which use various apocalyptic images to lend Christians courage in the hour of trial and battle, are eschatological. They promise, for example, that the eschaton will restore paradise with its store of life and blessings (2:7), that those who conquer will not fall victim to final death after the resurrection and judgment (2:11) but will receive eternal life, that their names will not be blotted out of the book of life and that Christ will confess them before his Father and the angels (3:5).

These eschatological promises for the most part imply a christological statement. This is true above all in the case of the words introducing the seven letters, each of which contains a title claimed by the exalted Christ.[18] They summarize, as it were, the positive and negative elements, containing threats, promises, or both.

In 2:1, for example, we read: "The words of him who holds the seven stars in his right hand, who walks among the seven gold lampstands" (cf. 3:1); in other words, the exalted Christ holds the Christian communities in his hand and is in their midst. The self-designation in 2:8 echoes 1:17–18: Christ is the first and the last, who died and came to life. In 2:12 and 2:18, which cite 1:16

15. Hahn, *Sendschreiben*, 381ff.
16. Ibid., 384–85.
17. See Otto Bauernfeind, "nikaō," *TDNT* 4:945.
18. See Holtz, *Christologie*, 137ff.; Hahn, *Sendschreiben*, 367ff.

and 1:14–15, only judgment is considered. The self-designation of the exalted Lord in 3:7 and 3:14 once again is more like a promise: "The words of the holy one, the true one, who has the key of David, who opens and no one shall shut, who shuts and no one opens" (3:7); in 3:14, Christ appears as God's affirmation, the faithful and true witness.

Taken as a group, these passages indicate that christology is dominated by the notion of sovereignty and redemption, and above all that in Revelation christology and eschatology constitute the primary elements of ethics and the Christian life.

4. The substance of what is required of Christians is also stated in the seven letters, primarily in terms of the specific conduct for which each church is praised or chastised. Because of the eschatological motivation, it is not surprising that the most frequent theme is the call to repent. The concept of *metanoia* ("change of mind," "repentance") is as central to Revelation as to the Gospels (cf. Rev. 2:5, 16, 21–22; 3:3, 19). Here, too, the word means conversion of the entire person, although the call is addressed solely to Christians. Repentance clearly involves a cognitive element; in 2:5, for example, we read: "Remember then from what you have fallen and repent." Repentance begins with recollection of what one has lost. Such recollection is an integral part of repentance, but they are not identical. Repentance is neither theoretical and intellectual nor cultic; it does not mean return from lawlessness to the law. This relates Revelation to Jesus and distinguishes it from Judaism.

This absence of conversion to the Mosaic law suggests that the law does not play a central role in Revelation. This observation, too, sets Revelation clearly apart from the Jewish apocalypses (2:24 may even explicitly reject the "burden" imposed by the law). The call to repentance is never motivated by or grounded on the authority of the law. In 3:19, the call derives from the preceding statement that God reproves and chastens those he loves. Verse 20, which follows, also motivates the call to repentance and emphasizes its urgency by pointing to the imminent coming of the Lord in the Parousia, when Christ will celebrate the eschatological banquet with his followers (cf. Mark 13:29; Luke 12:36; etc.). In contrast to the Synoptic tradition, however, Revelation calls on the reader not only to turn to God but to turn away from evil or the world, usually in terms of forsaking evil deeds (2:21–22; 9:20; 16:11). Repentance that does not manifest itself in works is not repentance. Therefore 2:5 can command in a single breath: "Remember from what you have fallen, repent and do the works you did at first."

5. It is quite generally true that works play an important role in Revelation, but without any overtones of merit (cf. 19:8: "it was granted them"—an expression that does not rule out the notion of reward and judgment, for "their deeds follow them," that is, into eternal life [14:13]). After Christ's introductory formula in the first person, most of the seven letters begin with the statement, "I know your works." According to 2:26, conquering depends on keeping Christ's works until the end, that is, the works already fore-shadowed in the life of Jesus. Therefore 3:8 can use "keeping Christ's words" as a parallel instead of "doing works"; according to Lohmeyer,[19] these ex-pressions are merged by 2:26 into "keeping my works." The word "law" does not occur at all. Twice the author speaks of "keeping the commandments of God," but only in parallel with "bearing testimony to Jesus" (12:17) or "keeping the faith of Jesus" (14:12). What gives works their value is the approval of Christ (cf. 2:2, 6). The term "works" probably means primarily works of love.

The admonition in Rev. 2:5 to "do the works you did at first" is preceded in v. 4 by the charge of "having abandoned the love you had at first." These words are not meant to evoke feelings of romantic melancholy or to recall the extraordinary inspiration and bubbling enthusiasm of the time just after initial conversion. They speak quite soberly of return to the former Christian way of life, which was characterized by love.

Interpreters have been misled repeatedly into thinking of the first fire of love between a man and a woman, probably because chapter 19 pictures the relationship between Christ and the Christian community in terms of mar-riage or bride and bridegroom. But 2:4 refers not to love of Christ or God, but to love of other Christians. This is suggested not only by the parallel ex-pression "the works you did at first" in 2:5 but also by the fact that 2:19, too, associates agape with works and service and that these are the only two passages that speak of Christian agape.

Probably there are also echoes of the apocalyptic expectation that love would grow cold in the final time of tribulation (Matt. 24:12); this is not an excuse but a warning not to fall prey to this fatal lack of love. This also explains the admonition of Rev. 3:2 to awaken and strengthen the members of the community who are asleep and on the point of death.

6. Still another element is important to the seer in the setting of the call to repentance: turning away from false teachers or, more explicitly, from mis-taken tolerance of syncretistic ideas that certain people preach as being Christian. In 2:16, the call to repent follows directly upon the statement that people holding the teaching of Balaam (v. 14) or the teaching of the Nic-olaitans (v. 15) are found in the community. According to 2:21, the proph-etess Jezebel has been given time to repent, but she has refused.

Probably the Balaamites, Nicolaitans, and followers of Jezebel are gnostic heretics, described in 2:24 as claiming to possess a gnosis that even plumbs the depths of Satan. The seer disapproves of them largely because they eat food offered to idols and engage in immorality. Since the text speaks not only of what these heretics do but also of what they teach (2:14–15, 20, 24), we

---

should probably picture them not simply as living worldly or lax lives, but as preaching libertinistic propaganda, which fits with the idea of unrestricted freedom common to Gnosticism. In Corinth, too, people used this argument to defend eating food sacrificed to idols and participating in the meals of heathen cults as well as immorality. In Revelation, the latter may refer to apostasy and unfaithfulness or syncretism, or else to sexual immorality such as free love. According to Lampe,[20] the seer differed from Paul in objecting to food offered to idols because the pressures of emperor worship had given "the uncompromising preservation of Christian identity precedence over the need to minimize outward unpleasantness and vexation." But he is also right to see the heretics' readiness to accommodate as reflecting a sense of spiritual perfection (3:17) that considers a future hope unnecessary.[21] Schüssler Fiorenza[22] even thinks it possible that the Nicolaitans preached "de facto syncretism and accommodation to the imperial cult of Rome."

Furthermore, the author does not object to a woman's playing a leading role as prophetess in the Christian community at Thyatira, but only to her false doctrine. The seer considered it very important that the community be alert against false teachers: 2:2 praises the community for opposing false apostles and refusing to accept everyone claiming the name and title of apostle.

7. The call to repentance goes hand in hand with a call to wholehearted and absolute commitment, which is emphasized strongly in Revelation. The words addressed to the Laodicean community are well known: "I know your works: you are neither cold nor hot. Would that you were cold or hot! So, because you are lukewarm, and neither cold nor hot, I will spew you out of my mouth" (3:15–16). The basic evil is indifference, compromise, the indecisive, lukewarm, vague Christianity that the seer describes as arousing the Lord's loathing. The same either/or is demanded here as in the Sermon on the Mount or James. An uncompromising and wholehearted "no" is better than a "yes and no," better than neutrality and mediocrity. Closely connected with this lukewarmness is the fanatical contentment of the Laodicean community, which is prosperous and self-satisfied, but in reality is wretched, pitiable, poor, blind, and naked (3:17–18). The seer attacks a realized eschatology that is convinced of present perfection as well as self-satisfaction. The community in Sardis is addressed in similar terms: they have the name, that is, the reputation, of being alive, but are actually dead (3:1). They practice Christianity in name only, a Christianity that is thought to be vital and alive but in fact already bears the marks of death. In both cases the seer still speaks of works, but the works are not "perfect in the sight of God" (3:2). Such works can be acceptable and honored in the eyes of the world, but

20. "Apokalyptiker," 113.
21. Ibid., 114.
22. "Religion," 267.

God judges by a different standard, and this standard is not met. It is therefore necessary to be awake and alert. All the letters end with the call, "He who has an ear, let him hear!" Alertness and sobriety are always characteristic features of apocalyptic exhortation (cf. Mark 13:33ff.; 1 Pet. 4:7ff.).

Finally, according to Revelation, this firmness and determination must be joined with steadfastness and endurance, which the author often praises (2:2, 3, 19; 3:10; cf. also 1:9; 13:10; 14:12). This does not refer to a general patience amid the problems and adversities of life, but iron resistance in the face of the trials and tribulations that arise when one confesses Jesus Christ, bearing up for his name's sake (2:3), "not denying his name" (3:8), or "bearing testimony to Jesus" (12:17; cf. also 14:12). Revelation 21:8 places cowardice first in its catalogue of vices, and 12:11 calls those who have not loved their lives conquerors. In all these passages we hear echoes of the conflict with the empire.

8. Although there are hints of how life was lived in the Christian community and its world, the seer scarcely touches on concrete ethical problems besides this conflict with the state and emperor worship, which keeps him in suspense and threatens him with pain and death. Only in chapter 18, in the announcement of the fall of Babylon and the lament over its destruction, do we detect overtones of social criticism,[23] which may be echoed in the economic distress spoken of in 6:6.

First, however, we must discuss chapter 17, the vision of the city of Rome. The harlot Babylon, which symbolizes Rome, the capital of the world, sits upon a beast, which symbolizes the satanic empire. The woman is adorned with gold, jewels, and pearls, probably intended to suggest the wealth and luxury of Rome. She also holds a golden cup in her hand, full of abominations and the impurities of her fornication. It is probably wrong to interpret this image as referring specifically to the excesses and pleasures of life in the metropolis. In biblical language, "abomination," the contents of the cup, refers more to something displeasing to God than to something morally and aesthetically repugnant, although the two can overlap. Rome is brought to judgment on account of her blasphemy and persecution of Christians (cf. 17:3, 6), but also on account of her economic power (like Tyre, the commercial center of the nations, which enriched "the kings of the earth" with her abundant wealth and merchandise [Ezek. 26:2ff.; cf. Isa. 23; Ezek. 26:1— 28:19]). In addition, "those polluted with abominations" in 21:8 appear in a series that includes murderers, fornicators, sorcerers, and idolators, so that there may be elements of moral decay implicit in chapter 17, even though it is impossible to be more specific. As in the name "mother of harlots and of

23. See Adela Yarbro Collins, "Revelation 18: Taunt-Song or Dirge?" in *L'Apocalypse johannique et l'Apocalyptique dans le NT*, BEThL 53 (Louvain: Leuven University Press, 1980), 185– 204, esp. 202–3. See also Aland, "Verhältnis" (B5), 220ff.

earth's abominations" (17:5), the point is probably that Rome is the center and source of every conceivable abomination.

Revelation 18 is somewhat more specific. Here v. 3 connects the fall of Babylon with her sin and gives this explanation: Rome has made all the nations drunk with her idolatry, and the merchants of the earth (in parallel with "the kings of the earth") have grown rich with the power of her wealth. Where there is political and economic power, the seer sees "a dwelling place of demons and a haunt of every foul spirit" (v. 2), so that all the Christian community can hope for here is a new exodus (v. 4). The author probably had little interest in how concentration of power and disastrous economic crises come about. This illustration of Rome's sin agrees with chapter 17: economic power and exploitation, arrogance and wealth, provoke judgment.

This is confirmed by the lament of the kings and merchants, shipmasters and sailors, in 18:9ff. The merchants lament the loss of their markets, "no one buys their cargo" (v. 11), which is detailed in a long list: gold and jewels, costly fabrics, spices, cosmetics, luxuries, and so forth. This list, which even includes traffic in slaves, gives an interesting insight into the social and cultural life of the wealthy upper class and indeed of the fashionable world in general. We do not hear the hatred and resentment of the downtrodden looking with satisfaction on the ruin and destruction of the upper class and intent only on a reversal of roles. In the tradition of prophetic social criticism, we hear the ironic voice of a prophet's wrath in the face of social injustice and wickedness.

Two points need to be noted. First, the author obviously wishes to keep a healthy distance from the seductive power exercised by wealth and the luxuries of civilization, even though he does not speak explicitly of the undertow he clearly fears. It is nevertheless striking that the two communities not censured in chapters 2—3 (Smyrna and Philadelphia) live in extreme poverty. Second, as in Jesus and the Epistle of James, we see again that emphasis on future hope does not blind the author's eyes to earthly needs and problems but rather strengthens his social conscience and sensibilities.

C. CONFLICT WITH THE STATE

1. Elsewhere in the New Testament there is only more or less indirect evidence of conflict between the will of God and that of the state. The Revelation of John, however, bears witness to the collision between the Christian faith on the one hand and the Roman Empire and emperor worship on the other. It provides an insight into the beginnings of persecution on the part of the Roman authorities and the powerless protest of the Christian communities. It is impossible to distinguish in detail the parts of the visions that are prophecies after the event (*vaticinia ex eventu*) from those that the seer sees as being yet to come. In any case, there must have been some instances of martyrdom: 2:13 mentions one martyred member of the commu-

nity by name; and 6:9–11, which describes the crying out of those slain for the Word of God and for their witness, presupposes it is not mere speculation or worry about the future when the seer sees the harlot of Babylon "drunk with the blood of the martyrs" (17:6) or speaks of Christians who have been beheaded (20:4; cf. also 12:11; 13:2ff.; 18:24; 19:2).

In my opinion, it is wrong to cite 3:10 as evidence that the persecutions all still lie in the future,[24] and 6:11 can hardly refer to the martyrs of the Old Testament[25] (cf. v. 9b; in 16:6, too, "the blood of saints and prophets" refers to Christians).

As long as early Christianity was not clearly distinct from Judaism, it shared the privileges of the Jews and the Roman toleration of Judaism. When the breach between church and synagogue became definitive, the conflict with Rome took on ominous proportions. The Christian faith as such was not yet subject to criminal penalties, but only refusal to participate in the state cult or to worship the emperor. This refusal was the real source of conflict with the state.

2. We cannot here discuss the origin, spread, and forms of the official cult that provoked the conflict. It had its beginnings and centers principally in the eastern parts of the empire, under the influence of oriental cults in which rulers were worshipped.[26] Although Caligula already claimed to be divine, as we learn from inscriptions calling him "the supreme revealed god," it was under Domitian that the emperor cult was exalted to the position of an official state religion serving the empire's own propaganda. It also appeared useful as a powerful ideological and religious bond uniting the various peoples and cultures of the empire. In the New Testament period, the institutions and forms of the cult of Caesar are attested by a wealth of temples, cultic images, altars, inscriptions, and coins. The province of Asia in particular, where the communities mentioned in 1:11 and chapters 2—3 were located, was a center of the imperial cult. Even in the reigns of Augustus and Tiberius, provincial temples were built there (at Pergamon and Smyrna) in honor of the goddess Roma and *Divus Augustus*. In the time of Domitian, an imperial temple was built at Ephesus; its remains have been excavated. The head and forearm of a colossal statue of Domitian (four times life size) have been preserved. Votive inscriptions to the divine ruler have been found at Ephesus, Pergamon, Laodicea, and Thyatira.

It is therefore no accident that under the emperor Domitian, who claimed divine honors as "Lord and God" (*dominus ac deus*) during his own lifetime, a bloody persecution based on religious grounds erupted for the first time because there was opposition to the empire and its emperor. It is against this background that we must understand Revelation, and especially chapter 13.

24. Aland, "Verhältnis," 216–17.
25. Ibid., 217–18.
26. In addition to Schütz, *Offenbarung*, see Albert Dihle, "Herrschaft," *RGG*[3] 3:278–80.

3. Drawing on an ancient mythological tradition, the seer paints a fantastic picture of a demonic monster symbolizing the Roman Empire.[27] A beast with ten horns and seven heads rises out of the sea; on the horns are ten diadems, and on the heads are blasphemous names. It resembles a leopard. Its feet are like those of a bear. Its mouth is like a lion's mouth.[28]

The seer probably borrowed the image of the monster with many heads and horns from the apocalyptic tradition of Judaism (cf. Daniel 7, which does not mention seven heads but uses similar symbolism). Whether this tradition derives ultimately from ancient Babylonian mythology (Tiamat, Behemoth, Leviathan) may remain an open question (cf. also 4 Esd. 6:49; Syriac Baruch 29:4; Test. of Judah 21:7; Ps. of Sol. 2:15).

This traditio-historical analysis naturally does not rule out historical interpretation. It is therefore wrong to claim that the seer is not concerned with "time and history, but only with subterranean forces that transcend history."[29] In both Daniel 7 and the Jewish apocalypses, eschatological imagery often alludes to political events and powers. In Revelation, too, there is much that makes sense only from this perspective (cf. also the transparency of the meaning in 13:8 and 17:3, manifest in the change of gender).

The meaning of this unimaginable and mysterious combination of bestial features is clear from comparison with Daniel 7, where four beasts rise in turn from the sea. Here they are combined in a single horrible creature. The point is clear: from the apocalyptic perspective of the seer, which is identical with that of God, all the atrocities and all the evil powers of earlier empires culminate in the Roman Empire. It has become a solitary beast of prey, appearing in bestial forms and devouring everything. In simple language: it is debased political power.[30]

Revelation 12:18 shows the connection between the coming of the dragon (Satan; cf. 12:9) to the sea and the rising of the beast from the sea, thus making it clear from the outset what realm the beast belongs to and in whose service it stands. This assumes, of course, that "he" is the original reading of 12:18, rather than "I" (found in Luther and some translations). This reading is supported by manuscript evidence and the author's purpose: he wishes to show that it is the dragon that occasions the appearance of the beast.

Revelation 13:2 asserts explicitly that the dragon gives the beast "his power and his throne and great authority." Since, however, the satanic dragon itself is characterized by seven heads and ten horns (12:3), the beast not only stands

27. See Heinrich Schlier, "Vom Antichrist," in *Die Zeit der Kirche* (Freiburg: Herder, 1956), 16–29; Schrage, *Staat* (B5), 69ff.

28. See Wilhelm Bousset, *Der Antichrist in der Überlieferung des Judentums, des NT und der alten Kirche* (Göttingen: Vandenhoeck & Ruprecht, 1895); Ernst Lohmeyer, "Antichrist," *RAC* 1:450–57; Roland Schütz, "Antichrist (im NT)," *RGG*³ 1:431–32; Josef Ernst, *Die eschatologischen Gegenspieler in den Schriften des NT*, BU 3 (Regensburg: Pustet, 1967), 80ff.

29. Lohmeyer, *Offenbarung*, 194.

30. Schlier, "Antichrist," 21.

in service of the dragon but is also its earthly counterpart. The Roman Empire is thus in fact the incarnation of Satan's power upon earth. The blasphemous names on the heads—probably an allusion to the sacral titles and apotheosis claimed by the emperor, which constitute blasphemy—indicate the real danger that issues from the beast: not only is it the incarnation of the dragon, it is also a satanic caricature of Christ—the antichrist, the satanic enemy of Christ and hence of God.

This is confirmed by several observations. First, the diadem, the sign of royal dignity on the horns of the beast, is elsewhere spoken of only in connection with Christ (19:12). Second, the dragon's giving its throne to the beast (13:2) is a parody of Christ's enthronement (3:21). We may also cite 2:13, which speaks of "Satan's throne" in Pergamon, although it is not entirely clear that this phrase alludes to the focus of the emperor cult.[31] Third, and of particular importance, is the reference in 13:3 to the beast's "mortal wound" and its healing (cf. v. 14). This description of the beast as having been slain and brought back to life is nothing less than a parody and usurpation of divine attributes. In 5:6, 12, Christ is described as having been "slain"; 2:8 states that he "died and came to life" (cf. also 20:4). Fourth, worshiping the beast (13:4) is a satanic counterpart to the true worship of the Lamb or God. Fifth, the picture is completed by the audacious question of the blind worshipers, who transfer the incomparability of God to the beast: "Who is like the beast?" (13:4; cf. Exod. 15:11).

In short, the state demands what is appropriate only to God and to Christ. In making these demands, the state is of the devil. It is not satanic because it is imperfect but because it is totalitarian. It does not have too little authority but too much, authority "over every tribe and people and tongue and nation" (13:7). It is demonic in its totalitarian deification. No wonder such a diabolic state acts as antichrist, aiming "to make war on the saints and to conquer them" (13:7). To the seer, it is only logical that "the whole earth" should follow the beast and worship it (13:3, 8).

4. Beginning with 13:11, the author describes another beast, this one rising out of the earth rather than the sea. The meaning of this second power hostile to God is clear from 16:13–14; 19:20; 20:10, which speak of the land monster as the "false prophet" who stands in service of the beast (13:2: "it makes the earth and its inhabitants worship the first beast"). It is thus associated with the empire, supporting its deification; it probably represents the provincial priesthood of the emperor cult.

This second beast has "two horns like a lamb" (note once more the perilous similarity to Christ), but speaks "like a dragon" (13:11), thus revealing its words in fact to be satanically inspired. Furthermore, it "works great signs, even making fire come down from heaven to earth" (13:13; note the perilous

31. See Werner Foerster, "Satanas," *TDNT* 7:161 n. 50; also Otto Schmitz, "thrones," *TDNT* 3:166–67.

ambivalence of such miracles). Through its words and wonders, through its impressive propaganda and fascinating power, the second beast leads the inhabitants of the world astray, inducing them to worship the first beast (13:14) and to make a cultic image (cf. Dan. 3:5ff.). One might say that it is responsible for the ideology and metaphysics of the state, its cult and symbolism.[32] But the second beast is also responsible for security: it punishes those who refuse to be marked by its sign (13:16–17) or to participate in the state religion by economic boycott (13:17) or execution (13:15).

There is no evidence for any such "marking" connected with the emperor cult. Probably the seer meant only to indicate a relationship to the emperor cult analogous to the "sealing" of Christians (chapter 7). According to 13:18, the "mark" of the beast (v. 16) or "the name of the beast or the number of its name" (v. 17) is 666. Attempts to explicate this mysterious number through gematria will probably never arrive at a universally accepted conclusion. The most likely explanation is that the number alludes to *Nero redivivus* in the Hebrew alphabet (*Neron qesar*). Those who think the variant 616 represents the original text suggest *kaisar theos* ("the emperor is God") in the Greek alphabet.

5. When we turn to the response of the Christian community, it is obvious that Christians would refuse to worship the image of the emperor. On this point, their stance toward the state must be disobedience rather than obedience. As the references to economic boycott and execution show, this response is a public matter and subject to criminal charges; it is not just a private decision left to the religious preference of the individual. Especially in the eastern regions of the empire, an offense against Rome's religion implies an offense against the Roman state.[33] When religion and politics are so fused, rejection of the emperor cult is *eo ipso* a political act, demonstrating resistance against the emperor and the state: it represents both "atheism" and anarchy. This brings with it persecution that can end in martyrdom, or at least confiscation of property and banishment.

In this situation, the seer does not call for revolt and rebellion or a holy war, but for nonviolent, passive resistance: "Here is a call for the endurance and faith of the saints" (13:10). Collins,[34] following some other scholars, claims to find fragments of the holy war tradition in 14:4 and 17:14. But nothing is said about giving "all the righteous a sword to execute God's judgment against all the wicked" (Ethiopic Enoch 91:12) or a call to take part in a "bloodbath" (1QM 1:10ff.). Only the sword that issues from the mouth of the Word can conquer the enemy (19:15, 21).[35]

32. See Cullmann, *State* (B5), 77–78.
33. See Theodor Mommsen, "Der Religionsfrevel nach römischen Recht," in *Gesammelte Schriften,* 8 vols. (Berlin: Weidmann, 1905–13), 3:389–422; Wilhelm Nestle, "Atheismus," *RAC* 1:869–70, with bibliography.
34. Collins, "Perspective," 248.
35. Cf. Lampe, "Apokalyptiker," 102.

The impotence of the Christians makes pure passivity the only option. In the opinion of the seer, they should not even try to shake off the demonic and despotic regime. There is no prospect of success in rebellion or evasion. Not only does the beast attack the saints with warlike cruelty, but the universal sway of its sovereign authority means than no one can escape its grasp (cf. 13:7). Therefore the seer issues his warning in 13:10: "If any one is to be taken captive, to captivity he goes; if any one is to be slain with the sword, with the sword he must be slain."

The textual tradition of this verse is not unanimous, and commentaries interpret it variously. The RSV and many commentaries do not pay enough attention to the influence of the parallel in Matt. 26:52 or to the practical impossibility in the actual situation of the reading that speaks of Christians taking up the sword. There is no hint of any threat against those who persecute the Christians. Nor is there any suggestion of a concrete active response. This is all the more striking because a purely passive attitude is not the only conceivable answer to persecution in the New Testament (cf. 1 Peter). Lampe[36] thinks that the disaster of the Jewish War influenced the author's preference for a "pacifistic" response.

This, then, is the meaning of 13:10: even if the fate of those who are persecuted is captivity, martyrdom, and death, they are to accept it as a test; they must not be intimidated, but must meet with ready confidence whatever befalls them in God's plan. The Christian community can know that the satanic rage of the dragon and the beasts has a limit set by God—forty-two months, according to 13:5. This is the famous apocalyptic term, found already in Daniel 7 (cf. also Rev. 12:14; 12:6). It shows that God has appointed a precise time for everything. In the view of the seer, it is the devil who throws Christians into prison (2:10), but even this is by God's permission (cf. the passive in 13:7, pointing implicitly to God as the subject). Indeed, even in these machinations of the devil, God ultimately pursues his own plan, leading finally to establishment of his kingdom. The fall of Babylon—that is, the fall of the godless Roman Empire, brought about by God—will be followed shortly by the victory of Christ (cf. Revelation 17—18).

The knowledge of Christians that they are "entered in the book of life" and thus enjoy heavenly citizenship and the promise of eternal life (13:8; 3:5) gives them strength to withstand the implacable power of the empire. When empire and emperor consider themselves divine, when they surround themselves with the aura of divinity and religious trappings and thus turn themselves into a universal diabolical power, the only possible Christian response is resistance, resistance to the death. Participation in the emperor cult is not trivial; it brings eternal damnation. But those who must go to martyrdom and death for the sake of their witness, that is, for refusing to participate in the

36. Ibid., 123.

emperor cult, are comforted by a voice from heaven itself: "Blessed are the dead who die in the Lord" (14:13). At the very beginning of Revelation, the letter to Smyrna cautions its readers to be faithful unto death (2:10). The community must know what it is facing and must be prepared, but need not fear (2:10a): it follows the Lamb (cf. 14:4) wherever the Lamb goes. The way through suffering and tribulation leads to sharing in the new eon, in which God himself "will wipe away every tear from their eyes, and death shall be no more, neither shall there be mourning nor crying nor pain any more" (21:4).

BIBLIOGRAPHY

Works listed in this bibliography are cited in the text with the author's name and short title followed by "(B)," "(B1)," etc.

B. General

Bultmann, Rudolf. *Theologie des NT.* 4th ed. NTG. Tübingen: Mohr, 1961. Eng. trans. of 1st ed.: *Theology of the NT.* New York: Charles Scribner's Sons, 1951–55.

Collange, Jean-Francois. *De Jésus à Paul.* Le champ éthique 3. Geneva: Labor et Fides, 1980.

Conzelmann, Hans. *Grundriss der Theologie des NT.* 3d ed. EETh 2. Munich: Kaiser, 1976. Eng. trans. of 1st ed.: *An Outline of the Theology of the NT.* New York: Harper & Row, 1969.

Dewar, Lindsay. *An Outline of NT Ethics.* LTL. London: Univ. London Press, 1949.

Dihle, A. "Ethik." in *RAC* 6:646–796.

Dodd, Charles Harold. *Gospel and Law.* BLA 3. New York: Columbia Univ. Press, 1951.

Duchrow, Ulrich. *Christenheit und Verantwortung.* 2d ed. FBESG 25. Stuttgart: Klett, 1983. Cited here from the 1st ed. (1970).

Flender, Helmut. "Das Verständnis der Welt bei Paulus, Markus und Lukas." *KuD* 14 (1968): 1–27.

Greeven, Heinrich. *Das Hauptproblem der Sozialethik in der neueren Stoa und im Urchristentum.* NTF, 3d ser., 4. Gütersloh: Bertelsmann, 1935. Reprint. Münster: Stenderhoff, 1983.

Houlden, James Leslie. *Ethics and the NT.* Harmondsworth, Eng.: Penguin, 1973. Reprint. New York: Oxford Univ. Press, 1982.

Jacoby, Hermann. *Neutestamentliche Ethik.* Königsberg: Thomas, 1899.

Käsemann, Ernst. *Der Ruf der Freiheit.* 5th ed. Tübingen: Mohr, 1972. Eng. trans. of the 4th ed. (1968): *Jesus Means Freedom.* Philadelphia: Fortress Press; SCM Press, 1970.

Kümmel, Werner Georg. "Sittlichkeit im Urchristentum." in *RGG*[3] 6:70–80.

Leipoldt, Johannes. *Der soziale Gedanke in der altchristlichen Kirche.* Leipzig: Koehler & Amelang, 1952. Reprint. Leipzig: Zentralantiquariat, 1970.

Lillie, William. *Studies in the NT Ethics.* Edinburgh: Oliver & Boyd, 1961.

Lohmeyer, Ernst. *Soziale Fragen im Urchristentum.* Wissenschaft und Bildung 172. Leipzig: Quelle & Meyer, 1921. Reprint. Darmstadt: Wissenschaftliche Buchgesellschaft, 1973.

Marshall, Laurence Henry. *The Challenge of NT Ethics*. London: Macmillan, 1964 [1964].

Osborn, Eric Francis. *Ethical Patterns in Early Christian Thought*. Cambridge: Cambridge Univ. Press, 1976.

Preisker, Herbert. *Das Ethos des Urchristentums*. Gütersloh: Bertelsmann, 1949. Originally published as *Geist und Leben* [1933]. Reprint. Darmstadt: Wissenschaftliche Buchgesellschaft, 1968.

Sanders, Jack T. *Ethics in the NT*. Philadelphia: Fortress Press, 1975; London: SCM Press, 1986.

Schelkle, Karl Hermann. *Theologie des NT III: Ethos*. KBANT. Düsseldorf: Patmos, 1970. English: *Theology of the NT III: Morality*. Collegeville, Minn.: Liturgical Press, 1971.

Schnackenburg, Rudolf. *Die sittliche Botschaft des NT*. 2d ed. HMT 6. Munich: Hueber, 1962. English: *The Moral Teaching of the NT*. London: Burns & Oates, 1975; New York: Seabury Press, 1979. Here cited from the 1st German ed. (1954; HMT 4).

Schulz, Siegfried. "Evangelium und Welt." In *NT und christliche Existenz* (Festschrift Herbert Braun), ed. H. D. Betz and L. Schottroff, 483–501. Tübingen: Mohr, 1973.

Spicq, Ceslaus. *Théologie morale du NT*. 4th ed. EtB. Paris: Lecoffre, 1965. Cited here from the 1st ed. (1965).

Strecker, Georg. *Handlungsorientierter Glaube*. Stuttgart: Kreuz, 1972.

————. "Strukturen einer neutestamentlichen Ethik." *ZThK* 75 (1978): 117–46.

Völkl, Richard. *Christ und Welt nach dem NT*. Würzburg: Echter, 1961.

Wendland, Heinz-Dieter. *Ethik des NT*. GNT 4. Göttingen: Vandenhoeck & Ruprecht, 1978 [1970].

White, R. E. O. *Biblical Ethics: The Changing Continuity of Christian Ethics*. 1. Atlanta: John Knox Press; Exter: Paternoster, 1979.

B1. Foundations

Becker, Jürgen. "Das Problem der Schriftgemässheit der Ethik." In *Handbuch der christlichen Ethik*, ed. A. Hertz, et al. 1:243–69. Freiburg: Herder, 1978.

Birch, Bruce C., and Larry L. Rasmussen. *Bible and Ethics in the Christian Life*. Minneapolis: Augsburg Pub. House, 1976.

Goppelt, Leonhard. "Die Herrschaft Christi und die Welt nach dem NT." *LR* 17 (1967): 21–50.

————. "Prinzipien neutestament licher und systematischer Sozialethik heute." In *Die Verantwortung der Kirche in der Gesellschaft*, ed. J. Bauer, L. Goppelt, and G. Kretschmar, 7–30. Stuttgart: Calwer, 1973.

Hahn, Ferdinand. "Neutestamentliche Grundlagen einer christlichen Ethik." *TThZ* 86 (1977): 31–41.

Klein, Güunter. "Christusglaube und Weltverantwortung als Interpretationsproblem neutestamentlicher Theologie." *VF* 18 (1973): 45–76.

Schnackenburg, Rudolf. "Neutestamentliche Ethik im Kontext heutiger Wirklichkeit." In *Anspruch der Wirklichkeit und christlicher Glaube* (Festschrift Alfons Auer), 193–207. Düsseldorf: Patmos, 1980.

Schneider, Gerhard. "Biblische Begründung ethischer Normen." *BiLe* 14 (1973): 153–64.

Schrage, Wolfgang. "Barmen II und das NT." In Hans-Georg Geyer et al., *Zum politischen Auftrag der christlichen Gemeinde*, 127–71. Gütersloh: Mohn, 1974.

Wendland, Heinz-Dietrich. "Gibt es Sozialethik im NT?" In *Die Botschaft an die*

soziale Welt. Studien zur evangelischen Sozialtheologie und Sozialethik 5, 85–103. Hamburg: Furche, 1959.
_____. "Die Weltherrschaft Christi und die zwei Reiche." Ibid., 68–84.

B2. Men and Women

Baltensweiler, Heinrich. *Die Ehe im NT.* AThANT 52. Zürich: Zwingli, 1967.
Friedrich, Gerhard. *Sexualität und Ehe, Rückfragen an das NT.* Stuttgart: Katholisches Bibelwerk, 1977.
Greeven, Heinrich. "Ehe nach dem NT." In *Theologie der Ehe*, 2d ed., ed. G. Krems and R. Mumm, 37–79. Regensburg: Pustet, 1972.
_____. "Zu den Aussagen des NT über die Ehe." *ZEE* 1 (1957): 109–25.
Leipoldt, Johannes. *Die Frau in der antiken Welt und im Urchristentum.* 3d ed. Leipzig: Koehler & Amelang, 1965. Cited here from the 2d ed. (1955).
Niederwimmer, Kurt. *Askese und Mysterium.* FRLANT 133. Göttingen: Vandenhoeck & Ruprecht, 1975.
Pesch, Rudolf. *Freie Treue.* Freiburg: Herder, 1971.
Preisker, Herbert. *Christentum und Ehe in den ersten drei Jahrhunderten.* Neue Studien zur Geschichte der Theologie und Kirche 23. 1927. Reprint. Aalen: Scientia, 1979.
Rengstorf, Karl Heinrich. *Mann und Frau im Urchristentum,* pp. 7–52. Arbeitsgemeinschaft für Forschung des Landes Nordrhein Westfalen—Geisteswissenschaften 12. Cologne: Westdeutscher Verlag, 1954.
Schnackenburg, Rudolf. "Die Ehe nach dem NT." In *Theologie der Ehe*, 2d ed., ed. G. Krems and R. Mumm, 9–36. Regensburg: Pustet, 1972.
Schottroff, Luise. "Frauen in der Nachfolge Jesu in neutestamentlicher Zeit." In *Traditionen der Befreiung*, ed. Willy Schottroff et al., 2:91–133. 2 vols. Munich: Kaiser, 1980.
Schrage, Wolfgang, and Erhard Gerstenberger. *Frau und Mann.* Stuttgart: Kohlhammer, 1980.
Stendahl, Krister. *The Bible and the Role of Women.* Facet Books. Philadelphia: Fortress Press, 1966.
Thraede, Klaus. "Ärger mit der Freiheit." In *"Freunde in Christus werden . . . ,"* 31–182. Berlin: Burckhardthaus, 1977.

B3. Property

Bornhäuser, Karl. *Der Christ und seine Habe nach dem NT.* BFChTh 38:3. Gütersloh: Bertelsmann, 1936.
Dautzenberg, Gerhard. "Biblische Perspektiven zu Arbeit und Eigentum." In *Handbuch der christlichen Ethik.* 2:343–62. (B1)
Hauck, Friedrich. *Die Stellung des Urchristentums zu Arbeit und Geld.* BFChTh, ser. 2, 3. Gütersloh: Bertelsmann, 1921.
Hengel, Martin. *Eigentum und Reichtum in der frühen Kirche.* Stuttgart: Calwer, 1973. English: *Property and Riches in the Early Church.* Philadelphia: Fortress Press; London: SCM Press, 1974.

B4. Slavery

Gülzow, Henneke. *Christentum und Sklaverei in den ersten drei Jahrhunderten.* Bonn: Habelt, 1969.

B5. The State

Aland, Kurt. "Das Verhältnis von Kirche und Staat in der Frühzeit." *ANRW* II/23 (1979), 60–246.

Cullmann, Oscar. *Der Staat im NT.* 2d ed. Tübingen: Mohr, 1961. English: *The State in the NT.* New York: Charles Scribner's Sons, 1956.

Dibelius, Martin. "Rom und die Christen im ersten Jahrhundert." In *Botschaft und Geschichte*, 2:177–228. Tübingen: Mohr, 1956.

Goppelt, Leonhard. "Der Staat in der Sicht des NT." In *Macht und Recht*, 9–21. Berlin: Lutherisches Verlagshaus, 1956.

Hengel, Martin. *Gewalt und Gewaltlosigkeit.* CwH 118. Stuttgart: Calwer, 1971. Eng. trans.: *Victory over Violence.* Philadelphia: Fortress Press, 1973.

———. *Die Zeloten.* 2d ed. Leiden: Brill, 1976. Cited here from the 1st ed. (1961).

Lohfink, Norbert, and Rudolf Pesch. *Weltgestaltung und Gewaltlosigkeit.* Düsseldorf: Patmos, 1978.

Schrage, Wolfgang. *Die Christen und der Staat nach dem NT.* Gütersloh: Mohn, 1971.

B6. Other Topics

Betz, Hans Dieter. *Nachfolge und Nachahmung Jesu Christi im NT.* BHTh 37. Tübingen: Mohr, 1967.

Bienert, Walther. *Die Arbeit nach der Lehre der Bibel.* Stuttgart: Evangelisches Verlagshaus, 1954.

Campenhausen, Hans von. *Die Askese im Urchristentum.* SGV 192. Tübingen: Mohr, 1949.

———. "Die Christen und das bürgerliche Leben nach den Aussagen des NT." In *Tradition und Leben*, 180–202. Tübingen: Mohr, 1960. English: "Faith and Culture in the NT." In *Tradition and Life in the Church*, 19–41. Trans. A. V. Littledale. Philadelphia: Fortress Press, 1968.

Furnish, Victor Paul. *The Love Commandment in the NT.* Nashville: Abingdon Press, 1972.

Grässer, Erich. "Neutestamentliche Erwägungen zu einer Schöpfungsethik." *WPKG* 68 (1979): 98–114.

Jentsch, Weiner. *Urchristliches Erziehungsdenken.* BFChTh 45:3. Gütersloh: Bertelsmann, 1951.

Schulz, Anselm. *Nachfolgen und Nachahmen.* StANT 6. Munich: Kösel, 1962.

Stuhlmacher, Peter. "Der Begriff des Friedens im NT und seine Konsequenzen." In *Historische Beiträge zur Friedensforschung*, ed. W. Huber, 21–69. 1970.

B7. Forms

Crouch, James E. *The Origin and Intention of the Corinthian Haustafel.* FRLANT 109. Göttingen: Vandenhoeck & Ruprecht, 1972.

Kamlah, Ehrhard. *Die Form der katalogischen Paränese im NT.* WUNT 7. Tübingen: Mohr, 1964.

Schroeder, D. "Die Haustafeln des NT." Dissertation, Univ. Hamburg, 1959.

Seeberg, Alfred. *Der Katechismus der Urchristenheit.* Munich: Kaiser, 1960 [1903].

Vögtle, Anton. *Die Tugend- und Lasterkataloge im NT.* NTA 16:4–5. Münster: Aschendorff, 1936.

Weidinger, Karl. *Die Haustafeln.* UNT 14. Leipzig: Hinrichs, 1928.

Wibbing, Siegfried. *Die Tugend- und Lasterkataloge im NT.* BZNW 25. Berlin: Töpelmann, 1959.

Zeller, Dieter, *Die weisheitlichen Mahnsprüche bei den Synoptikern.* FzB 17. Würzburg: Echter, 1977.

SCRIPTURE INDEX